Frommer's®

Bahamas
20th Edition

by Darwin Porter & Danforth Prince

WILEY

John Wiley & Sons, Inc.

Published by:

JOHN WILEY & SONS, INC.

111 River St.
Hoboken, NJ 07030-5774

ISBN 978-1-118-28751-4 (paper); ISBN 978-1-118-33359-4 (ebk); ISBN 978-1-118-33471-3 (ebk); ISBN 978-1-118-33074-6 (ebk)

Editor: Gene Shannon
Production Editor: Erin Geile
Cartographer: Guy Ruggiero
Photo Editor: Richard Fox
Production by Wiley Indianapolis Composition Services
Front Cover Photo: Freeport on Grand Bahama Island in the Bahamas, Lighthouse (High Rock Lighthouse) and surf. ©Nik Wheeler / Alamy Images
Back Cover Photo: Bahamian racing sloop at the annual [National Family Island Regatta]. George Town, [Great Exuma Island], Bahamas. ©George H.H. Huey / Alamy Images

For information on our other products and services or to obtain technical support, please contact our Customer Care Department within the U.S. at 877/762-2974, outside the U.S. at 317/572-3993 or fax 317/572-4002.

Wiley also publishes its books in a variety of electronic formats. Some content that appears in print may not be available in electronic formats.

Manufactured in the United States of America

5 4 3 2 1

CONTENTS

LIST OF MAPS

HOW TO CONTACT US

In researching this book, we discovered many wonderful places—hotels, restaurants, shops, and more. We're sure you'll find others. Please tell us about them, so we can share the information with your fellow travelers in upcoming editions. If you were disappointed with a recommendation, we'd love to know that, too. Please write to:

Frommer's Bahamas, 20th Edition
John Wiley & Sons, Inc. • 111 River St. • Hoboken, NJ 07030-5774

ADVISORY & DISCLAIMER

Travel information can change quickly and unexpectedly, and we strongly advise you to confirm important details locally before traveling, including information on visas, health and safety, traffic and transport, accommodations, shopping, and eating out. We also encourage you to stay alert while traveling and to remain aware of your surroundings. Avoid civil disturbances, and keep a close eye on cameras, purses, wallets, and other valuables.

While we have endeavored to ensure that the information contained within this guide is accurate and up-to-date at the time of publication, we make no representations or warranties with respect to the accuracy or completeness of the contents of this work and specifically disclaim all warranties, including without limitation warranties of fitness for a particular purpose. We accept no responsibility or liability for any inaccuracy or errors or omissions, or for any inconvenience, loss, damage, costs, or expenses of any nature whatsoever incurred or suffered by anyone as a result of any advice or information contained in this guide.

The inclusion of a company, organization, or website in this guide as a service provider and/or potential source of further information does not mean that we endorse them or the information they provide. Be aware that information provided through some websites may be unreliable and can change without notice. Neither the publisher nor author shall be liable for any damages arising herefrom.

ABOUT THE AUTHORS

Veteran travel writers **Darwin Porter** and **Danforth Prince** have written many popular guides within the Frommer's series, including books on the Caribbean, France, England, Germany, and Italy. This travel team wrote the first-ever Frommer's Guide to The Bahamas, and also a number of other Frommer guides to such island destinations as Bermuda, Puerto Rico, Jamaica, Barbados, the Dominican Republic, and the Cayman islands. Porter is also a leading Hollywood biographer, film critic, broadcaster, and columnist. His most recent biography, J. Edgar Hoover and Clyde Tolson: Investigating the Sexual Secrets of America's Most Famous Men and Women, was widely reviewed by both the scholastic and the tabloid press. Prince was formerly employed in the Paris bureau of The New York Times, and is the founder and president of Blood Moon Productions.

FROMMER'S STAR RATINGS, ICONS & ABBREVIATIONS

Every hotel, restaurant, and attraction listing in this guide has been ranked for quality, value, service, amenities, and special features using a **star-rating system.** In country, state, and regional guides, we also rate towns and regions to help you narrow down your choices and budget your time accordingly. Hotels and restaurants are rated on a scale of zero (recommended) to three stars (exceptional). Attractions, shopping, nightlife, towns, and regions are rated according to the following scale: zero stars (recommended), one star (highly recommended), two stars (very highly recommended), and three stars (must-see).

In addition to the star-rating system, we also use **seven feature icons** that point you to the great deals, in-the-know advice, and unique experiences that separate travelers from tourists. Throughout the book, look for:

special finds—those places only insiders know about

fun facts—details that make travelers more informed and their trips more fun

kids—best bets for kids and advice for the whole family

special moments—those experiences that memories are made of

overrated—places or experiences not worth your time or money

insider tips—great ways to save time and money

great values—where to get the best deals

The following abbreviations are used for credit cards:

AE American Express	DISC Discover	V Visa
DC Diners Club	MC MasterCard	

TRAVEL RESOURCES AT FROMMERS.COM

Frommer's travel resources don't end with this guide. Frommer's website, **www. frommers.com,** has travel information on more than 4,000 destinations. We update features regularly, giving you access to the most current trip-planning information and the best airfare, lodging, and car-rental bargains. You can also listen to podcasts, connect with other Frommers.com members through our active-reader forums, share your travel photos, read blogs from guidebook editors and fellow travelers, and much more.

THE BEST OF THE BAHAMAS

Geeorge Washington called the Bahamas the land of perpetual June. How right he was. This coral-based archipelago boasts 700 sun-drenched islands with near-perfect weather year-round. Four million annual visitors come for its pink sandy beaches, its splashy resorts like Atlantis on Paradise Island, and to its dive sites at the Andros Barrier Reef, the world's third-largest. Snorkelers discover stunning black coral gardens, and fishing nets every species from the Nassau grouper to shark. Although bombarded by American culture, it's still very British—you drive on the left and locals still take time for a "cuppa" tea.

Things to Do   Wander across endless baby's bottom sands shaded by casuarina pines waving in the tradewinds. Take a cruise from Nassau to privately leased islands with stunning beaches, straw-hut bars, and nature trails where you'll feel like Robinson Crusoe. Armed with snorkeling gear, dive into the blue waters to discover a world of rainbow-hued fish, coral reefs, sea gardens, blue holes, and "drop-offs" featured in James Bond movies. In Nassau, take in the pink colonial buildings, straw markets, casinos, restaurants, and nautical bars.

Beaches   The most popular beach in The Bahamas is **Cable Beach.** Just west of Nassau, it's lined with soft white sands and everything from jet skiing to banana boat rides. Across the waters from Nassau, **Cabbage Beach** on Paradise Island is a spectacular strip of sand ideal for swimming in gin-clear waters, sunning, and watersports. The best for last: The aptly named **Pink Sands Beach** on Harbour Island stretches a whopping 5km (3 miles) of near perfect sands and is idyllic for swimming year round, opening onto a reef-protected natural harbor.

Restaurants and Dining   Sink your teeth into chewy conch (pronounced "konk"), a sea creature evocative of a giant snail, a mainstay of the Bahamian diet and viewed as an aphrodisiac. In the big resorts, a wide swath of American and European cuisine is served, but it's a lot more fun to eat as the locals do—ask for a plate of "google eye" or Bahamian grouper, or the famous "boil" fish breakfast—muttonfish cooked in a savory peppery, lime-based broth and served with a chunk of johnnycake.

Nightlife & Entertainment   The most glamorous center of night life in The Bahamas is the sprawling Atlantis Casino on Paradise Island, the largest in the archipelago. The Crystal Palace Casino on Cable Beach across the water comes in second with games of chance ranging from baccarat to roulette. On the Out Islands, occasional bands play for dancing, but also recommended is a good book, plus moonlit walks along the beach before bedtime.

THE best BEACHES

o **Cable Beach** (New Providence Island): The glittering shoreline of Cable Beach proffers easy access to shops, casinos, restaurants, watersports, and bars. It's a sandy 6.5km-long (4-mile) strip, with a great array of facilities and activities. See p. 55.

o **Cabbage Beach** (Paradise Island): Think Vegas in the Tropics. It seems as though most of the sunbathers dozing on the sands here are recovering from the previous night's partying, and it's likely to be crowded near the mega-hotels, but you can find more solitude on the beach's northwestern extension (Paradise Beach), which is accessible only by boat or on foot. Lined with palms, sea grapes, and casuarinas, the sands are broad and stretch for at least 3km (1¾ miles). See p. 109.

o **Xanadu Beach** (Grand Bahama Island): Grand Bahama has 97km (60 miles) of sandy shoreline, but Xanadu Beach is most convenient to Freeport's hotels, several of which offer shuttle service here. There's more than two kilometers (1.3 miles) of white sand and (usually) gentle surf. Don't expect to have it to yourself, but if you want more quiet and privacy, try any of the beaches that stretch from Xanadu for many miles in either direction. See p. 134.

o **Tahiti Beach** (Hope Town, Elbow Cay, Abacos): Since this beach is so isolated at the far end of the island, you can be sure that only a handful of people will ever visit these cool waters and white sands. The crowds stay away because you can't drive here; you have to walk or ride a bike along sand and gravel paths from Hope Town. You can also charter a boat to reach the beach—which isn't too hard, since the Abacos are the country's sailing capital. See p. 187.

o **Ten Bay Beach** (Eleuthera): Ten Bay Beach lies a short drive south of Palmetto Point, just north of Savannah Sound. Once upon a time, the exclusive Cotton Bay Club chose to build a hotel here because of the fabulous scenery. There may not be any facilities now, but ever since the hotel closed, the white sands and turquoise waters here have been more idyllic and private than ever. See p. 210.

o **Pink Sands Beach** (Harbour Island, Eleuthera): Running the entire length of the island's eastern side, these pale-pink sands stretch for 5km (3 miles) past a handful of low-rise hotels and private villas. A coral reef protects the shore from breakers, making for some of the safest swimming in The Bahamas. See p. 228.

o **Saddle Cay** (Exumas): Most of the Exumas are oval-shaped islands strung end to end like links in a 209km (130-mile) chain. One notable exception is Saddle Cay, with its horseshoe-shaped curve near the Exumas' northern tip. It can be reached only by boat but offers an unspoiled setting without a trace of the modern world—and plenty of other cays and islets where you can play Robinson Crusoe for a few hours, if you like. See p. 232.

o **Stocking Island** (Exumas): One of the finest white sandy beaches in The Bahamas lies off Elizabeth Harbour, the archipelago's main harbor, which is close to the little capital of George Town on Great Exuma Island. You can reach Stocking Island easily by boat, and the sands of this offshore island are rarely crowded; snorkelers and divers love to explore its gin-clear waters. In addition to its beach of powdery white sand, the island is known for its blue holes, coral gardens, and undersea caves. See p. 241.

- **Cat Island** (Southern Bahamas): The white beaches ringing this island are pristine, opening onto crystal-clear waters and lined with coconut palms, palmettos, and casuarina trees—and best of all, you'll practically have the place to yourself. One of our favorite beaches here, near Old Bight, has a beautiful, lazy curve of white sand. Another fabulous one lies 5km (3 miles) north of New Bight, at the Fernandez Bay Village resort. This one, set against another backdrop of casuarinas, is unusually tranquil. A good shoreline here is the long, sandy stretch that opens onto Hawk's Nest Resort & Marina, on the southwestern side. None of the Cat Island beaches has any facilities (bring everything you need from your hotel), but they do offer peace, quiet, and seclusion. See p. 251.

THE best DIVING

- **New Providence Island:** Many ships have sunk near Nassau in the past 300 years, and all the dive outfitters here know the most scenic wreck sites. Other underwater attractions are gardens of elkhorn coral and dozens of reefs packed with life. The most spectacular dive site is **Shark Wall,** 16km (10 miles) off New Providence's southwest coast; it's blessed with incredible, colorful sea life and the healthiest coral offshore. You'll even get to swim with sharks (not as bait, of course). See p. 74.
- **Grand Bahama Island:** The island is ringed with reefs, and dive sites are plentiful, including the **Wall,** the **Caves** (site of a long-ago disaster known as Theo's Wreck), and **Treasure Reef.** Other popular dive sites include **Spit City** (yes, that's right), **Ben Blue Hole,** and the **Rose Garden** (no one knows how this one got its name). What makes Grand Bahama a cut above the others is the presence of a world-class dive operator, **UNEXSO,** the Underwater Explorer Society (© **800/992-DIVE** [3483] or 242/373-1244; www.unexso.com). See p. 138.
- **Lucayan National Park:** This park on Grand Bahama is the site of a 9.5km-long (6-mile) underground freshwater cave system, the longest of its type in the world. The largest cave contains spiral staircases that lead visitors into a freshwater world inhabited by shrimp, mosquito fish, fruit bats, freshwater eels, and a species of crustacean (*Spelionectes lucayensis*) that has never been documented elsewhere. In the 16-hectare (40-acre) preserve are examples of the island's five ecosystems— pine forests, rocky coppice, mangrove swamps, whiteland coppice, and sand dunes. Pause to sunbathe on a lovely stretch of sandy beach or hike along paths accented by orchids, hummingbirds, and barn owls. See p. 139.
- **Bimini:** Although Bimini is most famous for its game fishing, it boasts excellent diving, too. Five kilometers (3 miles) of offshore reefs attract millions of colorful fish. Even snorkelers can see black-coral gardens, blue holes, and an odd configuration on the sea floor that is allegedly part of the lost continent of Atlantis (a fun legend, at any rate). Divers can check out the wreck of a motorized yacht, the *Sapona* (owned by Henry Ford), which sank in shallow waters off the coast in 1929. See p. 153.
- **Andros:** Marine life abounds in the barrier reef off the coast of Andros, which is one of the world's largest and a famous destination for divers. The reef plunges 1,800m (5,906 ft.) to a narrow drop-off known as the **Tongue of the Ocean.** You can also explore mysterious blue holes, formed when subterranean caves filled with seawater, causing their ceilings to collapse and expose clear, deep pools. See p. 159 and 170.

The Bahamas' Best Beaches

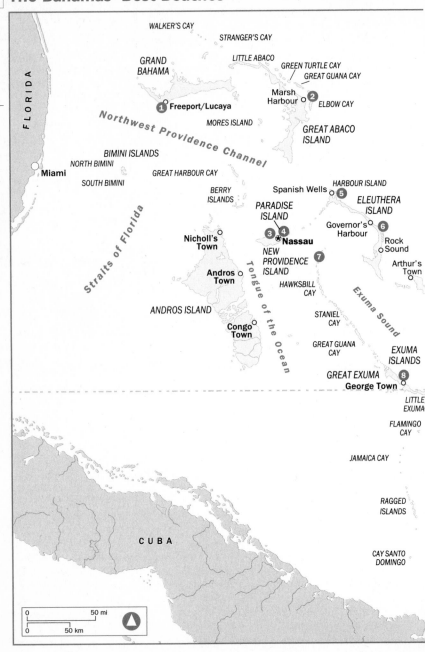

WALKER'S CAY

STRANGER'S CAY

GRAND
BAHAMA

LITTLE ABACO

GREEN TURTLE CAY

GREAT GUANA CAY

Marsh
Harbour ○ **2** ELBOW CAY

1 ○ **Freeport/Lucaya**

Northwest Providence Channel

MORES ISLAND

GREAT ABACO
ISLAND

FLORIDA

BIMINI ISLANDS

NORTH BIMINI

○ **Miami**

SOUTH BIMINI

GREAT HARBOUR CAY

Spanish Wells ○ **5**

HARBOUR ISLAND

ELEUTHERA
ISLAND

BERRY
ISLANDS

PARADISE
ISLAND

3 4

Governor's ○ **6**
Harbour

Straits of Florida

Nicholl's
Town ○

⊛ **Nassau**

NEW
PROVIDENCE
ISLAND

7

Rock
○ Sound

Arthur's
Town
○

Andros
Town ○

Tongue of the Ocean

HAWKSBILL
CAY

Exuma Sound

ANDROS ISLAND

STANIEL
CAY

EXUMA
ISLANDS

Congo
Town ○

GREAT GUANA
CAY

8

GREAT EXUMA

George Town

LITTLE
EXUMA

FLAMINGO
CAY

JAMAICA CAY

RAGGED
ISLANDS

C U B A

CAY SANTO
DOMINGO

0 ___ 50 mi
0 ___ 50 km

THE BEST BEACHES
Cabbage Beach **4**
Cable Beach **3**
Cat Island's beaches **9**
Pink Sands Beach **5**
Saddle Cay **7**
Stocking Island **8**
Tahiti Beach **2**
Ten Bay Beach **6**
Xanadu Beach **1**

A T L A N T I C

O C E A N

CAT ISLAND
9

Cockburn
Town   *SAN SALVADOR*

Stella   *RUM CAY*
Maris

Tropic of Cancer

*LONG
ISLAND*

Deadman's Cay

*CROOKED
ISLAND*

*ACKLINS
ISLAND*   *MAYAGUANA
ISLAND*

**TURKS AND CAICOS
ISLANDS**
NORTH   (U.K.)
CAICOS

PINE CAY   *MIDDLE CAICOS*

PROVIDENCIALES   *EAST CAICOS*
Grace
Bay   *CAICOS*   *GRAND*
ISLANDS   *SOUTH*   *TURK*
LITTLE INAGUA   *CAICOS*   *ISLAND*

SALT
CAY   *TURKS*
GREAT INAGUA   *ISLANDS*

- **Pelican Cays Land and Sea Park** (Abacos): Known for its undersea caves, seemingly endless coral reefs, and abundant plant and marine life, this national park, 13km (8 miles) north of Cherokee Sound at Great Abaco Island, is a highlight for scuba divers. See p. 181.

- **Harbour Island** (Eleuthera): In addition to lovely coral and an array of colorful fish, divers can enjoy some unique experiences here, such as the **Current Cut,** an exciting underwater gully that carries you on a swiftly flowing underwater current for 10 minutes. Four wrecked ships also lie nearby, at depths of less than 12m (39 ft.), including a barge that was transporting the engine of a steam locomotive in 1865, reportedly after the American Confederacy sold it to raise cash for its war effort. See p. 176.

- **Exuma Cays Land and Sea Park** (Exumas): A major attraction, this park was the first of its kind anywhere on the planet. The 35km-long (22-mile), 13km-wide (8-mile) natural preserve attracts divers to its 453 sq. km (175 sq. miles) of sea gardens with spectacular reefs, flora, and fauna. Inaugurated in 1958, it lies some 35km (22 miles) northwest of Staniel Cay and 64km (40 miles) southeast of Nassau; it's only accessible by boat. See p. 249.

- **Long Island** (Southern Bahamas): Snorkeling is spectacular on virtually all sides of this island. But experienced divers venturing into deeper waters offshore can visit underwater cages to feed swarms of mako, bull, and reef sharks. Dive sites abound, including the Arawak "green hole," a blue hole of incomprehensible depth. See p. 264.

THE best SNORKELING

- **New Providence and Paradise Islands:** The waters that ring densely populated New Providence and nearby Paradise Island are easy to explore. Most people head for the **Rose Island Reefs,** the **Gambier Deep Reef,** the **Booby Rock Channel,** the **Goulding Reef Cays,** and some easily seen, well-known underwater wrecks that lie in shallow water. Virtually every hotel on the island offers equipment and can book you onto a snorkel cruise to sites farther offshore. See p. 74 and 110.

- **Grand Bahama Island:** Resort hotels can hook you up with snorkeling excursions, such as the ones offered by **Reef Tours** (© 242/373-5880; www.bahamas vacationguide.com/reeftours), the best snorkeling outfitter, which can also arrange any kind of watersport from banana-boating to water-skiing. The clear waters around Grand Bahama are wonderful for snorkeling because they have a rich marine life. Snorkelers are fond of exploring **Ben's Cave,** a stunning cavern that's part of Lucayan Caves, as well as the coral beds at places like **Silver Point Reef** and **Gold Rock.** See p. 138.

- **Bimini:** Snorkelers are enthralled with the black-coral gardens that are easily accessible from shore and the colorful marine life around the island. Sometimes when conditions are right, snorkelers can frolic with a pod of spotted dolphins. Off North Bimini, snorkelers are attracted to a cluster of huge flat rocks that lie submerged in about 6m (20 ft.) of water near the coast. The most imaginative snorkelers claim that these rocks, which seem hand-hewn, were part of a road system that once traversed the lost continent of Atlantis. See p. 153.

- **Elbow Cay** (Abacos): With its 209km (130-mile) string of beautiful cays and some of the best beaches in The Bahamas, the Abacos are ideal for snorkeling, especially in the waters off Elbow Cay. Visibility is often excellent because the cay lies close to the Gulf Stream's cleansing waters. Marsh Harbour's **Mermaid Beach,** a particularly colorful reef, is another favorite.

- **Stocking Island** (Exumas): George Town is the capital of the Exumas, the Bahamian district celebrated for its crystal-clear waters so beloved by yachties. From George Town, Stocking Island lies across Elizabeth Harbour, only 1.6km (1 mile) away. This long, thin barrier island attracts snorkelers who explore its blue holes (ocean pools of fresh water floating on heavier saltwater). The island is also ringed with undersea caves and coral gardens in stunning colors. You'll find some of the most gorgeous beaches in the Southern Bahamas here. See p. 241.

- **San Salvador** (Southern Bahamas): Following in the wake of Columbus, snorkelers find a rich paradise on this relatively undiscovered island, with its unspoiled, unpopulated miles of beaches ideal for swimming, shelling, and close-in snorkeling (snorkeling close to shore). A week's stay is enough time to become acquainted with only some of the possibilities, including **Bamboo Point, Fernandez Bay,** and **Long Bay,** all within a few miles of Cockburn (the main village) on the island's west side. At San Salvador's southern tip are some of our favorite places for snorkeling: **Sandy Point** and nearby **Grotto Bay.** See p. 260.

- **Long Island** (Southern Bahamas): Shallow bays and sandy beaches offer many possibilities for snorkeling, and the staffs at both major resorts will direct you to the finest conditions near their stretches of beach. The island's southern end is especially dramatic because of its unique sea cliffs. Many east-coast beach coves also offer fantastic snorkeling opportunities. See p. 268.

THE best FISHING

- **New Providence Island:** The waters around New Providence teem with game fish. In-the-know fishermen long ago learned the best months to pursue their catch: November to February for wahoo found in the reefs, June and July for blue marlin, and May to August for the oceanic bonito and blackfin tuna. Nassau, in particular, is ideal for sportfishing. Most boat charters allow passengers to start fishing within 15 minutes after leaving the dock. The best outfitter is **Born Free Charters** (© **242/393-4144;** www.bornfreefishing.com). Anchoring and bottom-fishing are also options. See p. 73.

- **Grand Bahama Island:** The tropical waters along Grand Bahama lure anglers in search of "the big one" because this is home to some of the biggest game fish on earth. Off the coast, the clear waters are good hunting grounds for snapper, grouper, yellowtail, wahoo, barracuda, and kingfish. Many fishermen catch dolphin (the mahimahi kind, not Flipper), and Deep Water Cay is a fishing hot spot. The best outfitter is **Reef Tours** (© **242/373-5880;** www.bahamasvacationguide. com/reeftours). See p. 136.

- **Treasure Cay** (Abacos): Some of the best fishing grounds in the Abacos are in the sea bordering this remote island. At **Treasure Cay Marina** (© **242/365-8250;** www.treasurecay.com), fishermen from all over the world hire experienced skippers to take them out in search of barracuda, grouper, yellowtail, snapper, tuna, marlin, dolphinfish, and wahoo. Deep-sea, bottom-, and drift-fishing are yours for the asking. The cay's own bonefish flats are just a short boat cruise from the marina. See p. 194.

○ **Green Turtle Cay** (Abacos): The deep-sea fishing possibilities off the coast of this cay draw anglers from all over the world. An abundance of giant game fish as well as tropical fish live in these beautiful waters. Both dedicated fisherman and more casual anglers come to the little island seeking yellowfin tuna, a few dolphinfish, and big-game wahoo, among other catches. Green Turtle Cay also has some of the best fishing guides in The Bahamas, weather-beaten men who've spent a lifetime fishing the surrounding waters. **Green Turtle Club** (℗ 242/365-4271; www. greenturtleclub.com) is the best place to hook up with one of these guides. See p. 195.

○ **The Exumas:** Anglers from all over the U.S. descend on this beautiful archipelago for deep-sea fishing or bottom-fishing. Fishermen hunt for kingfish, wahoo, dolphinfish, tuna, and bonito in the deepest waters off the coastline. Many visitors also fly here just to go bonefishing. Among the outfitters who can hook you up is **Club Peace & Plenty** (℗ 242/336-2551; www.peaceandplenty.com), which rents the necessary equipment and can arrange for experienced guides to accompany you. See p. 242.

THE best SAILING

○ **New Providence Island:** Although sailing in the waters off New Providence isn't the equal of those yachting favorites the Exumas and the Abacos, boaters can still find many delights. A greater number of organized boating excursions is offered in New Providence than anywhere else in The Bahamas, especially by outfitters such as **Barefoot Sailing Cruises** (℗ 242/393-0820; www.barefootsailingcruises. com) and **Majestic Tours** (℗ 242/322-2606; www.majesticholidays.com). You can also choose from an array of sunset cruises, such as the ones the *Flying Cloud* (℗ 242/394-5067; www.flyingcloud.info) offers aboard its fleet of catamarans. The most popular—and the most scenic—trip is to tranquil **Rose Island,** 13km (8 miles) east of the center of Nassau and reached after sailing past several small uninhabited cays. (The drawbacks to this island, however, are that cruise-ship passengers flock here and many beach buffs like to come on day trips.) In addition, **Blue Lagoon Island,** 5km (3 miles) northeast of Paradise Island, is a magnet for boaters, offering seven white-sand beaches with seaside hammocks. See p. 72.

○ **Grand Bahama Island:** On the beautiful waters off this large island, you can go sailing aboard the *Ocean Wonder* (℗ 242/373-5880), which is supposedly the world's largest twin-diesel-engine glass-bottom boat. This vessel offers the best and most panoramic picture of underwater life off the coast of Grand Bahama—a view most often reserved for scuba divers. See p. 135.

○ **Marsh Harbour & Hope Town** (Abacos): Known among yachters for their many anchorages, sheltered coves, and plentiful marine facilities, the Abacos are considered one of the most perfect sailing areas in the world. You can charter boats of all shapes and sizes for a week or longer, with or without a crew. One of the finest anchorages in the Out Islands is in Marsh Harbour, the "Boating Capital of The Bahamas." This is where you'll find the **Moorings** (℗ 888/952-8420; www. moorings.com), one of the world's leading charter sailboat outfitters. Passengers will discover white-sand beaches and snug anchorages on uninhabited cays. Sailing here is one of the great experiences of visiting The Bahamas. See p. 180 and 187.

○ **The Exumas:** Yachties head to these beautiful sailing waters to see some of the country's most dramatic coastal scenery. The **Family Island Regatta,** the most popular boating spectacle in The Bahamas, is held here every spring. Most of the recreational boating happens in the government-protected **Exuma Cays Land and Sea Park,** an area of splendid sea gardens and rainbow-hued coral reefs that stretches south from Wax Cay to Conch Cay. You can rent motorboats at **Minns Water Sports,** in George Town (℃ 242/336-3483; www.mwsboats. com). See p. 242.

THE best GOLF COURSES

○ **New Providence Island:** The main draw is the 18-hole **Cable Beach Golf Club** (℃ 242/677-4175; www.crystalpalacevacations.com). The oldest golf course in The Bahamas, this par-71 green was the private retreat of British expatriates in the 1930s. Today, it's owned by Cable Beach casino marketers. Small ponds and water traps heighten the challenge, amid more than 5,901m (6,453 yd.) of well-maintained greens and fairways. See p. 74.

○ **Paradise Island:** Tom Weiskopf designed the **Ocean Club Golf Course** (℃ 242/363-2510; www.oneandonlyresorts.com), an 18-hole, par-72 course, and it's a stunner. With challenges that include the world's largest sand trap and water hazards (mainly the Atlantic Ocean) on three sides, the course has received praise from Jack Nicklaus and Gary Player. For the best panoramic ocean view—good enough to take your mind off your game—play the par-3 14th hole. See p. 109.

○ **Grand Bahama Island:** The Lucayan Country Club now boasts two separate courses. The **Reef Golf Course** (℃ 242/373-1333), a sandy course with links-style greens designed by Robert Trent Jones, Jr., opened in 2000. The Bahamian press called it a bit like a Scottish course, "but a lot warmer." The **Lucayan Golf Course** (℃ 242/373-1333) is a well-respected, renovated, tree-lined course originally laid out in 1964. Both courses have 18 holes and a par of 72. Though they aren't immediately adjacent, shuttle buses carry golfers from one course to the other at frequent intervals. See p. 136.

○ **The Exumas:** At long last, the Southern Bahamas has a world-class golf course: The **Sandals Emerald Bay Golf Club** (℃ 888/726-3257; www.sandals.com) opens onto Emerald Bay's waters. The par-72, 18-hole course was designed by Greg Norman, who created 6 oceanfront holes. The course is challenging yet not daunting, so it appeals to golfers of various skill levels. See p. 242.

THE best TENNIS FACILITIES

○ **Paradise Island:** Well-heeled tennis buffs check into the **One&Only Ocean Club** (www.oneandonlyresorts.com; ℃ 242/363-2501). In fact, many visitors come here just for the tennis, which can be played day or night on the six Har-Tru courts. Although beginners and intermediate players are welcome, the courts are often filled with top-notch competitors. The tennis complex at **Atlantis** (www.atlantis. com; ℃ 242/363-3000) is more accessible to the general public, with six courts (three clay and three hard surface), some lit for night games. See p. 100 and 111.

o **Grand Bahama Island:** Freeport/Lucaya is another top choice for tennis buffs. The island's best tennis is at the **Ace Tennis Center** at the **Radisson Grand Lucayan,** Royal Palm Way (www.ourlucaya.com; *C* **242/350-5294**). It has four courts with different playing surfaces. See p. 138.

THE best HONEYMOON RESORTS

o **Sandals Royal Bahamian** (Cable Beach, New Providence Island; www.sandals. com; *C* **800/SANDALS** [726-3257]) is one branch of a Jamaica-based chain of couples-only, all-inclusive hotels that are favorites among honeymooners. This one is more upscale than many of its Jamaican counterparts and offers 27 secluded honeymoon suites with semiprivate plunge pools. Staff members lend their experience and talent to on-site wedding celebrations: Sandals will provide everything from a preacher to flowers, as well as champagne and a cake. It's more expensive than most Sandals resorts, but you can usually get better prices than the official rack rates through a travel agent or a package deal. See p. 56.

o **One&Only Ocean Club** (Paradise Island; www.oneandonlyresorts.com; *C* **888/528-7157**) is elegant, low-key, low-rise, and exclusive. Guests include many older honeymoon couples. With waterfalls, fountains, reflecting pools, and a stone gazebo, its formal terraced gardens were inspired by the club's founder (an heir to the A&P grocery fortune) and are the most impressive in The Bahamas. At the center is a French cloister, with carvings from the 12th century. See p. 100.

o **Old Bahama Bay Resort and Yacht Marina** (Grand Bahama Island; www.old bahamabay.com; *C* **888/800-8959**) is perfect for honeymooners seeking a hideaway in a boutique-style hotel with cottages adjacent to a marina. The entertainment, shopping, and dining of Freeport/Lucaya are 40km (25 miles) away, so it's ideal for quiet luxury, solitude, and romance. See p. 125.

o **Kamalame Cay** (Staniard Creek, Andros; www.kamalame.com; *C* **800/790-7971**) requires deep pockets; it's one of the most exclusive resorts in the Out Islands, a perfect retreat for the couple longing to escape casinos and mega-resorts. With its 5km (3 miles) of white-sand beaches in both directions, this pocket of posh specializes in luxury and comfort. And don't worry if you've already taken your honeymoon; this is the perfect place to take a second one, or even a third. See p. 164.

o **Abaco Inn** (Elbow Cay, the Abacos; www.abacoinn.com; *C* **800/468-8799**) provides barefoot elegance and romance in the sands. This sophisticated little hideaway is one of the gems of the Abacos. Luxury villa suites with sunrise and sunset views are the way to go. You and your loved one should seek out a hammock in the gardens. See p. 184.

o **Sandals Emerald Bay Great Exuma** (Great Exuma, The Exumas; www.sandals. com; *C* **888/SANDALS** [726-3257]), is a tranquil, remote retreat, providing more luxuries than any other hotel in the Exumas or the Southern Bahamas. Rent a beachfront suite and listen to the sound of crashing waves. When you want to do something else for fun, you'll find a vast array of activities, ranging from golf to watersports. The on-site spa will restore your energy for the oncoming night. See p. 237.

- **Green Turtle Club Resort & Marina** (Green Turtle Cay, the Abacos; www.green turtleclub.com; © 800/370-4468) appeals to romantics who appreciate its winning combination of yachting atmosphere and well-manicured comfort. It's small and civilized in an understated way. The charming, clapboard-covered village of New Plymouth is nearby, accessible by motor launch or, even better, a 45-minute walk across windswept scrublands. See p. 197.
- **Pink Sands** (Harbour Island, Eleuthera; www.pinksandsresort.com; © 800/407-4776) allows for a spectacular getaway at an elite, 11-hectare (27-acre) beachfront estate owned by Chris Blackwell, the founder of Island Records. Its location on a 5km (3-mile) stretch of private pink sand, sheltered by a barrier reef, is just one of its assets. You can ask for a room that evokes an upscale bordello in Shanghai to put you in a romantic mood, and you can also enjoy the best meals on the island. See p. 222.
- **Stella Maris Resort Club** (Long Island, Southern Bahamas; www.stellamarisresort. com; © 800/426-0466) is right on the Atlantic, built on the grounds of an old plantation, and has become a Long Island social hub. Sailing is important here, as are diving and getting away from it all. Many of the guests hail from Germany, lending the place a European flair. The sleepy island itself is one of the most beautiful in The Bahamas, and honeymooners fit into the grand scheme of things perfectly. See p. 267.

THE best FAMILY VACATIONS

- **Sheraton Nassau Beach Resort** (Cable Beach, New Providence Island; www. starwoodhotels.com; © 800/325-3535) could keep a family occupied for their entire vacation. On the grounds of this vast resort is a pool area that features the most lavish artificial waterfall this side of Tahiti; Camp Junkanoo, with supervised play for kids 3 through 12; and a long list of in-house activities such as dancing lessons. See p. 59.
- **Atlantis Paradise Island** (Paradise Island; www.atlantis.com; © 800/285-2684) is one of the world's largest hotel complexes, with endless rows of shops and watersports galore. Both children and adults will enjoy the sprawling sea world with water slides, a lagoon, white-sand beaches, and underground grottoes, plus an underwater viewing tunnel and 240m (787 ft.) of cascading waterfalls. Its children's menus and innovative, creative kids' programs are the best in The Bahamas and perhaps even in the Caribbean. See p. 95.
- **Castaways Resort & Suites** (Grand Bahama Island; www.castaways-resort.com; © 866/410-9676) is a good choice for families on a budget. The pagoda-capped lobby is set a very short walk from the ice-cream stands, souvenir shops, and fountains of the International Bazaar. Children 11 and under stay free, and the in-house lounge presents limbo and fire-eating shows several evenings a month. The hotel also offers babysitting service and a free shuttle to William's Town Beach. See p. 122.
- **Regatta Point** (George Town, Great Exuma; www.regattapointbahamas.com; © 888/720-0011) offers efficiency apartments at moderate prices. Set on a palm-grove cay, it's family-friendly and has its own little beach. Bikes are available and Sunfish boats can be rented. There's also a grocery store nearby where you can pick up supplies. Many units are suitable for families of four or five. See p. 238.

THE best PLACES TO GET AWAY FROM IT ALL

- **Green Turtle Club Resort & Marina** (Green Turtle Cay, the Abacos; www.green turtleclub.com; ℭ **800/370-4468**), secluded and private, is a sailing retreat that consists of tastefully decorated rooms and villas (the latter have full kitchens). It opens onto a small private beach with a 35-slip marina, one of the archipelago's most complete yachting facilities. Many rooms open onto the pool, and the dining room is decorated in Queen Anne style. See p. 197.
- **Rock House Hotel** (Harbour Island, Eleuthera; www.rockhousebahamas.com; ℭ **242/333-2053**) is a glamorous and stylish inn—really, a glorified B&B. This posh little hideaway is drawing more and more of the glitterati to its shores. Set on a low bluff above the harbor, it is tranquility itself. No one will find you if you decide to hide out in its whimsically decorated bedrooms. See p. 223.
- **Fernandez Bay Village** (Cat Island, Southern Bahamas; www.fernandezbayvillage. com; ℭ **800/940-1905**) is home to a dozen or so stone-and-timber villas, the closest thing to urban congestion Cat Island ever sees. There's a funky, thatch-roofed beach bar that'll make you feel like you're in the South Pacific—a great place to enjoy a cold beer each afternoon after you leave the stunning sands and turquoise waters behind for the day. There's only one phone at the entire resort, and your bathroom shower will probably open to a view of the sky. See p. 254.
- **Club Med Columbus Isle** (San Salvador, Southern Bahamas; www.clubmed.com; ℭ **800/CLUB-MED** [258-2633]) was the first large resort to be built on one of the country's most isolated islands, site of Columbus's first landfall in the New World. It's unusually luxurious, and unusually isolated, for a Club Med, and it occupies a gorgeous beach. The sheer difficulty of reaching it adds to the get-away-from-it-all mystique. See p. 258.

THE best RESTAURANTS

- **Graycliff Nassau** (New Providence Island; ℭ **242/302-9150**), serves Nassau's finest continental cuisine in an antiques-filled colonial mansion in the center of town. Over the years, celebrity palates have been catered to here in a refined setting where top quality ingredients go into every dish, and the chefs use local produce when available. See p. 62.
- **Black Angus Grille** (Cable Beach, New Providence Island; ℭ **242/327-6200**). Steak lovers who demand the very best cuts are drawn to this pocket of posh in the Wyndham Nassau Resort, above the Crystal Palace Casino. If you win at the tables, you can spend some of the loot here on the best prime rib, filet mignon, and pepper steaks in the Greater Nassau area. Service is first-rate too. For those who aren't carnivores, an array of other dishes, such as freshly caught tuna, is also available. See p. 67.
- **Bahamian Club** (Atlantis, Paradise Island; ℭ **242/363-3000;** www.atlantis.com), a notch down from the superb Dune, this is still one of the leading restaurants in The Bahamas—and our favorite at the sprawling mega-resort of Atlantis. Strictly upscale, it presents superb French and international cuisine against a backdrop evoking the British Colonial era. See p. 104.

- **Dune** (One&Only Ocean Club, Paradise Island; ℂ **242/363-2501,** ext. 64739; www.oneandonlyresorts.com) is the most cutting-edge restaurant in Paradise Island/Nassau. It's the creation of French-born restaurant guru Jean-Georges Vongerichten, the moving force behind several of New York City's top dining spots. Everything that comes out of the kitchen benefits from a special touch—witness the chicken and coconut-milk soup accompanied by shiitake cakes. See p. 106.

- **Nobu** (Atlantis, Paradise Island; ℂ **242/363-3000;** www.atlantis.com) has opened a branch of this celebrated Japanese restaurant in The Bahamas. It's the island's most-talked-about, and arguably its best, attracting a string of celebrities. The setting is glamorous, and the cuisine is top-rated, prepared with either market-fresh ingredients or exotic imported ingredients. See p. 107.

- **Mangoes Restaurant** (Marsh Harbour, the Abacos; ℂ **242/367-2366;** www. mangoesmarina.com) serves up the best and most authentic Bahamian food in the Abaco chain. Visiting yachties and locals flock to this welcoming spot for its fine cuisine. Order a conch burger for lunch and then return in the evening for the catch of the day—straight from the sea and grilled to your specifications. The namesake mango sauce really dresses up a plate of grilled pork tenderloin. See p. 179.

- **The Landing** (Harbour Island, Eleuthra; ℂ **242/333-2707;** www.harbourisland landing.com), an attractive restaurant at the Harbour Island ferry dock, has awakened the area's sleepy taste buds. Brenda Barry and daughter Tracy feed you well from a choice of international dishes, often prepared from recipes gathered during their world travels. Under mature trees in their garden, you can feast on delicious pastas, freshly made gazpacho, pan-fried grouper, or warm duck salad. See p. 223.

- **Rock House Restaurant** (Harbour Island, Eleuthra; ℂ **242/333-2053;** www. rockhousebahamas.com), in the Rock House Hotel on increasingly chic Harbour Island, serves superb international cuisine. Its hip bodega aura evokes Miami, but it's thoroughly grounded on the island. At lunch, you can get a rock-lobster sandwich; at night, the chefs display their culinary prowess with an array of satisfying dishes. See p. 223.

THE best NIGHTLIFE

- **Cable Beach** has a lot more splash and excitement than Nassau, its neighbor on New Providence Island. Wandering around Cable Beach is also much safer than exploring Nassau's back streets at night. The main attraction is the **Wyndham Nassau Resort & Crystal Palace Casino** (www.wyndhamnassauresort.com; ℂ **242/327-6200**), with an 800-seat theater known for staging glitzy extravaganzas and a gaming room that will make you think you're smack-dab in the middle of Vegas. One of the largest casinos in the islands, the Crystal Palace features blackjack tables, roulette wheels, craps tables, hundreds of slot machines, and a baccarat table. (We think the Paradise Island casino has more class, though.) Despite all the glitter, you can still find cozy bars and nooks throughout the resort, if you'd prefer a tranquil evening. See p. 60.

- **Paradise Island** provides the flashiest nightlife in all of The Bahamas, hands down. Not even nearby Nassau and Cable Beach can come close. Nearly all of the action takes place at the incredible **Atlantis Paradise Island** (www.atlantis.com; ℂ **242/363-3000**), where you'll find high rollers from Vegas and Atlantic City alongside grandmothers from Iowa who play the slots when the family isn't looking. It's all gloss, glitter, and showbiz, with good gambling (though savvy locals say your odds of beating the house are better in Vegas). For a quieter night out, you can also find intimate bars, discos, a comedy club, and lots more in this sprawling behemoth of a resort. See p. 111.

THE BAHAMAS IN DEPTH

After George Washington visited The Bahamas, he wrote that they were "Isles of Perpetual June." Today, the 1,220km-long (758-mile) chain of islands, cays, and reefs is rightfully known as the playground of the Western world. The northernmost island is Grand Bahama, whose western point is about 120km (75 miles) almost due east of Palm Beach, Florida. The southernmost is Great Inagua, some 97km (60 miles) northeast of Cuba and less than 160km (100 miles) north of Haiti. (Henri Christophe, the onetime self-proclaimed Haitian king, supposedly built a summer palace here in the early 19th century.)

There are 700 of these islands, many of which bear the name "cay," pronounced *key*. ("Cay" is Spanish for "small island.") Some, such as Andros, Grand Bahama, Great Abaco, Eleuthera, Cat Island, and Long Island, are fairly large, while others are tiny enough to seem crowded if more than two people visit at a time.

Rising out of the Bahama Banks, a 181,300-sq.-km (70,000-sq.-mile) area of shoals and broad elevations of the sea floor where the water is relatively shallow, The Bahamas are flat, low-lying islands. Some rise no more than 3m (9¾ ft.) above sea level at the highest point, with Mount Alvernia on Cat Island holding the height record at just above 60m (197 ft.).

In most places, the warm, shallow water is so clear that it allows an easy view of the bottom, though cuts and channels are deep. The Tongue of the Ocean between Andros and the Exumas, for example, goes thousands of feet down.

THE BAHAMAS TODAY

The Bahamas is one of the Atlantic's most geographically complicated nations. A coral-based archipelago, its hundreds of islands, cays, and rocky outcroppings became politically independent in 1973 after centuries of colonial rule.

Great Britain actually granted The Bahamas internal self-rule in 1964 and the fledgling nation adopted its own constitution, but chose not to sever its ties with its motherland. It has remained in the Commonwealth, with the British monarch as its head of state. In the British tradition, The Bahamas has a two-house Parliament, a ministerial cabinet headed by a prime minister, and an independent judiciary. The queen appoints a Bahamian governor-general to represent the Crown.

As The Bahamas moves deeper into the millennium, the government and various investors have faced various setbacks in some of their grandiose development plans and improvements in its tourism infrastructure. The downturn in the world economy is blamed. When Hubert Ingraham became prime minister in 1992, he launched the country down the long road toward regaining its market share of tourism, which, under Prime Minister Lynden Pindling, had seen a rapid decline. Polls revealed that some first-time visitors vowed never to return to The Bahamas under the administration of the notorious Pindling, whose government had taken over a number of hotels and failed to maintain them properly.

When Ingraham took office, however, he wisely recognized that the government wasn't meant to be in the hospitality business and turned many properties back over to the professionals. Tourism in the post-Pindling era attracts some 4 million visitors from all over the world, now flocking here annually. In Nassau, it's easy to see where the government's money is being spent: on widened roads, repaved sidewalks, underground phone cables, massive landscaping projects, a cleanup campaign, and additional police officers walking the beat to cut down on crime.

Perry Gladstone Christie, prime minister from 2002 to 2007, continued to carry out those same policies to better Nassau. Ingraham was reelected to the position in 2007.

Unlike Haiti and Jamaica, The Bahamas has remained politically stable and made the transition from white-minority rule to black-majority rule with relatively little tension.

Economic conditions have slowly improved here as well, although unemployment remains high. There's not the wretched poverty in Nassau that there is in, say, Kingston, Jamaica—though many poor residents do still live in New Providence Island's Over-the-Hill section, an area to which few tourists venture (although the neighborhood is gritty and fascinating).

The biggest changes have occurred in the hotel sector. Developers vastly expanded the Atlantis Resort on Paradise Island, turning it into a virtual water world. In addition, Hilton has developed the decaying old British Colonial in Nassau, restoring it to life. Cable Beach is slated for massive redevelopment in the future. And Grand Bahama Island is in a state of flux as hotels along the entire Lucayan strip get upgraded.

If there's a downside to this boom, it's the emphasis on mega-hotels and casinos— and the corresponding de-emphasis on the Out Islands, which include the Abacos, Andros, Bimini, Cat Island, the Exumas, Long Island, and San Salvador. Large resort chains, with the exception of Sandals and Club Med, have ignored these islands; most continue to slumber away in relative seclusion and poverty. Other than the Sandals mega-resort that opened in the Exumas, development has been minor. Little change in this Out Islands–versus–the-rest situation is anticipated soon.

There's another trend to note in The Bahamas: The government and many citizens here have awakened to ecotourism. More than any government in the Caribbean except perhaps Bonaire, this nation has started to try to protect its ecology. Government, private companies, and environmental groups have drawn up a national framework of priorities to protect the islands. One of their first goals was to save the nearly extinct West Indian flamingo. Today, about 60,000 flamingos inhabit Great Inagua Island. Other programs aim to prevent the extinction of the green turtle, the white-crowned pigeon, the Bahamian parrot, and the New Providence iguana.

Many problems remain for this archipelago nation. While some Bahamians seem among the friendliest and most hospitable people in the world, others—particularly those in the tourist industry—can be downright hostile. To counter this, the government is working to train its citizens to be more helpful, courteous, and efficient. Sometimes this training has been taken to heart; at other times, however, it clearly has not. Service with a smile is not assured in The Bahamas.

Drug smuggling also remains a serious problem, and, regrettably, there seems to be no immediate solution. Because the country is so close to U.S. shores, it is often used as a temporary depot for drugs shipped from South America to Florida. The Bahamas developed a tradition of catering to the illicit habits of U.S. citizens as well; during the heyday of Prohibition, many Bahamians grew rich smuggling rum into America. Things have improved, but you'll still see stories in the newspapers about floating bales of marijuana turning up just off the country's coastline.

Though this illicit trade rarely affects the casual visitor, it's important to know that it exists—so don't agree to carry any packages to or from the U.S. for a stranger, or you could end up taking a much longer vacation than you had ever imagined.

LOOKING BACK AT THE BAHAMAS

History

THE EARLY YEARS After Columbus made his first landfall somewhere in The Bahamas, Ponce de León voyaged here in 1513 looking for the legendary Fountain of Youth. This journey, incidentally, led to the European discovery of Florida and the Gulf Stream—but not the magic fountain. Ponce de León's historian described the waters of the Little Bahama Bank, just north of Grand Bahama, as *bajamar* (pronounced "ba-ha-*mar*," Spanish for shallow water). This seems to be a reasonable source of The Bahamas' name.

It was Columbus, landing on October 12, 1492, who met the island residents, Arawak Indians called Lucayans. He renamed an island, called Guanahani by its native inhabitants, San Salvador. Over the years, there has been much dispute as to just which island this was. Long ago, it was decided that the discoverer's first landfall in the New World was a place known as Watling Island—the modern-day San Salvador. Recent claims, however, place the first landing on Samana Cay, 105km (65 miles) southeast of what's now called San Salvador. In 1986, *National Geographic* propounded and supported this island as being the place where Columbus made landfall.

The Lucayans Columbus encountered are believed to have come to the islands in about the 8th century A.D. from the Greater Antilles (but originally from South America); they were seeking refuge from the savage Caribs then living in the Lesser Antilles. The Lucayans were peaceful people. They welcomed the Spaniards and taught them a skill soon shared with the entire seagoing world: how to make hammocks from heavy cotton cloth.

The Spanish, who claimed the Bahamian islands for their king and queen, did not repay the Lucayans kindly. Finding neither gold nor silver mines nor fertile soil, the conquistadors cleared the islands of their inhabitants, taking some 40,000 doomed Lucayans to other islands in New Spain to work in mines or dive for pearls. References to the islands first discovered by Columbus are almost nil after that time for about the next 135 years.

THE COMING OF THE ENGLISH England formally claimed The Bahamas in 1629. No settlement took place, however, until the 1640s, when religious disputes arose in Bermuda and England. English and Bermudian settlers sailed to an island called Cigatoo, changed the name to Eleuthera (from the Greek word for freedom), and launched a tough battle for survival. Many became discouraged and went back to Bermuda, but a few hardy souls hung on, living on the products of the sea—fish, ambergris, and shipwreck salvage.

Other people from Bermuda and England followed, and New Providence Island was settled in 1656. They planted cotton, tobacco, and sugarcane, and established Charles Towne, honoring Charles II, at the harbor.

PIRATES & PRIVATEERS The promising agricultural economy was short-lived. Several governors of that era were corrupt, and soon the islands became a refuge for English, Dutch, and French buccaneers who plundered the ships of Spain, the country that controlled the seas. The Spaniards responded by repeatedly ravaging New Providence for revenge, causing many of the settlers to leave. The remainder apparently found the pirates a good source of income. Privateers, a slightly more respectable type of freebooter (they had their sovereign's permission to prey on enemy ships), also found The Bahamas' many islets, tricky shoals, and secret harbors to be good hiding places on ships sailing between the New and Old worlds.

Late in the 17th century, Charles Towne's name was changed to Nassau to honor King William III, then on the British throne, who also had the title of Prince of Nassau. But the change in nomenclature didn't ease the troubled capital, as some 1,000 pirates still called New Providence home.

Finally, the appeals of merchants and law-abiding islanders for Crown control were heard, and in 1717, the lord proprietors turned over the government of The Bahamas, both civil and military, to King George I, who commissioned Capt. Woodes Rogers as the first royal governor.

Rogers seized hundreds of the lawless pirates. Some were sent to England to be tried. Eight were hanged. Others received the king's pardon, promising thereafter to lead law-abiding lives. Rogers was later given authority to set up a representative assembly, the precursor of today's Parliament. Despite such interruptions as the capture of Nassau by the fledgling U.S. Navy in 1776 (over in a few days) and the surrender of the Crown colony to Spain in 1782 (of almost a year's duration), the government of The Bahamas since Rogers's time has been conducted in an orderly fashion. The Spanish matter was settled in early 1783 in the Peace of Versailles, when Spain permanently ceded The Bahamas to Britain, ending some 300 years of disputed ownership.

LOYALISTS, BLOCKADE-RUNNERS & BOOTLEGGERS After the American Revolution, several thousand Loyalists from the former colonies emigrated to The Bahamas. Some of these, especially southerners, brought their black slaves with them and tried their luck at planting sea-island cotton in the Out Islands, as the islands other than New Providence were called. Growing cotton was not a success, as the plants fell prey to the chenille bug, but by then, the former Deep South planters had learned to fish, grow vegetables, and provide for their families and servants in other ways.

The first white settlers of The Bahamas had also brought slaves with them, but with the United Kingdom Emancipation Act of 1834, the slaves were freed and the government compensated the former owners for their "property loss." It was a fairly peaceful transition, though it was many years before any real equality was seen.

The Civil War in America brought a transient prosperity to The Bahamas through blockade-running. Nassau became a vital base for the Confederacy, with vessels taking manufactured goods into the Carolinas and bringing out cotton. The Union's victory ended blockade-running and plunged Nassau into economic depression.

The next real boom the islanders enjoyed was engendered by U.S. Prohibition. As with the blockade-runners—but this time with faster boats and more of them—rum-runners churned the waters between The Bahamas and the southeastern states. From the passage of the 18th Amendment in 1919 to repeal of that law in 1933, Nassau, Bimini, and Grand Bahama served as bases for running contraband alcoholic beverages across the Gulf Stream to assuage Americans' thirst. Ceaseless battles were waged between the U.S. Coast Guard and this new generation of freebooters. When the U.S. repealed Prohibition, it dealt another shattering blow to the Bahamian economy.

THE WAR YEARS   On August 17, 1940, the Duke and Duchess of Windsor arrived in Nassau, following his appointment as governor of the colony. The duke had abdicated as King Edward VIII to marry the woman he loved, a divorced American named Mrs. Simpson. The people of The Bahamas were shocked that such a once-powerful figure had been assigned the post of governing their impoverished colony, which was viewed as a backwater of the British Empire. The duke set about trying to make The Bahamas self-sufficient and providing more employment.

World War II healed the wounds of the bootlegging days, as The Bahamas served as an Atlantic air and sea station. From this, the country inherited two airports built for U.S. Air Force use during hostilities with the Germans. The islands were of strategic importance when Nazi submarines intruded into Atlantic coastal and Caribbean waters. Today, U.S. missile-tracking stations still exist on some of the outlying islands.

THE POSTWAR YEARS   In the post–World War II years, party politics developed in The Bahamas as independence from Britain seemed more possible. In 1967, Lynden Pindling became prime minister after winning a close election.

He stayed in power until 1992 in an administration filled with scandal and graft. He was finally defeated in 1992 by Hubert Ingraham (discussed earlier). Perry Gladstone Christie then defeated Ingraham and was prime minister from 2002 until 2007, when Ingraham was returned to power.

During the election of 1972, the Bahamian people opted for total independence. The Bahamas agreed to be a part of the British Commonwealth, presided over by Queen Elizabeth II. Her future appointed representative would only be a governor-general, holding a ritualized position with mostly symbolic power.

The Commonwealth of The Bahamas came into being in 1973, making it the world's 143rd sovereign state. Its government was to be ministerial with a bicameral legislature and headed by a prime minister and an independent judiciary. The end to centuries of colonial rule was actually signaled in 1964, when The Bahamas was granted internal self-government pending drafting of a constitution, which was adopted in 1969. By choice, the island nation did not completely sever its ties with Great Britain, preferring to remain in the Commonwealth of Nations with the British monarch as its head of state.

RECENT SCANDALS As The Bahamas grows into a favorite stamping ground of celebrities, the archipelago has also become the scene of several recent scandals, each of which promoted a seemingly endless series of lawsuits and tabloid headlines.

There was the death of blonde, busty Anna Nicole Smith, who, although living in Nassau at the time, died in a Florida hotel room in February 2007. After a long legal battle, she was buried on New Providence Island next to her 20-year-old son, Daniel, who had died from a lethal combination of methadone and two kinds of antidepressants in a hospital room where his mother had previously given birth to Dannielynn, a daughter.

In January 2009, John Travolta's 16-year-old son, Jett, died in Nassau from complications associated with a seizure. In an incredibly convoluted case, which news people had a hard time explaining clearly to the public, ambulance driver Tarino Lightbourne and his attorney politician Pleasant Bridgewater were accused of demanding $25 million from the actor to keep them from revealing private information in the death of his son.

Bridgewater resigned her seat in The Bahamas Senate after she was charged in the case. This attempted extortion went to trial, but a mistrial was declared.

In 2011, because of a bad economy, many grandiose development plans were stalled, but the largest project, the Baha Mar overhaul of Cable Beach, has been officially launched.

ARCHITECTURE The unique geography and history of The Bahamas contributed to a distinctive architectural style—the **Bahamian clapboard house**—that is today one of the most broadly copied in the tropics. But it wasn't until the early 19th century that this design began to become perfected and standardized.

The earliest clapboard-sided houses were usually angled to receive the trade winds. Large window openings and high ceilings increased airflow, while awning-style push-out shutters shaded windows and helped direct breezes indoors even during rainstorms. Unlike larger and more impressive houses, where foundations were massive edifices of coral, brick, or stone, the first floors of Bahamian cottages were elevated on low stilts or light masonry pilings to further allow air to circulate. Raising the

DATELINE

700s Lucayans, seeking refuge from the cannibalistic Caribs, emigrate to The Bahamas from the Greater Antilles.

1492 Columbus makes his first landfall in the New World, most likely in San Salvador, although some historians dispute this.

1513 Ponce de León searches for the Fountain of Youth and discovers the Gulf Stream instead.

1629 England claims The Bahamas.

1640s First Western settlements are established, as the Company of Eleutherian Adventurers arrives.

1656 New Providence Island (site of Nassau) is settled.

1717 King George I orders Capt. Woodes Rogers, the first royal governor, to chase the pirates out of Nassau.

1776 The fledgling U.S. Navy captures Nassau but soon departs.

1782 The British Crown colony surrenders The Bahamas to Spain, which rules it for almost a year.

building also served the function of keeping the floor joists, beams, and planking above floodwaters during a hurricane surge.

Ruggedly built of timbers whose ends were often pegged (not nailed) together and pinned to stone pilings several feet above ground, Bahamian-style clapboard houses survived when many rigid stone-built structures collapsed during hurricanes. Modern engineers affirm that these structures' flexibility increases their stability in high winds.

Some of the best-preserved and most charming examples of the Bahamian cottage style can be found on Harbour Island, off the coast of Eleuthera, and, to a lesser extent, at Spanish Wells and Green Turtle Cay.

CRAFTS The most prevalent craft in The Bahamas is the weaving of **straw goods.** So widespread is this activity that the largest assemblage of saleable objects in the archipelago—Nassau's Straw Market—was named after this ancient art form. In its open-air stalls, you'll find every imaginable kind of basket, hat, purse, tropical furniture, and souvenir.

At their best, the objects are gracefully woven concoctions of palm fronds or palmetto leaves crafted into patterns bearing such old-fashioned names as shark's tooth, Jacob's ladder, Bahama Mama, peas 'n' grits, lace-edge, and fish gill. At their worst, the objects are almost unbearably touristy, amusing but tasteless souvenirs.

The finest straw work is said to come, incidentally, from the Out Islands, with Long Island producing some of the best. So tightly woven are hats from Long Island that they can function for short periods as water buckets.

The second-most-important craft in the islands is **wood carving.** Local art critics consider the best wooden carvings those that are intuitively inspired by the flora, fauna, and images of the islands. The worst ones tend to be crafted specifically for a fast buck at the tourist market. Your eye and intuition will tell you which is which.

Interestingly, The Bahamas does not produce clay from any natural source, so any terra-cotta object you find will almost certainly have been produced from foreign-bought materials and inspired by the pottery traditions of other places. Ceramics in The Bahamas tend to be reserved for formally trained sculptors who promote their work as fine art.

1783	Spain signs the Peace of Versailles, ceding The Bahamas to Britain.
1834	The United Kingdom Emancipation Act frees slaves throughout the British Empire.
1861–65	U.S. Civil War brings prosperity to The Bahamas by way of blockade-running. Nassau becomes a vital supply base for the Confederacy.
1919	The Bahamas revives from an economic slump by rum-running during America's Prohibition years.
1933	The American repeal of Prohibition causes an economic collapse on the islands.
1940	The Duke of Windsor, after renouncing England's throne, is named governor of The Bahamas as war rages in Europe.
1964	Sir Roland Symonette becomes the country's first premier. The Bahamas are granted internal self-government.
1967	Lynden Pindling is named premier in a close election.
1968	African-Bahamians assume control of their government.

continues

THE BAHAMAS IN POP CULTURE

Books

FICTION & POETRY   The greatest literary figure inspired by The Bahamas was not Bahamian at all. He was Ernest Hemingway, a through-and-through American. The Bahamas figured in some of his fiction, notably *Islands in the Stream*. Hemingway preferred Bimini because of its fishing, and he was the first person the locals saw land a bluefin tuna on rod and reel. "Papa," as he was known, stayed at Helen Duncombe's Compleat Angler Hotel.

Hemingway went to Bimini first in 1934 on his boat, *Pilar*, bringing writer John Dos Passos, among others, with him. He was also there in 1937, working on revisions for his manuscript *To Have and Have Not*. But the Bahamians remember him mainly for *Islands in the Stream*. No writer before or since has captured in fiction the seedy charm of Bimini's Alice Town.

There are no Hemingways anymore, but novelists still use The Bahamas as a backdrop for their fiction. Instead of fishing, however, there is usually a drug-scene theme. Typical of this genre is David Poyer's *Bahamas Blue* (St. Martin's). Poyer, also the author of *Hatteras Blue,* obviously loves the sea, but hates the drug runners who use it. In his book, the hero sets off to make a 122m (400-ft.) dive to recover 50 tons of cocaine off the coast. It's a thriller, and certainly evocative of the 1990s in The Bahamas.

For insight into Bahamian life, read Desmond Bagley's novel *Bahama Crisis* (HarperCollins) or Dennis Ryan's book of poetry *Bahamas: In a White Coming On* (Dorrance).

RELIGION & FOLKLORE   Daniel J. Crowley's *I Could Talk Old-Story Good: Creativity in Bahamian Folklore* (University of California Press) and Leslie Higgs's *Bush Medicine in The Bahamas* (Nassau Guardian) are both recommended.

1972 Bahamians vote for total independence from Britain.	2007 Hubert Ingraham returns to power as prime minister.
1973 On July 9, the Union Jack in New Providence is lowered for the last time, ending more than 3 centuries of British rule.	2011 After some fitful inaugural starts (and stops), redevelopment of Cable Beach on New Providence Island relaunched.Architecture & Crafts
1992 After 25 years in power, Prime Minister Pindling goes down in defeat. Hubert Ingraham, campaigning against corruption and recession, replaces him.	
2002 Perry Gladstone Christie defeats Ingraham to become prime minister.	

HISTORY   From Columbus to today's historians, many authors have found the background of The Bahamas a trove of rich material. There are numerous volumes to choose from, but we'll start with just a sampling.

The Story of The Bahamas (Macmillan), by Paul Albury, is a 294-page history that's the best of its kind. It relates these islands' checkered past, from pirates to shipwreckers to rumrunners. Robert H. Fuson's The Log of Christopher Columbus (International Marine Publishing) presents the words of the explorer himself, providing the first impressions of The Bahamas ever recorded by a European. From his 1492 log comes the following: "I made sail and saw so many islands that I could not decide where to go first."

Grand Bahama (Macmillan), by Peter Barratt, a town planner in charge of developing Freeport on Grand Bahama, writes of how a barren pine-covered island became a major tourist center.

Photographer/writer Hans W. Hannau prepared The Bahama Islands in Full Color (Argos, Inc.), a large pictorial volume of color photographs. Somewhat of a coffee-table book, it does contain much general information about The Bahamas.

TRAVEL   Isles of Eden: Life in the Southern Family Islands of The Bahamas (Benjamin Publishing), by Harvey Lloyd, with a foreword by former prime minister Lynden Pindling, describes the island people who live in this rarely visited archipelago that stretches 145km (90 miles) southeast of Nassau all the way to Haiti. Lloyd blends unusual island photography with social commentary, history, and personal recollections.

Yachtsman's Guide to The Bahamas (Tropical Island Publishers), a thoroughly researched, annually revised guide, is essential for visitors contemplating boat tours.

Film

The lush look of The Bahamas makes it a favorite with film crews. Among the films shot here were the James Bond movies Dr. No, Never Say Never Again, and Thunderball. Clifton Wall, off New Providence, is a dramatic sea wall near a dozen shallow and deep sites. One wreck here formed the backdrop for Never Say Never Again. The film crew sunk a 34m (110-ft.) freighter that had been seized by the Bahamian government as a dope runner. Considered the country's most photogenic wreck site, it was also used in the movie Wet Gold as well as in several television commercials. A few hundred yards away are the ruins of an airplane prop used in Thunderball. The movie's famous spear-gun sequence was shot at Thunderball Reef.

Parts of other films have also been shot in The Bahamas, including Splash! and Cocoon. In addition, Islands in the Stream, starring George C. Scott and Claire Bloom, is based on the Hemingway novel about a sculptor living in isolation in The Bahamas.

Music

The Bahamas maintains great pride in its original musical idioms, often comparing their vitality to the more famous musical traditions of Jamaica, Puerto Rico, and Trinidad. Other than the spirituals whose roots were shared by slaves in colonial North America, by far the most famous musical products of the archipelago are Goombay and its closely linked sibling, Junkanoo.

GOOMBAY   Goombay music is an art form whose melodies and body movements are always accompanied by the beat of goatskin drums and, when available, the liberal consumption of rum. Goombay is a musical combination of Africa's tribal heritage (especially that of the Egungun sect of the Yoruba tribe) mingled with the Native

BAHAMIAN folklore

Many different factors contributed to the formation of a potent and vital body of myths within The Bahamas. Among the strongest factors were the nation's unusual geography, its noteworthy history, and the often turbulent mingling of cultures. Some tales are a mélange of about a half dozen different oral traditions, including those of England, Africa, France, and neighboring islands of the Caribbean. Storytelling is a fine art, with a tradition that remains the strongest on the Out Islands, where television (and electricity) was long in coming.

Obeah, which has been defined as a mixture of European superstitions, African (especially Yoruban) religion, and Judeo-Christian beliefs, retains similarities to the voodoo of Haiti, the Santeria of Cuba and Brazil, and the Shango of Trinidad. Steeped in the mythic traditions of West Africa, it is an important part of Bahamian national heritage.

An obeah practitioner may chant, sing, or go into a trance to communicate with another dimension of reality. The most common method of obeah practice in The Bahamas today involves "fixing" a person with a spell, which can be "cleared" either by another obeah practitioner or by a formal medical doctor. Much more serious is to be "cursed" by an obeah master, the effect of which can be lifted only by that same person. Magic is divided into black and white spheres, with white magic being the more potent and the less evil.

Ghosts or spirits are known as "sperrids," and necromancy—the habit of soliciting communications from the dead—is a ritualistic form of obeah used to get information that can be put either to good or evil use. According to tradition, the sperrids dwell in the fluffy tops of the silk cotton trees that are widespread throughout The Bahamas. This belief probably has its origins in African traditions, where many tribes worship the cotton tree as the abode of the spirits of the dead. Although sperrids wander at will throughout the earth, causing mischief and unhappiness wherever they go, only the obeah man or woman can channel their power.

On some islands (including remote Cat Island), residents believed that a "working witch" could be hired to perform tasks. The most common form of a witch was that of a cat, rabbit, snake, or rat. Folk tales abound about the mythical powers of these witch-animals. Especially fearsome was any short, fat snake with a ribbon tied around it, a sure sign that the reptile was actually a witch in disguise.

Highly secret, as clandestine as you might imagine witchcraft to be within unpublicized covens of New England, obeah is a superstitious undercurrent running through the context of life on some islands. No outsider would be invited to the few ritualized events that might take place.

American and British colonial influences of the New World. Although its appeal quickly spread to other islands, its traditions remain strongest within The Bahamas.

The most outlandish moments of the Goombay world occur the day following Christmas (Boxing Day). Dancers outfit themselves in masquerade costumes whose bizarre accessories and glittering colors evoke the plumage of jungle birds. Once dismissed by the British colonials as the pastime of hooligans, Goombay is now the most widespread and broad-based celebratory motif in The Bahamas, richly encouraged by the island's political and business elite. Goombay musicians and dancers are almost always male, honoring a tradition whereby men and boys from the same family pass on the rhythms and dance techniques from generation to generation. Goombay is the Bantu word for "rhythm," while also referring to a type of African drum.

Today, Goombay has a gentle, rolling rhythm, a melody produced by either a piano, a guitar, or a saxophone, and the enthusiastic inclusion of bongos, maracas, and rhythm ("click") sticks. Lyrics, unlike the words that accompany reggae, are rarely politicized, dealing instead with topics that might have been referred to in another day as "saucy." Eventually, the sounds of Goombay would be commercialized and adapted into the louder and more strident musical form known as Junkanoo.

JUNKANOO   Until the 1940s, Junkanoo referred almost exclusively to the yuletide procession wherein revelers in elaborate costumes paraded down main streets accompanied solely by percussion music. (During the days of slavery, Christmas was the most important of the four annual holidays granted to slaves, and the one that merited the most exuberant celebrations.) The rhythms of Junkanoo became hypnotic, growing with the spectators' enthusiasm and the dancers' uninhibited movements. Essential to the tradition were the use of cowbells, traditional drums, and whistles.

Theories differ as to the origins of Junkanoo's name, but possible explanations include a Creole-pidgin derivation of French-speaking Haiti's term *gens inconnus,* which means "unknown people"—a reference to the masked dancers.

Around World War II, Bahamian musicians fleshed out the yuletide Junkanoo parade's percussion rhythms with piano, electric bass, and guitar. This sparked the beginning of its development into what is today, the most prevalent musical form in The Bahamas.

RECORDINGS   One of the best-selling albums in Bahamian history is the privately produced *An Evening with Ronnie.* Composer of more hit singles than almost any other Bahamian star, Ronnie Butler's album contains renditions of "Burma Road," "Crow Calypso," and "Native Woman."

Tony McKay emigrated to New York and New Orleans after becoming an international sensation with his Junkanoo music. His best-selling records include *Rushing Through the Crowd* and *Reincarnation.*

The internationally acknowledged Baha Men (formerly High Voltage) reinterpret Goombay songs from the mid–20th century in *Junkanoo.* Of special interest are their Junkanoo adaptations of classic Goombay songs by such stars as George Symonette and Blind Blake.

Some of the best Junkanoo stars on the Bahamian scene are members of the group K.B., whose folk renditions revolving around Out Island values have led to such blockbusting singles as "She Fat," a romantic ode to the allure of overweight women. You'll find it on K.B.'s album *Kickin' Bahamian.*

The well-known Eddie Minnis survives exclusively on the sales of his paintings and records. His album *Discovery,* produced for the Bahamian quincentennial, features melodies and lyrics inspired by the folk idioms of the Exumas and Eleuthera. He has also produced other albums, all of which are available at record stores in Nassau.

The Bahamas has always inspired some of the Atlantic's most fervent religiosity. The country's most popular interpreter of gospel music is a Freeport-based group called the Cooling Waters, whose releases have approached the top of the religious-song charts in The Bahamas *and* the U.S.

One of the most important groups of all is King Eric and his Knights, whose leader is considered one of the patriarchs of Bahamian music. He composed an album, *Island Boy,* whose best-selling single, "Once Is Not Enough," later became the country's theme song.

EATING & DRINKING

There is a bona fide Bahamian cuisine, but you'll have to leave the first-class hotels to find it. If you want to dine on authentic Bahamian food, look for the word BAHA-MIAN in caps beside the restaurant reviews in this guide. When you see the word INTERNATIONAL, know that this means typical fare likely to be offered anywhere, especially at places such as resorts in Florida.

In some remote places, especially the Out Islands, Bahamian food is the only type of cuisine offered. Of course, the major restaurants have continental chefs, but else-where, especially at little local establishments, you eat as the Bahamians eat.

Cuisine, sad to say, is not one of the most compelling reasons to come to The Bahamas. You can fare much better on the mainland, especially in Florida. Except for some notable exceptions (see "The Best Restaurants," in chapter 1), many restaurants serve fairly routine international fare of the surf-and-turf variety. Local seafood dishes consist mainly of grouper and conch. In the Out Islands, you'll likely get one or the other every night. More exotic fish is often flown in frozen from Miami, as is most meat and poultry.

The best restaurants are in Nassau, Cable Beach, Paradise Island, and, to a lesser extent, Freeport/Lucaya. That doesn't mean you can't eat satisfactorily elsewhere in The Bahamas. You can, but chances are you won't be collecting recipes.

The Cuisine

SOUP Bahamian fish chowder can be prepared in any number of ways. Old-time chefs tell us that it's best when made with grouper. To that, they add celery, onions, tomatoes, and an array of flavorings that might include A1 steak sauce (or Worcester-shire, or both), along with thyme, cooking sherry, a bit of dark rum, and lime juice.

Increasingly rare these days, turtle soup was for years a mainstay of the Out Islands. It and other turtle dishes still appear on some menus despite the turtle's status as an endangered species. If you have alternatives, choose another dish.

CONCH The national food of The Bahamas is conch (pronounced "konk"). This mollusk's firm white meat is enjoyed throughout the islands. It actually tastes some-what bland, at least until Bahamian chefs get their hands on it. Locals eat it as a snack (usually served at happy hours in taverns and bars), as a main dish, as a salad, and as an hors d'oeuvre.

Some people think it tastes like abalone because it does not have a fishy flavor like halibut, but rather a chewy consistency, which means that a chef pounds it to tenderize it.

Every cook has a different recipe for making conch chowder. A popular version includes tomatoes, potatoes, sweet peppers, onions, carrots, salt pork or bacon, bay leaf, thyme, and (of course) salt and pepper.

Conch fritters, shaped like balls, are served with hot sauce and are made with finely minced sweet peppers, onions, and tomato paste, among other ingredients. They are deep-fried in oil.

Conch salad is another local favorite, and it, too, has many variations. Essentially, it is uncooked conch marinated in Old Sour (a hot pepper sauce) to break down its tissues and add extra flavor. This tangy dish is served with diced small red (or green) peppers and chopped onion.

Cracked conch (or fried conch, as the old-timers call it) is prepared like a breaded veal cutlet. Pounded hard and dipped in batter, it is then sautéed. Conch is also served steamed, in Creole sauce, curried, "scorched," creamed on toast, and stewed. Instead of conch chowder, you might get conch soup. You'll also see "conch burgers" on menus.

OTHER SEAFOOD   The most elegant item you'll see on nearly any menu in The Bahamas is the local spiny lobster. A tropical cousin of the Maine lobster, it is also called crayfish or rock lobster. Only the tail is eaten, however, and it's not as sweet as the Maine species. You get fresh lobster only in season, from the beginning of April until the end of August. Otherwise, it's frozen.

Bahamian lobster, in spite of its cost, is not always prepared well. Sometimes a cook leaves it in the oven too long and the meat becomes tough and chewy. But when prepared right, like it is at Nassau's famed Graycliff restaurant (p. 51), it is perfection and worth the exorbitant cost.

The Bahamian lobster lends itself to any international recipe for lobster, including Newburg and Thermidor. A typical local preparation is to curry it with lime juice and fresh coconut, among other ingredients.

After conch, grouper is the second-most-consumed seafood species in The Bahamas. It's served in a number of ways, often batter-dipped or sautéed, and called "fingers" because of the way it's sliced. The fish can also come steamed and served in a spicy Creole sauce. Sometimes it comes dressed in a sauce of dry white wine, mushrooms, onions, and thyme. Because the fish has a mild taste, the other ingredients' extra flavor is needed.

Baked bonefish is also common, and it's very simple to prepare. The bonefish is split in half and seasoned with Old Sour (a hot pepper sauce) and salt, and then popped into the oven.

Baked crab is one of the best-known dishes in The Bahamas. A chef mixes eggs and the meat of either land or sea crabs with seasonings and bread crumbs. The crabs are then replaced in their shells and baked.

PEAS 'N' RICE & JOHNNYCAKE   If mashed potatoes are the national starch of the United States, then peas 'n' rice fulfills that role in The Bahamas. Peas 'n' rice, like potatoes, can be prepared in a number of ways. One popular method is to cook pigeon peas (which grow in pods on small trees) or black-eyed peas with salt pork, tomatoes, celery, uncooked rice, thyme, green pepper, onion, salt, pepper, and whatever special touch a chef wants to add. When it's served as a side dish, Bahamians often sprinkle hot sauce over the concoction.

Johnnycake, another famed Bahamian dish, dates from the early settlers, who were often simple and poor. They survived mainly on a diet of fish and rice, supplemented by johnnycake, a pan-cooked bread made with butter, milk, flour, sugar, salt, and baking powder. (Originally it was called "Journey Cake," which was eventually corrupted to "johnnycake.") Fishermen could make this simple bread on the decks of their vessels: They'd build a fire in a box that had been filled with sand to keep the flames from spreading to the craft.

TROPICAL FRUITS   Bahamians are especially fond of fruits, and they make inventive dishes out of them, including soursop ice cream and sapodilla pudding. Guavas are used to make their famous guava duff dessert. The islanders also grow and enjoy melons, pineapples, passion fruit, and mangoes.

Their most famous fruit is the papaya, which is called "pawpaw" or "melon tree." It's made into a dessert or chutney or eaten for breakfast in its natural state. It's also used in many lunch and dinner recipes. An old Bahamian custom of using papaya as a meat tenderizer has, at least since the 1970s, invaded North American kitchens. Papaya is also used to make fruity tropical drinks, such as the Bahama Mama shake.

And if you see it for sale in a local food store, take home some "Goombay" marmalade, which is made with papaya, pineapple, and green ginger.

RUMS, LIQUEURS & SPECIALTY DRINKS   Although rum came north from Cuba and Jamaica, Bahamians quickly adopted it as their national alcoholic beverage. Using their imagination, they invented several local drinks, including the Yellow Bird, the Bahama Mama, and the Goombay Smash.

The Yellow Bird is made with crème de banana liqueur, Vat 19 rum, orange juice, pineapple juice, apricot brandy, and Galliano. A Bahama Mama has Vat 19, citrus juice (perhaps pineapple, too), bitters, a dash of nutmeg, crème de cassis, and a hint of grenadine. The Goombay Smash usually consists of coconut rum, pineapple juice, lemon juice, Triple Sec, Vat 19, and a dash of simple syrup.

Nearly every bartender in the islands has a personal version of Planter's Punch. A classic recipe is to make it with lime juice, sugar, and Vat 19, plus a dash of bitters. It's usually served with a cherry and an orange slice.

If you want a typically Bahamian liqueur, try Nassau Royale. It is used to make an increasingly popular drink, the C. C. Rider, which includes Canadian Club, apricot brandy, and pineapple juice.

WHEN TO GO
The Weather

The temperature in The Bahamas averages between 75°F and 84°F (24°C–29°C) in both winter and summer, although it can get chilly in the early morning and at night. The Bahamian winter is usually like a perpetual late spring—naturally, the high season for North Americans rushing to escape snow and ice. Summer brings broiling hot sun and humidity. There's a much greater chance of rain during the summer and fall.

The Hurricane Season

The curse of Bahamian weather, the hurricane season, lasts (officially) from June 1 to November 30. But there is no cause for panic. More tropical cyclones pound the U.S. mainland than The Bahamas. Hurricanes are actually fairly infrequent here, and when one does come, satellite forecasts generally give adequate advance warning so that precautions can be taken.

If you're heading for The Bahamas during the hurricane season, you might want to visit the National Weather Service at www.nws.noaa.gov.

For an online 10-day forecast, check the Weather Channel at www.weather.com.

Average Temperatures & Rainfall (in.) in The Bahamas

	JAN	FEB	MAR	APR	MAY	JUNE	JULY	AUG	SEPT	OCT	NOV	DEC
TEMP. (°F)	70	70	72	75	77	81	81	82	81	79	73	72
TEMP. (°C)	21	21	22	24	25	27	27	28	27	26	23	22
RAINFALL (IN.)	1.9	1.6	1.4	1.9	4.8	9.2	6.1	6.3	7.5	8.3	2.3	1.5

Note that these numbers are daily averages, so expect temperatures to climb significantly higher in the noonday sun and to cool off a good deal in the evening.

The "Season"

In The Bahamas, hotels charge their highest prices during the peak winter period from mid-December to mid-April, when visitors fleeing from cold north winds flock to the islands. Winter is the driest season.

If you plan to visit during the winter, try to make reservations at least 2 to 3 months in advance. At some hotels, it's impossible to book accommodations for Christmas and the month of February without even more lead time.

SAVING MONEY IN THE OFF SEASON

The Bahamas is a year-round destination. The islands' "off season" runs from late spring to late fall, when tolerable temperatures (see "The Weather," above) prevail throughout most of the region. Trade winds ensure comfortable days and nights, even in accommodations without air-conditioning. Although the noonday sun may raise temperatures to uncomfortable levels, cool breezes usually make the morning, late afternoon, and evening more pleasant here than in many parts of the U.S. mainland.

Dollar for dollar, you'll spend less money by renting a summer house or fully equipped unit in The Bahamas than you would on Cape Cod, Fire Island, Laguna Beach, or the coast of Maine.

The off season—roughly from mid-April to mid-December (rate schedules vary from hotel to hotel)—amounts to a summer sale. In most cases, hotel rates are slashed from 20% to a startling 60%. It's a bonanza for cost-conscious travelers, especially families who like to go on vacations together. In the chapters ahead, we'll spell out in dollars the specific amounts hotels charge during the off season.

OTHER OFF-SEASON ADVANTAGES

Although The Bahamas may appear inviting in the winter to those who live in northern climates, your trip may be more enjoyable if you go in the off season. Here's why:

- After the winter hordes have left, a less hurried way of life prevails.
- Swimming pools and beaches are less crowded—perhaps not crowded at all.
- To survive, resort boutiques often feature summer sales.
- You can often appear without a reservation at a top restaurant and get a table for dinner.
- The endless waiting game is over: no waiting for a rented car, no long wait for a golf course tee time, and quicker access to tennis courts and watersports.
- The atmosphere is more cosmopolitan than it is in winter, mainly because of the influx of Europeans.
- Some package-tour fares are as much as 20% lower, and individual excursion fares may be reduced from 5% to 10%.
- Accommodations and flights are much easier to book.
- Summer is an excellent time for family travel, which is not always possible during the winter season.
- Finally, the best Bahamian attractions—sea, sand, surf, and lots of sunshine—remain absolutely undiminished.

OFF-SEASON DISADVANTAGES

Let's not paint too rosy a picture. Although the advantages of off-season travel far outweigh the disadvantages, there are nevertheless some drawbacks to traveling here in summer:

- You might be staying at a construction site. Hoteliers save their major renovations until the off season. You may wake up to the sound of hammers.
- Single tourists find the dating scene better in winter when there are more visitors, especially unattached ones.
- Services are often reduced. In the peak of winter, everything is fully operational. But in summer, many programs (such as watersports) might be curtailed in spite of fine weather.

The Bahamas Calendar of Events

For an exhaustive list of events beyond those listed here, check http://events.frommers.com, where you'll find a searchable, up-to-the-minute roster of what's happening in cities all over the world. For specific events, you can call your nearest branch of **The Bahamas Tourist Office** (see "Visitor Information," p. 298) at ✆ **800/BAHAMAS** (224-2627) or check their website at **www.bahamas.com** or **http://eventguide.com/bahamas**.

JANUARY

Junkanoo. This Mardi Gras–style festival begins 2 or 3 hours before dawn on New Year's Day. Throngs of cavorting, costumed figures prance through Nassau, Freeport/Lucaya, and the Out Islands. Jubilant men, women, and children wear elaborate headdresses and festive apparel as they celebrate their African heritage with music and dance. Mini-Junkanoos, in which visitors can participate, are regular events. Local tourist offices will advise the best locations to see the festivities.

New Year's Day Sailing Regatta, Nassau and Paradise Island. About 40 sailing sloops, ranging from 5 to 8.5m (16–28 ft.), converge off Montagu Bay in a battle for bragging rights. For information, call ✆ **242/394-0445.**

Annual Bahamas Wahoo Championships, Berry Islands. Anglers try to bait one of the fastest fish in the ocean, reaching speeds up to 113kmph (70 mph). For information, call ✆ **954/634-7496.** Mid-January.

FEBRUARY

The Mid-Winter Wahoo, Bimini. The Bimini Big Game Resort & Marina draws Hemingway look-alikes and other anglers to this winter event that is heavily attended by Floridians. For more information, call ✆ **800/BAHAMAS [224-2627]** or contact the tournament director, at the Bimini Tourist Office at ✆ **242/347-3529** (www.bahamas.com). Early February.

Farmer's Cay Festival. This festival is a rendezvous for yachtsmen cruising the Exuma Islands and a homecoming for the people of Farmer's Cay, Exuma. Boat excursions will depart Nassau at Potter's Cay for the festival at 8pm on Friday, and then return to Nassau at 8pm on Saturday from the Farmer's Cay Dock. For information, contact Terry Bain in Little Farmer's Cay, Exuma, at ✆ **242/355-4006,** or the Exuma Tourist Office at ✆ **242/336-2430.** First Friday and Saturday in February.

MARCH

Bacardi Billfish Tournament, Freeport. A weeklong tournament attracting the who's who of deep-sea fishing. Headquarters is the Port Lucaya Resort & Yacht Club. For more information, call ✆ **800/582-2921** or 242/373-9090, or visit www.portlucaya.com. Mid-March.

APRIL

Bahamas Family Island Regatta, George Town, the Exumas. Featuring Bahamian craft sloops, these celebrated boat races are held in Elizabeth Harbour. There's also a variety of onshore activities, including basketball, a skipper's party, and a Junkanoo parade. Call ☎ **242-336-2430** or check www.georgetowncruisingregatta.org for exact dates and information. Usually third week of April.

Bahamas Billfish Championship. This annual event is divided into four competitions, taking place at four different venues and times, spanning April to June. Anglers can fish any and all of the tournaments taking place at Marsh Harbour (third week of Apr), Harbour Island (first week of May), Spanish Cay (mid-May), and Treasure Cay (first week to second week of June). Since dates vary, contact the **Bahamas Billfish Championship** at 2 Oakland Blvd., Suite 195, Hollywood, FL 33020 (☎ **888/303-2242** or 954/920-5577; www.bahamasbill fish.com). April to June.

Bahamas White Marlin Open, the Abacos. This rendezvous off Abaco draws anglers seeking an action-packed billfish tournament. The headquarters is the Treasure Cay Resort & Marina. For more information, call ☎ **800/275-2260,** 954/920-5577, or 242/367-2158, or visit www.bahamas whitemarlinopen.com. Dates vary.

MAY

Long Island Regatta, Salt Pond, Long Island. This event sees some 40 to 50 sailing sloops from throughout The Bahamas compete in three classes for trophies and cash prizes. Onshore, dancing to indigenous "rake 'n' scrape" music, sporting events, and local food specialties for sale make for a carnival-like atmosphere. For more information, call ☎ **242/394-1535.** Late May.

JUNE

Eleuthera Pineapple Festival, Gregory Town, Eleuthera. This celebration devoted to the island's succulent pineapple features a Junkanoo parade, craft displays, dancing, a pineapple recipe contest, tours of pineapple farms, and a "pineathalon"—a .5km (⅓-mile) swim, 5.5km (3⅓-mile) run, and 6.5km (4-mile) bike ride. For more information, call ☎ **242/332-2142.** First week of June.

Bahamas Summer Boating Fling/Flotilla. Boating enthusiasts and yachters make the

1-day crossing from Florida to The Bahamas (Port Lucaya's marina on Grand Bahama Island) in a flotilla of boats guided by a lead boat. All "flings" depart from the Radisson Bahia Mar Resort & Yacht Center in Fort Lauderdale. For more information, contact the **Bahamas Tourism Center** in Florida at ☎ **954/236-9292.** End of June to beginning of August.

JULY

Annual Racing Time in Abaco, Marsh Harbour. This weeklong regatta features a series of sailboat races in the Sea of Abaco. Onshore festivities include nightly entertainment, cocktail parties, beach picnics, cultural activities, and a grand finale party. For registration forms and information, contact the Abaco Tourist Office at ☎ **242/367-3067.** Early July.

Independence Week. Independence celebrations are marked throughout the islands by festivities, parades, and fireworks. It all culminates on Independence Day. Call ☎ **242/322-1312.** July 10.

AUGUST

Emancipation Day. The first Monday in August commemorates the emancipation of slaves in 1834. A highlight of this holiday is an early morning "Junkanoo Rushout" starting at 4am in Fox Hill Village in Nassau, followed by an afternoon of "cookouts," cultural events such as climbing a greased pole, and the plaiting of the Maypole. First Monday in August.

Cat Island Regatta, Southern Bahamas. Sleepy Cat Island comes alive in the weekend of festive events, including sloop races, live "rake 'n' scrape" bands, quadrille dancing, old-fashioned contests and games, and local cuisine. Contact the **Regatta Desk** at ☎ **242/502-0600;** www.regattabahamas.com in Nassau. Early August.

SEPTEMBER

All Abaco Sailing Regatta. Local sailing sloops rendezvous at Treasure Cay Harbour for a series of championship races and onshore festivities. Contact the **Regatta Desk** in Nassau at ☎ **242/502-0600** or in Abaco at ☎ **242/367-3067.** Late September.

OCTOBER

Discovery Day. The New World landing of Christopher Columbus, traditionally said to be on the island of San Salvador, is celebrated throughout The Bahamas. Naturally, San Salvador has a parade every year on October 12.

North Eleuthera Sailing Regatta. Native sailing sloops take to the waters of North Eleuthera, Harbour Island, and Spanish Wells in a weekend of championship races. For information, contact the **Eleuthera Tourist Office** at ℂ **242/332-2142** or 242/333-3621. Mid-October.

Great Bahamas Seafood and Heritage Festival, Heritage Village, Arawak Cay. A cultural affair, this festival held in October showcases authentic Bahamian cuisine, traditional music, and storytelling. For more information, exact times, and a schedule of events, contact the **Ministry of Tourism** at ℂ **242/302-2000.**

NOVEMBER

Guy Fawkes Day. The best celebrations are in Nassau. Nighttime parades through the streets are held on many of the islands, culminating in the hanging and burning of Guy Fawkes, an effigy of the British malefactor who was involved in the Gunpowder Plot of 1605 in London. It usually takes place around November 5, but check with island tourist offices.

Bimini Big Game Fishing Club All Wahoo Tournament. Anglers take up the tough challenge of baiting one of the fastest fishes in the ocean. Headquarters is the Bimini Sands Resort & Marina. For information, contact ℂ **242/347-3391.** Mid-November.

Annual One Bahamas Music & Heritage Festival. This 3-day celebration is staged at both Nassau and Paradise Island to celebrate national unity. Highlights include concerts featuring top Bahamian performing artists, "fun walks," and other activities. For details, contact the **Nassau/Paradise Island Office** at the Ministry of Tourism, ℂ **242/302-2000.** Last week of November.

DECEMBER

Junkanoo Boxing Day. High-energy Junkanoo parades and celebrations are held throughout the islands on December 26. Many of these activities are repeated on New Year's Day (see "January," above). December 26.

Holidays

Banks, government offices, post offices, and many stores and restaurants are closed on the following public holidays in The Bahamas: January 1 (New Year's Day), Good Friday, Easter Sunday, Easter Monday, Whit Monday (7 weeks after Easter), the first Friday in June (Labour Day), July 10 (Independence Day), the first Monday in August (Emancipation Day), October 12 (Discovery Day), December 25 (Christmas), and December 26 (Boxing Day). When a holiday falls on a Saturday or Sunday, stores and offices are usually closed on the following Monday, too.

THE LAY OF THE LAND

With more than 700 islands and some 2,000 cays, The Bahamas spreads over 259,000 sq. km (100,000 sq. miles) of the Atlantic Ocean and encompasses countless natural attractions, including underwater reefs that stretch 1,220km (758 miles) from the Abacos in the northeast to Long Island in the southeast.

The Bahamas is the largest oceanic archipelago nation in the tropical Atlantic, with miles of crystal-clear waters rich in fish and other marine resources. Although New Providence is heavily populated, the rest of the Out Islands, including Grand Bahama, have relatively small populations. Unlike Puerto Rico, Jamaica, Barbados, and other Caribbean island nations, The Bahamas has large areas of undeveloped natural land. The islands also have the most extensive ocean-hole and limestone cave systems in the world.

The country's approximately 2,330 sq. km (900 sq. miles) of coral reefs include the world's third-largest barrier reef, off the coast of Andros. Reef marine life includes green moray eels, cinnamon clownfish, and Nassau grouper. The Bahamas was one of the first Caribbean countries to outlaw long-line fishing, recognizing it as a threat to regional ecology.

Another act of Parliament, the Wild Birds Protection Act, was passed to ensure the survival of all bird species throughout The Bahamas. Great Inagua Island is home to more than 60,000 pink flamingos, Bahamian parrots, and much of the world's population of reddish egrets. These birds live in the government-protected 743-sq.-km (287-sq.-mile) Inagua National Park.

These islands are also home to more than 1,370 plant species and some 13 endemic mammal species, the majority of them bats. Other resident mammals include wild pigs, donkeys, raccoons, and the Abaco wild horse. Whales and dolphins, including the humpback and blue whales and the spotted dolphin, are in the seas around the islands.

The **Bahamas National Trust** administers 12 national parks and protected areas covering more than 97,100 hectares (239,939 acres). Its headquarters, which is home to one of the Western Hemisphere's finest collections of wild palms, is in Nassau at the Retreat Gardens on Village Road (© **242/393-1317;** www.bnt.bs). Volunteers help arrange visits to the islands' national parks, the best of which are previewed below. Ecotourism highlights of The Bahamas include:

○ **Exuma Cays Land and Sea Park:** This park was the first of its kind anywhere on the planet and is a major attraction of The Bahamas. The 35km-long (22-mile), 13km-wide (8-mile) natural preserve encompasses 450 sq. km (174 sq. miles) of sea gardens with spectacular reefs, flora, and fauna. Inaugurated in 1958, it lies some 35km (22 miles) northwest of Staniel Cay (64km/40 miles southeast of Nassau) and is accessible only by boat. The Exumas provide one of the world's most colorful yachting grounds. Its nearest rivals in the Caribbean are the British Virgin Islands and the Grenadines.

○ **Inagua National Park:** Located on Great Inagua Island in the Southern Bahamas, this park is internationally famous as the site of the world's largest colony of wild West Indian flamingos. In Bahamian dialect, these birds are sometimes called *fillymingos* or *flamingas*.

○ **Union Creek Reserve:** This 18-sq.-km (7-sq.-mile) enclosed tidal creek on Great Inagua serves as a captive breeding research site at which to study giant sea turtles, with special emphasis on the endangered green turtle. In the distant past, the waters around Green Turtle Cay in the Abacos teemed with prehistoric-looking green turtles. However, because they were a valuable food source, they were over-hunted and their population diminished greatly.

Islands in Brief

The most developed islands for tourism are **New Providence,** site of Cable Beach and Nassau (the capital); **Paradise Island;** and **Grand Bahama,** home of Freeport and Lucaya. If you're after glitz, gambling, bustling restaurants, nightclubs, and a beach-party scene, these big three islands are where you'll want to be. Package deals are easily found.

Set sail (or hop on a short commuter flight) for one of the **Out Islands,** such as Andros, the Exumas, or the Abacos, and you'll find fewer crowds—and often lower prices, too. Though some of the Out Islands are accessible mainly (or only) by boat, it's still worth your while to make the trip if you like the idea of having an entire beach to yourself. These are really the places to get away from it all.

NEW PROVIDENCE ISLAND (NASSAU/CABLE BEACH)   New Providence isn't the largest Bahamian island, but it's the nation's historic heart, with a strong maritime tradition and the country's largest population (125,000). It offers groves of palms and casuarinas; sandy, flat soil; the closest thing in The Bahamas to urban sprawl; and superb anchorages sheltered from rough seas by nearby Paradise Island. New Providence also has the country's busiest airport and is dotted with hundreds of villas owned by foreign investors. Its two major resort areas are Cable Beach and Nassau.

Cable Beach is a glittering beachfront strip of hotels, restaurants, and casinos; only Paradise Island has been more developed. Its center is the Wyndham Nassau Resort & Crystal Palace Casino. Often, deciding between Cable Beach and Paradise Island isn't so much a choice of which island you prefer as a choice of which hotel you prefer. But it's easy to sample both, since it takes only about 30 minutes to drive between the two.

Nassau, the Bahamian capital, isn't on a great stretch of shoreline and doesn't have as many first-rate hotels as either Paradise Island or Cable Beach—with the exception of the British Colonial Hilton, which has a small private beach. The main advantages of Nassau are its colonial charm and lower price point. Its accommodations may not be ideally located, but they are relatively inexpensive, sometimes even during the winter high season. You can base yourself here and commute easily to the beaches at Paradise Island or Cable Beach. Some travelers even prefer Nassau because it's the seat of Bahamian culture and history—not to mention the shopping mecca of The Bahamas.

PARADISE ISLAND   If high-rise hotels and glittering casinos are what you want, alongside some of the best beaches in The Bahamas, there is no better choice than Paradise Island, directly off Nassau's coast. It has the best food, entertainment, hotels, and terrific beaches and casinos. Its major drawbacks are that it's expensive and often overcrowded. With its colorful history but unremarkable architecture, Paradise Island remains one of the most intensely marketed pieces of real estate in the world. The sands and shoals of the long, narrow island protect Nassau's wharves and piers, which rise across a narrow channel only 180m (591 ft.) away.

Owners of the 277-hectare (684-acre) island have included brokerage mogul Joseph Lynch (of Merrill Lynch) and Huntington Hartford (heir to the A&P supermarket fortune). More recent investors have included Merv Griffin. The island today is a carefully landscaped residential and commercial complex with good beaches, lots of glitter (some of it tasteful, some of it way too over-the-top), and many diversions.

GRAND BAHAMA ISLAND (FREEPORT/LUCAYA)   The island's name derives from the Spanish term *gran bajamar* ("great shallows"), which refers to the shallow reefs and sandbars that, over the centuries, have destroyed everything from Spanish galleons to English clippers on these shores. Thanks to the development schemes of U.S. financiers such as Howard Hughes, Grand Bahama boasts a well-developed tourist infrastructure. Casinos, beaches, and restaurants are now plentiful.

Grand Bahama's **Freeport/Lucaya** resort area is another popular destination for American tourists, though it has a lot more tackiness than Paradise Island or Cable

Beach. The compensation for that is a lower price tag on just about everything. Free-port/Lucaya offers plenty of opportunities for fine dining, entertainment, and gambling.

This island, especially popular with families, also offers the best hiking in The Bahamas and some of the finest sandy beaches. Its golf courses attract players from all over the globe and host major tournaments several times a year. You'll find some of the world's best diving here, as well as UNEXSO, the internationally famous diving school.

BIMINI   One of the smallest destinations in The Bahamas, Bimini is close enough to Miami (just 81km/50 miles) to be distinctly separate from the archipelago's other islands.

Bimini is actually a pair of islands with a total area of 23 sq. km (8¾ sq. miles); smaller North Bimini is better developed than South Bimini. Luxurious yachts and fishing boats are always docked at both islands' marinas. Throughout Bimini, there's a slightly run-down Florida-resort atmosphere mingled with some small-town charm (think old-time Key West, before the cruise-ship crowds ruined it).

Sportfishing here is among the best in the world. Once the setting for Ernest Hemingway's *Islands in the Stream,* Bimini attracts big-game fishers for big-league fishing tournaments. If you'd like to follow in the footsteps of such famous anglers as Zane Grey and Howard Hughes, this is your island. In addition, the scuba diving here ranks among the country's very best.

THE BERRY ISLANDS   Between Nassau and Florida's coast, these 30-odd islands—which comprise only about 77 sq. km (30 sq. miles) of land—attract devoted yachters and fishermen. This series of islets, cays, and rows of barely sub-merged rocks has extremely limited tourist facilities and is geared mostly toward well-heeled anglers, many of whom hail from Florida. Most of the full-time population (about 700 people) lives on Great Harbour Cay. These islands are a lot classier and more charming than Bimini.

ANDROS   Made up of three major land areas connected by a series of canals and cays called *bights,* Andros makes up the largest landmass in The Bahamas. It attracts divers, fishing enthusiasts, and sightseers.

Most of the island is uninhabited and unexplored. Its main villages are Nicholl's Town, Andros Town, and Congo Town; all are accessible by frequent boat and plane connections from Miami and Nassau. Lodging options range from large resorts to small, plain guesthouses that cater primarily to fishermen.

The world's third-largest barrier reef lies off the coast of Andros, and divers come from all over the world to explore it. The reef plunges 1,800m (5,906 ft.) at a narrow drop-off known as the Tongue of the Ocean. Bonefishing here is among the best on earth, as is the marlin and bluefin tuna fishing.

Known as the "Big Yard," the central portion of North Andros is mostly a dense forest of mahogany and pine where more than 50 orchid varieties bloom. In South Andros, there's a 100-sq.-km (39-sq.-mile) forest and mangrove swamp worth explor-ing. Any hotel concierge can arrange for a local guide to give you a tour of either of these natural attractions.

THE ABACOS   This cluster of islands and islets is a mecca for yachters and other boaters who flock here year-round—particularly in July, when the Regatta Time in Abaco race is held at the Green Turtle Club. For centuries, residents of the Abacos have built boats, although tourism is now the main industry.

beaches 101: PARADISE ISLAND, CABLE BEACH & MORE

In The Bahamas, the issue about public access to beaches is a hot and controversial subject. Recognizing this, the government has made efforts to intersperse public beaches near private ones, where access would otherwise be impeded. Although mega-resorts restrict nonguests from having easy access to their individual beaches, there are so many public beaches on New Providence Island and Paradise Island that all a beach lover has to do is stop the car at, or walk to, many of the unmarked, unnamed beaches that flank these islands.

If you stay in one of the large beachfront resorts, just head for the ocean via the sand in front the resort. Otherwise, below are a few details that will come in handy if your accommodations aren't oceanfront, or if you want to explore another beach:

Cabbage Beach ★★ (also called **West Beach**) On Paradise Island, this is the real showcase, with broad, white sands that stretch for at least 3km (1¾ miles). Casuarinas, palms, and sea grapes border it. While it's likely to be crowded in winter, you can find a little more elbowroom by walking to its northwestern stretch. You can reach Paradise Island from downtown Nassau by walking over the bridge, taking a taxi, or boarding a ferryboat at Prince George Wharf. Cabbage Beach does not have public facilities, but if you patronize one of the handful of bars and restaurants nearby, you can use its restrooms.

Cable Beach ★★ No particular beach is actually called Cable Beach, yet this is New Providence Island's most popular beachfront destination. The 6.5km (4-mile) stretch of resorts and white-sand beaches in the central northern coast has calypso music floating to the sand from hotel pool patios and vendors making their way between sunblock-slathered bodies. There are no public toilets here because guests of the resorts use their hotels' restrooms. If you're not a hotel guest or customer, you're not supposed to use the facilities. The Cable Beach resorts begin 5km (3 miles) west of downtown Nassau.

Caves Beach On the north shore, past Cable Beach, Caves Beach, which has soft sands, lies some 11km (6¾ miles) west of Nassau. It stands near Rock Point, right

With the exception of Eleuthera's Harbour Island, you'll find more New England charm here than anywhere else in The Bahamas. Loyalists who left after the American Revolution settled here and built Cape Cod–style clapboard houses with white picket fences. The best places to experience this old-fashioned charm are **Green Turtle Cay** and **Elbow Cay,** which are accessible from Marsh Harbour. **Marsh Harbour** itself has an international airport and a shopping center, although its hotels aren't as good as those on Green Turtle Cay and Elbow Cay.

Many of the Abacos are undeveloped and uninhabited. For the best of both worlds, visitors can stay on either Walker's, Green Turtle, or Treasure cays, and then charter a boat to tour the more remote areas.

ELEUTHERA Long and slender, this most historic of the Out Islands (the first English settlers arrived here in 1648) is actually a string of islands that includes the satellite communities of Spanish Wells (on St. George's Cay) and chic Harbour Island. The length of the island (177km/110 miles) and the distances between Eleuthera's communities require access via three airports. Frequent flights connect before the turnoff along Blake Road that leads to the airport. Since visitors often don't know of this beach, it's a good spot at which to escape the hordes. There are no toilets or changing facilities.

Delaporte Beach   Just west of the busiest section of Cable Beach, Delaporte is a public-access beach where you can go to escape the crowds. It opens onto clear waters and boasts white sands, although it has no facilities.

Goodman's Bay   This public beach lies east of Cable Beach on the way toward Nassau's center. Goodman's Bay and Saunders Beach (see below) often host local fund-raising cookouts, at which vendors sell fish, chicken, conch, peas 'n' rice, and macaroni and cheese. People swim and socialize to blaring reggae and calypso music. To find out when one of these beach parties is happening, ask the staff at your hotel or pick up a local newspaper. There is a playground here, too, and toilet facilities.

Paradise Beach ★★   This beach, on Paradise Island, is one of the best in the entire area. White and sandy, it's dotted with *chikees* (thatched huts), which are perfect when you've had too much sun. Mainly used by guests of the Atlantis Resort (p. 95), it lies at the island's far western tip. If you're not a guest, access is difficult. If you're staying at a hotel in Nassau and want to come to Paradise Island for a day at the beach, it's better to go to Cabbage Beach (see above).

Saunders Beach   East of Cable Beach, this is where many islanders head on their weekends off. To reach it, take West Bay Street from Nassau toward Coral Island. The beach is across from Fort Charlotte, just west of Arawak Cay. Like Goodman's Bay (see above), it often hosts local fund-raising cookouts that are open to the public. These can be a lot of fun. There are no public facilities.

Western Esplanade (also called **Junkanoo Beach** or **Lighthouse Beach**)   If you're staying at a hotel in downtown Nassau, such as the British Colonial Hilton (p. 51), this is a good beach to patronize close to town. The narrow strip of sand is convenient to Nassau and has toilets, changing facilities, and a snack bar.

Eleuthera to Nassau, which lies about 97 km (60 miles) east. Eleuthera is similar to the Abacos; visitors are drawn to the fabulous secluded beaches and miles of barrier reef.

Gregory Town is the island chain's pineapple capital. A bit farther south is Surfers Beach, one of the best surfing spots in The Bahamas. Several accommodations are available in this sleepy, slightly budget-oriented section of Eleuthera. The region's only major resort is the Club Med at Governor's Harbour; other inns are more basic. At the southern end of the island, Rock Sound is in a slump, waiting to see whether the fabled Cotton Bay Club will ever reopen.

Off the coast, **Harbour Island** offers excellent hotels and food, along with pastel-colored houses that evoke Cape Cod right down to their picket fences. The beaches here are famed for their sand tinged pink by crushed coral and shells. **Spanish Wells,** on St. George's Cay, another offshore island near Eleuthera, has extremely limited accommodations, and the residents—descendants of long-ago Loyalists—aren't very welcoming to visitors.

THE EXUMAS   Just 56km (35 miles) southeast of Nassau, this 588km-long (365-mile) string of islands and cays—most of them uninhabited—is the great yachting hub of The Bahamas, rivaling (some say surpassing) the Abacos. These waters, some of the country's prettiest, are also ideal for fishing. Many secluded beaches open onto tranquil cays. Portions of the James Bond thriller *Thunderball* were filmed at Staniel Cay. Daily flights serve the Exumas from Nassau, Miami, Fort Lauderdale, and Atlanta.

The locals are very hospitable, and if you stay here, you'll feel like you practically have the archipelago to yourself. **Great Exuma Island** is home to a few good inns, mainly in **George Town,** the commercial center of the Exumas. Every April, George Town hosts the inter-island Family Island Regatta, a major yachting event. Elsewhere on the island, a big new Four Seasons resort and golf course officially opened in 2004 at Emerald Bay, bringing a new type of crowd here. The Four Seasons offers a deep-water marina with 125 state-of-the-art slips for ocean-going yachts, along with a dock master.

Exuma Cays Land and Sea Park, protected by The Bahamas National Trust, comprises much of the coastline. The park is accessible only by boat and is one of the major natural wonders and sightseeing destinations of The Bahamas, with abundant undersea life, reefs, blue holes, and shipwrecks.

RESPONSIBLE TRAVEL

The Bahamas is one of the most eco-friendly destinations in the Western Hemisphere. There are some, of course, who still eat endangered species like the turtle and pollute the environment, but the government is aware that the pristine beauty of the islands, both the sea and the land, is one of the main reasons their vital tourist industry exists. Officials want to preserve it for future generations.

For a rundown on what **The Bahamas National Trust** is doing to protect bird and animal life, its national parks, and nature areas, refer to "The Lay of the Land" earlier in this chapter.

Conserving the wetlands has become of prime importance to the government. These wetlands are the source of potential for an expanded ecotourism industry and of vital importance to birds, animals, and fish.

The fishing industry is the third largest in The Bahamas, generating millions of dollars in exports because the vast coastal wetlands serve as marine nurseries.

Hurricanes, along with the destruction of wetlands by people, remain a constant threat to the environment. The flood-and-surge destruction from hurricanes alone can exceed $500 million in damage during a particularly destructive year when Mother Nature vents her fury on the archipelago.

Ecotours and adventures await you throughout The Bahamas. In Nassau and Paradise Island, **Bahamas Adventure Glass Bottom Kayaks** (© **800/688-5871;** www.bestonbahamas.com for bookings) allows you to sail the clear waters of New Providence Island while enjoying the marine life beneath you. Guided tours with equipment costs $77 or $40 for children 11 and under.

At the same number, you can also book a **Blackbeard Cay Stingray Adventure,** snorkeling and interacting with these gentle aquatic creatures. Prices are $42 or $37 for children 11 and under.

Nassau Segway Nature Tour takes you on a ride through Earth Village, a 162-acre preserve acclaimed by botanists as one of the most diverse ecosystems in The Bahamas. The cost is $75 for per person. For reservations, call © **800/688-5871.**

GENERAL RESOURCES FOR responsible travel

In addition to the resources for **The Bahamas** listed above, the following websites provide valuable wide-ranging information on sustainable travel.

o **Responsible Travel** (www.responsibletravel.com) is a great source of sustainable travel ideas; the site is run by a spokesperson for ethical tourism in the travel industry.

o **Sustainable Travel International** (www.sustainabletravelinternational.org) promotes ethical tourism practices, and manages an extensive directory of sustainable properties and tour operators around the world.

o **Carbonfund** (www.carbonfund.org), **TerraPass** (www.terrapass.org), and **Cool Climate** (http://coolclimate.berkeley.edu) provide info on "carbon offsetting," or offsetting the greenhouse gases emitted during flights.

o **Greenhotels** (www.greenhotels.com) recommends green-rated member hotels around the world that fulfill the company's stringent environmental requirements.

Environmentally Friendly Hotels (www.environmentallyfriendly hotels.com) offers more green accommodations ratings.

o **Sustain Lane** (www.sustainlane.com) lists sustainable eating and drinking choices around the U.S.; also visit **www.eatwellguide.org** for tips on eating sustainably in the U.S. and Canada.

o For information on animal-friendly issues throughout the world, visit **Tread Lightly** (www.treadlightly.org). For information about the ethics of swimming with dolphins, visit the **Whale and Dolphin Conservation Society** (www.wdcs.org).

o **Volunteer International** (www.volunteerinternational.org) has a list of questions to help you determine the intentions and the nature of a volunteer program. For general info on volunteer travel, visit **www.goabroad.com/volunteer-abroad** and **www.idea list.org**.

On Grand Bahama Island, you can experience ecotourism by taking the **Lucayan National Park and Cave Tour** (www.grandbahamanaturetours.com), discovering the pristine beauty of the 42-acre Lucayan National Park for $40 ($25 for children 10 and under). You can also take part in guided kayak expeditions through this tropical Eden for $89 per person. For reservations for both tours, call © **800/688-5871.**

Some hotels are obviously "greener" than others. **Small Hope Bay Lodge** (p. 166) on Andros Island has long adopted the ecotourism philosophy. The lodge conducts ecotours and is a nature-based resort. The lodge's aim is to protect the environment while still granting access to visitors who can enjoy it but also work to maintain and not destroy the surrounding nature.

Also on Andros is another eco-friendly resort, **Tiamo** (p. 167). On 4.9 hectares (12 acres) of land, this resort combines eco-sensitivity with first-class comforts in a setting of mangroves, wild sea grapes, and coconut palms. Some of its environmentally friendly elements include solar power and composting toilets. The staff also serves as nature guides, helping guests explore the bonefish flats or the inland "blue holes."

SPECIAL-INTEREST & ESCORTED TRIPS

Package Tours

Before you search for the lowest airfare on your own (see earlier in this chapter), you may want to consider booking your flight as part of a package deal—a way to travel independently but pay group rates.

A package tour is not an escorted tour, in which you're led around by a guide. Except by cruise ships visiting certain islands, the option of being escorted around six or so Bahamian islands on an escorted tour does not exist.

Package tours are simply a way to buy the airfare, accommodations, and other elements of your trip (such as car rentals, airport transfers, and sometimes even activities) at the same time and often at discounted prices.

One good source of package deals is the airlines themselves. Most major airlines offer air/land packages, including **American Airlines Vacations** (© **800/321-2121;** www. aavacations.com), **Delta Vacations** (© **800/654-6559;** www.deltavacations.com), and **United Vacations** (© **888/854-3899;** www.unitedvacations.com). Several big **online travel agencies**—Expedia, Travelocity, Orbitz, Site59, and Lastminute.com—also do a brisk business in packages.

Liberty Travel (© **888/271-1584;** www.libertytravel.com) is one of the biggest packagers in the U.S. Northeast, and it usually boasts a full-page ad in Sunday papers. There's also **TourScan, Inc.,** 107 Three Corners Red, Guilford, CT 06437 (© **800/962-2080** in the U.S.; www.tourscan.com), which researches the best-value vacation at each hotel and condo.

For British travelers, package tours to The Bahamas can be booked through **Kuoni Travel,** Kuoni House, Dorking, Surrey RH5 4AZ (© **0844/488-0274;** www.kuoni. co.uk), which offers both land and air packages to destinations such as Nassau and Freeport, and to some places in the Out Islands. They also offer packages for self-catering villas on Paradise Island.

Club Med (www.clubmed.com; © **888/WEB-CLUB** [932-2582]) has various all-inclusive options throughout the Caribbean and The Bahamas.

Travel packages are also listed in the travel section of your local Sunday newspaper. Or check ads in the national travel magazines, such as *Arthur Frommer's Budget Travel Magazine, Travel + Leisure, National Geographic Traveler,* and *Condé Nast Traveler.*

Active Vacations

The more than 700 islands in the Bahamian archipelago (fewer than 30 of which are inhabited) are surrounded by warm, clear waters—ideal for fishing, sailing, and scuba diving. (Detailed recommendations and the costs of these activities are previewed under the individual destinations listings.) The country's perfect weather and its many cooperative local entrepreneurs allow easy access to more than 30 sports throughout the islands.

WATERSPORTS

FISHING The shallow waters between the hundreds of cays and islands of The Bahamas are some of the most fertile fishing grounds in the world. Even waters where marine traffic is relatively congested have yielded impressive catches in the past, although overfishing has depleted schools of fish, especially big-game fish.

Grouper, billfish, wahoo, tuna, and dozens of other species thrive in Bahamian waters, and dozens of charter boats are available for deep-sea fishing.

Frontiers International (© **800/245-1950** or 724/935-1577; www.frontiers travel.com) features fly- and spin-fishing tours of The Bahamas and is a specialist in saltwater-fishing destinations. In addition, reef fishing, either from small boats or from shorelines, is popular everywhere, with grouper, snapper, and barracuda being the most commonly caught species.

Specialists and serious amateurs of the sport often head for any of the following destinations listed below.

The island of **Bimini** is known as the "Big-Game Fishing Capital of the World." Here anglers can hunt for the increasingly elusive swordfish, sailfish, and marlin. For tournament listings, see the "Bahamas Calendar of Events," earlier in this chapter. Bimini maintains its own Hall of Fame, where proud anglers have their catches honored. World records for the size of catches don't seem to last long here; they are usually quickly surpassed.

Walker's Cay in the Abacos and **Chub Cay** in the Berry Islands are famous for both deep-sea and shore fishing. Some anglers return to these cays year after year. Grouper, jacks, and snapper are plentiful. Even spearfishing without scuba gear is common and popular.

Andros boasts the world's best bonefishing. Bonefish (also known as "gray fox") are medium-size fish that feed in shallow, well-lit waters. Known as some of the most tenacious fish in the world, they struggle ferociously against anglers who pride themselves on using light lines from shallow-draft boats. **Andros Island Bonefish Club** in North Andros (© **242/368-5167;** www.androsbonefishing.com) specializes in fishing adventures off some of the most remote and sparsely populated coastlines in the country.

SAILING   The Bahamas is one of the top yachting destinations in the Atlantic. Its more than 700 islands and well-developed marinas provide a spectacular and practical backdrop for sailing enthusiasts. For a listing of frequent regattas, see the "Bahamas Calendar of Events," earlier in this chapter. The mini archipelago of the **Abacos** is called "The Sailing Capital of the World." You might think it deserves the title until you've sailed the **Exumas,** which we think are even better.

Don't be dismayed if you don't own a yacht. All sizes and types of crafts, from dinghies to blue-water cruisers, are available for charter, and crew and captain are optional for experienced sailors. If your dreams involve experiencing the seagoing life for an afternoon or less, many hotels offer sightseeing cruises aboard catamarans or glass-bottom boats, often with the opportunity to snorkel or swim in the wide-open sea.

The Abacos have many marinas. The best boat rentals are at the **Moorings** (© **888/952-8420** or 727/535-1446; www.moorings.com). In the Exumas it's sometimes difficult to rent boats because most yachters arrive with their own.

SCUBA DIVING   The unusual marine topography of The Bahamas offers an astonishing variety of options for divers. Throughout the more than 700 islands are innumerable reefs, drop-offs, coral gardens, caves, and shipwrecks. In many locations, you may feel that you are the first human ever to explore the site. Since fewer than 30 of the Bahamian islands are inhabited, you can usually dive in pristine and uncrowded splendor.

Andros Island boasts the third-largest barrier reef in the world. Chub Cay, in the Berry Islands, and Riding Rock, San Salvador, also offer premium spots to take a plunge in an underwater world teeming with aquatic life. The intricate layout of the Exumas includes virtually every type of underwater dive site, very few of which have ever been explored. The Abacos, famous for yachting, and the extensive reefs off the coast of Freeport are also fabulous dive sites.

Freeport, incidentally, is home to the country's most famous and complete diving operation, **UNEXSO** (*©* **800/992-DIVE** [3483] or 242/373-1244; www.unexso. com). It offers a 5.2m-deep (17-ft.) swimming pool where divers can work toward certification, and the popular "Dolphin Experience," in which visitors are allowed to pet, swim, snorkel, and dive with these remarkable animals.

You can easily learn to dive for the first time in The Bahamas. Lots of Bahamian hotels offer resort courses for novices, usually enabling a beginner to dive with a guide after several hours of instruction. You'll probably start out in the swimming pool for your initial instruction and then go out with a guide from the beach. A license (called a certification card, or "C" card) proving the successful completion of a designated program of scuba study is legally required for solo divers. Many resort hotels and dive shops offer the necessary 5-day training course. Participants who successfully complete the courses are awarded certifications by diving organizations such as PADI or NAUI.

For useful information, check out the website of the Professional Association of Diving Instructors (PADI) at www.padi.com. You'll find a description of the best dive sites and a list of PADI-certified dive operators. *Rodale's Scuba Diving Magazine* also has a helpful website at www.scubadiving.com. Both sites list dive-package specials and display gorgeous color photos of some of the most beautiful dive spots in the world.

OTHER OUTDOOR ACTIVITIES

BIKE & SCOOTER RENTALS   Most biking or scooter riding is done either on New Providence Island (Nassau) or on Grand Bahama Island; both have relatively flat terrain. Biking is best on Grand Bahama Island because it's bigger, with better roads and more places to go. Getting around New Providence Island is relatively easy once you're out of the congestion of Nassau and Cable Beach. In Nassau many hotels will rent you a bike or motor scooter.

On Grand Bahama Island, you can rent bikes at most big hotels (see chapter 5 for phone numbers and addresses of hotels). You can also rent motor scooters starting at about $60 per day. The tourist office at Freeport/Lucaya will outline on a map the best biking routes.

In the Out Islands, roads are usually too bumpy and potholed for much serious biking or scooter riding. Bike-rental places are almost nonexistent unless your hotel has some vehicles.

GOLF   The richest pickings are on Grand Bahama Island. The **Reef Course** is the first new golf course to open in The Bahamas since 1969. Designed by Robert Trent Jones, Jr., it features water along 13 of its 18 holes. The oldest course on Grand Bahama Island is the **Lucayan Golf Course,** a wooded course with elevated greens and numerous water hazards designed for precision golf. See chapter 5 for details, and also refer to "The Best Golf Courses," in chapter 1.

Quality golf in The Bahamas, however, is not restricted to Grand Bahama Island. The **Cable Beach Golf Course** is the oldest golf course in the country. The widely publicized **Ocean Club Golf Club** has unusual obstacles—a lion's den and a windmill—which have challenged the skill of both Gary Player and Jack Nicklaus. It also boasts the world's largest sand trap. See chapters 3 and 4 for more information, and also refer to "The Best Golf Courses," in chapter 1.

A spectacular Greg Norman–designed course opened in Great Exuma, part of the massive new **Sandals** resort. See chapter 9.

Golf is also available at a course in the Abacos at the **Treasure Cay Golf Club.** The design is challenging, with many panoramic water views and water obstacles. See chapter 7 for more information.

HIKING   The Bahamas isn't the greatest destination for serious hikers. The best hiking is on Grand Bahama Island, especially in **Lucayan National Park,** which spreads across 16 hectares (40 acres) and is some 32km (20 miles) from Lucaya. A large map at the entrance to the park outlines the trails. The park is laced with trails and elevated walkways. The highlight of the park is what may be the largest underground cave system in the world, some 11km (6¾ miles) long. Spiral steps let you descend into an eerie underground world.

Also on Grand Bahama Island, the **Rand Memorial Nature Centre** is the second-best place for hiking. It offers some 40 wooded hectares (99 acres) that you can explore on your own or with a tour guide. A .8km (.5 mile) stretch of winding trails acquaints you with the flora and fauna that call Grand Bahama home, everything from a native boa constrictor to the Cuban emerald hummingbird, whose favorite food is the nectar of the hibiscus.

HORSEBACK RIDING   The best riding possibilities are at **Pinetree Stables** on Grand Bahama Island (© **242/373-3600** or 305/433-4809; www.pinetree-stables. com). Its escorted ecotour trail rides are especially interesting. Rides are offered two times a day Tuesday through Sunday; be sure to book rides a few days in advance. See chapter 5 for more information.

Virtually the only place on New Providence Island (Nassau) that offers horseback riding is **Windsor Equestrian Centre & Happy Trails Stables,** Coral Harbour (© **242/362-1820;** www.windsorequestriancentre.com), which features both morning and afternoon trail rides and requires a reservation. These tours include transportation to and from your hotel. The trail rides are guided through the woods and along the beach. See chapter 3for more information.

Horseback riding is hardly a passion on the other islands.

TENNIS   Most tennis courts are part of large resorts and are usually free for the use of registered guests during the day. Charges are imposed to light the courts at night. Nonguests are welcome but are charged a player's fee; they should call in advance to reserve. Larger resorts usually offer on-site pro shops and professional instructors. Court surfaces range from clay or asphalt to such technologically advanced substances as Flexipave and Har-Tru.

New Providence, with more than 80 tennis courts, wins points for offering the greatest number of choices. At least 21 of these lie on Paradise Island. See chapter 4. After New Providence, Grand Bahama has the largest number of courts available for play—almost 40 in all. See chapter 5. Within the Out Islands, tennis courts are available on the Berry Islands, the Abacos, Eleuthera, and the Exumas. See chapters 6, 7, 8, and 9 for more information.

NEW PROVIDENCE (NASSAU/CABLE BEACH)

3

New Providence could almost be England—but for the weather, that is, and for the staunch sense of Bahamian nationalism. The shops draw a lot more business than the museums, but no other city in The Bahamas is as rich in history. You can climb up the 18th-century Queen's Staircase to Fort Fincastle or learn about the traditions of the Junkanoo festival at the Junkanoo Expo. It's an intoxicating, laid-back city, one that offers a good dose of British colonial charm, where tropical foliage lines streets and horse-drawn surreys trot by.

Things to Do **Cable Beach** is perfect for families, with its soft white sand, gentle waves and children's clubs. Away from the beach, take a swashbuckling trip back in time at the interactive **Pirates of Nassau** museum. Examine religious and folklore paintings at Nassau's **National Art Gallery of The Bahamas** or learn about the rich history and colorful costumes of the Junkanoo festival at the **Junkanoo Expo.** In Nassau's harbor, numerous **glass-bottom boats** wait to take you through the colorful sea gardens off New Providence Island.

Shopping Most of New Providence shopping is on **Bay Street** in Nassau. Look for cut-price jewelry, cosmetics, and hand-rolled cigars, as well as a plethora of T-shirts and souvenirs. The **Nassau International Bazaar,** with its cobbled alleyways and garreted storefronts, houses some 30 shops in its idyllic waterfront location. Hotel arcades are also worth browsing, as well as duty-free antique shops. Junkanoo carnival masks from artists' studios bring a little Caribbean flavor into your home.

Nightlife & Entertainment As the sun goes down, **Cable Beach** offers fine dining, glitzy casinos, cabaret shows, moonlight cruises, romantic evening strolls, and parties on the sand. In the old town of **Nassau,** you can dance to *soca* and calypso in intimate clubs, or rattle your ribcage with pounding techno on **Paradise Island.** At local joints around the island, you can enjoy favorites such as "Funky Nassau" and older, more nostalgic tunes like "Goin' Down Burma Road" or "Get Involved."

Restaurants & Dining New Providence accents its Bahamian fare with ethnic specialties such as Asian, Latin and European cuisine. Thus,

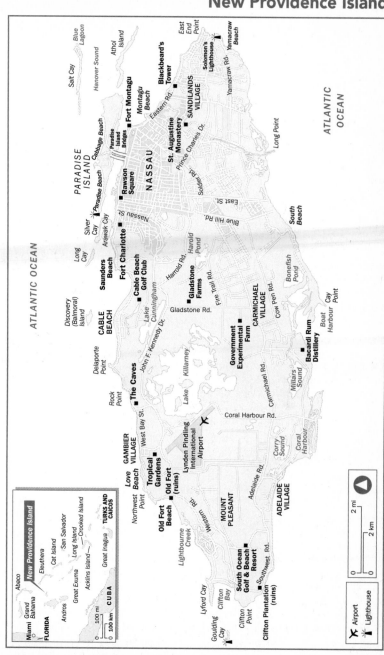

you can expect to find everything from steak and kidney pie (dating from the days of British colonial rule) in the celebrity-chef dining rooms of **Nassau** to the favorite **conch salad,** served at roadside shacks on the way to **Cable Beach.** Fresh seafood should not be missed, especially grouper, snapper, and conch.

ORIENTATION

Arriving

BY PLANE   Flights land at **Lynden Pindling International Airport** (© 242/702-1010; www.nas.bs), formerly known as Nassau International Airport, 13km (8 miles) west of Nassau, in the pine forests beside Lake Killarney.

No regularly scheduled bus service goes from the airport to Nassau, Cable Beach, or Paradise Island. Your hotel may provide **airport transfers** if you've made arrangements in advance; these are often included in package deals. You'll find any number of **car-rental** offices here (p. 48), though we don't really think you need one.

If you don't have a lift arranged, take a **taxi** to your hotel. From the airport to the center of Nassau, expect to pay around $27; to Cable Beach, $18; and to Paradise Island, $34, a rate that includes the bridge toll for passage between New Providence and Paradise islands. These rates apply to two persons and their luggage, with each additional passenger paying $3 each. Drivers expect to be tipped 15%, and some will remind you should you "forget." You don't need to exchange currency before departing the airport: U.S. dollars are fine for these (and any other) transactions.

BY CRUISE SHIP   Nassau has spent millions of dollars expanding its port so that a number of cruise ships can dock at once. Sounds great in theory, but practically speaking, facilities in Nassau, Cable Beach, and Paradise Island become extremely overcrowded as soon as the big boats arrive. You'll have to stake out your space on the beach, and you'll find downtown streets, shops, and attractions overrun with visitors every day you're in port.

Cruise ships dock near Rawson Square, the heart of the city and the shopping area— and the best place to begin a tour of Nassau. Unless you want to go to one of the beach strips along Cable Beach or Paradise Island, you won't need a taxi. You can go on a shopping expedition near where you dock: The Straw Market is at nearby Market Plaza; Bay Street, the main shopping artery, is also close; and the Nassau International Bazaar is at the intersection of Woodes Rogers Walk and Charlotte Street.

The government has added **Festival Place** (© **242/323-3182**) to the Prince George Wharf (where cruise ships arrive). Designed as a welcome point and service center for cruise-ship visitors, it's a multicolored structure with about 35 shops selling sundries, gift items, duty-free luxury goods, and Bahamian-themed arts, crafts, and souvenirs. There's also a tourist information booth (© **242/323-3182** or 323-3183) and various snack bars and cafes. You can lounge and have a daiquiri while you listen to the live calypso entertainment, or get your hair braided. This mall-like facility is open daily from 8am to 7pm, but if cruise ships are in port, closing may be extended to as late as 10pm. From a point nearby, you can catch a ride by horse and surrey, or take a water taxi across the channel to Paradise Island (p. 48).

Visitor Information

The Bahamas Ministry of Tourism maintains a tourist information booth at **Lynden Pindling International Airport** in the arrivals terminal (© **800/BAHAMAS** [224-2627] or 242/377-6806; www.bahamas.com). Hours are daily from 9am to 10pm.

FAVORITE NEW PROVIDENCE experiences

Listening to the sounds of Goombay. At local joints—such as Club Fluid and Da Tambrin Tree—you can enjoy an intoxicating beat and such island favorites as Andros-born Elon Moxey's "Catch the Crab" and K.B.'s "Civil Servants" (a satire of the sometimes pervasive governmental bureaucracy in The Bahamas). Deeply ingrained in the Bahamian musical psyche is a song that eventually became a huge international hit, "Funky Nassau." Older, more nostalgic tunes include "Goin' Down Burma Road," "Get Involved," and "John B. Sail."

Taking a glass-bottom boat ride. Right in the middle of Nassau's harbor, numerous boats wait to take you through the colorful sea gardens off New Providence Island. In the teeming reefs, you'll meet all sorts of sea creatures that inhabit this underwater wonderland.

Spending a day on Blue Lagoon Island. It's like an old Hollywood fantasy of a tropical island. Located off Paradise Island's eastern end, Blue Lagoon Island boasts seven sandy beaches. Boats from the ferryboat docks will take you there and back.

You can also stop by the information desk at the offices of the **Ministry of Tourism,** Bolam House, George Street (© **242/302-2000**), open Monday through Friday from 9am to 5pm, or the information booth at **Festival Place** (© **242/323-3182** or 323-3183), where the cruise ships dock. This kiosk is usually open daily 8am to 7pm.

The Lay of the Land

Most of Nassau's hotels are city hotels and are not on the water. To stay right on the sands, choose a hotel in Cable Beach (described later in this chapter) or on Paradise Island (see chapter 4).

Rawson Square is the heart of Nassau, positioned just a short walk from **Prince George Wharf,** where the big cruise ships, many of them originating in Florida, berth. Here you'll see the Churchill Building, which contains the offices of the Bahamian prime minister, along with other government ministries.

Busy **Bay Street,** the main shopping artery, begins on the south side of Rawson Square. This was the turf of the infamous Bay Street Boys, a group of rich, white Bahamians who once controlled political and economic activity on New Providence.

On the opposite side of Rawson Square is **Parliament Square,** with its government houses, House of Assembly, and statue of a youthful Queen Victoria. These are Georgian and Neo-Georgian buildings, some from the late 1700s.

The courthouse is separated by a little square from the **Nassau Public Library and Museum,** which opens onto Bank Lane. It was the former Nassau Gaol (jail). South of the library, across Shirley Street, are the remains of the **Royal Victoria Hotel,** which opened the same year the American Civil War began (1861) and hosted many a blockade runner and Confederate spy.

A walk down Parliament Street leads to the **post office.** Philatelists may want to stop in—some Bahamian stamps are true collectors' items.

Moving southward, farther away from the water, Elizabeth Avenue takes you to the **Queen's Staircase.** One of the major landmarks of Nassau, it climbs to Bennet's Hill and Fort Fincastle.

If you return to Bay Street, you'll discover the oversized tent that contains the **Straw Market,** a handicrafts emporium where you can buy all sorts of souvenirs.

GETTING AROUND

By Taxi

You can easily rely on taxis and skip renting a car. The rates for New Providence, including Nassau, are set by the government. Although working meters are required in all taxis, some of them don't work. Consequently, the government has established a well-defined roster of rates for passage between the airport and various points around the island. When you get in, the fixed rate is $3, plus 40¢ for each additional quarter-mile. Each passenger 2 years and older pays an extra $3. For sightseeing purposes, taxis can also be hired at the hourly rate of $50 for a five-passenger cab. Luggage is carried at a surcharge of $1 extra per piece, although the first two pieces are free. To call a cab, dial (C) **242/323-5111.** It's easy to get a taxi at the airport or at any of the big hotels.

If you'd like a personalized tour of the island, your best bet is to use **Romeo's Executive Limousine & Taxi Service** ((C) **242/363-4728;** www.romeoslimos. com). Romeo Farrington is quite informative about the island, its legends and lore. He personalizes all tours. A typical island tour, lasting from 2½ to 3 hours, costs $80 per hour for two passengers.

By Car

You really don't need to rent a car. It's a lot easier to rely on taxis when you're ready to leave the beach and do some exploring.

However, if you choose to drive (perhaps for a day of touring the whole island), some of the biggest U.S. car-rental companies maintain branches at the airport, and in some cases, at locations in downtown Nassau as well. **Avis** ((C) **800/331-1212** or 242/377-7121; www.avis.com) maintains an airport location, an office on Bay Street in downtown Nassau, and a branch on Cumberland Street on Paradise Island, and when business warrants, an office at the Prince George Docks in Nassau as well. Avis' three major competitors, **Budget** ((C) **800/527-0700** or 242/377-7405; www. budget.com), **Dollar/Thrifty** ((C) **800/800-3665** or 242/377-8300; www.dollar. com), and **Hertz** ((C) **800/654-3131** or 242/377-8684; www.hertz.com) each maintain offices at the airport, with flexible arrangements for delivering cars to other points on the island to anyone who's interested.

Remember: Drive on the left!

By Bus

The least expensive means of transport is via any of the buses (some locals refer to them as "jitneys") that make runs from downtown Nassau to outposts all over New Providence. The fare is $1.25, and the exact amount, in a combination of coins or with coins and a dollar bill, is required. The jitneys operate daily from 6:30am to 7pm.

Buses to the Cable Beach area and points west of that include the much-used **no. 10,** the **no. 10A,** and **"the Western bus."** They depart from the corner of Bay Street and George Street, with stops at various clearly designated spots along Bay Street. Buses headed to the eastern (mostly residential and rarely accessed by short-term visitors) part of New Providence Island depart from the Frederick Street North depot.

By Boat

Water taxis operate daily from 9am to 6pm at 20-minute intervals between Paradise Island and Prince George Wharf in nearby Nassau, just across the channel.

On Your Own Sturdy Feet

This is the only way to see Old Nassau, unless you rent a horse and carriage. All the major attractions and principal stores are within walking distance. You can even walk to Cable Beach or Paradise Island, although it's a hike in the hot sun.

Confine your walking to the daytime, and beware of the occasional pickpocket or purse snatcher. In the evening, avoid walking the streets of downtown Nassau, where, from time to time, muggings have been reported.

Ferryboats link the wharves at the end of Casuarina Drive on Paradise Island to Rawson Square, which lies across the channel on New Providence Island. The ferry operates daily from 9am to 6pm, with departures every half-hour from both sides of the harbor.

Both the ferryboats and the water taxis charge the same fixed rate: $6 per person, each way, for passage across the channel.

By Moped

Lots of visitors like to rent mopeds to explore the island. Unless you're an experienced rider, stay on quiet roads until you feel at ease; don't start out in all the congestion on Bay Street. Some hotels maintain rental kiosks on their premises. If yours doesn't, try **Bowcar Scooter Rental** (*②* 242/328-7300) at Festival Place near the cruise-ship dock. It charges $65 per day, which includes insurance and mandatory helmets for both drivers and passengers. Mopeds are rented daily between 8am and 5pm.

[FastFACTS] NEW PROVIDENCE

ATMs Major banks with ATMs in Nassau include the **Royal Bank of Canada** (*②* 242/322-8700; www.rbcroyalbank.com), **Scotia Bank** (*②* 242/397-3000; www.scotiabank.com), and **First Caribbean Bank** (*②* 242/356-8000; www.firstcaribbeanbank.com). Some accept cards only in the **Cirrus** network (*②* 800/424-7787; www.mastercard.com), while others take only **PLUS** (www.visa.com). ATMs at the Paradise Island and Cable Beach casinos dispense quick cash. Be aware that, whereas ATMs within large hotels and casinos tend to

dispense U.S. dollars, ATMs within banks and at the airport dispense Bahamian dollars. Since both U.S. and Bahamian currencies are readily accepted anywhere, it's not a crucial issue, but it's a good idea to read the information on the individual ATM before proceeding with your transaction.

Babysitting Hotel staff can help you hire an experienced sitter. Expect to pay between $12 and $15 per hour, plus $4 per hour for each additional child.

Dentists The **Princess Margaret Hospital,** on Sands Road at Shirley Street(*②* 242/322-2861;

www.phabahamas.org), has a dentistry department.

Doctors For the best service, go to the **Princess Margaret Hospital,** on Sands Road at Shirley Street(*②* 242/322-2861; www.phabahamas.org).

Drugstores In downtown Nassau, **Deveaux's Drugs and Convenience Store,** 99 Market St. at Wood's Alley (tel. 242/322-3941) is your best bet. It's open Monday to Saturday 8am to 6:30pm.

Emergencies Call *②* 911 or 919.

Eyeglass Repair The **Optique Shoppe,** 22 Parliament St., at Shirley Street

(**© 242/322-3910**), is convenient to the center of Nassau. Hours are Monday through Friday from 9am to 5pm and Saturday from 9am to noon.

Hospitals The government-operated **Princess Margaret Hospital**, on Sands Road at Shirley St. (**© 242/322-2861;** www. phabahamas.org), is one of the country's major hospitals. The privately owned **Doctors Hospital**, 1 Collins Ave. (**© 242/302-4600;** www.doctorshosp.com), is the region's most modern private healthcare facility.

Hot Lines For assistance of any kind, call **© 242/326-HELP** (4357).

Internet Access Check out **Cyberjack the Incredible** at the **Mall on Marathon Road** (**© 242/ 394-6254**), which charges 18¢ per minute to get online using one of its computers or your own laptop. The mall, lying at the intersection with Robinson Road, is 3 miles south of the center of Nassau. Take Mackey Street to Wuff Road, which leads to Marathon Road. If you're on Cable Beach, take the Tonique Williams-Darling Highway and the East West Highway north to the

intersection of Marathon Road and Robinson Road. Most of the larger hotels offer guests Internet access for a fee, which can in some cases be as high as 50¢ per minute.

Laundry & Dry Cleaning **Superwash,** at Nassau Street and Boyd Road (**© 242/323-4018**), offers coin-operated machines 24 hours a day, 7 days a week. Drop-off service is available for a small additional fee. In the same building is the **New Oriental Dry Cleaner** (**© 242/ 323-7249**).

Newspapers & Magazines The *Tribune* and the *Nassau Guardian*, both published in the morning, are the country's two competing daily newspapers. Hotels and tourist information desks distribute various helpful magazines, brochures, and booklets.

Police Dial **© 911** or 919.

Post Office **The Nassau General Post Office,** at the top of Parliament Street on East Hill Street (**© 242/ 322-4917**), is open Monday through Friday from 9am to 5pm and Saturday from 8:30am to 12:30pm. Note that you can also buy stamps from most postcard

kiosks. A postcard sent airmail to the U.S. or Canada costs 50¢; a letter to the same destinations costs 65¢ per half-ounce.

Safety Avoid walking along lonely side streets in downtown Nassau at night, when robberies and muggings sometimes occur. Because the local government is particularly punitive against crimes against tourists, most visitors from outside The Bahamas are never affected—but it's always better to be safe than sorry. Cable Beach and Paradise Island tend to be safer than downtown Nassau after dark.

Taxes There is no sales tax on any purchase made within The Bahamas, though there is a hotel tax, assessed at between 10% and 18%, depending on the category of hotel you stay in. Visitors leaving The Bahamas pay a $20 departure tax ($23 if you're departing for a point outside of The Bahamas from the airport on Grand Bahama Island), a tariff that's automatically included in the price of any airline or cruise-ship ticket. This departure tax only applies to travelers aged six and older.

WHERE TO STAY

In the hotel descriptions that follow, we've listed regular room prices, or "rack rates," but these are simply for ease of comparison. They are likely to be accurate for smaller properties, but you can almost always get a better price at the larger hotels and resorts.

Read the section entitled "Special-Interest & Escorted Trips," in chapter 2, before booking a hotel separately from your airfare. If you do book your own reservations, always inquire about honeymoon specials, golf packages, summer weeks, and other potential discounts. In many cases, a travel agent can get you a package deal that would be cheaper than the official rates.

Hotels add a tax of between 10% and 18%, depending on the category of hotel you stay at, to your rate. Sometimes this is quoted in advance as part of the net price; other times, it's added as an unexpected afterthought to your final bill. When you are quoted a rate, always ask if the tax is included. Many hotels also add a 15% service charge to your bill. Be sure to ask about these charges in advance so you won't be shocked when you receive the final tab.

Taxes and service charges are not included in the reviews below, which lead off with a selection of hotels within the heart of Nassau, followed by accommodations in Cable Beach. Most visitors prefer to stay at Cable Beach since its resorts are right on the sand. But you can also stay in Nassau and commute to the beaches at Cable Beach or Paradise Island; it's less convenient but cheaper. Those who prefer the ambience of Old Nassau's historic district and convenience to the best shops may decide to stay in town.

Nassau

EXPENSIVE

British Colonial Hilton This restored hotel exudes a palpable air of the long-ago days when The Bahamas was firmly within Britain's political and social orbit. This landmark seven-story structure is the biggest and most comprehensive hotel in downtown Nassau, a business-focused workhorse and focal point for meetings of public charities and business associations who want to avoid the tourist throngs of Cable Beach or Paradise Island. Don't expect glitz, glitter, or any intensely marketed sense of theme-related fantasy—the Hilton is after business travelers rather than the casino crowd. It also lacks the aristocratic credentials of Graycliff (see below). Nonetheless, the hotel is dignified and friendly, though rather sedate. Bedrooms are on the small side but have a discreetly upscale décor that was brushed up considerably during the 2010 renovation There's a small beach a few steps away, but it's not very appealing, as it's on the narrow channel separating New Providence from Paradise Island, with no wave action at all.

1 Bay St., Nassau, The Bahamas. www.hiltoncaribbean.com. © **800/HILTONS** (445-8667) in the U.S. and Canada, or 242/322-3301. Fax 242/302-9009. 288 units. Year-round $199–$425 double; $340–$550 suite. AE, DC, DISC, MC, V. Bus: 10. **Amenities:** 2 restaurants (including Aqua, p. 63); 2 bars; babysitting; concierge; health club & spa; outdoor pool; room service; nearby watersports equipment/rentals. *In room:* A/C, TV, hair dryer, Wi-Fi ($9.95).

Graycliff ★★★ One of the most luxurious inns in The Bahamas is steeped in glamour and imbued with memories of its past guests—the Duke and Duchess of Windsor, Sir Winston Churchill, Aristotle Onassis, even the Beatles. Originally an 18th-century private home reflecting Georgian colonial architecture, it's now a boutique-inspired compound of cottages and garden villas, in a setting of ponds, splashing fountains, and limestone patios in a dignified section of downtown Nassau. Even though it's not on the beach, guests who can afford to stay anywhere select this address because of its Old World style and grace. Beach lovers go by taxi to either nearby Goodman's Bay or the Western Esplanade Beach, adjacent to Arawak Cay.

The historic garden rooms in the main house are spacious and individually decorated with antiques, though many prefer the more modern garden units. The Yellow Bird, Hibiscus, and Pool cottages are idyllic, but the most luxurious unit is the

Where to Stay & Eat in Nassau

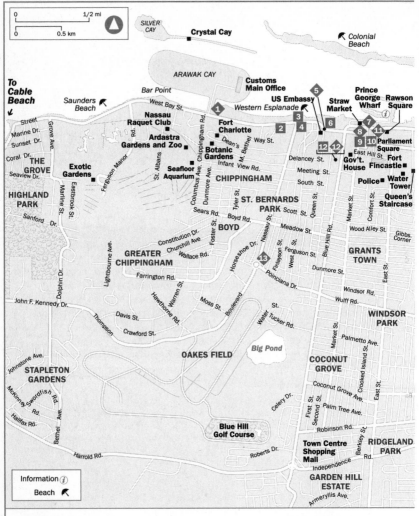

HOTELS ■

British Colonial Hilton **6**
El Greco Hotel **4**
Grand Central Hotel **10**
Graycliff **12**
Nassau Junkanoo Resort **3**
Nassau Palm Resort **2**
Towne House, the **9**

RESTAURANTS ◆

Aqua **7**
Athena Café & Bar **8**
Café Matisse **11**
Café Skans **8**
Chef Chea's **14**
Conch Fritters Bar & Grill **5**
Double Dragon **15**

East Villa Restaurant &
  Lounge **18**
Graycliff **12**
Green Parrot Harbourfront
  Restaurant **17**
Humidor Churrascaria **12**
Luciano's of Chicago **16**
Montagu Gardens **20**

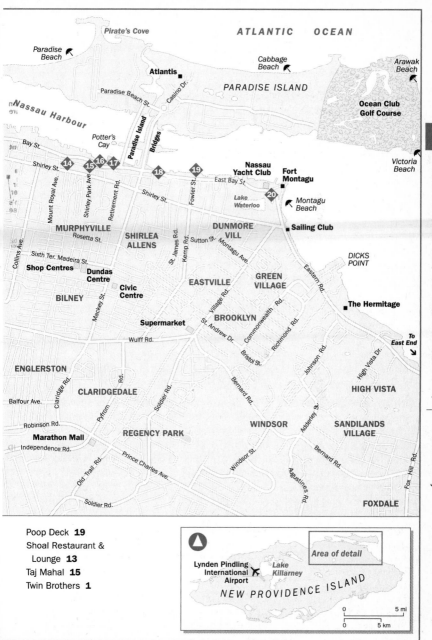

ATLANTIC OCEAN

Pirate's Cove

Paradise Beach

Cabbage Beach

Arawak Beach

Atlantis

Paradise Beach St.

Casino Dr.

PARADISE ISLAND

Ocean Club Golf Course

Nassau Harbour

Potter's Cay

Paradise Island Bridges

Victoria Beach

Bay St.

Shirley St.

14

15 **16** **17**

18

19

Nassau Yacht Club

Fort Montagu

East Bay St.

20

Montagu Beach

Mount Royal Ave.

Shirley Park Ave.

Retirement Rd.

Shirley St.

Fowler St.

Lake Waterloo

Sailing Club

Collins Ave.

MURPHYVILLE

Rosetta St.

SHIRLEA ALLENS

DUNMORE VILL

Montagu Ave.

Eastern Rd.

DICKS POINT

Sixth Ter. Madeira St.

Shop Centres

Dundas Centre

Civic Centre

St. James Rd.

Kemp Rd.

Sutton St.

EASTVILLE

GREEN VILLAGE

The Hermitage

BILNEY

Mackey St.

Village Rd.

BROOKLYN

Commonwealth Rd.

Richmond Rd.

Johnson Rd.

To East End

Supermarket

Wulff Rd.

St. Andrew Dr.

Bristol St.

High Vista Dr.

ENGLERSTON

Claridge Rd.

Pyfrom Rd.

CLARIDGEDALE

Bernard Rd.

HIGH VISTA

Balfour Ave.

Soldier Rd.

Adderley St.

SANDILANDS VILLAGE

Robinson Rd.

WINDSOR

Marathon Mall

REGENCY PARK

Prince Charles Ave.

Windsor St.

Bernard Rd.

Fox Hill Rd.

Independence Rd.

Old Trail Rd.

Augustine's Rd.

FOXDALE

Soldier Rd.

Poop Deck **19**

Shoal Restaurant & Lounge **13**

Taj Mahal **15**

Twin Brothers **1**

Lynden Pindling International Airport

Lake Killarney

Area of detail

NEW PROVIDENCE ISLAND

0   5 mi

0   5 km

Mandarino Suite, with its private balcony. One of the pools evokes a Tuscan-inspired neoclassical fantasy.

8–12 W. Hill St., Nassau, The Bahamas. www.graycliff.com. ℂ **800/476-0446** or 242/302-9150. Fax 242/326-6188. 20 units. Winter $375–$425 double, $475–$700 cottage; off-season $325–$370 double, $425–$550 cottage. AE, MC, V. Bus: 10, 15, or 21A. **Amenities:** 2 restaurants (Graycliff, p. 62; and Humidor Churrascaria, p. 62); 2 bars; babysitting; Jacuzzi; 2 outdoor pools; room service; sauna. *In room:* A/C, TV, hair dryer, minibar, Wi-Fi (free).

MODERATE

El Greco Hotel   This well-managed bargain choice attracts many European travelers. The Greek owners and staff genuinely seem to care about their guests—in fact, the two-story hotel seems more like a small European B&B than your typical Bahamian hotel. The location is across the street from Junkanoo Beach/Lighthouse Beach/ Western Esplanade and a short walk from Arawak Cay's sometimes raucous nightlife. It's also a quick walk from the shops and restaurants of downtown Nassau. The midsize rooms are set around a courtyard that contains bougainvillea-draped statues. Accommodations aren't that exciting, but they are clean and comfortable, with ceiling fans, carpeted floors, and a bright, Mediterranean-esque decor.

W. Bay St., Nassau, The Bahamas. www.hotels-nassau-bahamas.com. ℂ **242/325-1121.** Fax 242/325-1124. 30 units. Year-round $86–$120 double; $150–$210 suite. AE, MC, V. Free parking. Bus: 10. **Amenities:** Bar; babysitting; outdoor pool. *In room:* A/C, TV, hair dryer, Wi-Fi (free).

INEXPENSIVE

Grand Central Hotel ✦   This longtime favorite for frugal travelers dates back to the early 1940s. It is still going strong and has been much improved in recent years. There is no pool, and it's a bit of a walk to the beach, but this house, and the adjoining former private home, has much to recommend it. Bedrooms are midsize, well maintained, and comfortable, with pine furnishings. Some rooms have balconies, opening onto views of bustling Charlotte Street or the cruise ships beyond.

Charlotte St., Nassau, The Bahamas. www.grand-central-hotel.com. ℂ **242/322-8356.** Fax 242/325-0218. 35 units. Year-round $72–$87 double. AE, MC, V. *In room:* A/C, TV.

Nassau Junkanoo Resort   This no-nonsense, efficiently designed hotel rises prominently across busy West Bay Street from the narrow sands known variously as Junkanoo Beach, Lighthouse Beach, Long Wharf Beach, and the Western Esplanade. Partly because of its compact rooms, it's the least desirable, and also the least expensive, of the also-recommended hotels (Nassau Palm, El Greco) that lie nearby within this congested downtown neighborhood. But during the peak of winter, when other competitors might be sold out, it offers comfortable, unpretentious lodgings in a six-story venue that might be appealing if you don't expect tons of amenities or superlative service.

W. Bay and Nassau Sts., Nassau, The Bahamas. www.nassaujunkanooresort.com. ℂ **242/322-1515.** Fax 242/322-1514. 63 units. Year-round $95–$105 double, with an optional surcharge of $7 per day for housecleaning. AE, DC, DISC, MC, V. Bus: 10 or 16. **Amenities:** Bar; outdoor pool. *In room:* A/C, TV, hair dryer, Wi-Fi (free).

Nassau Palm Resort ✦   A short walk west of downtown Nassau, within a cluster of other cost-conscious hotels that includes both the El Greco (see above) and the Quality Resort (see below), this hotel lies across busy West Bay Street from the relatively narrow confines of Junkanoo Beach (also known as Lighthouse Beach or the Western Esplanade). Though not as dramatic as Cable Beach, a few miles west, it's a safe urban beach with tranquil waters and a lot of shells. This place is a good value for those who don't demand particularly attentive service and who don't want to pay the higher prices charged by the more deluxe hotels along Cable Beach. Bedrooms are outfitted in a standard motel style, most with a view of Nassau Harbour, and come with extras you don't always find in a moderately priced choice, such as alarm clocks, two-line phones, and desks.

W. Bay St., Nassau, The Bahamas. www.nassau-hotel.com. © **242/356-0000.** Fax 242/323-1408. 183 units. Year round $89–$109 double; $120 suite. AE, DISC, MC, V. Bus: 10 or 17. **Amenities:** Restaurant (breakfast only); bar; concierge; health club & spa; 2 outdoor pools. *In room:* A/C, TV, fridge, hair dryer, Wi-Fi ($16 per day).

The Towne House 🍴 If your demands aren't great, this modest hotel offers affordable rates, plus a location within walking distance of the center of Nassau and Lighthouse Beach. The hotel features simply but comfortably furnished midsize bedrooms, along with a swimming pool and a sun deck. If you don't want to go out at night, the Talking Stick Bar and Restaurant serves three meals a day, its menu mostly Bahamian with some international dishes.

40 George St., Nassau, The Bahamas. www.townehotel.com. © **242/322-8450.** Fax 242/328-1512. 46 units. Winter $90 double, $115 suite; off-season $75 double, $95 suite. Rates include breakfast. MAP (lunch or dinner) $16 per person extra. AE, MC, V. **Amenities:** Restaurant; bar; Internet (free); outdoor pool. *In room:* A/C, TV.

Cable Beach

Cable Beach has always figured high in the consciousness of The Bahamas. Ever since Atlantis premiered on Paradise Island, Cable Beach has flourished, and occasionally suffered, in the shadow of its more dramatic counterpart.

Cable Beach derived its name from the underwater telephone and telegraph cable that brought electronic communications from the outside world. For years, it was a rural outpost of New Providence Island, flanked by private homes and a desirable shoreline that was a destination for local residents. Its first major tourist boost came with the construction of the Ambassador Beach Hotel, now the site of Breezes Bahamas. In the 1980s, a building boom added a string of condos, timeshares, and hotels, all designed to serve the needs of sun-seekers and casinogoers. The district now has a wide variety of restaurants and sports facilities, lots of glitz and glitter, and one of the country's two biggest casinos (in terms of square footage).

In 2005, a consortium of investors, coalescing under the name **Baha Mar Resorts** (© **242/677-9000;** www.bahamar.com), pinpointed Cable Beach as the eventual site of one of the Atlantic's most far-reaching resort developments. (The project's investors also own and operate Cable Beach Resorts and Crystal Palace Casino.) In 2007, they inaugurated a plan that will dramatically alter the present landscape of Cable Beach, adding to the overall competitiveness of Nassau in general and its northern seafront in particular. By 2014, expect big changes that might make Cable Beach one of the world's most talked-about casino and resort destinations—that is, if all phases of the redevelopment are completed as planned. In 2010, the complex witnessed a major upgrade of the beachfront, with the addition of sea-fronting boardwalks and gazebos along with a dance floor and a sophisticated sound system. In 2011, plans were concretized for the radical alteration of traffic along West Bay Street, the opening of a sales office in Hong Kong, and the signing of management contracts for the eventual construction of new hotels run by Hyatt, Rosewood, and the Morgans Hotel Group.

Upcoming changes will include the dusty conclusion of the physical alterations to the layout of West Bay Street: the dredging of new lakes and marinas, creating water traps for a redesigned golf course, demolishing some older buildings within the Cable Beach compound, and enlarging the existing casino. The project also calls for constructing a new string of resort hotels, each catering to a different market. A Mondrian hotel, for example, will accent avant-garde design and, it's hoped, attract a youthful, trend-setting clientele. Eventual plans call for the construction of additional hotels whose names, natures, and marketing visions will unfold as plans at this mega-development continue evolving.

Even in its current form, Cable Beach has many loyal fans, some of whom find Paradise Island too expensive, too contrived, and too Disney-esque. Stay tuned for further developments—and expect endless delays, with investment money tight in these bad economic times.

VERY EXPENSIVE

Breezes Bahamas ★   In 1996, the SuperClubs chain spent $125 million transforming a tired old relic—the Ambassador Beach Hotel—into this all-inclusive resort, viewed today as a highly durable staple along Cable Beach. Today, its biggest competitor is the nearby Sandals Royal Bahamian (see below), which is more imposing, more stylish, more expensive, and more upscale. Rowdier and more raucous, however, and located on a prime 450m (1,476-ft.) beachfront along Cable Beach, Breezes attracts a more middle-of-the-road crowd; it's unpretentious and more affordable (though it isn't exactly cheap, and we think it's a bit overpriced for what it is).

The U-shaped resort has two wings of rooms plus a main clubhouse facing a large, sometimes overcrowded terrace with a swimming pool that serves as the social centerpiece. Couples and single travelers are equally accepted here, and the rate includes everything—the room, meals, snacks, unlimited wine (not the finest) with lunch and dinner, even premium-brand liquor at the bars, plus activities and airport transfers. Accommodations are not as luxurious as those at Sandals (picture pastel-painted furniture with Formica tops), but rates are deliberately lower.

Diners can sample unremarkable international fare at the food court, although the Italian restaurant serves better food. A beachside grill and snacks are available throughout the day. Entertainment includes a high-energy disco, a piano bar, and a nightclub. Karaoke is inevitable, but the professional Junkanoo live shows, which are presented every Saturday night, are more entertaining, and local bands often perform. For most of the year, there is a minimum stay required of between 2 and 7 nights, depending on bookings and the season.

Cable Beach, Nassau, The Bahamas. www.breezes.com. **②** **877/BREEZES** (273-3937) or 242/327-5356. Fax 242/327-5155. 391 units. Year-round $350–$450 double; $550–$590 suite. Rates include all meals, drinks, tips, airport transfers, and most activities. AE, DISC, MC, V. Free parking. Bus: 10. No children 15 and under; no children 18 and under, unless accompanied by an adult 21 or older. **Amenities:** 4 restaurants; 4 bars; state-of-the-art health club; Internet ($18/hr.); 3 outdoor pools; 3 tennis courts (lit for night play); watersports equipment/rentals. *In room:* A/C, TV, CD player, hair dryer.

Sandals Royal Bahamian ★   This all-inclusive, couples-only property originated as a very posh hotel, the Balmoral Beach, in the 1940s. In 1996, the Jamaica-based Sandals chain poured $20 million into radically redesigning and upgrading the resort. Now, everywhere, you'll find trappings of Edwardian England in the tropics: manicured gardens, neoclassical/Palladian architectural themes, and hidden courtyards

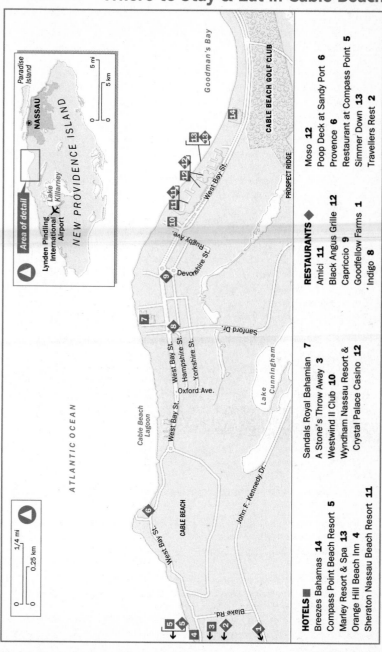

HOTELS ■

Breezes Bahamas **14**
Compass Point Beach Resort **5**
Marley Resort & Spa **13**
Orange Hill Beach Inn **4**
Sheraton Nassau Beach Resort **11**
Sandals Royal Bahamian **7**
A Stone's Throw Away **3**
Westwind II Club **10**
Wyndham Nassau Resort &
Crystal Palace Casino **12**

RESTAURANTS ◆

Amici **11**
Black Angus Grille **12**
Capriccio **9**
Goodfellow Farms **1**
'Indigo **8**
Moso **12**
Poop Deck at Sandy Port **6**
Provence **6**
Restaurant at Compass Point **5**
Simmer Down **13**
Travellers Rest **2**

3

NEW PROVIDENCE (NASSAU/CABLE BEACH) | Where to Stay

JUNKANOO festivals

No Bahamian celebration is as raucous as **Junkanoo.** Its special rituals originated during the colonial days of slavery, when African-born newcomers could legally drink and enjoy themselves only on certain strictly predetermined days of the year. In how it's celebrated, the Junkanoo festival closely resembles Carnival in Rio and Mardi Gras in New Orleans. Its major difference lies in the costumes and the timing (the major Junkanoo celebrations occur the day after Christmas, a legacy of the English celebration of Boxing Day on Dec 26, and on New Year's Day). A more touristy 4-week midsummer event, the **Junkanoo Summer Festival** (✆ **242/302-2085;** www.bahamas.com), takes place every Saturday in July from noon to 10pm along Woodes Rogers Walk, in the heart of downtown Nassau, at a point overlooking the Straw Market and the cruise ship harbor.

In the old days, Junkanoo costumes were crafted from crepe paper, often in primary colors, stretched over wire frames. (One sinister offshoot of the celebrations was that Junkanoo costumes and masks were used to conceal the identity of anyone seeking vengeance on a white person, or on another slave.) Today, locals have more money to spend on costumes and festivals than they did in the past. The finest costumes can cost up to $15,000 and are sometimes sponsored by local bazaars, lotteries, church groups, and charity auctions. Everyday folks from all walks of Bahamian life join in, often with homemade costumes that are sensuous or humorous.

The best time and place to observe Junkanoo is New Year's Day in Nassau, when throngs of cavorting, music-making, and costumed figures prance through the streets. Find yourself a good viewing position on Bay Street. Less elaborate celebrations take place in major towns on the other islands, including Freeport on Grand Bahama Island.

You can learn more about Junkanoo at the **Educulture Museum** at Ivern House, 31 W. St. at Delancey (✆ **242/328-DRUM** [3786]; www.educulturebahamas.com). The owner, Arlene Nash Ferguson, who has been joining in Junkanoo parades from the age of 4, is an expert on Bahamian culture and tradition and a font of information. She's one of the most gracious hosts in Nassau. This admission-free attraction can be visited Monday to Friday 9am to 5pm. The small museum is installed in the owner's childhood home. On display is the history of Junkanoo, with some of its more flamboyant costumes. This is a favorite with kids, too, since there's a room where they're given such instruments as drums and cowbells and told to create their own Junkanoo sounds.

tastefully accented with sculptures. The resort is located on a beach a short walk west of Cable Beach's more glittery mega-hotels.

A favorite for honeymooners, Sandals offers well-furnished and often elegant rooms, all classified as suites and positioned within either the resort's core Manor House or within the Windsor Building, an annex built shortly after the resort's takeover by Sandals. Others, including some of the most upscale, occupy outlying villas known collectively as the Royal Village. The villas are preferable thanks to their rigorously secluded settings and easy access to nearby semiprivate plunge pools. Bedrooms, regardless of their location, have thick cove moldings and formal English furniture. The rooms that face the ocean offer small terraces with views of an offshore sand spit, Sandals Key.

In addition to spectacular buffets, dining options include white-glove service and continental dishes at **Baccarat,** Japanese cuisine at **Kimonos,** and Italian fare at **Casanova.** The pool here is one of Nassau's most appealing, with touches of both Vegas and ancient Rome (outdoor murals and replicas of ancient Roman columns). Complimentary shuttle service goes to the casino and nightlife options at the nearby Wyndham Crystal Palace complex.

W. Bay St., Cable Beach, Nassau, The Bahamas. www.sandals.com. (¢)**888/SANDALS** (726-3257) or 242/327-6400. Fax 242/327-6961. 403 units. Year-round $3,400–$7,500 per couple for 7 days. Rates include all meals, drinks, and activities. AE, DISC, MC, V. Free parking. Bus: 10. Couples only; no children allowed. **Amenities:** 8 restaurants; 9 bars; concierge (for guests in higher-priced units); health club & spa; 7 outdoor pools; 2 tennis courts (lit for night play); watersports equipment/ rentals. In room: A/C, TV, hair dryer, Wi-Fi ($14/day).

EXPENSIVE

Sheraton Nassau Beach Resort ★ ☺ Prominently visible in the center of Cable Beach (its best asset) is this seven-story high-rise, connected by a shopping arcade to the Crystal Palace Casino. The nearby Wyndham (p. 60) is glitzier and has better facilities, but the Sheraton is still one of the best choices for families (many of its rooms contain two double beds, so they can accommodate up to four). You'll think of Vegas when you see the rows of fountains in front, the acres of marble inside, and the hotel's propensity for hosting large wedding parties. The big, brassy building forms a horseshoe-shaped curve around a landscaped beachfront garden; its Aztec-inspired facade of sharp angles incorporates prominent balconies. Bedrooms are modern and comfortable, reflecting a lighthearted interpretation of Tommy Bahama style, replete with dark-wood furniture and understated tones completely devoid of the floral prints of yesteryear. Big windows open onto views of either the garden or the beach.

W. Bay St., Cable Beach, Nassau, The Bahamas. www.starwoodhotels.com. (¢)**800/325-3535** or 242/327-6000. Fax 242/327-5968. 694 units. Year round $235–$544 double; $975 suite. AE, MC, V. Free parking. Bus: 10. **Amenities:** 4 restaurants, including Amici (p. 67); 3 bars; babysitting; kids' club; exercise room; 3 outdoor pools; room service; 2 tennis courts (lit for night play). In room: A/C, TV, hair dryer, Internet (free).

Westwind II Club ☺ Set on the western edge of Cable Beach's hotel strip, 9.5km (6 miles) from the center of Nassau, the Westwind II is a cluster of two-story buildings that contain two-bedroom, two-bathroom timeshare units made available to the public when not occupied by their investor-owners. The size and facilities of these units, including full kitchens (there's a grocery store nearby), make them ideal

---

The Art of Massage

The **Red Lane Spa,** at the Sandals Royal Bahamian in Nassau, has repeatedly made the top 10 list of spa resorts in the *Condé Nast Traveler* readers' choice survey. The decor features walls and floors of Italian Saturnia stone, rich mahogany doors, and a collection of pre-Raphaelite prints in gilded frames. One service offered, "In Each Other's Hands," allows couples to learn the art of massage from a professional so they can practice on each other in the comfort of their hotel room.

for families. All the diversions of the mega-hotels are nearby, but in the complex itself, you can enjoy privacy and a low-key atmosphere. (A masonry wall separates the compound from street traffic.) Each unit is pleasantly outfitted with white tile floors, rattan furniture, and a balcony or terrace. Price differences are based on whether the units face the beach, the pool, or the garden. Don't stay here if you expect resort luxuries or facilities; Westwind II is more for self-sufficient, do-it-yourself types.

W. Bay St., Cable Beach, Nassau, The Bahamas. www.westwindii.com. © **866/369-5921** or 242/327-7211. Fax 262/327-7529. 52 units. Winter $295–$340 double; off-season $230–$270 double. AE, DC, DISC, MC, V. Bus: 10. **Amenities:** Bar; babysitting; 2 outdoor pools; 2 tennis courts (lit for night play). *In room:* A/C, TV, kitchen, Wi-Fi ($15/day).

Wyndham Nassau Resort & Crystal Palace Casino ★ ☺ This flashy mega-resort on the lovely sands of Cable Beach is so vast and all-encompassing that some of its guests never venture into Nassau during their stay on the island. The futuristic-looking complex incorporates three high-rise towers, a central core topped with massive greenhouse-style domes, and a cluster of beachfront gazebos—all linked by arcades, covered passageways, and mini-pavilions. Guest rooms come in several categories, ranging from standard island view to ocean vista, each with private balcony. Corner suites are the way to go, with lots of space, wraparound balconies, and water views through floor-to-ceiling glass.

The Wyndham will be the centerpiece of a radical expansion of the hotel lineup here, as described in our introduction to Cable Beach (p. 55). Aside from the massive **Crystal Palace Casino** (p. 91), one of the two largest casinos in The Bahamas, the complex contains a wide array of dining and drinking facilities. Its restaurants are among New Providence's best; a particular favorite of ours is the appealingly experimental **Moso**. Even if you're not a guest of the hotel, you might want to take advantage of the bars, restaurants, or casino action here.

W. Bay St., Cable Beach, Nassau, The Bahamas. www.wyndhamnassauresort.com. © **877/999-3223** in the U.S., or 242/327-6200. Fax 954/327-6818. 559 units. Year-round $130–$225 double; $250–$560 suite. AE, DC, MC, V. Free self-parking; valet parking $5. Bus: 10. **Amenities:** 4 restaurants (including Black Angus Grille, p. 67); 4 bars; babysitting; concierge; state-of-the-art health club; room service. *In room:* A/C, TV, fridge, hair dryer, Wi-Fi ($15).

MODERATE

Orange Hill Beach Inn ★ 🛅 This simple, durable hotel, set on 1.4 landscaped hillside hectares (3½ acres), lies about 13km (8 miles) west of Nassau and 1.5km (1 mile) east of Love Beach, which has great snorkeling. It's perfect for those who want to escape the crowds and stay in a quieter part of New Providence; it's easy to catch a cab or jitney to Cable Beach or downtown Nassau. Many of the guests are Europeans, especially during summer.

Accommodations come in a variety of sizes, though most are small. Each room has a balcony or patio, and some have kitchenettes. An on-site bar serves sandwiches and salads throughout the day, while the restaurant offers simple but good dinners. Diving excursions along New Providence's southwestern coast are a popular activity, and the hotel provides free regular jitney service to and from local grocery stores, a fact that's much appreciated by guests who prepare meals within their kitchenettes.

W. Bay St. (just west of Blake Rd.), Nassau, The Bahamas. www.orangehill.com. © **888/399-3698** or 242/327-7157. Fax 242/327-5186. 32 units. Winter $138–$175 double; off-season $118–$158 double. MC, V. Free parking. Bus: 10. **Amenities:** Restaurant; bar; outdoor pool; Wi-Fi (free in lobby). *In room:* A/C, TV.

West of Cable Beach

EXPENSIVE

Compass Point Beach Resort ★   The whimsical Compass Point is self-con-sciously funky and out-of-the-way. The island's most westerly resort—directly beside Love Beach, several minutes' drive west from Cable Beach—is the closest thing to Jamaica in The Bahamas. In fact, it's associated with the Jamaica-based Island Out-post chain, owned by Christopher Blackwell, the music-industry entrepreneur who discovered and promoted Bob Marley's talent. Accommodations are within airy, old-fashioned, brightly painted wooden cottages, each simply but artfully furnished in a manner that encourages barefoot living if not altogether nudity. Prices vary according to the unit's view and size, and whether or not it's raised on stilts above the rocky landscape (units on stilts get more breezes and better views).

W. Bay St., Gambier, Nassau, The Bahamas. www.compasspointbeachresort.com. © **866/431-2874** or 242/327-4500. Fax 242/327-9904. 16 units. Year round $220–$380 double; $340–$420 2-bedroom apt for 4. AE, MC, V. Bus: 10. **Amenities:** Restaurant (p. 69); bar; outdoor pool; Wi-Fi (free in lobby). *In room:* A/C, TV/DVD, CD player, fridge, hair dryer.

Marley Resort & Spa ★   The former home of Bob Marley has been turned into New Providence's funkiest boutique hotel, with touches of genuine elegance and a Caribbean/African theme. The home is devoted to the good life and to the "life, leg-end, and inspiration" of the King of Reggae himself. As the managers so aptly put it, "Come embrace the feeling of One Love and One Heart in One Place."

The property was originally the governor's mansion until Rita Marley purchased it as a summer getaway for the Marleys, including Bob. The resort lies close to other buildings, beside a stretch of Cable Beach, and is filled with sculpted hard-carved doors, mosaic tiles, intricate stonework, limestone walls, and lots of dark-grained woods, especially mahogany. Naturally, the memory of Marley is perpetuated in nos-talgic mementos.

The names of the suites center on Marley song titles—"Kinky Reggae," "Talkin' Blues," and "Jammin'," among others. The most comfortable and spacious way to stay here is to rent one of the three Royal Suites on the second floor, each with its own private balcony offering views of the water. Our favorite is "Royal Rita."

West Bay St., Cable Beach, The Bahamas. www.marleyresort.com. © **866/737-1766** or 242/702-2800. Fax 242/327-4393. 16 suites. Year round $252 double; $315–$756 suite. AE, MC, V. **Amenities:** Restau-rant; room service; music gallery; "Natural Mystic Spa." *In room:* A/C, TV, hair dryer, Wi-Fi (free).

A Stone's Throw Away ★★ 📧   At last, New Providence has a gourmet-level B&B, a secluded hideaway conceived by French and Belgian owners, 21km (13 miles) west of Nassau. Ringed with verandas and evocative of a building that's much older than it really is, this boutique hotel for discerning visitors has already been discovered by some celebrities (though, for privacy's sake, management doesn't name names). The colonial-style inn's public rooms evoke an old plantation home. On the ground floor, guest rooms open onto gardens and a pool area, while the upper two floors provide panoramic lake views. Accommodations are luxuriously furnished with plush towels, Indonesian teak beds, and mahogany antiques. The staff serves three meals a day, including finely honed continental dinners.

Tropical Garden Rd. and W. Bay St., Gambier, Nassau, The Bahamas. www.astonesthrowaway.com. © **242/327-7030.** Fax 242/327-7040. 10 units. Nov–May $200–$290 double, $290 suite; off season $175–$235 double, $235 suite. AE, MC, V. **Amenities:** Restaurant; bar; outdoor pool; room service. *In room:* A/C, TV/DVD, Internet (free), minibar.

WHERE TO EAT

Nassau

Nassau restaurants open and close often. Even if reservations aren't required, it's a good idea to call first just to verify that a place is still in business and that the hours haven't changed. European and American cuisine are relatively easy to find. Surprisingly, it used to be difficult to find Bahamian cuisine, but in recent years, more restaurants have begun to offer authentic island fare.

EXPENSIVE

Chef Chea's ★ CONTINENTAL/BAHAMIAN   Opened in 2010, this dining room evokes the Nassau of years ago when the Duke of Windsor (King George VI's brother) ruled over the colony. Chef Christopher Chea, a former employee of the Atlantis Resort, is Le Cordon Bleu trained as reflected by his menu, which is more continental than local. You can peruse the menu by the soft glow of Art Deco chandeliers, in an elegant but subdued atmosphere that's close to the Nassau side of the Paradise Island Bridge, near the better-known Luciano's Restaurant. You can order tasty dishes such as oven-roasted duck, short ribs, or a juicy T-bone steak. Guests often begin with such starters as meaty portobello mushroom slices or a savory conch salad. Main courses often feature plump lobster ravioli or a classic and flavorful coq au vin. Whatever you order, save room for one of the best slices of cheesecake you'll encounter in The Bahamas. It's flavored with mango.

Dowdeswell & Armstrong sts. (✆ **242/323-3201.** Reservations recommended. Lunch main courses $18–$35, dinner main courses $29–$40. AE, MC, V. Mon–Fri 11:30am–3pm; Mon–Sat 6–10pm. Bus: 10 or 17.

Graycliff ★★ CONTINENTAL   Part of the Graycliff Hotel, an antiques-filled colonial mansion located in Nassau's commercial core (opposite the Government House), this deeply entrenched restaurant retains a history and nostalgia for the old days of The Bahamas as a colonial outpost of Britain. The chefs use local Bahamian products whenever available and turn them into old-fashioned cuisine that appeals to tradition-minded visitors, many of whom return here year after year. Try such dishes, neither completely traditional nor regional, as grouper soup in puff pastry or plump, juicy pheasant cooked with pineapples grown on Eleuthera. Lobster, another specialty, comes half in beurre blanc and half with a sauce prepared from the head of the lobster. Other options include escargots, foie gras, and lamb. The pricey wine list is praised as one of the finest in the country, with more than 250,000 bottles. This hotel and restaurant are managed by the same entrepreneurs who run a cigar-making facility; as such, its collection of Bahama-derived cigars is the world's most comprehensive.

Graycliff Hotel, 12 W. Hill St. (✆ **242/302-9150.** www.graycliff.com. Reservations required. Jacket advised for men. Main courses $48–$85. AE, MC, V. Mon–Fri 12:30–2:30pm; daily 6:30–9:30pm. Bus: 10, 15, or 21A.

Humidor Churrascaria ★ BRAZILIAN   Brazilian *rodizio*, the art of grilling large amounts of chicken, sausage, pork, and beef, has finally come to Nassau within this annex of the fabled Graycliff Hotel. Set in the same building as Graycliff's cigar factory and shop, within a generously proportioned, high-ceilinged enclave that's vaguely reminiscent of the long-ago British regime, it's fun, colorful, and filling. A staff wearing gaucho-inspired shirts invites you to the salad bar and then makes endless runs from the grill to your plate with skewers of assorted grilled meats—plus occasional *raciones* of grilled pineapple—as part of a ritual that evokes South America's pampas and plains. The only option available is the set-price dinner noted below. Vegetarians or the not-terribly-hungry can easily make do with a meal composed entirely from the salad bar.

Graycliff Hotel, 12 W. Hill St. ℂ **242/302-9150.** www.graycliff.com. Reservations required. Fixed-price, all-you-can-eat *churrasco* dinner $45. Access to salad bar without any *churrasco* $25. AE, MC, V. Mon–Sat 6:30–10pm. Bus: 10, 10A, or 21A.

MODERATE

Aqua ★ INTERNATIONAL Anchor yourself at a window seat in the British Colonial Hilton to watch the cruise ships from Florida arrive or depart. This restaurant is best at night, when you can enjoy lights along the harbor or from neighboring Paradise Island. A tantalizing array of appetizers, soups, and salads can get you started. The chef shows imagination in creating unusual taste sensations such as a Bahamian lobster Wellington with a mushroom tapenade, chili oil, and pimento coulis, or else a chicken satay with an avocado salsa. A creative soup is coconut sweet potato variation with a dash of brandy crème fraîche, and the most delightful salad is made with cranberries, orange wedges, and heart of lettuce, all tossed together with a pomegranate vinaigrette. The chef's specialties are a Bahamian conch sampler—conch salad, conch chowder, and conch fritters. Two or four diners can try the Aqua "Sample Tower," with marinated squid, seaweed salad, conch fritters and salad, and honey sesame shrimp among other ingredients. You can also order such classics as grilled beef tenderloin in a peppercorn jus or grilled baby lamb chops with a guava chutney.

British Colonial Hilton, 1 W. Bay St. ℂ **242/322-3301.** www.hiltoncaribbean.com. Reservations recommended. Main courses $18–$28 lunch, $18–$45 dinner; lunch buffet $29; dinner buffet (Fri–Sat) $39; breakfast buffet $22. AE, MC, V. Daily 6:30am–10:30pm.

Athena Café and Bar GREEK/AMERICAN/INTERNATIONAL Cheerful, straightforward and Greek, this bastion of Mediterranean cuisine occupies the second floor of a building in downtown Nassau that's outfitted with faux-statuary and memorabilia that you might have found in a Greek tavern anywhere in the world. Come here for diner-style breakfasts, especially feta-cheese omelets and pancakes; followed by lunches and dinners that focus on souvlaki, gyros, sandwiches, salads, moussaka, and diner-style food that's sometimes a welcome change from a constant diet of Bahamian food. Peter Mousis and his family work hard to keep this restaurant's reasonable prices, loyal clientele, and well-maintained premises.

Bay at Charlotte Street. ℂ**242/326-1296.** Reservations not required. Main courses $15–$26. DC, MC, V. Mon–Thurs 8am–7:30pm, Fri–Sat 8am–8:30pm, Sunday 9am–4pm.

Café Matisse ★ INTERNATIONAL/ITALIAN Set directly behind Parliament House, in a mustard-colored building built a century ago as a private home, this restaurant is on everybody's short list of downtown Nassau favorites. It serves well-prepared Italian and international cuisine to businesspeople, government workers, and all kinds of dealmakers. Guests are seated in an enclosed courtyard and on two floors of the interior, which is decorated with colorful Matisse prints. The sophisticated Bahamian-Italian team of Greg and Gabriella Curry prepare menu items that include calamari with spicy chili-flavored jam, served with tomatoes and fresh mozzarella; a mixed grill of seafood; grilled filet of local grouper served with a light tomato-caper sauce; spaghetti with lobster; grilled rack of lamb with gravy; a perfect filet mignon in a green-peppercorn sauce; and a zesty curried shrimp with rice.

Bank Lane at Bay St., just north of Parliament Sq. ℭ **242/356-7012.** www.cafe-matisse.com. Reservations recommended. Main courses $17–$28 lunch; $24–$46 dinner. AE, DISC, MC, V. Tues–Sat noon–3pm and 6–11pm. Bus: 17 or 21.

East Villa Restaurant and Lounge CHINESE/BAHAMIAN You might imagine yourself in 1980s Hong Kong in this well-designed modern house across the road from the Nassau Yacht Club headquarters, a short drive east of downtown Nassau's commercial core. It's somewhat upscale and completely devoid of the sense of bureaucracy associated with restaurants in some of the island's larger resorts. Sometimes attracting affluent Florida yachters to its dimly lit precinct, its aquariums bubble in a simple but tasteful contemporary setting. Zesty Szechuan flavors appear on the menu alongside less spicy Cantonese alternatives, including sweet-and-sour chicken and steamed vegetables with cashews and water chestnuts. Lobster tail in the spicy Chinese style is one of our favorites. Dishes can be ordered mild, medium, or hot. On the Bahamian side of the menu, cracked conch, Bahamian lobster tail, grilled steaks, and pan-fried grouper cutlets with scallops are highlights.

E. Bay St. ℭ **242/393-3377.** Reservations required. Main courses $9–$25 lunch; $12–$50 dinner. AE, MC, V. Sun–Fri noon–3pm and 6–10pm. Bus: 9A, 9B, 11, or 19.

Luciano's of Chicago ★ ITALIAN/SEAFOOD/STEAK One of Nassau's best upscale restaurants lies within a low-slung, red-painted building. A branch of a successful Chicago-based franchise, it emphasizes stiff drinks, two-fisted portions, and macho charm. Many visitors prefer the terrace, which affords a view of the towers and glittering lights of Atlantis just across the water. There's also a smoothly upscale dining room, air-conditioned and outfitted in tones of beige and brown. The menu includes a tempting roster of steaks; a romaine salad topped with basil-and-garlic-marinated sweet peppers; pot-roasted and marinated chicken served with sautéed garlic and kalamata olives; and country-style rigatoni with sweet Italian sausage, pancetta, and a light tomato-flavored cream sauce. A soup that's particularly successful is made from escarole, white beans, and Italian sausage.

E. Bay St., just before the northbound entrance to the Paradise Island Bridge. ℭ **242/323-7770.** www.lucianosnassau.com. Reservations recommended. Main courses $11–$30 lunch; $23–$46 dinner. AE, DC, DISC, MC, V. Mon–Fri 11:30am–3:30pm; daily 6–10pm. Bus: 10.

Montagu Gardens ★ CONTINENTAL Due to its relative isolation, diners often ignore this restaurant at the edge of Lake Waterloo, installed in an old mansion at the eastern end of Bay Street. However, the cuisine, especially the flame-grilled fresh native seafood, is worth the trip. Montagu is also one of New Providence's most romantic dining spots, especially its courtyard garden. Not only does the chef get the best seafood on the island (he does wonders with that old standby, Bahamian grouper), but he is also noted for his Angus beef, which he carves into T-bones, filet mignons, and rib-eyes. These succulent dishes can be prepared to order. Other inspired courses include baby back ribs and, on occasion, a perfectly seasoned and roasted rack of lamb.

E. Bay St. ℭ **242/394-6347.** Reservations required. Main courses $18–$40. AE, MC, V. Mon–Sat 11:30am–3pm and 6–10pm.

Poop Deck at East Bay BAHAMIAN/SEAFOOD Raffish and informal, this is the older version of a restaurant that has expanded with another branch at Cable Beach. This original is less touristy, hosting a clientele of sailors, yachtspeople, and workers from the nearby marinas and boatyards. Many of them find perches on the second-floor terrace, which overlooks the harbor and Paradise Island. If you like dining with a view, you won't find a better spot in the heart of Nassau. At lunch, order the perfectly seasoned conch chowder, a grilled chicken Caesar salad, or a juicy beef burger. The waiters are friendly, the crowd is convivial, and the festivities continue into the evening, usually with lots of drinking. Native grouper fingers served with peas 'n' rice is the Bahamian soul-food dish. Some of the best seafood selections are the fresh lobster, the grilled mahi-mahi with lime and sea salt, and the stuffed mushrooms with crabmeat. The creamy linguine with crisp garlic bread is another fine choice.

Nassau Yacht Haven Marina, E. Bay St. (*) **242/393-8175.** www.thepoopdeckrestaurants.com. Reservations recommended for dinner, not necessary at lunch. Main courses $11–$27 lunch; $21–$56 dinner. AE, DC, DISC, MC, V. Daily 11:30am–10:30pm. For the branch at the Nassau Yacht Haven: Bus 10, 19, or 23. For the branch on W. Bay St.: Bus 10 or "the Western bus."

Shoal Restaurant and Lounge ★ ◆ BAHAMIAN

Many of our good friends in Nassau swear this is one of the best joints for authentic local food. We rank it near the top for a venue that's utterly without glamour, serving sensible down-home food at a spot far removed from the typical tourist path. After all, where else can you get a good bowl of okra soup these days? This may or may not be your fantasy, but to a Bahamian, it's like what pot liquor and turnip greens with corn bread are to a Southerner. Many diners follow a bowl of soup (either split pea or the above-mentioned okra) with conch, either cracked or perhaps curried. But you can also order some unusual dishes, such as Bahamian-style curried mutton with native spices and herbs, stewed oxtail, or braised short ribs. Peas 'n' rice accompanies virtually everything served here. Because of its early closing, the place is appropriate only as a venue for lunch and for very early dinners. (Surprisingly, among locals at least, there is something of a rush hour here for early dinners at around 4pm.)

Nassau St., near Poinciana Dr. (*)**242/323-4400.** Reservations not required. Main courses $10–$30. AE, DISC, MC, V. Sun–Fri 7am to 5pm. Bus: 16.

Taj Mahal NORTHERN INDIAN

This is Nassau's best and most frequently recommended Indian restaurant. Within a room lined with Indian art and artifacts, you'll dine on a wide range of savory and zesty Punjabi, tandoori, and curried dishes. Some of the best choices are the lamb selections, though concessions to local culture, like curried or tandoori-style conch, have begun cropping up on the menu. Consider a tandoori mixed platter, which, with a side dish or two, might satisfy two diners. All of the *korma* dishes, which combine lamb, chicken, beef, or vegetables in a creamy curry sauce, are very successful. Take-out meals are also available.

48 Parliament St., at Bay St. (*)**242/356-3002.** Reservations recommended. Main courses $20–$35. AE, MC, V. Daily noon–3pm and 6:30–11pm. Bus: 10 or 17.

Twin Brothers ★ 🎁 BAHAMIAN

If you're visiting old Arawak Cay, you get not only the best daiquiris in The Bahamas, but fresh, well-prepared food in a convivial atmosphere that's "hopping," as the locals call it. The McCardy twins emigrated from Eleuthera at the age of 21, heading for Nassau where they began making daiquiris—strawberry, banana, whatever—at the old Straw Market and earned a kind of local fame, especially with their sour sop daiquiri.

When their customers demanded food as well, the twins launched themselves into the restaurant game. In a nautical setting, you can begin with one of Nassau's tastiest conch salads, which you can watch as it's prepared. Wash it down with a mango lemonade (a first for some visitors). Served with a side of potato salad, the fried shrimp is succulent. You can also order a meaty and juicy Bahamian lobster tail. The

The British tradition of afternoon tea is still observed on the last Friday of each month, from January to August, at the hilltop mansion of the governor-general in Nassau. You can spend a memorable afternoon here, enjoying musical numbers and sampling some local treats. For an invitation to tea, call the **People-to-People Unit of the Ministry of Tourism** at ℭ 242/323-1853.

catch of the day can be grilled, fried, boiled, or steamed, and your conch can either be cracked or scorched. Sides include creamy coleslaw or cheesy macaroni or else fried plantains or peas 'n' rice.

Arawak Cay. ℭ **242/328-5033.** www.twinbrothersbahamas.com. Reservations recommended. Main courses $13–$40. DISC, MC, V. Daily 11:30am to 10:30pm. Bus: 10.

INEXPENSIVE

Café Skans GREEK/AMERICAN/BAHAMIAN   Owned and operated by a hardworking Greek family, this straightforward, Formica-clad diner offers flavorful food that's served without fanfare in generous portions. Set in the midst of Nassau's densest concentration of shops, it attracts local residents and office workers from the government buildings nearby. Menu items include Bahamian fried or barbecued chicken, conch chowder, bean soup with dumplings, souvlaki or gyros in pita bread, burgers, steaks, and seafood platters. This is also where workaday Nassau comes for breakfast.

Bay St., near Market St. ℭ **242/322-2486.** Reservations not accepted. Breakfast items $5–$14; sandwiches $6–$12; main-course platters $7–$26. MC, V. Mon–Sat 8am–5pm; Sun 8am–3pm. Bus: 10 or 17.

Conch Fritters Bar & Grill ☺ BAHAMIAN/INTERNATIONAL   A true local hangout with real island atmosphere, this lighthearted, family-friendly restaurant changes its focus several times throughout the day. Lunches and dinners are high-volume, high-turnover affairs mitigated by attentive staff. Guests invariably include older diners and parents with young children in tow. Food choices are standard but quite good, including cracked conch, fried shrimp, grilled salmon, blackened rib-eye steak, burgers, sandwiches, and six different versions of chicken, including a combination platter with barbecued ribs. Specialty drinks from the always-active bar include the Goombay Smash. Musicians perform Friday and Saturday (and sometimes Thursdays as well, depending on the business) from 7 to 10pm.

Marlborough St. (across from the British Colonial Hilton). ℭ **242/323-8801.** Reservations not needed. Burgers, sandwiches, and platters $10–$50. AE, MC, V. Daily 11am–11pm (until midnight Fri–Sat). Bus: 10.

Double Dragon CANTONESE/SZECHUAN   The chefs at this unpretentious eatery hail from the province of Canton in mainland China, so that locale inspires most of the food here. You'll find the place in an unscenic, raffish-looking waterfront neighborhood a short drive east of downtown Nassau. If you've ever wondered about the differences between Cantonese and Szechuan cuisine, a quick look at the menu will highlight them. Lobster, chicken, or beef, for example, can be prepared Cantonese style, with mild black-bean or ginger sauce; or in spicier Szechuan versions with red peppers, chilies, and garlic. Honey-garlic chicken and orange-flavored shrimp are always popular and succulent. Overall, this place is a fine choice if you're eager for a change from grouper and burgers.

E. Bay St. (btw. Mackey St. and Williams Court). ℂ**242/393-5718.** Reservations not needed. Main courses $10–$24. DISC, MC, V. Mon–Fri noon–3:30pm; daily 4:30–10pm. Bus: 10 or 19.

The Green Parrot Harbourfront Restaurant BAHAMIAN   Less formal and less expensive than the grander restaurant next door (the also-recommended Luciano's) this is an island-inspired indoor/outdoor eatery that celebrates the Bahamian sense of wind, seawater, sand, and stiff drinks, with views out over Nassau's harbor and the channel separating Nassau from Paradise Island. No one will mind if you nurse a party-colored drink for a while before moving on to meals that might begin with a satay of spiny lobster with hoisin honey glaze and wasabi, smoked jumbo shrimp with chili-flavored lime mayonnaise, and (when available) conch salad or ceviche from local seafood. Salads and burgers are available at lunch and dinner, always with the provision that you can "build your own" based on a half-dozen cheeses, toppings, or sauces outlined on the menu. More substantial main courses include linguine with conch, shrimp, and lobster in a basil-flavored tomato sauce; steaks, or the eternal staple, local cracked conch with tartar sauce. Don't confuse this place with the also-recommended Green Parrot at Hurricane Hole, an even less pretentious eatery across the channel, under the Bridge on Paradise Island.

East Bay Street. ℂ**242/322-9248.** www.greenparrotbar.com/harbour-front. Burgers, salads, and sandwiches $14–$18; main course $19–$27. AE, MC, V. Daily 11am–midnight. Bus 10.

Cable Beach

VERY EXPENSIVE

Black Angus Grille ★ STEAK/SEAFOOD   This is a truly excellent steakhouse that's positioned amid a cluster of dining options immediately above Cable Beach's Crystal Palace Casino. Relaxed but macho-looking and undeniably upscale, it's Cable Beach's most consistently busy restaurant—a function of its good food and, according to its manager, of the predilection of gamblers for juicy steaks after a nerve-jangling session at the gaming tables. Those succulent steaks are well prepared and cooked to your specifications. There's prime rib, filet mignon, and pepper steak, along with grilled tuna with a white-bean salad, blackened conch filet, Caesar salad, and an array of dessert soufflés that include versions with chocolate, praline, and orange.

Wyndham Nassau Resort, above the Crystal Palace Casino, W. Bay St. ℂ**242/327-6200.** www.wyndhamnassauresort.com. Reservations recommended. Main courses $29–$48. AE, DC, DISC, MC, V. Daily 6–11pm. Bus: 10.

EXPENSIVE

Amici ★ ITALIAN   The most glamorous of the Sheraton's restaurants, the highly recommended Amici works hard to maintain its status as a culinary showcase for the flavorful Italian cuisine that many guests crave after too long an exposure to an all-Bahamian diet. Following a radical renovation in 2007, its two-story garden setting features ceiling fans, dark-wood furniture reminiscent of a trattoria in Italy, and big windows framing a beach view. Popular and long-enduring dishes here include scampi cocktails, Caesar salad, fettuccine alfredo, Florentine-style breast of chicken on a bed of spinach, spicy shrimp, and braised pork shank with olive oil, hot peppers, and angel-hair pasta.

Sheraton Nassau Beach Resort, W. Bay St. ℂ**242/327-6000.** www.starwoodhotels.com. Reservations recommended. Main courses $24–$50. AE, DC, DISC, MC, V. Daily 6–10:30pm. Bus: 10.

Capriccio ITALIAN/INTERNATIONAL   Set beside a prominent roundabout, about .5km (⅓ mile) west of the mega-hotels of Cable Beach, this restaurant lies within a much-weathered, faux-baroque Italian building with Corinthian columns and an outdoor terrace. Inside, it's a lot less formal, outfitted like an upscale luncheonette, but with lots of exposed granite, busy espresso machines, and kindly Bahamian staff who understand Italian culinary nuance. At lunch, you get pretty ordinary fare such as salads, sandwiches, and a few hot platters like cracked conch. But the cooks shine at night, offering dishes such as chicken breast with sage and wine sauce, veal cutlets served Milanese style or with Marsala sauce, spaghetti with pesto and pine nuts, and seafood platters.

W. Bay St. ℭ **242/327-8547.** Reservations recommended. Lunch items $10–$21; dinner main courses $19–$35. AE, MC, V. Mon–Sat 11:30am–10pm; Sun 5–10pm. Bus: 10 or 17.

Indigo ★ INTERNATIONAL   Locals flock to this dive, and visitors find its funky atmosphere appealing as well. In the pre-dinner hours, the bar is bustling and animated. There's some Bahamian culture on show as well, as the walls are decorated with original oils, mostly of native island scenes. Friday and Saturday are the big nights here, when a steel-pan band is brought in. The joint can get classy, too. The food, consisting of pastas, steaks, chicken, lobster, curries, and fresh fish, is well-prepared but rather standard, except for the sushi, which comes as a surprise. Other Asian-style dishes are given a distinct Bahamian touch. The conch chowder evokes a South Seas flavor via the addition of coconut and curry powder.

W. Bay St. (at the Sandals traffic circle). ℭ **242/327-2524.** Reservations not necessary. Main courses $12–$36. AE, DISC, MC, V. Mon–Sat noon–10pm.

Poop Deck at Sandyport INTERNATIONAL/SEAFOOD   This is one of the three most imposing, desirable restaurants west of Cable Beach, convenient for the owners of the many upscale villas and condos, including those at Lyford Cay, that occupy New Providence's western edge. More international and upscale than its more raffish counterpart on East Bay Street (p. 67), it's set within a peach-colored concrete building that's highly visible from West Bay Street. Despite the rosy exterior, it's a bit sterile-looking inside. This island restaurant evolved from a roughneck bar that occupied this site during the early 1970s. Lunch is usually devoted to well-prepared burgers, pastas, sandwiches, paellas, and salads. Dinners are more substantial, featuring filet mignon, seafood and steak combos, cracked conch, fried shrimp, and fresh fish. There's also a tempting list of Spanish-style tapas, authentic to Iberia, priced at around $6 per portion, including exotic versions of cured ham. The house drink is a Bacardi Splish-Splash, a buzz-inducing blend of Bacardi Select, Nassau Royal Liqueur, pineapple juice, cream, and sugar-cane syrup.

Poop Deck Dr., off W. Bay St. ℭ **242/327-DECK** (3325). www.thepoopdeckrestaurants.com. Reservations recommended. Main courses $11–$30 lunch; $21–$60 dinner. AE, DISC, MC, V. Tues–Sat noon–10:30pm; Sun noon–10pm. Bus: 10 or "the Western bus."

Provence ★ FRENCH MEDITERRANEAN   Nassau's best Mediterranean cuisine is showcased within this sunny yellow restaurant. Lying near West Bay Street's western terminus, it's extremely popular with well-heeled locals (some of whom aren't particularly enchanted with the island's blockbuster casino hotels and their eateries). Decor includes big-windowed sea views and oil paintings of landscapes that evoke the southern French coast. Provence prepares its *cuisine du soleil* with superb simplicity—Atlantic salmon with citrus butter, for example—so as not to mar the natural flavor. Other dishes are heavily spiced, such as the rib-eye steak in a fire-breathing pepper sauce. The chefs also turn out a delightful bouillabaisse and a Moroccan-style seafood *tagine*. Daily seafood specials may include pan-seared sea bass, our favorite, or black grouper filet. Everybody seems to like the lobster cocktails and the rack of lamb.

Old Towne Sandyport. © **242/327-0985.** www.provencerestaurant.net. Reservations required. Main courses $11–$22 lunch; $28–$55 dinner. AE, DISC, MC, V. Mon–Fri 11:30am–3pm; Mon–Sat 6–10:30pm. Bus: 10 or "the Western bus."

West of Cable Beach

Goodfellow Farms ★ 🏠BAHAMIAN   A visit to this country store and open-air lunch restaurant on the western end of the island is a journey back in time to the way The Bahamas used to be. This vegetable farm supplies fresh produce to Nassau restaurants and to visiting yachties, but you can sample it daily. Most visitors, however, show up for their midday meal, ordering from a menu that changes weekly. Our favorite items are the freshly grown gourmet greens and the large array of specialty vegetables, although you can also enjoy high-quality cheeses and cuts of meat that include lamb, organic chicken, and fresh seafood, especially mahimahi, sea bass, and jumbo lump crabmeat. An on-site retail shop is stocked with all sorts of delectable food items.

Nelson Rd., Mt. Pleasant Village. © **242/377-5000.** www.goodfellowfarms.com. Reservations recommended, essential on Fri night. Lunch main courses $14–$17. MC, V. Lunch served daily, year-round, 11am–3pm. Retail store Mon–Sat 9am–4pm. Drive west toward Old Fort Bay and Lyford Cay; at the traffic circle at Lyford Cay Plaza, exit up the hill toward Templeton. The farm is signposted.

Restaurant at Compass Point ★ BAHAMIAN   Dining here might remind those who experienced the '60s of how they felt after ingesting one of those hallucinogenic brownies during their college years. The ceiling is orange, the bar is a study in marine blues, the view sweeps out over the sea, and everywhere you'll see the vivid Junkanoo, or reggae, colors of the West Indies. It's a charming and somewhat out-of-the-way retreat from the densely populated urban scenes of downtown Nassau and nearby Cable Beach. Lunches are simple and uncomplicated affairs, with turkey club sandwiches, meal-size salads, and burgers. Dinners are more elaborate and steeped in West Indian tradition, including dishes such as cracked conch, seafood-stuffed snapper, and pan-fried grouper with peas, rice, and plantains. Try the shrimp tempura or lobster stir-fried with mango and goat peppers. Because of its position facing the setting sun, the bar is a well-known spot from which to look for the elusive "green flash"; if that's your aim, the bartender can explain this to you and prepare you a bright-yellow Compass Bliss.

Compass Point Resort, W. Bay St., Gambier. © **242/327-4500.** www.compasspointbeachresort. com. Reservations recommended. Lunch platters $9–$15; dinner main courses $29–$42, more for lobster. AE, MC, V. Sun–Thurs 11am–10pm (last order); Fri–Sat 11am–11pm. Bar closes at midnight. Bus: 10 from Nassau and Cable Beach.

Simmer Down CARIBBEAN   More than any other restaurant in The Bahamas, this one, and the inn that contains it (p. 61), is devoted to the legendary Jamaican superstar Bob Marley, whose memory lives on through artwork and memorabilia scattered around the dining room and bar. Be warned that curious onlookers from nearby hotels might pop in for a drink here, and at other moments the restaurant might be closed altogether based on advance bookings. The menu focuses on Caribbean cuisine, particularly from Jamaica, and includes some classic Marley family recipes and some of Bob's favorite dishes. Organic produce and fresh seafood highlight the menu.

If you're keen on organizing a picnic and want to gather your provisions, consider heading about 3km (1¾ miles) west of Cable Beach. Within a shopping complex known as Caves Village, you'll find the **Gourmet Market** (© 242/327-1067; www.gourmetmarketnassau.com), the island's most upscale grocery store. Functioning like a magnet for villa owners within the nearby exclusive gated community of Lyford Cay, it sells fruits, cheeses, fish, wines, and pastries. And yes, they'll make sandwiches and even assemble, with or without strong guidance from you, picnic meals to go. It's open Monday to Friday 8:30am to 6pm, Sat 9am to 6pm.

Start with an appetizer of Bahamian crab cake or savory seafood and cheese terrine, followed by jerk chicken or spicy jerk fish (this was Bob's favorite). A specialty is roasted organic pineapple rum duck, or else you can try "Rita's Favorite," roasted rack of lamb. Desserts are sumptuous, including guava upside down cake with brandy cream or chocolate banana pudding with vanilla ice cream and Jamaican rum.

On a stage in the courtyard, live entertainment, especially reggae, is sometimes presented. On site is Marley's Boutique, a funky Jamaica-inspired outlet selling arts and crafts, plus high-end resort wear designed by Cedelia Marley, the late reggae star's daughter, under the label "Catch a Fire."

In the Marley Resort & Spa, West Bay St., Cable Beach. © **272/702-2800.** www.marleyresort.com. Reservations required. Main courses $26–$41. AE, MC, V. Daily 7:30–10:30am, noon–3pm, and 6–10pm.

Travellers Rest ★ 🍴 BAHAMIAN/SEAFOOD   Set in an isolated spot about 2.5km (1½ miles) west of Cable Beach's mega-hotels, this restaurant feels far away from it all—like you're dining on a remote Out Island. The cozy cement-sided house, established as a restaurant in 1972, stands in a grove of sea-grape and palm trees facing the ocean. Because it's near the airport, travelers whose flights are delayed sometimes opt to chill out here until departure. You can dine outside, but if it's rainy (highly unlikely), go inside the tavern, with its small bar decorated with local paintings. In this laid-back atmosphere, feast on well-prepared grouper fingers, barbecued ribs, curried chicken, steamed or cracked conch, or minced crayfish. Finish with guava cake, the best on the island. The conch salad served on weekends is said to increase men's virility.

W. Bay St., near Gambier (14km/8¾ miles west of the center of Nassau). © **242/327-7633.** Main courses at both lunch and dinner $15–$30. Daily 11:30am–11pm. Bus: 10, 12B, or "the Western bus."

BEACHES & OUTDOOR PURSUITS

One of the great sports centers of the world, New Providence and the islands that surround it are marvelous places for swimming, sunning, snorkeling, scuba diving, boating, water-skiing, and deep-sea fishing, as well as playing tennis and golf.

3

NEW PROVIDENCE (NASSAU/CABLE BEACH)   Beaches & Outdoor Pursuits

Hitting the Beach

In The Bahamas, as in Puerto Rico, the issue regarding public access to beaches is a hot and controversial subject. Recognizing this, the government has made efforts to intersperse public beaches with easy access between more private beaches where access may be impeded. Although mega-resorts discourage nonresidents from accessing their individual beaches, there are so many local public beaches that all you'd have to do is drive or walk to any of the many unmarked, unnamed beaches.

Most visitors stay in one of the large beachfront resorts that have the ocean meeting the sand right outside of their doors. For those hoping to explore more of the coast, here's a list of recommended beaches that are absolutely accessible to the public:

CABLE BEACH ★★ No particular beach is actually called Cable Beach, yet this is the most popular stretch of sand on New Providence Island. Cable Beach is the name given not to a single beach, but to a string of resorts and beaches in the center of New Providence's northern coast, attracting the most visitors. This beachfront offers 6.5km (4 miles) of soft white sand, with many different types of restaurants, snack bars, and watersports offered by the hotels lining the waterfront. Calypso music floats to the sand from hotel pool patios, where vacationers play musical chairs and see how low they can limbo. Vendors wend their way between sunscreen-slathered bodies selling armloads of shell jewelry, T-shirts, beach cover-ups, and fresh coconuts for sipping the sweet "water" straight from the shell. Others offer hair-braiding services or sign up visitors for water-skiing, jet-skiing, and banana-boat rides. Kiosks advertise parasailing, scuba-diving, and snorkeling trips, as well as party cruises to offshore islands. Waters can be rough and reefy, but then calm and clear a little farther along the shore. There are no public toilets here because guests of the resorts use their hotel facilities. If you're not a hotel guest and not a customer, you're not supposed to use the facilities. Cable Beach resorts begin 5km (3 miles) west of downtown Nassau, and even though they line much of this long swath of beach, there are various sections where public access is available without crossing through private hotel grounds.

CAVES BEACH On the north shore, past the Cable Beach hotels, Caves Beach is 11km (6¾ miles) west of Nassau. It stands near Rock Point, right before the turnoff along Blake Road that leads to the airport. Since many visitors don't know of this place, it's a good spot to escape the hordes. It's also an attractive beach with soft sands. There are no toilets or changing facilities.

DELAPORTE BEACH Just west of Cable Beach's busiest section is this public-access beach where you can escape the crowds. It opens onto clear waters and boasts white sands, although it has neither facilities nor toilets.

GOODMAN'S BAY This public beach lies east of Cable Beach on the way toward Nassau's center. Goodman's Bay and Saunders Beach (see below) often host local fund-raising cookouts, during which vendors sell fish, chicken, conch, peas 'n' rice, and macaroni and cheese. People swim and socialize to blaring reggae and calypso tunes. To find out when one of these beach parties is happening, ask the staff at your hotel or pick up a local newspaper. There's a playground here, plus toilet facilities.

OLD FORT BEACH ★ To escape the crowds on weekdays, we often head here, a 15-minute drive west of Lynden Pindling International Airport (take W. Bay St. toward Lyford Cay). This lovely beach opens onto Old Fort Bay's turquoise waters,

A Beach for Lovers

Continuing west along West Bay Street, you'll reach **Love Beach**, across from Sea Gardens, a nice stretch of sand lying east of Northwest Point. Love Beach, although not big, is a special favorite of lovers (hence the name). The snorkeling is superb, too. It's technically private, but no one bothers visitors, even though locals fervently hope it won't become overrun like Cable Beach.

near western New Providence. The least developed of the island's beaches, it attracts many homeowners from the swanky Lyford Cay gated community. In winter, it can be quite windy, but in summer, it's as calm as the Caribbean.

SAUNDERS BEACH East of Cable Beach, this is where many islanders go on the weekends. To reach it, take West Bay Street from Nassau toward Coral Island. This beach lies across from Fort Charlotte, just west of Arawak Cay. Like Goodman's Bay (see above), it often hosts local fund-raising cookouts open to the public. These can be a lot of fun. There are no public facilities.

WESTERN ESPLANADE If you're staying at a hotel in downtown Nassau, such as the British Colonial, this is a good beach to patronize close to town. On this narrow strip of sand convenient to Nassau, you'll find toilets, changing facilities, and a snack bar. It's also known as Junkanoo Beach or Lighthouse Beach.

Biking

A half-day bicycle tour with **Bahamas Outdoors Ltd. (© 242/362-1574;** www.bahamasoutdoors.com) takes you on a 5km (3-mile) ride along scenic forest and shoreline trails in the Coral Harbour area on the island's southwestern coast. New Providence resident Carolyn Wardle, an expert on the region's ecology, bird life, and history, provides ongoing commentary. The itinerary follows a series of easy trails, usually on hard-packed earth, along seashores and through pink forests. En route, you'll see sleepy Adelaide Village (settled by freed slaves in the 1830s) and spot local birds, either with the naked eye or aided by binoculars. Shorts and a T-shirt are the recommended attire. Tours rarely include more than a half-dozen participants at a time; most are morning events that last around 4 hours. The cost is $79 per person for a half-day tour, and $149 (winter only) for a full day tour; there is a two-person minimum.

If you'd like to go it alone, know that some of the major hotels on Paradise Beach and Cable Beach rent bicycles to their guests. You can bike along Cable Beach or along the beachfront at Paradise Island, but roads through downtown Nassau are too narrow, and traffic too congested, to make the ride genuinely pleasant or even particularly safe.

Boat Cruises

A number of operators offer cruises from the harbors around New Providence, with trips ranging from daytime voyages—for snorkeling, picnicking, sunning, and swimming—to sunset and moonlight cruises.

Barefoot Sailing Cruises, Bay Shore Marina, on East Bay Street (© **242/393-0820;** www.barefootsailingcruises.com), operates the 12m (41-ft.) *Wind Dance*, which leaves for all-day cruises involving many sailing and snorkeling possibilities.

This is your best bet if you're seeking a more romantic cruise and don't want 100 people aboard. The cruises usually stop at Rose Island, a charming, picture-perfect spot with an uncrowded beach and palm trees. You can also sail on a ketch, the 17m (56-ft.) *Riding High*. Cruise options are plentiful, including sailing, snorkeling, and exploring for $75 per person for a half-day and $115 for a full day. A 2-hour sunset cruise, departing between 5 and 8pm two to three times a week (depending on the season, the weather, and advance bookings), costs $65 per person.

The *Flying Cloud,* Paradise Island West Dock (© 242/394-5067; www.flying cloud.info), is a twin-hulled sailing catamaran that carries 50 people for day and sunset trips. It's a good bet for those who want a more intimate cruise and shy away from the heavy volume carried aboard the Majestic Tours catamarans (see below). Snorkeling equipment is included in the cost, which is $70 per person for a half-day charter. A 2½-hour sunset cruise also goes for $70. Evening bookings are on Monday, Wednesday, and Friday. On Sunday, a 5-hour cruise leaves at 10am, includes a simple lunch, and costs $85 per person.

Majestic Tours, Hillside Manor, Cumberland Street (© **242/322-2606;** www. majestictoursbahamas.com), offers tours aboard the *Robinson Crusoe* to an uninhabited offshore cay, Rose Island, for up to 200 passengers, who sunbathe, swim, snorkel, collect seashells, and wander across a sunflooded, scrub-covered landscape, escaping at least temporarily from the realities of urban life. On Wednesday, Friday, and Sunday, cruises run from 10am to 4:30pm, costing $70 for adults and $35 for kids 4 to 12. Sunset dinner cruises run from 7 to 10pm on Tuesday and Friday; the cost is $60 for adults, half-price for children.

Fishing

Fishing choices are plentiful: You can troll for wahoo, tuna, and marlin in the deep sea, or cast in the shallows for snapper, grouper, and yellowtail. Anchoring and bottom-fishing are calmer options. May to August are the best months to catch oceanic bonito and the blackfin tuna, June and July for blue marlin, and November through February for the wahoo found in reefy areas. Arrangements for fishing trips can be made at any of the big hotels, but unfortunately, there's a hefty price tag.

Born Free Charters (© **242/393-4144;** www.bornfreefishing.com), one of the most reliable companies, maintains a fleet of three vessels, each between 11 and 14m long (36–46 ft.), that can seat six comfortably. You can rent them for a half-day ($600–$800) or a full day ($1,200–$1,600). Each additional person pays $50. We recommend this company because it offers so many types of fishing and gives lots of leeway regarding where you want to fish and how much time you want to spend.

Occasionally, boat owners will configure themselves and their boats as businesses for deep-sea fishing. Unless you're dealing with a genuinely experienced guide, however, your fishing trip may or may not be a success. **John Pratt** has emerged over the years as one of the most consistently reliable deep-sea fishermen. He maintains a 14m (46-ft.) fishing boat, making it available for full- or half-day deep-sea fishing excursions. It docks every night at the island's largest marina, the 150-slip **Nassau Yacht Haven Marina,** on East Bay Street (© **242/393-8173** or 242/422-0364; www.nassauyachthaven.com), where a member of the staff will direct you. Alternatively, you can call © **242/422-0364** to speak to Mr. Pratt directly. It takes about 20 minutes of boat travel to reach an offshore point where dolphin and wahoo may or may not be biting, depending on a raft of complicated seasonal factors. ***Note:*** These trips need to be booked several weeks in advance.

Golf

Some of the country's best golfing is in Nassau and on nearby Paradise Island (p. 93). Although "dormant," or storm-damaged, courses on the extreme western end of New Providence might one day be rejuvenated, at press time, the only functioning golf course on New Providence Island that is open to nonmembers is the **Cable Beach Golf Club ★★**, West Bay Street, Cable Beach (*②* **242/677-4175;** www.crystal palacevacations.com). An intricately designed 9-hole course, it benefited from a major redesign in 2011. Earlier redesigns at the debut of the millennium reshaped the fairways, repositioned putting greens, and introduced new hazards and water-lined holes throughout two-thirds of its layout. Better year-round playing conditions were ensured by introducing a salt-tolerant grass (paspalum) that is greener, firmer, and more upright, withstanding the salty breezes and tropical heat while providing a premium putting surface. The alterations were overseen by veteran designer Fred M. Settle, Jr.

Many of the players who tee off are guests of hotels on Cable Beach. Year-round greens fees for 9 holes of play range from $80 to $100, depending on the season, and include the use of an electric golf cart. Discounts, depending on the season, are usually granted to pre-reserved residents of the Sheraton Nassau Beach Hotel and the Wyndham Nassau Resort. Rental of golf clubs costs an additional $35 per person.

Horseback Riding

Windsor Equestrian Centre & Happy Trails Stables, Coral Harbour, on the southwest shore (*②* 242/362-1820; www.bahamahorse.com or www.windsor equestriancentre.com), offers 90-minute horseback trail rides, which are limited to a maximum of eight riders at a time, for $150 per person. The price includes free transportation to and from your hotel. The stables are signposted from the Lynden Pindling International Airport, which is 3km (1¾ miles) away. Children must be 12 and older, riders must weigh less than 91kg (201 lb.), and reservations are required.

Snorkeling & Scuba Diving

There's great snorkeling off most of New Providence's shore, especially at **Love Beach.** Most hotels and resorts will rent or loan snorkeling equipment to guests. Several of the companies mentioned under "Boat Cruises" (p. 72) offer snorkel trips. Also see "Easy Side Trips to Nearby Islands" (p. 87) for descriptions of additional snorkeling excursions.

Our favorite snorkel site is **Goulding Cay,** off the island's western tip. Underwater, you'll find a field of hard corals, especially the elegant elkhorn. The clear waters and shallow coral heads make it ideal for filmmakers. In fact, it's been featured in many films, from a number of James Bond movies to *20,000 Leagues Under the Sea.* More elkhorn coral is found to the south at **Southwest Reef,** which also shelters stunning star coral in water less than 2.4m (8 ft.) deep. To the north is **Fish Hotel,** which is not much on coral but graced with large schools of fish, especially red snapper, jacks, and grunts.

There are more dive sites around New Providence than you can see in one visit, but a few of our recommendations are: the intriguing **Shark Wall ★★**, 16km (10 miles) off the coast; the **Rose Island Reefs;** the **Southwest Reef; Razorback;** and **Booby Rock Reef.** Dive outfitters can also lead you to many old shipwrecks off the coast, along with caves and cliffs. Wrecks include the *Mahoney* and *Alcora,* plus the wreck featured in the James Bond film *Never Say Never Again.* Divers can also explore the airplane propeller used in another Bond film, *Thunderball*. All outfitters will take you to one or more of these sites.

Bahamas Divers, Nassau Yacht Haven Marina, on East Bay Street (© **800/398-3483** in the U.S., or 242/393-5644; www.bahamadivers.com), offers packages that include a half-day of snorkeling at offshore reefs for $50 per person, or a half-day scuba trip with experienced, certified divers for between $70 and $129, depending on the destination. Half-day excursions for certified divers to deeper outlying reefs, drop-offs, and blue holes can be arranged, usually for $109 to $150 for a two-tank dive. Novice divers sometimes sign up for a carefully supervised course that includes instruction with scuba equipment in a swimming pool, followed by a shallow shore-front dive accompanied by an instructor, also for $135 per person. Participants receive free transportation from their hotel to the boats. Children must be 10 and older, and reservations are required, especially during the holiday season.

Stuart Cove's Dive Bahamas, on Southwest Bay Street, South Ocean (© **800/879-9832** in the U.S. or 242/362-4171; www.stuartcove.com), is about 10 minutes from top dive sites, including the coral reefs, wrecks, and underwater airplane structure featured in James Bond thrillers. For the island's most exciting underwater adventure, divers head to the **Caribe Breeze wreck,** depicted in the film *Open Water*. Here the staff feeds reef sharks some 15m (49 ft.) below the surface; from a position of safety, divers in full scuba gear witness the show. Steep sea walls and the Porpoise Pen Reefs (named for Flipper) are also on the agenda. A two-tank dive in the morning costs $109; an all-day program goes for $155. All prices for boat dives include tanks, weights, and belts. An open-water P.A.D.I certification course starts at $960. Bring along two friends, and the price drops to $615 per person. Three-hour escorted boat snorkeling trips cost $65; children 11 and under are included for $30. A special feature is a series of shark-dive experiences priced at $150. At **Shark Arena,** divers kneel while a dive master feeds the toothsome predators off a long pole. On the **Shark Buoy** dive at a depth of about 9m (30 ft.), sharks swim among divers while the dive master feeds them.

SEEING THE SIGHTS

Most of Nassau can be explored on foot, beginning at **Rawson Square** in the center, where Bahamian fishers unload a variety of produce and seafood—crates of mangoes, oranges, tomatoes, and limes, plus lots of crimson-lipped conch. To experience this slice of Bahamian life, go any morning Monday through Saturday before noon.

The best way to see some of Nassau's major public buildings is to take our walking tour (p. 81), which will give you not only an overview of the historic highlights, but

 Fifteen Miles of Great Scenery for $1.25

In Nassau, local tourism officials are promoting a bus route, the **no. 10,** that takes you on a road trip that covers 15 scenic miles along West Bay Street, passing historic forts, ocean vistas, well-to-do neighborhoods, secluded coves, and strands of golden-sand beaches.

The cost is only $1.25 per ride, a super bargain compared to the other means of transport used by visitors—chauffeured limos, horse-and-carriage rides, loaded bus tours, rented cars, or even motor bikes.

3

NEW PROVIDENCE (NASSAU/CABLE BEACH) | Seeing the Sights

75

TO MARKET, TO MARKET AT potter's cay

One of the liveliest places in Nassau during the day is **Potter's Cay,** a market that thrives beneath the Paradise Island Bridge. From the Out Islands, fishing boats and heavily laden sloops arrive early in the morning to unload the day's catch. Spiny lobster is the most expensive seafood, but grouper reigns supreme along with fresh crab, jack, and mackerel.

If grouper is king, then "sweet, sexy conch," as the locals say, is queen. Vendors make the freshest conch salad right on the spot; if you haven't eaten the delicacy before, this is the place to try it.

What we don't like to see are fishmongers chopping up sea turtles, a highly endangered species. However, the vendors are not of the politically correct sort, and they're more interested in catering to the Bahamians' lifelong love of turtle flesh than they are in preserving the species for future generations.

Not just fish is sold here. Sloops from the Out Islands also bring in cartons of freshly harvested vegetables, including the fiery hot peppers so beloved by locals, along with an array of luscious exotic fruits. **Tip:** Many of these vendors have a wicked sense of humor and will offer you a taste of tamarind, claiming it's the "sweetest taste on God's earth." Invariably, tricked visitors spit it out: The taste is horrendously offensive.

You can also see mail boats leaving and coming to this quay. Watching their frenetic departure or arrival is one of the island's more amusing scenes.

also an overall feel for the city. After that, concentrate on specific sights you'd like to take in; Ardastra Gardens and Coral Island Bahamas are notable options.

The Top Attractions

Ardastra Gardens, Zoo & Conservation Center ★ The main attraction of the Ardastra Gardens, almost 2 hectares (5 acres) of lush tropical plants about 1.5km (1 mile) west of downtown Nassau near Fort Charlotte, is the parading flock of **pink flamingos.** The Caribbean flamingo, national bird of The Bahamas, had almost disappeared by the early 1940s, but was brought back to significant numbers through the efforts of the National Trust. They now flourish in the rookery on Great Inagua. A flock of these exotic feathered creatures has been trained to march in drill formation, responding to human commands with long-legged precision. The flamingos perform daily at 10:30am, 2:10pm, and 4:10pm.

Other exotic wildlife here include boa constrictors (very tame), macaws, kinkajous (honey bears) from Central and South America, peacocks and peahens, capuchin monkeys, iguanas, lemurs, margays, brown-headed tamarins (monkeys), and a crocodile. There are also numerous waterfowl in Swan Lake, including black swans from Australia and several species of wild ducks. Parrot feedings take place at 11am, 1:30pm, and 3:30pm.

You can get a good look at Ardastra's flora by walking along the signposted paths. Many of the more interesting and exotic trees bear plaques listing their names.

Chippingham Rd. © **242/323-5806.** www.ardastra.com. Admission $16 adults, $8 children 4–12. Daily 9am–4:10pm (last entrance). Bus: 10.

What to See & Do in Nassau

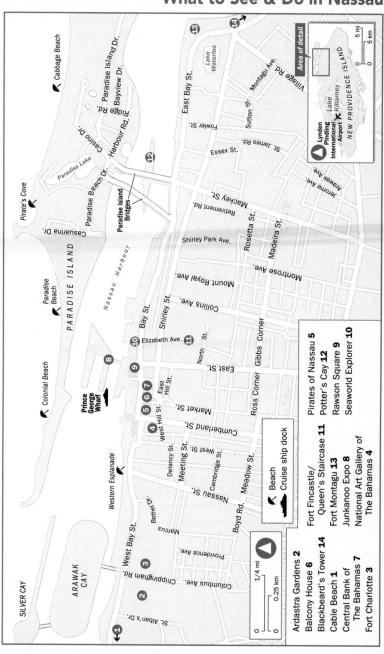

Ardastra Gardens **2**
Balcony House **6**
Blackbeard's Tower **14**
Central Bank of
The Bahamas **7**
Fort Charlotte **3**

Fort Fincastle/
Queen's Staircase **11**
Fort Montagu **13**
Junkanoo Expo **8**
National Art Gallery of
The Bahamas **4**

Pirates of Nassau **5**
Potter's Cay **12**
Rawson Square **9**
Seaworld Explorer **10**

↖ Beach
⚓ Cruise ship dock

The Retreat, Village Road (℃ **242/393-1317;** www.bnt.bs), on the southern outskirts of downtown Nassau, is the home of The Bahamas National Trust. A clapboard-sided green-and-white building, it was originally conceived as the homestead of the Langlois family and purchased from them by the National Trust in 1925. Whereas there's nothing of particular interest inside the house (it contains mostly workaday offices), its gardens are worth a visit. They comprise 4.4 hectares (11 acres) of the most unspoiled greens on New Providence and contain about 200 species of exotic palm trees. The grounds, which are for the most part flat, can be navigated with a map available on-site. A gift shop sells books and memorabilia approved by and associated with the National Trust. Visit Monday through Friday from 9am to 5pm; admission is $2 for adults and $1 for children 5 to 12 and students up to 18.

National Art Gallery of The Bahamas ★   At long last, this archipelago nation has a showcase in which to display the works of its talented artists. In a restored 18th-century building in the center of Nassau, the gallery features Bahamian art, which, as an entity, has existed for only 50 years. Curators claim that the present collection is only the nucleus of a larger, long-range strategy to beef up the present number of works. Most of the paintings on exhibit are divided into historical and contemporary collections. Pioneering Bahamian artists are honored, as are younger and more modern painters. Among island artists, Amos Ferguson is one of the most acclaimed. His somewhat naïve yet sophisticated technique is at its best in the painting *Snowbirds:* He used house paint on cardboard to create a remarkable portrait. Maxwell Taylor and Antonius Roberts are two other heavily featured Bahamian painters.

Villa Doyle, W. Hill St. in downtown Nassau. ℃**242/328-5800.** www.nagb.org.bs. Admission $5 adults, $3 seniors and students, free for children 12 and under. Tues–Sat 10am–4pm. Bus: 10.

Seaworld Explorer ★   If you're curious about life below the waves but aren't a strong swimmer, hop aboard this 45-person submarine. Tours last 90 minutes and include 45 to 55 minutes of actual underwater travel at depths of about 3.5m (11 ft.). Big windows allow big views of a protected ecology zone offshore from Paradise Island Airport. The remainder of the time is devoted to an above-water tour of landmarks on either side of the channel that separates Nassau from Paradise Island.

W. Bay St. at Elizabeth Ave. ℃**242/356-2548.** www.seaworldtours.com. Reservations required. $45 adults, $25 children 2–12. Tours daily at 9:30am, 11:30am, and 1:30pm year-round; call for latest details. Bus: 10.

More Attractions

Balcony House   This landmark house's original design exemplifies late-18th-century Southeast American architecture. The pink two-story structure is named for its overhanging and much-photographed balcony. Restored about 20 years ago, the house has been returned to its original design, recapturing a historic period. The mahogany staircase inside is thought to have been salvaged from a wrecked ship in the 1800s. At press time, the house was closed for renovations, but despite budgetary restraints, it might be open by the time of your visit. Call in advance before you go.

MEET THE bahamians

The **People-to-People Program,** estab- lished by the Ministry of Tourism, pro- vides an opportunity for visitors to learn more about the culture of The Bahamas by interacting with the Bahamians them- selves. The program matches visitors, often entire families, with more than 1,500 Bahamian volunteers of similar ages and interests for a day or evening activity, which could include boating, fish- ing, shopping at the local outdoor mar- ket, enjoying a back-street tour, or, more often, visiting them in their home for a traditional meal of peas 'n' rice, fried fish, and guava duff. These encounters have resulted in lasting friendships between visitors and locals. Philip Archer, a pro- gram volunteer for more than 20 years, has received hundreds of invitations to visit families from different countries. Cel- ebrating its 34th anniversary in 2011, the People-to-People Program has expanded beyond Nassau to Abaco, Bimini, Eleu- thera, Grand Bahama Island, North Andros, the Exumas, and Cat Island. To participate in the program in Nassau/ Paradise Island and the Out Islands, e-mail peopletopeople@bahamas.com. To participate in the program, direct an e-mail to tourism@bahamas.com, or click on www.bahamas.com/bahamas/ people-people.

Trinity Place and Market St. ℂ **242/302-2621.** Free admission, but donations advised. Mon–Wed and Fri 9:30am–4:30pm. Bus: 10.

Blackbeard's Tower   These crumbling remains of a watchtower are said to have been used by the infamous pirate Edward Teach in the 17th century. The ruins are only mildly interesting—there isn't much trace of buccaneering. What's interesting is the view: With a little imagination, you can almost see Blackbeard, who also purport- edly lived here (though this is hardly well documented), peering out at unsuspecting ships.

Fox Hill, 8km/5 miles east of Fort Montagu. ℂ **242/364-8310.** Free admission. Daily 24 hr. Reach- able by jitney.

Central Bank of The Bahamas   The nerve center that governs the archipelago's financial transactions is also the venue for a year-round cycle of temporary exhibitions of paintings that represent the nation's multifaceted artistic talent. The cornerstone of the building was laid by Prince Charles on July 9, 1973, when the country became independent from Britain. Queen Elizabeth II officially inaugurated the bank in 1975.

Trinity Place and Frederick St. ℂ **242/302-2600.** www.centralbankbahamas.com. Free admission. Mon–Fri 9:30am–4:30pm. Bus: 10.

Fort Charlotte   Begun in 1787, Fort Charlotte is the largest of Nassau's three major defense buildings, built with plenty of dungeons. It used to command the western harbor. Named after King George III's consort, it was built by Gov. Lord Dunmore, who was also the last royal governor of New York and Virginia. Its 42 can- nons (only seven remain on-site) never fired a shot—at least, not at an invader. Within the complex are underground passages, which can be viewed on a free tour (guides are very happy to accept a tip).

Off W. Bay St. on Chippingham Rd. (opposite Arawak Cay) ℂ **242/325-9186.** Admission $5 adults, $2 for children 12 and under. Daily 8am–3pm. Bus: 10.

Few visitors make the trip anymore, but it used to be a tradition to go over the hill to Nassau's most colorful area. **"Over-the-Hill"** is the actual name of this poor residential district, where descendants of former slaves built rainbow-hued houses, leaving the most desirable lands around the harbor to the rich folk. This, not the historic core of Nassau around Rawson Square, is truly the heart of Bahamian-African culture. The thump of the Junkanoo-Goombay drum can be heard here day and night. The area never sleeps, or so it is said—and certainly not on Sunday morning, when you can drive by the churches and hear hell and damnation promised loudly to all sinners and backsliders.

This fascinating part of Nassau begins .5km (⅓ mile) south of Blue Hill Road, which starts at the exclusive Graycliff Hotel. But once you're "Over-the-Hill," you're a long way from the hotel's vintage wine and Cuban cigars. Some people—usually savvy store owners from abroad—come here to buy local handicrafts from individual vendors. The area can be explored on foot (during the day only), but many visitors prefer to drive. **Note:** This area is well worth a visit, but keep your eyes open; most of Nassau's criminal incidents happen in this part of town.

Fort Fincastle Reached by climbing the Queen's Staircase, this fort was constructed in 1793 by Lord Dunmore, the royal governor. You can take an elevator ride to the top and walk on the observation floor (a 38m-high/125-ft. water tower and lighthouse) for a panoramic view of the harbor. The tower is New Providence's highest point. This fort's so-called bow is patterned like a Mississippi paddle-wheel steamer; it was built to defend Nassau against a possible invasion, though no shot was ever fired.

Though the ruins hardly compete with the view, you can walk around on your own here. Be wary, however, of the very persistent young men who will try to show you around; they'll try to hustle you, but you really don't need a guide to see some old cannons.

Elizabeth Ave. ☎ **242/322-7500.** Free admission. Mon–Sat 8am–5pm. Bus: 10 or 17.

Fort Montagu Built in 1741, this fort—the island's oldest—stands guard at the eastern entrance to Nassau's harbor. The Americans captured it in 1776 during the Revolutionary War. Less interesting than Fort Charlotte and Fort Fincastle (described above), the ruins of this place are mainly for fort buffs. Regrettably, it can be visited only from the outside, but many visitors find the nearby park, with well-maintained lawns, plenty of shade, and vendors peddling local handicrafts, more interesting than the fort itself.

Eastern Rd. No phone. Free admission. No regular hours. Bus: 10 or 17.

Pirates of Nassau ☺ This museum, which opened in 2003, celebrates the dubious "golden age of piracy" (1690–1720). Nassau was once a bustling, robust town where buccaneers grew rich from gold and other goods plundered at sea. Known as a paradise for pirates, it also attracted various rogues and the wild women who flooded into the port to entertain them—for a price, of course. The museum re-creates those bawdy days in exhibits illustrating pirate lore. You can walk through the belly of a pirate ship, the *Revenge,* as you hear "pirates" plan their next attack, smell

THE "pirate" OF THE BAHAMAS

These days Johnny Depp—otherwise known as Captain Jack Sparrow in *Pirates of the Caribbean*—can be seen coming and going with his family from the Nassau airport.

He's heading for his own private island (not open to the general public) in the Exumas, the 45-acre Little Hall's Pond Cay, which he bought as a private, completely solar-powered getaway in 2004. He dedicated a part of his own island paradise to the late actor Heath Ledger, star of *Brokeback Mountain* and a close friend of Depp's.

He also named two of the island's beaches for two of his other close friends, Marlon Brando and Hunter S. Thompson. He didn't neglect his family either, naming one beach for Vanessa Paradis, his longtime companion, and others for his daughter, Lily Rose, and his son, Jack. Of course, if he should extend an invitation to you, you can see what a cool $3.6 million can buy.

the dampness of a dungeon, and even hear the final prayer of an ill-fated victim before he walks the gangplank. It's fairly cheesy, but fun for kids. Exhibits also tell the saga of Capt. Woodes Rogers, who was sent by the English crown to suppress pirates in the Caribbean.

Marlborough and George sts. © **242/356-3759.** www.pirates-of-nassau.com. Admission $12 adults, $6 children 4–17, free for children 3 and under. Mon–Sat 9am–6pm; Sun 9am–noon. Bus: 10.

WALKING TOUR: HISTORIC NASSAAU

START:	**Rawson Square.**
FINISH:	**Prince George Wharf.**
TIME:	**2 hours.**
BEST TIMES:	**Monday through Saturday between 10am and 4pm.**
WORST TIMES:	**Sunday, when many places are closed and lots of cruise ships are in port.**

Begin your tour at:

1 Rawson Square

The center of Nassau, Rawson Square lies directly inland from Prince George Wharf, where many of the big cruise ships dock. Everyone seems to pass through this crossroads, from the prime minister, bankers, and local attorneys to cruise-ship passengers, shoppers from Paradise Island, and Junkanoo bands. On the square is the Churchill Building, used by the prime minister and some government ministries. Look for the statue of Sir Milo Butler, a former shopkeeper who became the first governor of The Bahamas after Britain granted its independence in 1973.

Across Rawson Square is:

2 Parliament Square

A statue of a youthful Queen Victoria dominates the square. To the right of it stand more Bahamian government office buildings, and to the left is the House of Assembly, the New World's oldest governing body in continuous session. In the building behind the statue, the Senate meets; this is a less influential body than the House of Assembly. Some of these Georgian-style buildings date from the late 1700s and early 1800s. Immediately south of Parliament Square, in a Georgian-inspired building between Parliament Street and Bank Lane, is the Supreme Court. The bewigged and begowned judges here, looking very British, interpret Bahamian law and dispense high-authority justice.

3 Café Matisse ☕

If you'd like to relax, try Café Matisse, Bank Lane and Bay Street, behind Parliament Square (☎ 242/356-7012). The house specialty is pizza topped with fresh local seafood. Lunch is served Tuesday through Saturday from noon to 3pm.

The Supreme Court building stands next to the:

4 Nassau Public Library and Museum

This 1797 building was once the Nassau Gaol (jail); it became the public library in 1873. Chances are you will have seen greater libraries, but what's amusing here is the small prison cells lined with books. Another item of interest is the library's collection of historic prints and old documents dating from colonial days. It's open to visitors Monday through Thursday from 10am to 8pm, Friday from 10am to 5pm, and Saturday from 10am to 4pm.

Across from the library on Shirley Street is the former site of the:

5 Royal Victoria Hotel

The hotel that once occupied this site was the haunt of Confederate spies, royalty, smugglers of all sorts, and ladies and gentlemen. The American journalist Horace Greeley pronounced it "the largest and most commodious hotel ever built in the Tropics," and many agreed with him. The hotel experienced its heyday during the American Civil War. At the Blockade Runners' Ball, some 300 guests reportedly consumed 350 magnums of champagne. Former guests have included two British prime ministers, Neville Chamberlain and his successor, Winston Churchill. Prince Albert, consort of Queen Victoria, also stayed here once. The hotel closed in 1971. After it was destroyed by fire, it was demolished and razed to the ground. Today, the site accommodates one of Nassau's showcase parking lots. Incidentally, the parking lot seems to be such a source of pride to the city that it is unlikely the Royal Victoria will ever be rebuilt, at least in that spot.

After imagining the former splendor of the Royal Victoria, head south along Parliament Street. At the end of it stands the:

6 Nassau General Post Office

If you're a collector, you may want to purchase colorful Bahamian stamps, which might be valuable in future years. You can also mail letters and packages here.

Walk east (right) on East Hill Street. Turn left onto East Street, then right onto Shirley Street, and head straight on Elizabeth Avenue. This will take you to the landmark:

7 Queen's Staircase

This stairway, built in 1793 by slaves who cut the 66 steps out of sandstone cliffs, leads to Bennet's Hill.

Walking Tour: Historic Nassau

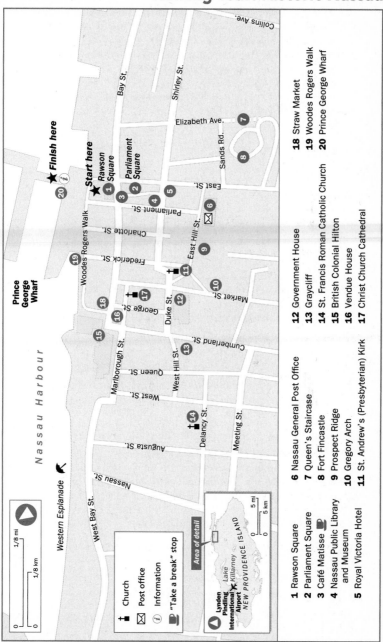

1 Rawson Square
2 Parliament Square
3 Café Matisse
4 Nassau Public Library and Museum
5 Royal Victoria Hotel

6 Nassau General Post Office
7 Queen's Staircase
8 Fort Fincastle
9 Prospect Ridge
10 Gregory Arch
11 St. Andrew's (Presbyterian) Kirk

12 Government House
13 Graycliff
14 St. Francis Roman Catholic Church
15 British Colonial Hilton
16 Vendue House
17 Christ Church Cathedral

18 Straw Market
19 Woodes Rogers Walk
20 Prince George Wharf

Church
Post office
Information
"Take a break" stop

83

These stairs provide access from Old Nassau's center to:

8 Fort Fincastle

Lord Dunmore built this fort in 1793. Designed in the shape of a paddle-wheel steamer, it was a place from which to look out for marauders who never came. It was eventually converted into a lighthouse because it occupied the highest point on the island. The tower rises more than 60m (197 ft.) above the sea, providing a panoramic view of Nassau and its harbor.

A small footpath leads down from the fort to Sands Road. Once you reach it, head west (left) until you approach East Street again, and then bear right. When you come to East Hill Street (again), go left because you will have returned to the post office.

Continue your westward trek along East Hill Street, which is the foothill of:

9 Prospect Ridge

This was the old dividing line between Nassau's rich and poor. The rich (usually white) people lived along the waterfront, often in beautiful mansions. Bahamians of African descent went over the hill to work in these rich homes during the day, but returned to Prospect Ridge to their own homes (most often shanties) at night.

Near the end of East Hill Street, you come to:

10 Gregory Arch

This tunnel was cut through the hill in 1850. After it opened, working-class black Bahamians were happy to not have to go over the steep hill anymore; they could instead go through this arch to return home.

At the intersection with Market Street, turn right. On your right, you'll see:

11 St. Andrew's (Presbyterian) Kirk

Called simply "the Kirk," the church dates from 1810 but has seen many changes over the years. In 1864, it was enlarged, and a bell tower was added along with other architectural features. This church had the first non-Anglican parishioners in The Bahamas.

On a steep hill, rising to the west of Market Street, you see on your left:

12 Government House

This house is the official residence of the archipelago's governor-general, the queen's representative to The Bahamas. (The post today is largely ceremonial, as an elected prime minister does the actual governing.) This pink-and-white neoclassical mansion dates from the early 19th century. Poised on its front steps is a rather jaunty statue of Christopher Columbus.

Opposite the road from Government House on West Hill Street is:

13 Graycliff

A Georgian-style hotel and restaurant, this stomping ground of the rich and famous was constructed by Capt. John Howard Graysmith in the 1720s. In the 1920s, it achieved notoriety when it was run by Polly Leach, a pal of gangster Al Capone. Later, under royal ownership, it attracted such famous guests as Winston Churchill and the Duke and Duchess of Windsor.

Upon leaving Graycliff, you'll see, embedded in a hill, a plaque that commemorates the spot where Nassau's oldest church once stood.

On the corner of West Hill and West streets is Villa Doyle, the former home of William Henry Doyle, chief justice of the Bahamian Supreme Court in the late 1800s.

Opposite Villa Doyle stands:

14 St. Francis Roman Catholic Church

Constructed between 1885 and 1886, it was the country's first Catholic church. New York's archdiocese raised the funds to construct it.

Continue along West Street until you reach Marlborough. Walk the short block that leads to Queen Street and turn right, passing the American Embassy. At the corner of Queen Street and Marlborough rises the:

15 British Colonial Hilton

Built in 1923, the nation's most famous hotel was once run by Sir Harry Oakes, who was at the time the most powerful man on the islands and a friend of the Duke of Windsor. Oakes's murder in 1943, still unsolved, was called "the crime of the century." This historic location was the site of Fort Nassau, as well as the set for several James Bond thrillers. In 1999, it became a Hilton hotel.

One part of the hotel fronts George Street, where you'll find:

16 Vendue House

One of Nassau's oldest buildings, Vendue House was once called the Bourse (Stock Exchange) and was the site of many slave auctions. It is now a museum.

Not far from Vendue House on George Street is:

17 Christ Church Cathedral

Dating from 1837, this Gothic Episcopal cathedral is the venue of many important state ceremonies, including the opening of the Supreme Court, during which a procession of bewigged, robed judges emerges, followed by barristers, and accompanied by music from the police band.

Continue north on George Street to the Bay Street intersection, where you'll find the:

18 Straw Market

The market—largely destroyed by a fire in fall 2001, and still not rebuilt—is now housed within a tentlike temporary structure that opens onto Bay Street (at George St., about 2 blocks from its original premises). It has long been a favorite of cruise-ship passengers. You'll find not only straw products, but also all sorts of souvenirs and gift items. Bahamian women at the market weave traditional baskets and braid visitors' hair with beads. Hours are daily from 7am to around 8pm, though each vendor (there are around 200 of them) sets his or her own hours.

Continue north toward the water until you reach:

19 Woodes Rogers Walk

The walk was named for a former governor of the colony who was thrown into debtors' prison in London before coming back to Nassau as the royal governor. Head east on it for a panoramic view of the harbor, with its colorful mail and sponge boats. Markets sell vegetables, fish, and lots of conch.

The walk leads to:

20 Prince George Wharf

The wharf was constructed in the 1920s, the heyday of American Prohibition, to provide harbor space for hundreds of bootlegging craft defying the American blockade against liquor. Queen Elizabeth II's yacht, the HMS Britannia, has been a frequent visitor. Cruise ships also dock here.

Organized Tours

There's a lot to see in Nassau. Many tour options can be customized to suit your taste and take you through the colorful historic city and outlying sights of interest.

Walking tours, arranged by the Ministry of Tourism, leave from the tourist information booth at Festival Place every day intermittently and, depending on demand, at 10am. Tours last an hour and include descriptions of some of the city's most venerable buildings, with commentaries on Nassau's history, customs, and traditions. The cost is $10 per person for all ages. Call ✆ **242/395-8382** to confirm that tours are running. Reservations are helpful but not essential.

Majestic Tours, Hillside Manor, Cumberland Street (✆ **242/322-2606;** www. majestictoursbahamas.com), offers a number of trips, both night and day. A 2½-hour city-and-country tour leaves daily at 2pm, visiting major points of interest, including forts, the Queen's Staircase, the water tower, and the former site of the Straw Market (passing but not entering it). The cost is $45 per person. An extended city-and-country

 JOURNEY INTO THE wild

Take a day off from the beach and join one of the wildlife tours offered by **Bahamas Outdoors** (✆ **242/362-1574** or 242/457-0329; www.bahamasoutdoors. com). We highly recommend speaking to Carolyn Wardle, president of Bahamas Outdoors, for insight into the best of the island's remaining wildlife habitats. Born in Surrey, England, and a resident of New Providence for decades, Ms. Wardle, a passionate conservationist (she's a director of the Society for the Conservation and Study of Caribbean Birds), is well known to residents of New Providence's more isolated regions. Armed with sturdy shoes, a Bahamas Outdoors T-shirt, sunglasses, a hat, and binoculars, she knows the island's wildlife habitats (forest, seashore, and freshwater ponds) better than anyone on the island. Consider signing on for a half-day tour, priced at $79 per person, or a full-day

tour, at $109–$149 per person, depending on the destination and venue you select. Tours rarely include more than a half-dozen participants and can be conducted either in a vehicle (with frequent stops along the way for closer observation) or on an all-terrain bike. Depending on your stated preferences, the focus of your island tour could include birds, native flora and fauna, butterflies, national parks, historic sites, or—best of all—a combination of all of them. Access to binoculars and a battered collection of field guides is included. The full-day tours also include a picnic lunch.

It's advisable to make reservations at least a day in advance. Most tours begin in front of the participants' hotel at a prearranged time. Bird-watching tours tend to begin earlier (around 7am) than biking and/or historic and nature tours, which start just a bit later.

tour also leaves daily at 2pm and includes the Ardastra Gardens; the cost is $60 per person, half-price for children 12 and under. Many hotels have a Majestic Tours Hospitality Desk in their lobby, where you can get information and make reservations for these tours. Other hotels have brochures and can tell you where to sign up.

Easy Side Trips to Nearby Islands

Remote **Rose Island** is a sliver of land poking out of the sea just northeast of Nassau's Prince George waterfront. Shelling is one of the lures of this little islet. If you want to escape the crowds of Nassau for an island retreat, you can take a boat here, relax in a hammock, snorkel among the coral reefs, and enjoy the white-sand beach before and after a sizzling barbecue lunch with white wine. Excursions to Rose Island are offered by **Barefoot Sailing Cruises,** Bay Shore Marina, East Bay Street (*©* **242/393-0820;** www.barefootsailingcruises.com), and **Majestic Tours,** Hillside Manor, Cumberland Street (*©* **242/322-2606;** www.majesticholidays.com). With Majestic Tours, expect to pay $45 to $70 per adult for a trip lasting from 10am to 4:30pm. For more information on boat cruises, see p. 72.

If you want to see the Exuma island chain on a daylong excursion, try **Powerboat Adventures,** Shirley Park Avenue at Shirley St. (*©* **242/323-8888;** www.power boatadventures.com), which provides an excellent overview of the area. The boat departs Nassau Harbour at 9am and arrives in the Exuma Cays about an hour later. There are several stops, including snorkeling at a private cay (Ship Channel), visiting the iguanas on Allan's Cay, feeding stingrays along the shore, and enjoying a barbecue lunch. A full bar is available all day, and drinks are included in the cost, which is $199 for adults and $140 for children 2 to 12. Transportation from your hotel to the port of embarkation is included. The experience finishes around 5pm.

SHOPPING

Nassau's shopping options are more upscale than they once were, with the arrival of swanky jewelers and a burgeoning fashion scene. There are still plenty of T-shirts claiming that "It's Better in The Bahamas," but you can also find diamonds and platinum watches. The range of goods is staggering; in the midst of all the junk souvenirs, you'll see an increasing array of china, crystal, watches, and clothing from such names as Herend, Lalique, Baccarat, Bally, and Ferragamo.

But can you really save money compared to what you would pay stateside? The answer is "yes" on some items, "no" on others. To figure out what's a bargain and what's not, you've got to know the price of everything back home, turning yourself into a sort of human calculator.

Don't try to bargain with the salespeople in Nassau stores as you would with merchants at the local market. The price marked is the price you must pay, though you won't be pressed to make a purchase. The salespeople here are generally courteous and helpful.

There are no import duties on 11 categories of luxury goods, including china, crystal, fine linens, jewelry, leather goods, photographic equipment, watches, and fragrances. Antiques, of course, are exempt from import duty worldwide. But even though prices are "duty free," you can still end up spending more on an item in The Bahamas than you would back home; it's a tricky situation.

If you're contemplating a major purchase, such as a Swiss watch or expensive perfume, it's best to do some research in your local discount outlets or online before you leave home. While the alleged 30% to 50% discount off stateside prices might apply in some cases, it's not true in others. Certain cameras and electronic equipment, for instance, are listed in The Bahamas at, say, 20% below the manufacturer's "suggested retail price." That sounds good, except the manufacturer's suggested price might be a lot higher than what you'd actually pay in retail stores back home. Some shoppers take along catalogs from the U.S. or print out online references to determine if they are indeed getting a bargain; it's not a bad idea.

A lot of price-fixing seems to be going on in Nassau. For example, a bottle of Chanel perfume is likely to sell for pretty much the same price anywhere, regardless of the store.

How much you can take home depends on your country of origin. For details about Customs requirements, refer to "Entry Requirements," in chapter 11.

The principal shopping areas are **Bay Street** and its side streets downtown, as well as the shops in the arcades of hotels. Not many street numbers are used along Bay Street; just look for store signs.

Bahamian Art

If you've had your fill of the flood of upscale gems and fashion items you're likely to find in downtown Nassau, near the cruise port, or on Paradise Island, stop by one of the best art galleries in Nassau, **Doongalik Studios,** 18 Village Rd. (© **242/394-1886**). Owned and operated by Pam Burnside, the recent widow of Jackson Burnside (one of the architects of the Atlantis' resort's Marina Village) it's located near Montague Beach, on Nassau's mostly residential far east end. Come here for insight into who is creating contemporary art in The Bahamas. Oil paintings by locally famous artists (including John Cox, John Paul, Jessica Colebrooke, and Amos Ferguson) range from $20 for a print on paper to oil paintings and sculptures, some of them fashioned from driftwood, priced at many thousands of dollars.

Brass & Copper

Brass & Leather Shops   With two branches on Charlotte Street, this local chain offers English brass, handbags, luggage, briefcases, belts, scarves, and ties from such designers as Furla, Tumi, Briggs & Riley, and others. If you look carefully, you can find some good buys here. 12 Charlotte St., btw. Bay and Shirley sts. © **242/322-3806.** www.brass-leather.com.

Cigars

Remember, U.S. citizens are prohibited from bringing Cuban cigars back home because of the trade embargo. If you buy them, enjoy them in The Bahamas.

Graycliff Cigar Company ★   In 1994, an emigrant businessman from Lake Como, Italy, moved to Nassau to supervise his investment, the Graycliff Hotel, and liked it so much there that he decided to stay. Eventually, he established the country's best-known and most respected cigar factory. It employs about 16 mostly Cuban-expatriate cigar rollers, who, within full view, use non-Cuban tobacco to create 10 different styles of sought-after cigars. These are sold on the premises and priced around $5 to $30 each, depending on quality. There's also a 41cm (16-in.) "big bamboo," priced at $50, that makes whoever smokes it look almost like a caricature, and that is guaranteed to get its consumer very, very high. Best of all, these cigars, crafted with the finest techniques, are completely legal to import back into the U.S. 12 West Hill St. © **242/302-9150.** www.graycliff.com.

Crystal, China & Gems

Solomon's Mines   Evoking the title of a 1950s MGM flick, this is one grand shopping adventure. This flagship store, with many branches, is one of the largest duty-free retailers in the Caribbean, a tradition since 1908. Entering the store is like making a shopping trip to London or Paris. The amount of merchandise is staggering, from a $50,000 Patek Philippe watch to one of the largest collections of Herend china in the West. Most prices on timepieces, china, jewelry, crystal, Herend, Baccarat, Ferragamo, Bally, Lalique, and other names are discounted 15% to 30%—and some of the merchandise and oddities here are not available in the U.S., such as the stunning African diamonds. The selections of Italian, French, and American fragrances and skin-care products are the best in the archipelago. Bay St.© **242/356-6920.** A 2nd location is at Charlotte and Bay Sts. © **242/356-6920,** ext. 240.

Fashion

Cole's of Nassau   This boutique offers the most extensive selection of designer fashions in Nassau. Women can find everything from swimwear to formal gowns, sportswear to hosiery. Cole's also sells gift items, sterling-silver designer and costume jewelry, hats, shoes, bags, scarves, and belts. Parliament St. © **242/322-8393.**

Fendi   This is Nassau's only outlet for the well-crafted accessories made by this famous luxe-goods company. With handbags, luggage, shoes, watches, wallets, and portfolios to choose from, the selection may well solve some of your gift-giving quandaries. Charlotte and Bay sts. © **242/322-6300.**

Handicrafts

Sea Grape Boutique   This is one of the island's genuinely fine gift shops, with an inventory of exotic decorative items that you'll probably find fascinating. It includes jewelry crafted from fossilized coral, sometimes with sharks' teeth embedded inside, and clothing that's well suited to the sometimes-steamy climate. W. Bay St. (next to Travellers Rest). © **242/327-1308.**

Jewelry

Colombian Emeralds   Famous around the Caribbean, this international outlet is not limited to emeralds, although its selection of that stone is the best in The Bahamas. You'll find an impressive display of diamonds and other precious gems. The gold jewelry here sells for about half the price it does stateside, and many of the gems are discounted 20% to 30%. Ask about the "cybershopping" program. Bay St. © **242/322-2230.** www.columbianemeralds.com.

John Bull   The jewelry department here offers classic selections from Tiffany & Co., cultured pearls from Mikimoto, the creations of David Yurman and Carrera y Carrera, Greek and Roman coin jewelry, and Spanish gold and silver pieces. It's the best name in the business. The store also features a wide selection of watches, cameras, perfumes, cosmetics, leather goods, and accessories. It is one of the country's best places to buy a Gucci or Cartier watch. Bay St. © **242/302-2800.** www.johnbull.com.

Leather

In addition to the stores mentioned below, another good source for leather goods is the **Brass & Leather Shops,** described under "Brass & Copper," above.

Gucci This shop, opposite Rawson Square, is the best place to buy leather goods in Nassau. The wide selection includes handbags, wallets, luggage, briefcases, gift items, scarves, ties, eveningwear for men and women, umbrellas, shoes, sandals, watches, and perfume, all by Italy's famous producer of luxury items. Saffrey Sq., Bay St., at Bank Lane. ℂ **242/325-0561.**

Leather Masters This well-known retail outlet carries an internationally known collection of leather bags, luggage, and accessories by Ted Lapidus, Lanvin, Lancel, Etienne Aigner, and I Santi of Italy, plus luggage by Piel and Travel Pro. Non-leather items include pens, lighters, watches by Colibri, silk scarves, neckties, and cigar accessories. 8 Parliament St. ℂ **242/322-7597.**

Linens

The Linen Shop This is Nassau's best outlet for linens, featuring beautifully embroidered bedding, Irish handkerchiefs, and tablecloths. Look also for the most exquisite children's clothing and christening gowns in town. Ironmongery Building, Bay St., near Charlotte St. ℂ **242/322-4266.**

Markets

The **Nassau International Bazaar** consists of some 30 shops selling international goods in a new arcade. A pleasant place for browsing, the million-dollar complex runs from Bay Street down to the waterfront (near Prince George Wharf). With cobbled alleyways and garreted storefronts, it looks like a European village.

Prince George Plaza, on Bay Street, is popular with cruise-ship passengers. Many fine shops (Gucci, for example) occupy space here. When you get tired of shopping, dine at the open-air rooftop restaurant that overlooks Bay Street.

Perfumes & Cosmetics

Nassau has several good perfume outlets, notably **John Bull** and **Little Switzerland,** which also stock a lot of non-perfume merchandise.

Beauty Spot The country's largest cosmetics shop, this outlet sells duty-free cosmetics by Lancôme, Chanel, YSL, Elizabeth Arden, Estée Lauder, Clinique, Christian Dior, and Biotherm, among others. It also operates facial salons. Bay and Frederick Sts. ℂ **242/325-3649.**

Perfume Bar This little gem has exclusive rights to market Boucheron. It also stocks the Clarins line (though not exclusively). Bay St. ℂ **242/325-1258.**

Perfume Shop In the heart of Nassau, within walking distance of the cruise ships, the Perfume Shop offers duty-free savings on world-famous perfumes for women and men, including Eternity, Obsession, and Chanel. Bay and Frederick sts. ℂ **242/322-2375.**

NEW PROVIDENCE AFTER DARK

Gone are the days when tuxedo-clad gentlemen and elegantly gowned ladies drank and danced the night away at such famous nightclubs as the Yellow Bird and the Big

Bamboo. You can still find dancing, along with limbo and calypso, but for most visitors, the major attraction is gambling.

Cultural entertainment in Nassau is limited, though the **Dundas Centre for the Performing Arts,** on Mackey St., sometimes stages ballets, plays, and musicals. Call ℂ **242/393-3728** to find out what's scheduled during your visit.

Rolling the Dice

As another option, you can easily head over to Paradise Island and drop into the massive, spectacular casino at **Atlantis** (p. 95).

Wyndham Nassau Crystal Palace Casino   This dazzling casino is the only one on New Providence Island and is now run by the Wyndham Nassau Resort. Thanks to constant improvements, it stacks up well against the other major casinos of the Caribbean. Incorporating more than 3,250 sq. m (34,983 sq. ft.) into its flashy-looking premises, it's animated, bustling, and filled with the serious business of people having fun with their money and temptations. The gaming room features hundreds of slot machines—only a few of which resemble the low-tech, one-armed bandits that were in vogue 20 years ago. You'll find blackjack tables, roulette wheels, craps tables, a baccarat table, and a sophisticated electronic link to Las Vegas that provides odds on most of the world's major sporting events. There's also a serious commitment to poker. W. Bay St., Cable Beach. ℂ **242/327-6200.** www.wyndhamnassauresort.com.

The Club & Music Scene

Da Tambrin Tree ★ 🎒   If you'd like to escape from the tourist joints and experience a slice of Bahamian life as lived by the locals, head for this nighttime dive. It lies a 10- to 15-minute taxi ride from the center of Nassau. The music is loud and compelling, and the place is the most fun club in Nassau. Something is always happening here, everything from a Wednesday night karaoke and gong show to a jam session with the best DJs on the island. Happy hour begins at 5pm, and the club often stays open until dawn, depending on business. Summerwind Plaza, Harold Rd. ℂ **242/356-7200.** Cover ranges from free to $20 (includes 2 drinks).

Rainforest Theatre   Accessible directly from the Crystal Palace Casino on Cable Beach, this 800-seat theater is a major nightlife attraction. Revues tend to be small-scale, relatively restrained, and very definitely on the safe and family-friendly side of the great cultural divide. Fake palm trees and touches of glitter set the scene for the onstage entertainment. Hours vary with the season, the act, and the number of guests booked into the hotel at the time. It's also a venue for "specialty events," things you might not have automatically expected. One of these is the Bahamian National Body Building Championships, during which the theater's roster of repertoire cabaret, feathers, and glitter, are either curtailed or cancelled. Billboards located prominently throughout the hotel hawk whoever is headlining at the moment. Crystal Palace Casino, W. Bay St., Cable Beach. ℂ **242/327-6200.** Tickets $35–$50.

Space   Set within the cellar of a two-story building in the heart of downtown Nassau, this club rocks and rolls. It is the newest hot spot for the beautiful set, many of them between 25 and 45, on New Providence Island. Musical venues are dedicated to soca, reggae, hip-hop, R&B, and whatever's hip and trendy in places like South Beach, Miami, and NYC at the moment. It's open Wednesday to Sunday from 9pm to 2am. W. Bay Street, near Frederick St. ℂ **242/433-4004.** Cover $10–$25.

The Bar Scene

Charlie's on the Beach/Cocktails & Dreams The focus at this sparsely decorated club is local gossip, calypso and reggae music, and stiff drinks, all of which make for a high-energy night out in Nassau. The setting is a simple warehouselike structure a few blocks west of the British Colonial Hilton, though management warns that during some particularly active weekends (including spring break), the entire venue might move, for the short term, to a larger, as-yet-undetermined location. Open Wednesday and Friday through Sunday from 9pm to 4am. W. Bay St., near Long Wharf Beach. © **242/328-3745.** Free or $15 cover, depending on the night.

Señor Frog's How can you hate a bar that manages to satirize itself as richly as this one does? The interior is deliberately and somewhat claustrophobically over-crowded with frogs, faux palm trees, and battered wooden tables. Choices range from midday salsa and chips to "Let's sample all of the margaritas available on this menu" contests conducted informally among heavy-drinking cruise-ship drop-ins. Expect merengue music (especially on weekends, when tables are pushed aside to form an ersatz dance floor) and a menu loaded with burgers, fajitas, and tacos. W. Bay St., near the British Colonial Hilton. © **242/323-1777.** www.senorfrogs.com. No cover.

PARADISE ISLAND

J ust off Nassau's north shore lies paradise, with a sweeping tropical beach edged by a luxurious grove of casuarina trees. Paradise Island's centerpiece is the mammoth Atlantis Paradise Island Resort & Casino, a pulsing nightlife mecca and a sightseeing attraction in its own right. Think Vegas in the tropics. Away from the resort's lively casinos, sunsets at The Cloister and strolls in beautiful Versailles Gardens provide peaceful respite. Tired of paradise? Cross to Nassau on foot, by boat, or by car for sightseeing and shopping.

4

Things to Do Try your luck at the **Atlantis Paradise Casino,** one of the most imaginatively decorated casinos in the Caribbean. Away from the glitz and glamor, wander around the statues of the peaceful **Versailles Gardens,** a popular location for weddings. The sugar-white sand of **Cabbage Beach** invites sunbathing and swimming. For one of the most beautiful pink and mauve sunsets in all The Bahamas, sit amid stone remains of the 12th-century French monastery at **The Cloister.**

Shopping The energy from the Atlantis Paradise Casino spills over at the **Shops at the Atlantis,** an impressive collection of high-end couture boutiques and designer emporiums. All the top labels are here, from Cartier to Versace, alongside fine jewelry, giftware, and perfume. For Bahamian handicrafts and artwork, browse the shops at **Marina Village.** For cut-price jewelry, cosmetics, and hand-rolled cigars, as well as a plethora of T-shirts and souvenirs, cross the Paradise Island Bridge into Nassau and head to **Bay Street.**

Nightlife & Entertainment The razzle-dazzle of gaming tables and a thousand clanging slot machines vie for your attention at the lavish **Atlantis Paradise Casino.** Away from the casino, sip cocktails and gawk at yachts in **Marina Village,** squeeze onto a packed dance floor in a flashy club or enjoy a late-night latte in the **Royal Towers**—the tallest and most imaginative edifice in The Bahamas. Dress casually but leave the beachwear in the hotel.

Restaurants & Dining Paradise Island offers the broadest mix of restaurants in The Bahamas, from elegant beachfront bistros with harbor views to earthy surf-and-turf spots clustered around the **Atlantis Paradise Island Casino.** If you want a brand name, **Nobu** and **Bobby Flay at the Mesa Grill** have a presence. Enjoy gourmet takes on seafood fresh from the Atlantic, broiled grouper almondine, for instance, or Nassau conch chowder. Paradise is pricey, though. Budget-minded visitors may want to cross over the bridge into downtown Nassau.

ORIENTATION

Arriving

Most visitors to Paradise Island arrive in Nassau and commute to Paradise Island by ground transport.

When you arrive at **Lynden Pindling International Airport** (formerly known as Nassau International Airport; see chapter 3 for information on flying into Nassau), you won't find bus service to take you to Paradise Island. Many package deals include hotel transfers from the airport. Otherwise, if you're not renting a car, you'll need to take a taxi. Taxis in Nassau are metered and take cash only; it usually costs around $35 to go from the airport to your hotel. The driver will also ask you to pay the northbound one-way $1 bridge toll, a charge that will be added onto your metered fare at the end of the ride.

Visitor Information

Paradise Island does not have a visitor information office, so refer to the tourist facilities in downtown Nassau (see chapter 3). The concierge or guest-services staff at your hotel can also give you information about local attractions.

Island Layout

Paradise Island's finest beaches lie on the Atlantic (northern) coastline, while the docks, wharves, and marinas are on the southern side. Most of the island's largest and glossiest hotels and restaurants, as well as the casino and a lagoon with landscaped borders, lie west and north of the roundabout. The area east of the roundabout is less congested, with only a handful of smaller hotels, a golf course, the Versailles Gardens, The Cloister, the airport, and many of the island's privately owned villas.

GETTING AROUND

You don't need to rent a car here. Most visitors walk around Paradise Island's most densely developed sections and hire a taxi for the occasional longer haul.

The most popular way to reach nearby Nassau is to **walk across the toll bridge.** There is no charge for pedestrians.

To tour Paradise Island or New Providence by **taxi,** make arrangements with either a taxi driver or your hotel's reception desk. Taxis wait at the entrances to all the major hotels. The hourly rate is about $60 in cars or small vans.

If you are without a car and don't want to take a taxi or walk, you can hop one of the **ferryboats** to Nassau, which leave from the dock on Casino Drive every 30 minutes between 9am and 6pm daily; the 10-minute ride costs $6 one-way. Quicker and easier than a taxi, the ferry deposits you right at Prince George Wharf, in downtown Nassau.

Water taxis also operate between Paradise Island and Nassau's Prince George Wharf. They depart at 15- to 30-minute intervals from 8:30am to 6pm daily. Round-trip fare is $6.

If you're a guest at one of the properties associated with **Atlantis** (see below), hop aboard one of the complimentary **shuttle buses** for drop-offs at any of the resort's accommodations. Atlantis guests can also take a complimentary tour of the island, which departs daily at noon.

Unlike New Providence, no public buses are allowed on Paradise Island.

WHERE TO STAY

In the off season—from mid-April to mid-December—prices are slashed by at least 20% and sometimes a lot more, though the weather isn't as ideal. But because Paradise Island's summer business has increased dramatically, you'll never see some of the 60% reductions that might be offered by cheaper properties in the Greater Nassau area. For inexpensive accommodations, refer to the listings for New Providence Island in chapter 3. Paradise Island isn't cheap!

Very Expensive

Atlantis Paradise Island ★★★ ☺ This creatively designed mega-resort, the biggest in The Bahamas, functions as a vacation destination and theme park in its own right. A blockbuster in every sense of the word, it contains the most creative interiors, the most intriguing aesthetics, and the most elaborate waterscapes of any hotel in the country. It's the most recent incarnation of a resort that originated in the early days of Paradise Island's tourism industry, passing through rocky and sometimes less glamorous days before reaching its current form as a destination that appeals to adults (its gambling facilities are the largest in The Bahamas) and to ecologists (its focus on protecting marine life adds a welcome dose of "save the planet" to an otherwise relentlessly consumerist theme, and dozens of waterways crisscross the flat, sandy terrain on which the resort sits). Atlantis is also a potent lure for children, and the child that remains within many of us, thanks to its evocation of a "lost continent" whose replicated ruins evoke—you guessed it—Atlantis.

But whereas the newest buildings manage to conjure science fiction and ancient mythology at the same time (no easy feat), its older buildings still retain a whiff of the old Merv Griffin days of the 1980s. But thanks to skillful landscaping and the miles of canals whose currents carry swimmers with flotation devices on meandering runs down mythical rivers, no one seems to notice.

The entire sprawling compound opens onto a long stretch of sandy beach with a sheltered marina. Think Vegas in the Tropics, with a mythological theme and an interconnected series of lagoons, lakes, rivers, waterfalls, and water tubes thrown in, and you'll get the picture. One advantage to the place is that there's a lot of visual distraction and high-energy, upbeat stimulation; the downside is that it's huge, impersonal, and at times downright bureaucratic. The service from the sometimes bored staff just can't keep up with the number of guests here.

Overall, it's an appropriate (albeit rather pricey) choice for a family vacation, since the price includes direct access to endless numbers of watery gimmicks. Children's programs are comprehensive and well-choreographed, and many parents simply turn their kids loose onto the extensive grounds, understanding that a battalion of lifeguards and supervisors keep the show rolling and the safety levels up to par. Singles and young couples who want a lot of razzle-dazzle appreciate the place, too, though some people find it over-the-top and too firmly mired in the limitations of its own "lost continent" theme.

The resort offers such a range of sports, dining, and entertainment options that many guests never venture off the property during their entire vacation. It's expensive, but for your money, you'll find yourself neck-deep amid many of the diversions you might expect from a theme park. And if you opt for one of the resort's less plush accommodations, especially within the Beach Tower, the sticker shock won't seem as severe.

Where to Stay & Eat on Paradise Island

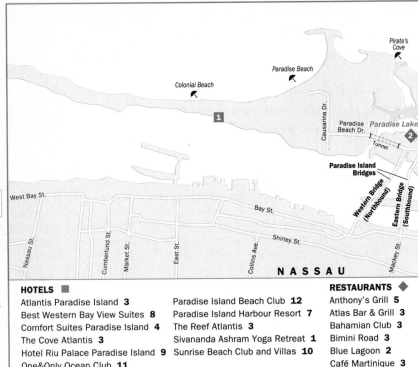

HOTELS ■

Atlantis Paradise Island **3**
Best Western Bay View Suites **8**
Comfort Suites Paradise Island **4**
The Cove Atlantis **3**
Hotel Riu Palace Paradise Island **9**
One&Only Ocean Club **11**
Paradise Harbour Club & Marina **14**

Paradise Island Beach Club **12**
Paradise Island Harbour Resort **7**
The Reef Atlantis **3**
Sivananda Ashram Yoga Retreat **1**
Sunrise Beach Club and Villas **10**

RESTAURANTS ◆

Anthony's Grill **5**
Atlas Bar & Grill **3**
Bahamian Club **3**
Bimini Road **3**
Blue Lagoon **2**
Café Martinique **3**

Accommodations feature distinctly different levels of opulence, based, for the most part, on where they're located. The most grand and expensive units lie in semi-secluded annexes whose facilities are not open to the hotel's general clientele. These include the **One&Only Ocean Club** and the **Cove Atlantis,** a 600-unit, all-suite hotel-within-a-hotel that opened in 2007. Both pockets of heightened posh were designed as separate and semi-independent entities within the resort, and each is described in separate reviews below.

As the resort has expanded, accommodations within its central core are emerging as more affordable options. And of those units, the plushest lie within the **Royal Towers**—the tallest and most imaginative edifice in The Bahamas, replete with decorative seahorses, winged dragons, and huge conch shells sprouting from cornices and rooflines. Rooms in the Royal Towers' **Imperial Club** come with concierge service and upgraded amenities. The most deluxe accommodations anywhere within the Atlantis fiefdom (going for $25,000 a night) are in the **Bridge Suite,** an architectural oddity that, many stories above ground level, links the two spires of the Royal Towers.

The Reef, in a category of luxury all its own, is a condo complex whose one- and two-bedroom units, each with full kitchen, are rented out as hotel accommodations according to a complicated schedule.

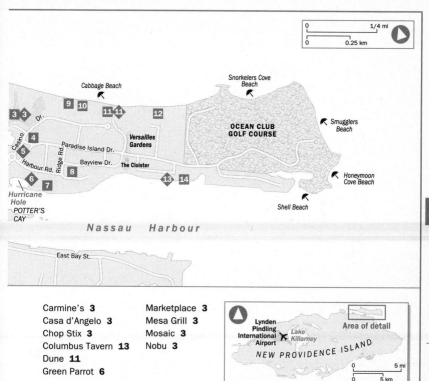

Cabbage Beach

Snorkelers Cove Beach

Smugglers Beach

OCEAN CLUB GOLF COURSE

Honeymoon Cove Beach

Shell Beach

Versailles Gardens

Paradise Island Dr.

Bayview Dr.

The Cloister

Ridge Rd.

Harbour Rd.

Casino

Hurricane Hole

POTTER'S CAY

Nassau Harbour

East Bay St.

Carmine's **3**
Casa d'Angelo **3**
Chop Stix **3**
Columbus Tavern **13**
Dune **11**
Green Parrot **6**

Marketplace **3**
Mesa Grill **3**
Mosaic **3**
Nobu **3**

Lynden Pindling International Airport

Lake Killarney

Area of detail

NEW PROVIDENCE ISLAND

Less posh and less plush are rooms within the **Coral Towers,** and least expensive of the entire lot are units within the still-serviceable but older **Beach Tower,** with a floor plan shaped like an airplane propeller, dating back to the dimly remembered 1980s. But even in the older, less pricey sections, accommodations are comfortable, well accessorized, and afford occupants full access to the sprawling water parks that are otherwise accessible only on a limited basis to nonresidents. Most units sport a balcony or terrace with water views.

Any old hotel might have tropical gardens, but Atlantis goes one better by featuring the world's largest collection of outdoor open-air marine habitats, each of them aesthetically stunning. A few of these were conceived for snorkelers and swimmers, but most were designed so that guests could observe the marine life from catwalks above and from glassed-in underwater viewing tunnels. Even folks who don't stay here, including thousands of cruise-ship passengers, can take part in orchestrated tours. These jaunts include 11 different exhibition lagoons, containing millions of gallons of water and at least 200 species of tropical fish. On-site marine habitats include separate lagoons for sharks, dolphins, and stingrays, plus individual habitats for lobsters, piranhas, and underwater exotica.

Swimmers can meander along an underwater snorkeling trail called **Paradise Lagoon** to explore a five-story replica of an ancient ziggurat-shaped Mayan temple, the sides of which incorporate water slides with slippery, wet, and wild runs, including an 18m (59-ft.) nearly vertical drop. Riders emerge from the sculpted mouths of giant Mayan gods like human sacrifices as they race giddily down the course of the water slide.

In 2007, additional water attractions, known collectively as **Aquaventure,** were added, bringing the surface area devoted to water features to 50 hectares (124 acres). The most visible monument within Aquaventure is a mythical-looking building called the **Power Tower,** site of even more imaginative water slides, each skillfully landscaped into the surrounding vegetation. Aquaventure's labyrinth of meandering streams and waterfalls is accessible, without charge, for guests staying at Atlantis. Nonresidents, however, are strictly barred from entering unless they buy a day pass, which costs $110 for adults, $80 for children 4 to 12. Depending on capacity within Atlantis at the time of your visit, day passes might not be available, but when they are, day-pass holders get access to all marine habitats, water slides, beach and pool facilities, and Aquaventure.

One major entertainment venue within Atlantis that's open, without charge, to the general public is **Marina Village,** inspired by an old Bahamian harborfront with a string of clapboard-sided houses (think historic Key West, Florida, but with a lot more money). Flanking a marina that draws some of the world's most spectacular yachts, it's self-enclosed and has dozens of shops, bars, and restaurants, plus gazebos and live musicians.

The focal point of Atlantis's extravagance is the massive **Atlantis Casino,** the best-designed and most imaginatively conceived casino in The Bahamas. Set over a lagoon's watery depths, it contains three bars and two restaurants.

Within the diverse and scattered elements of this extended resort, you'll find some 40 separate food and beverage outlets, some of which open, close, and are reconfigured at sometimes dizzying rates. None of them comes cheap: Expect to pay a lot to dine or drink in the resort. For detailed descriptions of Atlantis's most worthy eateries, see "Where to Eat" and "Paradise Island After Dark," later in this chapter.

Casino Dr., Paradise Island, The Bahamas. www.atlantis.com. © **800/ATLANTIS** (285-2684) in the U.S., or 242/363-3000. Fax 242/363-6300. 2,317 units. Rates in Beach Tower, Coral Towers, and Royal Towers: winter $480–$800 double, from $980 suite; off-season $360–$680 double, from $840 suite. AE, MC, V. **Amenities:** 20 restaurants; 18 lounges and clubs; babysitting; children's programs

Not a Registered Guest?

Guided tours of the resort are available to those not staying overnight. Called **Discover Atlantis,** the hour-long affair costs $39 for adults, $29 for kids aged 4 to 12. If you sign up, know that some of the resort's most intriguing areas remain off-limits to everyone except registered guests. Despite that, there's a lot to see on this tour. But in the end, the experience is rather tightly choreographed, not permitting free time to float down the lazy rivers. If anything, it's meant to pique your interest in Atlantis and up your motivation to return one day as a registered guest. For information, call © **242/363-3000.** Besides the tour, the general public has access to the **casino, nightclubs,** and Marina Village's **shops** and **restaurants.**

PROUDLY REMAINING adult AT ATLANTIS

Faced with increasing numbers of families with children, and with the perception that its acres of water slides and canals are a glorified summer camp for the offspring of parents who can afford it, there's an awareness that Atlantis needs quiet corners where grown-ups can be grown-ups.

If you fall into that category, we advise that you check into either the **Cove Atlantis,** the **Reef Atlantis,** the **One&Only Ocean Club,** or one of the more upscale rooms within the **Royal Towers.** None of these venues officially restricts children, but the Beach and Coral towers tend to house the greatest numbers of foursomes—usually a nuclear family with their kids or festive 20-somethings on reprieve from their lives in the frigid north.

If you've opted for lodgings within the Cove, spend time at the **adults-only swimming pool.** Its staffers are hip, and 20 cabanas await you and your significant other.

On your first night at Atlantis, go for drinks and dinner at **Nobu.** We find the Asian food here delicious and fascinating—enough so that most North American kids will find it bizarre. The pre-dinner scene at the bar, where women look foxier than in the glaring sun of a Bahamian noon, is definitely not for children. Awaken, too, to the nocturnal charms of **Aura,** the appealingly permissive nightclub where celeb-gazing is something of an art form.

Finally, book a long session at **Mandara Spa.** If you see anyone inside who's 17 or under, it's likely they're in line to inherit a very substantial fortune. Otherwise, even though adults adore it, it's not the sort of place teeny-boppers necessarily crave.

(ages 3–17); concierge; health club & spa; 17 outdoor pools; room service; 5 tennis courts (lit for night play). *In room:* A/C, TV, hair dryer, minibar, Wi-Fi ($15/day).

The Cove Atlantis ★★★   Housed within a handsome turquoise-and-coral tower whose fanciful detailing matches the resort's mythical theme, this hotel was configured as a semiprivate hideaway. Don't expect anything conventional about this place: It serves partially (but not completely) as an adults-oriented venue, taking pains to dilute a growing perception that Atlantis has too much of a family emphasis. Inaugurated in 2007, it boasts an avant-garde design that combines the best of minimalist Japan and ultra-high-end postmodern Florida. All units are luxurious and high-tech, with step-down living rooms, personal butlers, and every imaginable amenity. Whereas one of the two pools reserved only for Cove guests is family-friendly, the adults-only social centerpiece is an 836-sq.-m (9,000-sq.-ft.) "ultrapool" that is strictly off-limits to anyone under 18. It's ringed by 20 private cabanas, which can be rented by the day for sybaritic adults seeking seclusion. On the lobby level, there's a branch of Bobby Flay's **Mesa Grill** (p. 106). Immediately adjacent to the Cove, and open to any Atlantis guest or day-pass holder, is **Mandara Spa,** whose design was inspired by the architecture of Bali and incorporates stone, bamboo, and tropical hardwoods.

Casino Dr., Paradise Island, The Bahamas. www.atlantis.com. Ⓒ **800/ATLANTIS** (285-2684) in the U.S., or 242/363-3000. Fax 242/363-6300. 600 suites. Winter $789–$1,660 suite; off-season $629–$900 suite. AE, MC, V. **Amenities:** 2 restaurants; 2 bars; access to 18-hole golf course; health club & spa; 3 outdoor pools; room service. *In room:* A/C, TV, hair dryer, minibar, Wi-Fi ($15/day).

One&Only Ocean Club ★★★ Tranquil, secluded, and intimate, this is Paradise Island's most exclusive address, with sky-high prices to accompany the refined ambience and pampering service (the best in The Bahamas). Although it's owned by the same entity that controls the much larger Atlantis, huge efforts have been expended to separate it from the guests at the less personalized, more family-oriented mega-resort. In fact, though Atlantis's facilities are available to the residents here, that same privilege does not extend in the opposite direction. As such, you'll find a boutique-style hotel that, to a large degree, is cloistered from the much splashier venue nearby. The spacious and elegantly furnished rooms are comfortable, with king-size beds, gilt-framed mirrors, and dark-wood armoires.

The resort's real heart and soul lie in the surrounding gardens, designed by the island's former owner, Huntington Hartford II, heir to the A&P grocery fortune. This resort, in fact, was once the site of his private home. The formal gardens surround a rebuilt medieval French cloister set on 14 hectares (35 acres) of manicured lawns. Graceful 12th-century arcades are visible at the crest of a hill, across a stretch of terraced waterfalls, fountains, a stone gazebo, and rose gardens. Begin your tour of the gardens at the large swimming pool, which feeds a series of reflecting pools that stretch out toward the cloister. A kid-friendly pool is replete with aqua toys and a waterfall. This is also one of the best-developed tennis resorts in The Bahamas, and the white-sand beach adjacent to the hotel is the finest in the area. What could arguably be called Paradise Island's top restaurant is the resort's **Dune** (p. 106), created by culinary legend Jean-Georges Vongerichten.

Ocean Club Dr., Paradise Island, The Bahamas. www.oneandonlyresorts.com. ✆ **888/528-7157** in the U.S., or 242/363-2501. Fax 242/363-2424. 105 units. Winter $825–$1,000 double, from $1,500 suite; off-season from $625 double, from $1,100 suite. AE, MC, V. Free parking. **Amenities:** 2 restaurants; 3 bars; babysitting; concierge; 18-hole golf course; health club & spa; 2 outdoor pools; room service; 6 tennis courts (lit for night play). *In room:* A/C, TV, hair dryer, Internet (free), kitchen, minibar.

The Reef Atlantis ★★★ Inaugurated in 2007, and purpose-built as a condominium complex, this resort (along with the Cove) is Atlantis's tallest building. It's also the most flamboyantly state-of-the-art, permeated with the theme that defines virtually everything else around it. Although its decor most closely matches accommodations within the Cove, its level of contemporary comfort surpasses everything else at Atlantis. Opt for a room here if you're entertaining a group of four or more, if having a spectacularly high-tech kitchen is important to you, or if you have so much money that cost is absolutely no object. All of Atlantis's diversions and distractions are open to short-term residents of the Reef, and some renters have liked the place so much that they bought a unit.

Casino Dr., Paradise Island, The Bahamas. www.atlantis.com. ✆ **800/ATLANTIS** (285-2684) in the U.S., or 242/363-3000. Fax 242/363-6300. 550 suites. Winter $550–$700 studio for two, from $890 suite; off-season $425–$600 studio for two, from $670 suite. AE, MC, V. Rates include unrestricted access to all Atlantis attractions and amenities. *In room:* A/C, TV, hair dryer, kitchen, Wi-Fi (free).

Expensive

Hotel Riu Palace Paradise Island ★ ☺ In 2009, the owners reconfigured this resort into a venue wherein every accommodation is a suite. Opening onto a 5km (3-mile) stretch of beach, and within walking distance of Atlantis, this 14-story ecru-colored high-rise offers some of Paradise Island's most comfortably appointed bedrooms (many with balconies that afford sweeping water views). It's more understated than Atlantis, and usually a lot cheaper and more user-friendly and manageable in terms of size and layout. Your kids would likely be happier at Atlantis, but Riu is a viable runner-up for the family set.

Welcoming drinks are served in the lobby bar amid palm trees and tropical foliage. Guests can easily leave the shelter of the poolside terrace and settle onto one of the waterside chaise lounges on the beach. For an extra charge, you can skip the all-inclusive dinner fare and dine at Tengoku, a Japanese-themed restaurant, or Sir Alexander, for refined continental cuisine made with first-rate ingredients. Live entertainment is available 6 nights a week.

6307 Casino Dr., Paradise Island, The Bahamas. www.riu.com. © **888/666-8816** in the U.S., or 242/363-3500. Fax 242/363-3900. 379 units. Winter $680–$840 suite; off-season $638–$800 suite. Rates are all-inclusive. AE, DC, MC, V. **Amenities:** 4 restaurants; 3 bars; babysitting; concierge; health club & spa; outdoor pool; tennis court (lit for night play); watersports equipment/rentals; Wi-Fi (free in lobby). *In room:* A/C, TV, hair dryer, minibar.

Paradise Island Beach Club ★ This timeshare complex is set near Paradise Island's eastern tip, adjacent to a relatively isolated strip of spectacular beachfront. Distinctly more low-key and laissez-faire than larger hotels, such as the Atlantis, nearby, it's more of a self-catering condo complex than a full-fledged resort. Many guests cook at least some meals in their own kitchens and head elsewhere, often to bigger hotels, for restaurants, watersports, gambling, and entertainment. Overall, the setting is comfortable and cozy—you'll feel like you have your own apartment with easy access to both the beach and a taxi stand, where cabs are available to take you to other points on Paradise Island or New Providence. Accommodations each contain two bedrooms (for a maximum of six persons), with wicker and rattan furnishings, nice touches such as double basins in each bathroom, and views that may include ocean panoramas. The on-site pool bar opens for breakfast and serves drinks throughout the day until 5pm. The entertainment of the island's more densely developed sections lies just a short walk away. There's maid service every day, as you'd expect in any hotel, except on Sunday, when guests make do on their own.

Ocean Ridge Dr., Paradise Island, The Bahamas. www.mypibc.com. © **242/363-2523.** Fax 242/363-2130. 44 units. Year-round $350–$380 2-bedroom apt. AE, MC, V. **Amenities:** Restaurant; bar; pool bar; exercise room; 2 outdoor pools; Wi-Fi (free in lobby). *In room:* A/C, TV, hair dryer, kitchen.

Paradise Island Harbour Resort ★ ☺ This older 12-floor property is adjacent to the waters of Nassau Harbour, opening onto a marina with very little beach. Just a short stroll from Atlantis with all its attractions, it has been retrofitted into an all-inclusive resort. Bedrooms are midsize with twin or king-size beds, plus well-maintained bathrooms. The decor is comfortable, airy, and sunny, with tropically inspired colors and upholstery. The food served is palatable, though service can be slow. However, nightly live shows spice up the night, including fire dancing and Bahamian bands on occasion.

Harbour Dr., Paradise Island, The Bahamas. www.paradiseislandbahama.com. © **888/645-5550** or 242/363-2561. Fax 242/363-1220. 246 units. Winter $225–$285 double, $385 suite; off-season $200–$275 double, $365 suite. Rates are all-inclusive. AE, DC, DISC, MC, V. **Amenities:** 2 restaurants; 2 bars; babysitting; children's programs; concierge; health club with Jacuzzi; watersports equipment/rentals. *In room:* AC, TV, fridge, hair dryer, Wi-Fi ($10/day).

Sunrise Beach Club and Villas ★ ☺ Sunrise is a good bet for quieter families who want to avoid the circus at Atlantis and enjoy a more subdued, relaxed vacation.

Atlantis's 2,323-sq.-m (25,005-sq.-ft.) **Mandara Spa** (© **242/363-3000;** www. mandaraspa.com) is a Zen-inspired enclave of calm and serenity designed to make guests feel like gods and goddesses. Services include exotic body scrubs and wrap treatments with names like Caribbean Coffee Scrub, Tropical Coconut Scrub, and Sunburn Cooler.

This cluster of Spanish-style low-rise town houses occupies one of the most desirable stretches of beachfront. Midway between Hotel Riu and the One&Only Ocean Club, it's a short walk from the casino and a variety of sports and dining options. The hotel is usually full of Germans, Swiss, and Austrians, many of whom stay for several weeks. Accommodations are clustered within five groupings of red-roofed town houses, each with access to the resort's two pools (one of which has a waterfall) and a simple snack bar. Expect pastel colors, summery furniture, a private patio or veranda, and a kitchen, plus king-size beds, floor-to-ceiling mirrored headboards, and average-size bathrooms. The best units are the three-bedroom apartments, situated directly on the beach.

Casino Dr., Paradise Island, The Bahamas. www.sunrisebeachclub.com. © **888/754-5315** or 242/363-2234. Fax 242/363-2308. 28 units. Winter $331–$426 1-bedroom unit, $579 2-bedroom unit; off-season $221–$255 double, $463 2-bedroom unit. AE, MC, V. **Amenities:** Bar; babysitting; Internet ($12); 2 outdoor pools. *In room:* A/C, TV, hair dryer, kitchen.

Moderate

Best Western Bay View Suites ★ More than 20 kinds of hibiscus and many varieties of bougainvillea beautify this 1.6-hectare (4-acre) condo complex. The property is near the geographic center of Paradise Island, only a 10-minute walk to either the harbor or Cabbage Beach (the complex has no beach of its own). The dining options of Atlantis are only a few minutes away, but the modest Terrace restaurant here is nothing to be ashamed of. A shopping center is 3 minutes away, and a full-time personal cook can be arranged on request. Accommodations come in a variety of sizes—the largest can hold up to six—and some open onto views of the harbor. Each unit has its own kitchen with dishwasher, plus a patio or balcony and daily maid service. Penthouse suites have roof gardens with views. *Tip:* Rooms near the center of the resort are closest to the pools and laundry facilities.

Bayview Dr., Paradise Island, The Bahamas. www.bwbayviewsuites.com. © **800-WESTERN** (937-8376) or 800/757-1357 in the U.S., or 242/363-2555. Fax 242/363-2370. 75 units. Winter $240 1-bedroom suite, $415 town house for 4, from $435 villa for 6; off-season $200 1-bedroom suite, $335 town house for 4, from $345 villa for 6. Weekly rates are slightly lower. AE, DC, MC, V. **Amenities:** Lunch-only restaurant; bar; babysitting; 3 outdoor pools; tennis court (lit for night play). *In room:* A/C, TV, hair dryer, kitchen, Wi-Fi (free).

Comfort Suites Paradise Island ♦ A favorite with honeymooners, this three-story all-suite hotel is across the street from Atlantis and makes for a low-key, laid-back alternative to the behemoth. You get all the splash and wonder, but don't have to stay when the cruise-ship crowds descend. Though the hotel has its own pool bar and restaurant, guests are also granted free entrance and signing privileges at Atlantis's drinking and dining spots, as well as access to the mega-resort's pool, beach, and

Ex-Beatle George Harrison and a host of other yoga devotees over the years have checked into **Sivananda Ashram Yoga Retreat** (ℂ 800/441-2096 or 242/363-2902; fax 242/363-3783; www.sivananda.org), which is reached only by boat from Paradise Island. For some 40 years, it's been completely removed from the rest of Paradise Island's frantic gambling, heady lifestyle, and high prices. Today, the retreat teaches the healing arts and spiritual practices.

Lecturers from all over the world come here to give seminars and practice meditation. When not devoting their time to yoga, guests rest on a lovely sandy beach, all part of a compound that reaches from Nassau Harbour to the Atlantic. Guests attend two daily meditation sessions, the first starting at 5am. Two yoga classes per day are also required, but you're free daily from 10am to 4pm. A boat shuttles guests into Nassau so they can see its sights.

Participants are housed in the simple main house or in small one-room bungalows. The most desirable units, a dozen of them, front the beach. There are also 35 private single rooms, plus seven dormlike spaces. Vegetarian meals are included in the rate of $99 to $109 for a single, $79 to $129 for a double, or $69 to $79 for a three- or four-bed dormitory. Tent space is available for $69 per night. The ashram welcomes non-residents in for a communal yoga class, priced at $10 per lesson, or as part of day passes, priced at $45 per person, a price which includes two meals, two of the regularly scheduled yoga classes, and participation in whatever program, activity, or study group has been scheduled for the day of your arrival. Should you opt to do this, a phone call in advance is a good idea.

sports facilities. Accommodations are priced according to their views: over the island, the pool, or the garden. Bedrooms are standard motel size; the medium-size bathrooms are stocked with beach towels.

Paradise Island Dr., Paradise Island, The Bahamas. www.comfortsuitespi.com. ℂ **877/424-6423** in the U.S. or Canada, or 242/363-3680. Fax 242/363-2588. 228 units. Winter $279–$373 double; off-season $172–$373 double. Rates include continental breakfast. AE, DISC, MC, V. **Amenities:** Restaurant; bar; small health club; outdoor pool; tennis court (lit for night play). In room: A/C, TV, fridge, hair dryer, Wi-Fi (free).

Paradise Harbour Club & Marina   This place is noteworthy for its sense of isolation, despite being on heavily developed Paradise Island. Built in 1991 near the island's extreme eastern tip, the hotel has rambling upper hallways, terra-cotta tile floors, and clean, well-organized bedrooms. If available, opt for one of the top-floor units so you can enjoy the view. Some of the property's quaint services, all free, include a water taxi to downtown Nassau, a beach shuttle (albeit in a golf cart), and use of snorkeling gear, fishing poles, and bikes. Another weekly shuttle runs residents to and from a local grocery store as a means of stocking up on food supplies.

Paradise Island Dr., Paradise Island, The Bahamas. www.festiva-paradise.com. ℂ **800/594-3495** or 242/363-2992. Fax 242/363-2840. 23 units. Winter $145 junior suite, $202–$250 1-bedroom suite; off-season $130 junior suite, $167–$220 1-bedroom suite. MC, V. **Amenities:** Restaurant; bar; babysitting; exercise room with Jacuzzi; room service; watersports equipment/rentals. In room: A/C, TV, hair dryer, kitchen (in some), minibar, Wi-Fi (free).

WHERE TO EAT

Paradise Island offers an array of the most dazzling, and the most expensive, restaurants in The Bahamas. If you're on a strict budget, cross over the bridge into downtown Nassau, which has far more affordable places to eat. Though pricey, meals on Paradise Island are often unimaginative—surf and turf appears on many a menu, so, unfortunately, you may not get what you pay for. The greatest concentration of restaurants is near the casino, but there are other good options outside the Atlantis complex, including Dune at the One&Only Ocean Club.

Expensive

Bahamian Club ★★ STEAK   With an upscale British colonial feel and an atmosphere like that of an elegant and somewhat macho country club, this is a big (but civilized) clubby spot, with spacious vistas, mirrors, gleaming mahogany, and forest-green walls. The excellent food is prepared with top-quality ingredients from the U.S. and served in two-fisted portions. Meat is king here, with all those old favorites like roasted prime rib and Cornish hen, plus the island's best T-bone, along with a selection of veal and lamb chops. The retro menu also lists the inevitable Dover sole, lobster Thermidor, and grilled salmon, as well as appetizers that hearken back to the good old days, such as fresh jumbo-shrimp cocktail and onion soup. Try the Bahamian conch chowder for some local flavor. Side dishes are excellent, especially the penne with fresh tomato sauce and the roasted shiitake mushrooms. Proper attire is required—that means no jeans or sneakers.

Coral Towers at Atlantis, Casino Dr. ✆ **242/363-3000.** www.atlantis.com. Reservations required. Main courses $28–$65. AE, DC, DISC, MC, V. Usually Wed–Mon 6–11pm, though days and hours may vary.

Blue Lagoon ★ SEAFOOD   Views of the marina, along with music from a one-man band, complement a candlelit meal here—a nice escape from the casino's glitter and glitz. Many of the seafood dishes, including stone-crab claws and Nassau conch chowder, are excellent. The ubiquitous broiled grouper, in this case stuffed with shrimp and covered with a cheese sauce, is on the menu, as are dishes such as brochette of seafood with a creole sauce; steak au poivre with a brandy sauce; baked chicken, Eleuthera-style (with pineapple); and duck à l'orange. The chef even whips up a good Caesar salad for two. Yes, you've probably had better versions of these dishes elsewhere, but they are competently prepared, even though the meats are shipped in frozen.

Club Land'or, Paradise Dr. ✆ **242/363-2400.** www.clublandor.com. Reservations required. Main courses $28–$70. AE, MC, V. Mon–Sat 5–10pm.

Hopping, Skipping & Jumping with Dining Hours

Restaurants here, especially in hotels, are not known for keeping fixed dining hours. Hours of operation can vary with the season and the hotel's occupancy level. Dining rooms—again, mainly in hotels—can open and close for no reason that's immediately obvious. If you're planning on going to a particular restaurant, call in advance even if reservations aren't required.

Café Martinique ★★★ FRENCH   The most elegant and upscale restaurant on Paradise Island occupies a replica of the kind of town house that might belong to a billionaire who happened to live in, say, Martinique and happened to have imported art and antiques from Belle Epoque Paris. This mixture of haute Paris with a French Colonial twist is enormously appealing, as is the wrought-iron birdcage elevator that brings you upstairs to the dining room. Begin your evening in the supremely comfortable bar area, replete with French Caribbean carved mahogany antiques. In the tastefully posh and well-upholstered dining area, masses of flowers and dessert trolleys await your pleasure—not to mention the cuisine of superchef Jean-Georges Vongerichten. Begin with such delectable items as tartare of tuna with puffed *gaufrettes* of potato and chive sauce, or sautéed foie gras with mango. The main courses are sublime, especially the blackened and grilled chicken with glazed kumquats and cilantro, filet of Dover sole (either meunière or almondine), and Paradise Island's most upscale cheeseburger (filet steak, chopped, served with truffled mayonnaise). The restaurant is known for its grills, everything from prime rib for two to a succulent veal chop.

In Marina Village at Atlantis, Casino Dr. ℂ **242/363-3000.** Reservations required. Main courses $36–$65. AE, DC, DISC, MC, V. Daily 6–11pm, though days and hours may vary.

Casa d'Angelo ★ ITALIAN   Posh, richly upholstered, and decorated with art and objects reminiscent of old-world Italy, Paradise Island's premier Italian restaurant creates classic dishes prepared with skill, served with flair, and comparable to the kind of elegant manicured cuisine you'd expect from a top-notch Italian restaurant in Florida. Some of the best main courses include sautéed Fra Diavolo–style calamari and clams served over crostini; tuna carpaccio with spinach, olives, artichoke hearts, and orange sauce; risotto with porcini mushrooms, truffle oil, goat cheese, and thyme; and grilled swordfish steak with garlic, white wine, tomatoes, capers, black olives, onions, and fresh oregano.

Coral Towers at Atlantis, Casino Dr. ℂ **242/363-3000.** www.atlantis.com. Reservations required. Main courses $35–$66. AE, DC, MC, V. Daily 6–10pm, though days and hours may vary.

Chop Stix CANTONESE   Many people come here just to hang out in the bar. But if you're in the mood for a good Chinese meal, you'll be ushered to a table in a circular dining room, engaging and stylish, with a ceiling draped with fabric that evokes a richly decorated tent. The sophisticated decor seems to encourage both your sense of humor and your sense of camp; it suggests Shanghai during the British colonial age. Some of the island's best appetizers are served here—try the steamed shrimp dumplings or the Thai chicken spring rolls. This might be followed by the wok-seared grouper with garlic sauce or the coconut curry chicken with mango.

Coral Towers at Atlantis, Casino Dr. ℂ **242/363-3000.** www.atlantis.com. Reservations recommended. Main courses $25–$60. AE, DC, DISC, MC, V. Tues–Sat 6–10pm, though days and hours may vary.

Columbus Tavern ★ SEAFOOD   Through the large open windows of this restaurant, you can watch the boats in Nassau Harbour. A laid-back alternative to the glitter of the nearby mega-resort, this is the only native seaside restaurant and bar on Paradise Island. It's nestled between the Ocean Club Golf Course and the Paradise Harbour Club & Marina. Seafood is prepared here any way you specify—steamed, baked, whole, or fried. The chef's delectable specialties include lobster flambé or a steak Diane prepared tableside. But most guests gravitate to the "Fisherman's Fiesta," a combo platter that includes blackened lobster, fresh shrimp, or scallops in a tasty

Creole sauce. Other classics are filet of Nassau grouper sautéed and topped with a creamy garlic, white wine, and shallot sauce, or else roasted Cornish hen glazed with a lemon pepper sauce. The Guava Duff, an old Bahamian dessert specialty, will win your heart.

Paradise Island Dr. ☎ **242/363-2534.** www.columbustavernbahamas.com. Reservations recommended for dinner. Lunch main courses $13–$21; dinner main courses $27–$42. AE, MC, V. Daily 11am–4pm and 4:30–10:30pm.

Dune ★★★ INTERNATIONAL   One of Paradise Island's most cutting-edge restaurants is a beachfront annex of the One&Only Ocean Club. It offers very attentive service, a sweeping view of the ocean, a teakwood floor that makes you feel like you're aboard a yacht, and a gray-and-black decor that looks like it was plucked from a chic enclave in Milan. Near the restaurant's entrance is a thriving herb garden from which many of the culinary flavorings are derived. The chefs here invariably select the finest ingredients and handle them with razor-sharp technique. Every dish has a special something, especially the shrimp dusted with orange powder and served with artichokes and arugula. The tuna spring rolls with soybean salsa are splendid, as is the chicken and coconut-milk soup served with shiitake cakes. The goat cheese and watermelon salad is an unexpected delight. Grouper filet—that Bahamian standard—is at its savory best here when served with zesty tomato sauce.

One&Only Ocean Club, Ocean Club Dr. ☎ **242/363-2501,** ext. 64739. www.oneandonlyresorts. com. Reservations required. Main courses $23–$39 lunch; $38–$65 dinner. AE, DC, DISC, MC, V. Daily 7–11am, noon–3pm, and 6–10:30pm, though days and hours may vary.

Marketplace ★ 🍴 BUFFET/INTERNATIONAL   Unless you're hopelessly jaded or blasé, you can't leave here without feeling amazed by how abundant and elaborate the buffets at a casino resort can really be. Decorated with old vases and terra-cotta tiles, this one evokes a sprawling market in which all the food just happens to be beautifully prepared, elegantly displayed, and showcased in breathtaking variety and quantity—making it the best buffet on Paradise Island. Before you start loading stuff onto your plate, browse your way past the various cooking stations and do some strategic planning. From fresh fruit to omelets, you can make breakfast as light or as heavy as you want. At dinner, you'll find everything from fresh seafood and made-to-order pastas to carved roast beef and lamb. No intimate affair, this place seats some 400 diners. Sit inside or on the patio overlooking a lagoon.

Royal Towers at Atlantis, Casino Dr. ☎ **242/363-3000.** www.atlantis.com. Reservations not needed. Buffets $29 breakfast, $63 dinner. AE, DC, MC, V. Daily 7–11am, and 5:30–10pm.

Mesa Grill ★★ SOUTHWESTERN   In 2007, Atlantis carved this Southwestern-chic enclave out of a beachfront spot on the lobby level of the Cove, its boutique-style hotel-within-a-hotel. Don't presume that this is a down-home joint for chili, beer, and barbecue. It's actually rather haute, distinctly gourmet, and run by celebrity chef Bobby Flay. Begin a meal here with a shrimp-and-roasted-garlic cornmeal tamale with fresh corn and cilantro sauce, or perhaps the raw tuna nachos with mango hot sauce and avocado cream. Follow that with the 16-spice chicken or honey-glazed salmon. There are at least three succulent preparations of grilled steaks, plus an excellent vegetarian main course: the cornmeal-crusted chili relleno filled with goat cheese, wild mushrooms, and a smoked red-pepper sauce. Well-flavored side dishes include collard greens, sweet-potato gratin, black-eyed peas with rice, and cilantro-pesto mashed potatoes. **Note:** Children 12 and under are discouraged from dining here.

The Cove Atlantis. © **242/363-3000,** ext. 59250. www.atlantis.com. Reservations required. Main courses $33–$55. AE, DC, MC, V. Daily 5:30–10:30pm (last seating), though days and hours may vary.

Mosaic ★ 🗲 BAHAMIAN/MEDITERRANEAN   This is perhaps the best buffet restaurant in all the islands, and it serves a big spread for breakfast, lunch, and dinner. It's an all-you-can-eat type of establishment, and is popular with families. The restaurant changes from day to evening in its aura, using lighting to play off the polished chrome, Wedgewood, and limestone. A lot of the cuisine is inspired by the Mediterranean. Just because it's a buffet doesn't mean that all dishes are already prepared. Several cooking stations will prepare dishes on demand from the fresh catch of the day to churrasco grilled steaks.

Casino Dr. © **242/363-3000.** www.atlantis.com. Reservations recommended. Buffets $33 at breakfast, $35 at lunch, $68 at dinner. AE, DC, MC, V. Daily 7–11am, noon–2:30pm, and 5:30–10pm.

Nobu ★★★ JAPANESE/ASIAN   It's the most talked-about, hip, and sought-after restaurant in Atlantis, thanks to its avant-garde Asian food and its association with an ongoing round of celebrities. It's the culinary statement of chef Nobu Matsuhisa, whose New York City branch caused a sensation among the glitterati when it opened in the '90s. Some diners prefer to start with Nobu's special cold dishes, including lobster seviche—but since conch is queen in The Bahamas, you might opt instead for conch seviche. The best appetizer we've sampled is the yellowtail sashimi with jalapeño. If you like your dishes spicy, try the rock shrimp with wasabi sauce or the Chilean sea bass with black-bean sauce. The tempura selection is vast, ranging from pumpkin to shiitake. Most patrons order some items from the wide selection of sushi and sashimi, including exotica such as live conch, sea urchin, or freshwater eel. Of course, you can also order well-prepared standards such as tuna, octopus, and salmon. If you want Paradise Island's most lavish and exotic meal, request the *omakase*, the chef's signature fixed-price menu.

Atlantis Casino, Casino Dr. © **242/363-3000.** www.atlantis.com. Reservations required. Main courses $12–$50; sushi and sashimi $4–$37; sushi or sashimi dinner $49; chef's special *omakase* menu $150–$200. AE, DC, DISC, MC, V. Daily 6–11pm, though days and hours may vary.

Moderate

Bimini Road ★ BAHAMIAN/INTERNATIONAL   The name refers to a mysterious underwater rock formation off the coast of Bimini that resembles a ruined triumphal boulevard. Partly because of its relatively reasonable prices and partly because it showcases Bahamian cuisine more proudly than any other restaurant at Atlantis, this eatery is among the most consistently popular and crowded dining spots. The red-leatherette banquettes and Formica tables suggest a Goombay version of a diner in the Out Islands. Yet a second glance reveals a sophisticated and hysterically busy open kitchen (entertainment in its own right) and walls covered with tropical murals, some influenced by the Junkanoo festival. Start with specialties like scorched conch salad or Rum Bay boiled fish in a citrus broth. Other island favorites include the catch of the day, which can be grilled, blackened, or fried. A tasty dish is chicken mojo—boneless breast with spices and a lime mojo sauce, charcoal-roasted and served over native rice. The only problem with this place is the crowd of expectant diners who cluster, somewhat uncomfortably, near the entrance waiting for a table. A phone call in advance for information about wait times might help you avoid this inconvenience.

Marina Village at Atlantis, Casino Dr. © **242/363-3000**. www.atlantis.com. Reservations accepted only for parties of 6 or more. Main courses $22–$50. AE, DISC, MC, V. Daily 6–11pm, though days and hours may vary.

Carmine's ITALIAN   A lot of the signals that emanate from Carmine's communicate "family." Here we're talking about a large, loud, and in-your-face Italian family who work out their emotional conflicts with gusto, verve, and platters piled high with an amazing amount of food. Set at Marina Village's most distant point from the casino, this is the local branch of a New York City–based chain. Even though it was custom-built, it feels like a team of decorators gentrified this boathouse by adding many square yards of mahogany bar tops, terra-cotta tiles, and monumental wine racks. This place prides itself on serving portions that could feed a party of four to six. As such, it's at its best when groups gather together to order several platters for collective consumption. If you're a single diner or a couple, head instead for other dining haunts such as Café Martinique or Bahamian Club.

Marina Village at Atlantis, Casino Dr. © **242/363-3000**. www.atlantis.com. Reservations accepted only for parties of 6 or more. Main courses $30–$50. AE, DC, DISC, MC, V. Daily 6–11pm, though days and hours may vary.

Green Parrot AMERICAN   You might enjoy a panorama of the Nassau Harbour from your table at this informal open-air restaurant and bar, a fave of some expats and denizens of Nassau, along with a scattering of vacationers. During the day, it sells a lot of burgers and well-stuffed sandwiches, later gearing up for happy hour, karaoke, and a native group performing on Thursday and Saturday nights. Starters include typical sports-bar fare (buffalo wings, onion rings, chicken or cheese quesadillas, or chicken tenders). The most popular lunch item is the "Works Burger," a whopper with American and Swiss cheese along with grilled onions and mushrooms. The non-carnivore can opt for a veggie burger, a cracked conch po' boy, or any of four meal-sized salads. At dinner, go for the catch of the day, which can be grilled or blackened. Other tasty mains include a grilled New York steak, cracked conch, and curried chicken.

Hurricane Hole Marina. © **242/322-9248**. www.greenparrotbar.com. Reservations not needed. Main courses $12–$15; burgers and sandwiches $8–$15. MC, V. Sun–Thurs 11:30am–11pm; Fri–Sat 11:30am–midnight.

Inexpensive

Anthony's Grill AMERICAN/CARIBBEAN   Its owners think of this place as an upscale version of Bennigan's or T.G.I. Friday's, but the decor is thoroughly Caribbean, thanks to psychedelic tropical colors, underwater sea themes, and jaunty maritime decorative touches. Tucked into a shopping center a short walk from the main entrance to the Atlantis resort, and evoking a very different ambience from its neighbor, it has a bar dispensing everything from conventional mai tais to embarrassingly oversized 48-ounce "sparklers"—with a combination of rum, amaretto, vodka, and fruit punch that is about all most serious drinkers can handle. Menu items include burgers, barbecued or fried chicken, ribs with Caribbean barbecue sauce, meal-size salads, and pizzas topped with everything from lobster to jerk chicken.

Paradise Island Shopping Plaza, at Paradise Island and Casino drives. © **242/363-3152**. www. anthonysgrillparadiseisland.com. Main courses $9–$15 lunch; $14–$32 dinner. AE, DISC, MC, V. Daily 7:30am–11pm.

Atlas Bar & Grill AMERICAN   The blare of its dozen or so TVs competes with the jangling of slot machines. This is the sports bar with the most elaborate array of screens on Paradise Island. It's set up in two separate ovals, each of which rings, at different perimeters, an oval-shaped bar. Decor includes lots of statues depicting Atlas and his many macho struggles. What should you get here? Consider a burger with beer, a burger with scotch, or a burger with a soda. There's also jambalaya, spare ribs, and pastas.

Atlantis Casino, Casino Dr. *©***242/363-3000.** www.atlantis.com. Reservations not necessary. Main courses $10–$36. AE, DC, MC, V. Daily 11am–4pm; Thurs–Sun 4pm–3am, though days and hours (especially at dinner) may vary.

BEACHES & OUTDOOR PURSUITS

Visitors interested in more than lazing on the beach have only to ask hotel staff to make the necessary arrangements. Guests at Atlantis, for example, have access to a surprising number of diversions without so much as leaving the hotel property: They can splash in private pools; play tennis, ping-pong, and shuffleboard; ride the waves; snorkel; or rent WaveRunners, jet skis, banana boats, and catamarans from contractors located in kiosks.

Hitting the Beach

On Paradise Island, **Cabbage Beach ★★** (also known as **West Beach**) is the real showcase. Its broad white sands stretch for at least 3km (1¾ miles) and are bordered by casuarinas, palms, and sea grapes. It's likely to be crowded in winter, but you can find more elbow room by walking to the beach's northwestern stretch. You can reach Paradise Island from downtown Nassau by walking over the bridge, taking a taxi, or boarding a ferryboat at Prince George Wharf. Cabbage Beach does not have public restrooms, but if you patronize one of the handful of bars and restaurants nearby, you can use its facilities. Note that during the construction of Atlantis's soon-to-come waterfront timeshare property, access to some sections of this beach might be off-limits.

Our other favorite beach in this area is the white-sand **Paradise Beach ★★**, which is used mainly by guests of the Cove Atlantis and the Reef Atlantis hotels, as it lies at the island's far western tip. If you're not a resident, access is difficult. If you're staying at a hotel in Nassau and want to come to Paradise Island for a day at the beach, it's better to go to Cabbage Beach. However, sunsets viewed from the sands of Paradise Beach look particularly beautiful.

Fishing

Anglers can fish close to shore for grouper, dolphinfish, red snapper, crabs, even lobster. Farther out, in first-class fishing boats fitted with outriggers and fighting chairs, they troll for billfish or giant marlin.

The best way to pursue this pastime is to go to your hotel's activities desk, where the staff can set you up with a local charter operator for a half or full day of fishing. Also see "Beaches & Outdoor Pursuits" in chapter 3.

Golf

Ocean Club Golf Course ★★, Paradise Island Drive (*©* **242/363-2510;** www. oneandonlyresorts.com), at the island's east end, is an 18-hole championship golf course designed by Tom Weiskopf that overlooks both the Atlantic Ocean and Nassau Harbour. Attracting every caliber of golfer, the par-72 course is known for its hole 17, which plays entirely along the scenic Snorkelers Cove. Greens fees, including use of

FAVORITE PARADISE ISLAND experiences

Watching the sunset at The Cloister. Here, amid the reassembled remains of a 12th-century French stone monastery once owned by William Randolph Hearst, you can enjoy one of the most beautiful pink and mauve sunsets in all of The Bahamas.

Spending an evening at the casino. The Atlantis Casino—the only one on Paradise Island—is one of the world's most impressive and imaginatively decorated. Many visitors arrive on the island just to test their luck at this gaming destination. Once you're here, make it a point to check out the huge clusters of handblown glass arranged into amazing sculptures, conceived by American glass-blowing master Dale Chihuly. This casino contains at least four of his pieces, each one massive, hyper-fragile, and awe-inspiring. Looking for a dining venue? The echoing interior passageway that connects the various parts of this resort is home to a medley of shops and restaurants, some of them among the finest in The Bahamas.

a golf cart, are $120 to $300 for 18 holes of play, depending on the season, without reductions for guests at any individual hotels. Rental clubs and shoes are available.

Golfers seeking more variety will find one other course on New Providence Island, the **Cable Beach Golf Club** (p. 74).

Snorkeling & Scuba Diving

Bahama Divers, Nassau Yacht Haven Marina, on East Bay Street (℗ **800/398-3483** or 242/393-5644; www.bahamadivers.com), is the area's best all-around center for watersports, specializing in scuba diving and snorkeling. A two-tank morning dive goes for $109 to $150, depending on its venue and location, and a single-tank afternoon dive costs $70 to $100, and a half-day snorkeling trip is $50. Dive packages are also offered.

For more scuba sites in the area, see "Snorkeling & Scuba Diving" under "Beaches & Outdoor Pursuits" in chapter 3.

Tennis

No other hotel in The Bahamas pays as much attention to tennis as the **One&Only Ocean Club,** Ocean Club Drive (℗ **242/363-2501;** www.oneandonlyresorts.com), which has six Har-Tru courts, four lit for night play. Guests here can practically roll out of bed and onto the courts, which are often filled with first-class competitors, although beginners and intermediate players are welcome. One&Only Ocean Club guests have free access to the courts; they can also play with the resident pro for $75 per hour. Nonguests are not admitted.

Other hotels with courts include **Atlantis,** Casino Drive (℗ **242/363-3000;** www.atlantis.com), with six hard-surface and clay courts. Atlantis guests (nonguests are not admitted) pay $25 per hour for access to the courts; they can play with the resident pro for an additional $70 per hour. Ball rentals go for $10 per hour, tennis racquets for another $10 per hour.

SEEING THE SIGHTS

Most of the big hotels here maintain activity-packed calendars, especially for that occasional windy, rainy day that comes in winter. Similar to life aboard a large cruise ship, the resorts offer diversions (some of them age-specific) that include water-volleyball games, bingo, fish-feeding demonstrations, and movie screenings. And that doesn't include the disco parties for teens and preteens that tend to be scheduled for late afternoons or early evenings. To an increasing degree, hotels such as Atlantis have configured themselves as destinations in their own right.

Atlantis Paradise Island ★★   Regardless of where you're staying—even if it's at New Providence Island's most remote hotel—you'll want to visit this lavish theme park, hotel, restaurant complex, casino, and entertainment center. It is, hands down, Paradise Island's biggest attraction. You could spend all day here—and all night, too—wandering the resort's shopping arcades, sampling the eateries' international cuisine, or gambling at roulette wheels, slot machines, poker games, and blackjack tables. And once you're here, don't even think about leaving without a walk along the marina or a visit to the Dig, a theme-driven marine attraction that celebrates the eerie, tragic legend of the lost continent of Atlantis. During the day you can wear casual clothes, but at night you should dress up a bit, especially to try one of the better restaurants.

The most crowded time to visit is between 9am and 5pm on days when cruise ships are berthed in the nearby harbor—usually every Tuesday, Friday, and Saturday. The casino is at its most packed between 8 and 11pm any night of the week. There is no cover to enter: You pay just for what you eat, drink, and gamble away (and that could be considerable). Ironically, it's illegal for Bahamian citizens or residents to gamble. That restriction, however, most definitely does not apply to visitors from other countries. Except for the price of the liquor, entertainment within the bars—which usually includes live salsa, Goombay, and calypso music provided by local bands—is free.

Casino Dr. ℂ **242/363-3000.** Free admission. Daily 24 hr.

The Cloister ★   Located in the Versailles Gardens of the One&Only Ocean Club, this 12th-century cloister built by Augustinian monks in southwestern France was reassembled here stone by stone. Huntington Hartford, the A&P heir, purchased the cloister from the estate of William Randolph Hearst. Regrettably, after the newspaper czar originally bought the cloister, it was hastily dismantled in France for shipment to The Bahamas. However, the parts had not been numbered—they all arrived unlabeled on Paradise Island. The reassembly of the complicated monument baffled most, and defied conventional methods of construction, until artist and sculptor Jean Castre-Manne set about doing it piece by piece. It took him 2 years, and what you see today presumably bears some similarity to the original. The gardens, which extend over the rise to Nassau Harbour, are filled with tropical flowers and classical statues. Though the monument retains a timeless beauty, recently erected buildings have encroached on either side, marring Hartford's original vision.

One&Only Ocean Club, Ocean Club Dr. ℂ **242/363-2501.** www.oneandonlyresorts.com. Free admission. Daily 24 hr.

   A Special Place of Beauty

Paradise Island's loveliest spot is Ocean Club's **Versailles Gardens,** far removed from the glitz and faux glamour of Atlantis. Within its seven terraces, the sites of many a wedding, are statues of some of Huntington Hartford's favorite people, including Mephistopheles, Franklin D. Roosevelt, and Doctor Livingstone. The gardens are open anytime, day or night, and admission is free.

SHOPPING

Many of Nassau's major stores also have outlets on Paradise Island. For serious shopping, however, cross over the Paradise Island Bridge into downtown Nassau (see chapter 3).

The **Shops at Atlantis** (℃ **242/363-3000;** www.atlantis.com) is the largest concentration of shopping and boutiques on Paradise Island, rivaling anything else in The Bahamas in terms of size, selection, and style. The boutiques are subdivided into two different sections: The well-appointed **Crystal Court Shops** corridor meanders between the Royal Towers and the Coral Towers, encompassing 3,252 sq. m (35,004 sq. ft.) of prime high-traffic retail space. The waterfront **Marina Village Shops** are newer. Another handful of emporiums is scattered randomly throughout other parts of the resort. It's all about flagrantly conspicuous consumption that's sometimes fueled by the gaming frenzy in the nearby casino.

The resort contains three branches of **Colombian Emeralds** (one in the Marina Village, another in Atlantis's Beach Tower, another in Atlantis's Royal Tower), where the colored gemstones far outnumber the relatively limited selection of diamonds. Other boutiques include **Versace,** which has not only clothing but also a charming home division; **Bulgari,** producer of some of the world's most enviable jewels, as well as watches, gifts, and perfumes; and **Gucci** and **Ferragamo,** in case you forgot your best dancing shoes. For bathing suits, **Cole's of Nassau,** selling swimwear by Gottex, Pucci, and Fernando Sanchez, maintains two separate branches within the Atlantis resort. Watch seller **John Bull,** known for its Bay Street store in Nassau, has an intriguing assortment of timepieces, jewelry, and designer accessories. Other shops within the Atlantis include David Yurman for exotic "postmodern" jewelry designs, and boutiques maintained by Tiffany's, Cartier, Coach Leather Goods, Guess sportswear, and all manner of emporiums devoted to fun-in-the-sun accessories, fashion, and gift items.

PARADISE ISLAND AFTER DARK

Paradise Island has the country's best nightlife, and most of it centers on Atlantis.

Atlantis Paradise Island ★★★ There's no other spot in The Bahamas, with the possible exception of the Crystal Palace complex on Cable Beach, with such a wide variety of after-dark attractions, and absolutely nothing that approaches its inspired brand of razzle-dazzle. Even if you stay in Nassau or Cable Beach, you'll want to drop by this artfully decorated, self-contained temple to decadence, even if gambling isn't your passion. Love it or hate it, this place is simply a jaw-dropper.

The **Atlantis Casino** is the most lavishly planned, most obviously themed venue of its kind this side of Vegas. Its managers claim that it's the only casino in the world built above a body of water. Designed in homage to the lost continent of Atlantis, it appears to have risen directly from the waters of the lagoon. The gaming area is centered on buildings representing a Temple of the Sun and a Temple of the Moon, with a painted replica of the zodiac chart overhead. Rising from key locations are four of the most elaborate sculptures in the world. Massive and complex, they were crafted by teams of artisans spearheaded by Dale Chihuly, the American-born master whose glass-blowing skills are heralded globally. Other than the decor, the casino's gaming tables, open daily from 10am to 4am, are the main attraction in this enormous place, and about a thousand whirring and clanging slot machines operate 24 hours a day.

Recent additions include a lineup of poker tables and the **Pegasus Race & Sports Book,** with an illuminated and computerized display that lists the odds for many of the world's upcoming sporting events. Thanks to instantaneous communications with a centralized betting facility in Las Vegas, the staff here will make odds on a staggering number of sports events, both professional and collegiate, as well as horse racing and greyhound racing. This facility also contains a miniamphitheater with plush armchairs and views over a battery of TV screens, each displaying one of the sporting and/or racing events for which odds are being calculated and money is changing hands.

Upstairs from the casino is **Aura,** a totally upscale nightclub experience that manages to attract a few local hipsters as well as Atlantis guests. Come anytime during casino hours for a drink. A sweaty, flirty crowd parties all night on the dance floor. The club gets going around 10pm nightly, with a cover of $50 for females and $100 for males, unless they're guests of Atlantis, in which case they enter without charge. (Note that the cover for nonguests is usually waived for women if they're hip or beautiful enough.) Drinks inside carry big-city price tags, usually hovering around $17 for a scotch and soda. Ringing the casino are at least 3,252 sq. m (35,004 sq. ft.) of retail shopping space, with even more located nearby in Marina Village (see "Shopping," above), and an impressive cluster of hideaway bars and restaurants.

Also in Atlantis, **Joker's Wild** is the only real comedy club in The Bahamas, with a talented company of funny people who work hard to make you laugh. Showtimes are Tuesday through Sunday at 9:30pm. There's a per-person cover of $20 to $35 for everyone. At least two comedians appear on any given night, and most of them hail from either the U.S. or the U.K. Midway btw. Beach and Coral towers, on Casino Dr. *C* **242/363-3000.** www.atlantis.com.

The Bar Scene

Bimini Road At many bars in this sprawling resort, the bartenders seem to ignore you. Not here—they're a lively bunch, slinging drinks like the sour-apple Gussie Mae in a setting imbued with a Junkanoo theme. The place is especially popular with yachties, who tie up at the nearby marina. A costumed dance troupe performs 4 nights a week (times vary), and live bands pump out island music. The restaurant (p. 107) serves food daily from 5 to 11pm. Both bars here (one on the terrace, the other indoors) are open daily until 1:30am. Marina Village at Atlantis, Casino Dr. *C* **242/363-3000.** www.atlantis.com.

Dune Bar This luxe dining room (p. 106) is also the setting for the island's most sophisticated lounge; it's becoming increasingly popular as a plush meeting spot for singles. The action centers around a translucent white marble bar illuminated from behind. The terrace here can be undeniably romantic. One&Only Ocean Club, Ocean Club Dr. *C* **242/363-2501.** www.oneandonlyresorts.com. Call for hours, which vary.

Plato's Lounge This is Atlantis's most popular bar, a sensual spot where you can escape the din of the slot machines and relax in an upscale environment that's flanked with replicas of Greek texts that might have been hand-lettered by Plato himself when he wrote about the lost continent of Atlantis. A pianist sets the mood during cocktail hour, and you'll get the sense that you're right in the heart of everything. In the sunlit hours, the site doubles as a cafe, serving pastries and snacks from 6am until 4pm. Open until 1am nightly. Royal Towers at Atlantis, Casino Dr. *C* **242/363-3000.** www.atlantis.com.

GRAND BAHAMA (FREEPORT/ LUCAYA)

5

Fabulous beaches, unspoiled beauty, and warm waters continue to make Grand Bahama Island, just 50 miles east of Florida, a year-round destination. Of its two main urban centers, Freeport is a stimulating mix of restaurants, shops and nightlife, while Lucaya, called the "Garden City," pleases with its restaurants, fine beaches, and marketplace shops. The rest of the island is filled with long stretches of beach, broken by inlets and fishing villages. Away from the beach Rand Nature Centre, its national park, invites peaceful strolls along paths of casuarina, palmetto, and pine trees.

Things to Do Grand Bahama has enough shoreline space for everyone, and you'll find plenty of spots in the sand to sun at **Xanadu Beach** and **Lucaya Beach.** If you want to get away from it all, **Fortune Beach** is a gem of secluded white sand. Get in the water to commune with dolphins on a **dolphin dive** at the Underwater Explorer Society. For a more fragrant and surprising experience, immerse yourself in the invigorating scent of pine trees as you wander through **Lucayan National Park,** with its underwater caves, forest trails, and quiet beach.

Shopping The brightly painted huts at **Port Lucaya Marketplace,** along the waterfront, are filled with handicrafts and souvenirs. At Freeport's **International Bazaar,** you can fill your shopping bag full of duty-free cameras, perfumes, and clothing. A **straw market** next door to the International Bazaar contains items with that special Bahamian touch—brightly hued baskets, hats, handbags, placemats, and an endless array of T-shirts.

Nightlife & Entertainment Lively restaurants and bars keep things hopping at **Port Lucaya,** while DJs keep the dance floors rocking in the clubs around the International Bazaar in **Freeport.** Spin the slot machines at the **Isle of Capri** casino at **Our Lucaya Beach Resort.** For the island's best live music, check out what's playing at **Count Basie Square** in the Port Lucaya Marketplace.

Restaurants & Dining Bahamian cuisine dominates the dining rooms in Grand Bahama, but you can also expect everything from steak

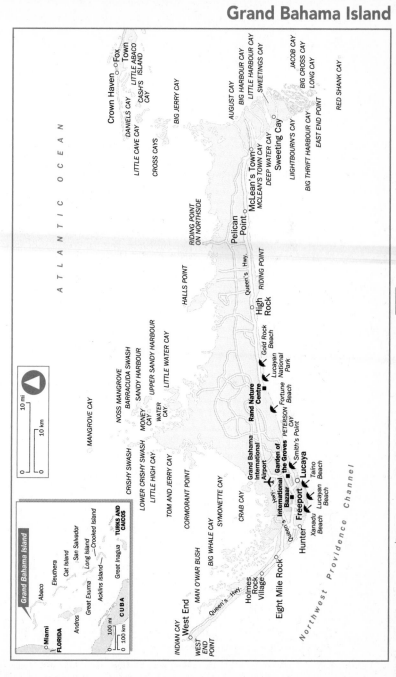

and kidney pie (from the days of British colonial rule) in the backstreets of **Freeport** to creative Italian and Pacific Rim fare at the resort restaurants. Along **Taíno Beach** and at **Lucaya,** beach shacks serve up sumptuous specialties such as conch, grouper, Bahamian lobster and **conch salad,** the Bahamian favorite. A traditional dish to try is **meat souse** (boiled mutton), accompanied with fried plantain, macaroni pie, or peas 'n' rice.

ORIENTATION

Arriving

A number of airlines fly to Freeport's **Grand Bahama International Airport** (FPO; ✆ 242/352-6020) from the continental United States. **American Airlines** (✆ 800/ 433-7300; www.aa.com) and **Bahamasair** (✆ 800/222-4262 or 242/352-8346; www. bahamasair.com) both offer daily flights from Miami. **Continental Connection** (✆ 800/231-0856; www.continental.com) flies to Freeport from Miami and West Palm Beach once daily, and from Fort Lauderdale five times daily. **Delta Connection** (✆ 800/221-1212; www.delta.com) has daily service from Atlanta. **United** (✆ 800/864-8331; www.united.com) flies frequently from Fort Lauderdale; **US Airways** (✆ 800/428-4322; www.usairways.com) operates flights to Freeport from Charlotte, NC, and Philadelphia.

Many visitors arrive in Nassau and then hop on one of the five daily Bahamasair flights to Freeport. These 30-minute hops usually cost around $160 round-trip.

No buses run from the airport to the major hotel zones, but many hotels provide airport transfers, especially if you've bought a package deal. If yours does not, no problem; **taxis** meet arriving flights and can take you from the airport to hotels in Freeport or Lucaya for about $18 to $38. The ride shouldn't take more than about 10 minutes.

Visitor Information

Information is available at the **Grand Bahama Tourism Board,** in the Fidelity Financial Centre, West Mall Drive at Poinciana Drive (✆ **242/352-8356;** www. grandbahama.bahamas.com). It's open Monday to Friday 9am to 5pm. That organization maintains three smaller information booths, each open daily, at least in theory, from 9am to 5pm. If there's no actual representative inside at the time of your visit, because of slow business, a recorded message will promise to call you back if you leave a contact phone number. They're located at **Grand Bahama International Airport** (✆ **242/352-2052**), at **Port Lucaya Marketplace** (✆ **242/373-8988**), and at the cruise-ship docks adjacent to **Lucayan Harbour** (✆ **242/350-8600**).

Island Layout

Other than the perhaps unexpected novelty of driving on the left, getting around Freeport/Lucaya is fairly easy due to the flat terrain. Although Freeport and Lucaya are frequently mentioned in the same breath, newcomers should note that Freeport is a landlocked collection of hotels and shops rising from the island's center, while the better-maintained and more appealing Lucaya, about 4km (2½ miles) away, is a bustling waterfront section of hotels, shops, and restaurants clustered next to a saltwater pond on the island's southern shore.

Freeport lies midway between Grand Bahama's northern and southern shores. Bisected by some of the island's largest roads, it was originally conceived as the site of the biggest hotels. Until a few years ago, the **International Bazaar** here was one of the country's most visited. Now in a lackluster state of disrepair, it's merely a theme-oriented mall that has seen better days. Immediately adjacent is the local **straw market,** where you can buy inexpensive souvenirs and Bahamian handicrafts.

To reach **Port Lucaya** from Freeport, head east from the International Bazaar along East Sunrise Highway, and then turn south at the intersection with Seahorse Road. The intersection—actually an oversize roundabout—is marked with a prominent stone marker that says PORT LUCAYA. Less than a mile from that roundabout, you'll be in the heart of the Lucaya complex. Know in advance that the shops and restaurants on the marina side of Seahorse Road are identified as being within the **"Port Lucaya"** subdivision. Conversely, the Radisson hotels, their restaurants, and their shops, all of which are clustered on the landward side of Seahorse Road, are identified as **"Our Lucaya."**

Port Lucaya's architectural centerpiece is **Count Basie Square,** named for the great entertainer who used to have a home on the island. A short walk east or west of the square will take you to most of the hotels, rising above the narrow strip of sand that separates the sea from a saltwater pond.

Life on Grand Bahama Island doesn't get more glamorous after you leave the Lucaya area. To the west of Freeport and Lucaya, the West Sunrise Highway passes grim industrial complexes that include the Bahamas Oil Refining Company. Once you pass the built-up waterfront sprawl of Freeport's western end, you can take Queen's Highway northwest all the way to **West End,** some 45km (28 miles) from Freeport's center. Along the way you pass the not-very-picturesque wharves of **Freeport Harbour,** where cruise ships dock. Just to the east lies **Hawksbill Creek,** a nondescript village that's home to some of the local port workers.

Much less explored is Grand Bahama's isolated **East End.** Its most distant tip lies about 72km (45 miles) from the center of Freeport and is reached via the Grand Bahama Highway. Despite its name, the route is bumpy and potholed in places and, along extensive stretches of its central area, is either blocked by piles of sand, rock, and fallen trees or is under construction. For access to the East End's most distant reaches from Freeport or Lucaya, allow about 2 hours of driving time. You'll first pass the **Rand Nature Centre,** about 5km (3 miles) east of Freeport. About 11km (6¾ miles) on is **Lucayan National Park,** and 8km (5 miles) farther lies the hamlet of **Free Town;** east of that is **High Rock,** known for its Emmanuel Baptist Church. The road now becomes considerably rougher until it ends in **McLean's Town,** which celebrates Columbus Day with an annual conch-cracking contest. From here, you can take a water taxi across Runners Creek to the exclusive **Deep Water Cay Club,** which caters to serious anglers.

Note: In Freeport/Lucaya, but especially on the rest of Grand Bahama Island, you will almost never find a street number on a hotel or a store. Sometimes in the more remote places, including sparsely populated areas on Lucaya's outskirts, you won't even find street signs. In lieu of numbers, locate places by their relation to hotels, beaches, or landmarks.

GETTING AROUND
By Taxi

The government sets the taxi rates, and the cabs are metered (or should be). Metered rates are $3 for the first .3km (¼ mile) and 40¢ for each additional 1.6km (1 mile).

Extra passengers over the age of 2 pay $3 each. If there's no meter, agree on a price with the driver in advance. Typical taxi rates from the cruise dock are as follows: Xanadu Beach Hotel, $23; Port Lucaya Marketplace, $28; Flamingo Beach Resort, $27; and Viva Fortuna Beach, $34. Rates from the airport are as follows: Port Lucaya or Our Lucaya, $23; Viva Fortuna, $25; Royal Oasis, $22; and Xanadu $18.

You can call for a taxi, though most cabs wait at the big hotels or the cruise dock to pick up passengers. One major dispatcher is **Freeport Taxi Company,** Logwood Road (✆ **242/352-6666**), open 24 hours. Another is **Grand Bahama Taxi Union,** at Grand Bahama International Airport, Old Airport Road (✆ **242/352-7101**), also open 24 hours.

By Car

If you plan to confine your exploration to the center of Freeport, with its International Bazaar, and Lucaya, with its beaches, you can rely on public transportation. However, if you'd like to explore the rest of the island (perhaps to find a more secluded beach), a rental car is the way to go. Terrain here is universally flat, a fact that's appreciated by drivers trying to conserve gasoline. Try **Avis** (✆ **800/331-1212** or 242/332-7666; www.avis.com) or **Hertz** (✆ **800/654-3131** or 242/352-9250; www.hertz.com), which both maintain offices in small bungalows near Grand Bahama International Airport. From inside the terminal, an employee of either company will contact a colleague, who will direct you to the curb outside the baggage pickup point. Then someone will arrive in a company car or van to drive you to the car pickup location.

One of the best companies is **Dollar Rent-a-Car,** Old Airport Road (✆ **800/800-3665** or 242/352-9325; www.dollar.com), which rents everything from a new Kia Sportage to a VW Jetta. Rates start at $50 per day for a small car with automatic transmission and air conditioning, Mileage is unlimited, but the collision damage waiver (CDW) costs another $18 per day ($350 deductible). Remember to drive on the left, as British rules apply.

By Bus

Public bus service runs from the International Bazaar and downtown Freeport to Lucaya. The typical fare is $1.50 for adults, 50¢ for children. Check with the Grand Bahama Tourism Board (p. 116) for bus schedules; there is no number to call for information.

By Scooter

A scooter is a fun way to get around, as most of Grand Bahama is flat with well-paved roads. Scooters can be rented at most hotels or, for cruise-ship passengers, in the Freeport Harbour area. Occasionally, you'll spot stands along the roads in Freeport and Lucaya, as well as in major parking lots, charging from $45 to $65 per day. Helmets are required and provided by the outfitter.

On Foot

You can explore the center of Freeport or Lucaya on foot, but if you want to venture into the East End or West End, you'll need to rent a car, hire a taxi, or try Grand Bahama's erratic public transportation.

[FastFACTS] GRAND BAHAMA

ATMs Most banks here have ATMs that accept Visa, MasterCard, American Express, and any other bank or credit card on the Cirrus, Honor, Novus, and PLUS networks. Americans need not bother exchanging their money into Bahamian dollars because the currencies are on par, and U.S. dollars are readily accepted everywhere.

Doctors For the fastest and best service, head to **Rand Memorial Hospital** (see "Hospitals," below).

Emergencies Call ✆ **911,** or dial **0** for the operator.

Eyeglass Repair The biggest specialist in eyeglasses and contact lenses is the **Optique Shoppe,** 7 Regent Centre, downtown Freeport (✆ **242/352-9073**).

Hospitals If you need medical care, go to the government-operated, 86-bed **Rand Memorial Hospital,** East Atlantic Drive (✆ **242/352-6735,** or 352-2689 for ambulance; www.pha bahamas.org).

Laundry & Dry Cleaning Try **Jiffy Cleaners Number 3,** West Mall at Pioneer's Way (✆ **242/352-7079**), open Monday 8am to 1pm, Tuesday to Saturday 8am to 6pm.

Newspapers & Magazines The *Freeport News* is a morning paper published Monday to Saturday, except holidays. Nassau's two dailies, the *Tribune* and the *Nassau Guardian*, are also available here, as are some New York and Miami papers, especially the *Miami Herald*, usually on the date of publication. American newsmagazines, such as *Time* and *Newsweek*, are flown in on the day of publication.

Pharmacies For prescriptions and other pharmaceutical needs, go to Health Enhancing Pharmacy, 1 West Mall (✆ **242/352-7327**). Hours are Monday through Saturday from 8am to 8pm and Sunday from 8am to 3pm.

Police Dial ✆ **911.**

Post Office The main post office (✆ **242/352-9371**) is on Explorer's Way, in Freeport.

Safety Avoid walking or jogging along lonely roads. There are no particular danger zones, but stay alert: Grand Bahama is no stranger to drugs and crime.

Taxes There is no sales tax on any purchase made within The Bahamas, though there is a 12% hotel tax. Visitors leaving The Bahamas pay a $20 departure tax, a tariff that's automatically included in the price of any airline or cruise-ship ticket.

Weather Grand Bahama Island, in the north of The Bahamas, has winter temperatures varying from around 61° to 75°F (16°–24°C) daily. Summer variations range from 79°F to the high 80s (26°C to the low 30s Celsius). In Freeport/Lucaya, phone ✆ **915** for weather information.

WHERE TO STAY

Most accommodations are in the Freeport area, near the International Bazaar, or in the Lucaya area, which is closer to the beach. *Remember:* In most cases, a resort levy of 8% and a 15% service charge will be added to your final bill. Be prepared, and ask if it's already included in the price you're quoted.

Freeport
EXPENSIVE

Island Seas Resort A three-story timeshare property that rents units to non-members, this peach-colored resort opens onto a secluded beach midway between downtown Freeport and Port Lucaya. The location is convenient to both the Port

Where to Stay & Eat in Freeport/Lucaya

HOTELS ■

Bell Channel Inn Hotel **17**
Bishop's Beach Club **21**
Castaways Resort & Suites **4**
Dundee Bay Villas **8**
Flamingo Bay Hotel & Marina **20**
Island Palm Resort **2**
Island Seas Resort **10**
Ocean Reef Yacht Club & Resort **12**
Old Bahama Bay Resort & Yacht Harbour **3**
Paradise Cove Beach Resort **3**
Pelican Bay at Lucaya **15**
Radisson Grand Lucayan Beach & Golf Resort **13**
Royal Islander Hotel **4**
Royal Palm Resort & Suites **1**
Sunrise Resort & Marina **9**
Taino Beach Resort **18**
Viva Wyndham Fortuna Beach **21**

Grand Bahama International Airport

Grand Bahamian Hwy.

Settlers Way

Pioneers Way   **FREEPORT**

Santa Maria Ave.

Cadwallader Dr.

Explorers Way

Nansen Ave.

West Atlantic Drive

West Mall Drive.

East Mall Drive

Frobisher Drive

Pioneers Way East

Ellis Lightfoot Ave.

Bahamia Princess Ruby Golf Course

Adventurers Way

SUNRISE PARK

West Sunrise Hwy.

Coral Rd.

International Bazaar

Princess Casino

Poinciana St

Ranfurly Circus

Tamarind St.

Gambier St.

Bahamia Princess Emerald Golf Course

Santa Maria Ave.

Hydroflora Gardens

East Sunrise Hwy.

Pinetree Stables

E. Beach Dr.

Pinta Ave.

The Mall South

Drumfish St.

Glover St.

CARAVEL BEACH

Beachway Dr.

Tahiti St.

ROYAL BAHAMIAN ESTATES

Pinta Ave.

Lunar Blvd.

Xanadu Beach

JOHN JACK PT.

Port-of-Call St.

BAHAMAS TERRACE

Bahama Reef

WILLIAM'S TOWN

MADIOCA PT.

East Palm Beach

Silver Pt. Dr.

Northwest Providence Channel

SILVER PT.

RESTAURANTS ◆
Becky's Restaurant **7**
China Beach **13**
Geneva's **6**
Giovanni's Café **16**
Iries **13**
Luciano's **14**

Mediterranean Restaurant
& Bar ("Le Med") **14**
Outrigger's Native Restaurant/
White Wave Club **19**
Pepper Pot **11**
Pisces **16**
Prop Club **13**

Ruby Swiss European
Restaurant **5**
Sabor **15**
Willy Broadleaf **13**
Zorba's **16**

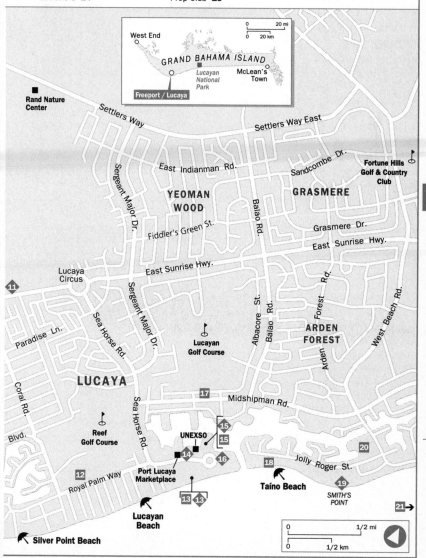

Lucaya Marketplace and the Lucaya and Reef golf courses. The resort offers its own water fun with a pool, hot tub, and waterfall—plus a tiki-hut restaurant and bar. Because the condos are individually owned, each has unique furnishings and decor. All of the one- and two-bedroom units contain a full kitchen and balcony. Although technically they're not associated with the hotel, many watersports outfitters are located right on the beach.

William's Town, Freeport, Grand Bahama, The Bahamas. www.islandseas.com. © **800/801-6884** or 242/373-1271. Fax 242/373-1275. 197 units. Year-round $219–$499 1-bedroom unit; $319–$499 2-bedroom unit. AE, DISC, MC, V. **Amenities:** Restaurant; bar; bikes; exercise room; Internet (free in lobby); outdoor pool; tennis court (lit for night play). In room: A/C, TV/DVD, kitchen.

MODERATE

Castaways Resort & Suites ★ ☺ Castaways is a modest and unassuming hotel that's almost immediately adjacent to the International Bazaar in downtown Freeport. A mix of vacationers and business travelers come here for the clean, well-maintained motel-style accommodations and the moderate prices. Pink-walled, green-shuttered rooms surround a quartet of landscaped courtyards, creating shelter from the traffic outside. It's not on the water, but a free shuttle will take you to nearby William's Town Beach. The four-story hotel is surrounded by gardens and has an indoor-outdoor garden lobby with a gift shop and kiosks selling island tours and watersports opportunities. The Flamingo Restaurant serves Bahamian and American fare daily from 7:30am to 10pm; it also has one of the island's best breakfasts. The pool area has a wide terrace and adjoining playground, plus a bar serving sandwiches and cool drinks.

E. Mall Dr., Freeport, Grand Bahama, The Bahamas. www.castaways-resort.com. © **866/410-9676** or 242/352-6682. Fax 242/352-5087. 118 units. Winter $125–$155 double, $185–$195 suite; off-season $105–$135 double, $150–$160 suite. Children 12 and under stay free in parent's room. AE, MC, V. **Amenities:** Restaurant; 2 bars; babysitting; fitness center, outdoor pool. In room: A/C, TV, DVD and VCR in some, hair dryer, Wi-Fi (free).

Royal Palm Resort & Suites ☺ Don't confuse this hotel with some of its competitors, whose names and amenities are roughly equivalent. The staff here mentioned to us that taxis often arrive with passengers booked at other properties with similar names, such as the Royal Islander, the Island Palm, and the more expensive Island Seas. This particular choice is a well-maintained, two-story pink motel that's the closest lodging to the airport. Though inland from the beach, it provides an oasis of resort-style living, with its wings wrapping around a pool. About half the rooms were renovated in 2012. Rooms are outfitted in tropical motel style: tile floors, simple furniture, and floral upholsteries. Each sleeps up to four people, making this an economical choice for families. Although it's usually a bit more expensive than either the Royal Islander or the Island Palm, its repeat clientele—about 50% of whom are here for business reasons—don't seem to mind.

E. Mall Dr. at Settlers Way, Freeport, Grand Bahama, The Bahamas. © **888/790-5264** or 242/352-3462. Fax 242/352-5759. 48 units. $75–$90 double. AE, DC, MC, V. **Amenities:** Restaurant; pool bar; children's playground; Internet (free in cafe); outdoor pool; tennis court (lit for night play). In room: A/C, TV, hair dryer, Wi-Fi (free).

INEXPENSIVE

Dundee Bay Villas ✦ These well-furnished and affordable accommodations open onto ocean or canal views, with a good beach only 100 yards away. The place has a sort of down-home feeling, providing that home for you means Florida. All of the studios and the one-, two-, and three-bedroom units are comfortably decorated in a sort of tropical motif and come with fully equipped kitchens. To save money, many guests cook some of their own meals here. The two- and three-bedroom units are sought out by families. The larger ones with a loft can sleep eight comfortably and include a step-up jetted tub in the master bathroom.

15 Dundee Bay Dr., Freeport, Grand Bahama, The Bahamas. www.dundeebayvillas.com. © **866/771-7778** or 242/352-8038. Fax 416/247-4561. 10 units. Year-round $75–$100 studio; $99–$189 1-bedroom unit; $149–$189 2-bedroom unit; $169–$219 3-bedroom unit. AE, DISC, MC, V. **Amenities:** Outdoor pool; Wi-Fi in lobby (free). *In room:* A/C, TV, kitchen.

Island Palm Resort 🏄 Set within the commercial heart of Freeport, this simple three-story motel—the less expensive sibling of the also-recommended Island Seas Resort—incorporates four buildings separated by parking lots and greenery. An easy walk to virtually everything in town and 2km (1¼ miles) from the International Bazaar, it offers good value in no-frills, eminently serviceable rooms with well-kept bathrooms. Complimentary shuttle service ferries guests to nearby William's Town Beach (also called Island Seas Beach), where you can jet-ski and snorkel at its sibling property, the Island Seas.

E. Mall Dr., Freeport, Grand Bahama, The Bahamas. www.islandseas.com © **800/790-5264** or 242/352-6648. Fax 242/352-6640. 143 units. Year-round $179–$199 1-bedroom suite; $229–$249 2-bedroom suite. Extra person $15. AE, DISC, MC, V. **Amenities:** Bar; outdoor pool; Wi-Fi (free in lobby). *In room:* A/C, TV.

Royal Islander Hotel ☺ This hotel was built during an unfortunate Disney-style period in Freeport's expansion during the early 1980s. Its improbable-looking pyramidal roofs, inspired by a trio of Mayan pyramids, were rendered somewhat less obvious in 2004 when they were covered with dark-gray metal. Hospitable rooms are arranged around a verdant courtyard that seems far removed from the busy traffic and sterile-looking landscape outside. Rooms on the street level have white-tile floors, while those upstairs have wall-to-wall carpeting. Bathrooms are on the small side. Throughout, the motif is Floridian tropical, with some pizzazz and rates that tend to be lower than the Best Western across the street. Lots of families check in here, so it's a safe environment for those with kids, who will enjoy the on-site playground. They can also take advantage of the free hourly shuttles to the more opulent Xanadu, under the same ownership, without paying that resort's higher prices. There's a snack bar and a small restaurant on the premises, but otherwise you'll have to wander a short distance, perhaps to the International Bazaar across the street, to find dining and diversions.

E. Mall Dr., Freeport, Grand Bahama, The Bahamas. www.royalislanderhotel.com. © **242/351-6000.** Fax 242/351-3546. 100 units. Year-round $82–$102 double. Children 14 and under stay free in parent's room. AE, MC, V. **Amenities:** Restaurant; snack bar; bar; children's playground; outdoor pool. *In room:* A/C, TV, Wi-Fi ($10).

Lucaya

EXPENSIVE

Pelican Bay at Lucaya ★★ Here's a hotel with more architectural charm than any other small property on Grand Bahama. It was built in 1996 (and refurbished in 2005) on a peninsula jutting into a labyrinth of inland waterways, with moored yachts on several sides. Pelican Bay evokes a Dutch seaside village with rows of whimsically trimmed town houses, each painted a different color. Its location couldn't be better, immediately adjacent to Port Lucaya Marketplace, where restaurants and entertainment spots abound. Lucayan Beach, one of the best stretches of white sand on the island, is a 5-minute walk away. The equally appealing Taíno Beach lies immediately to the east, on the opposite side of a saltwater channel with hourly ferryboat service. UNEXSO, which provides some of the best dive facilities in The Bahamas, is next door. If that's not enough, the extensive amenities of Our Lucaya Resort, a very short walk away, are also available for use. Accommodations—especially suites—are about as stylish as you'll find on Grand Bahama, rivaled only by the Radisson compound at Our Lucaya. Each has a veranda or balcony, usually with water views; floors of buffed, tinted concrete; and rustic art objects and handicrafts from all over the world.

Seahorse Rd., Port Lucaya, Grand Bahama, The Bahamas. www.pelicanbayhotel.com. © **800/852-3702** in the U.S., or 242/373-9550. Fax 242/373-9551. 183 units. Winter $185 double, $214–$229 suite; off-season $165 double, $195–$215 suite. AE, MC, V. **Amenities:** Restaurant (Sabor, p. 131); bar; babysitting; Jacuzzi; 3 outdoor pools. *In room:* A/C, TV, fridge, hair dryer, minibar (in suites), Wi-Fi ($14).

Radisson Grand Lucayan Golf and Beach Resort ★★★   This resort is one of the country's largest—and without a doubt it's the finest, most appealing, and best-accessorized property on Grand Bahama Island. The resort is set beside Lucayan Beach, one of the top white strands in The Bahamas.

The size and scale of this resort has been radically downsized since its original conception in 1998, but in its leaner, trimmed-down scope, it's easier to navigate, with a design and with accessories and style that's the most avant-garde on the island. It occupies a grand 10-story, white-sided tower (known to some locals as Breakers Cay) whose edges bend in a postmodern S-curve beside the beach. It also contains an impressive array of dining options, each with a different theme and ambience. At presstime, seven of them were open, with plans to bring online, during high season, four or five more. The most intriguing are reviewed under "Where to Eat," below. The hotel also boasts the most appealing swimming pool on Grand Bahama Island: Separated from the powder-white sands of Lucayan Beach by a trio of lap pools, each 15m (49 ft.) long and 1.2m (4 ft.) deep, with edges replicating the hotel's sinuous "S" shape. The pools culminate in a watery crescent whose infinity edge seems to merge directly into the Atlantic. The swim-up bar and hot tubs add more watery appeal.

Recent years have seen the addition of a spa, a convention center, and an upscale shopping mall. There's an increasing emphasis on golf here, thanks to the opening of the spectacular **Reef Golf Course** (p. 137). And tennis players will enjoy the innovative **Ace Tennis Center,** which features replicas of the world's best-known court surfaces—like the red clay of the French Open, the manicured grass of Wimbledon, the Rebound Ace of the Australian Open, and the DecoTurf of the U.S. Open.

Royal Palm Way, Grand Bahama, The Bahamas. www.grandlucayan.com. © **866/870-7148** in the U.S., or 242/373-1333. Fax 242/327-5968. 725 units. Year-round $159–$244 double; $259–$1,500 suite. $30 extra per day for 3rd and 4th occupants. AE, DC, DISC, MC, V. **Amenities:** 7 restaurants; 9 bars; babysitting; concierge; two 18-hole golf courses; health club and spa; room service; 4 tennis courts (lit for night play); watersports equipment/rentals; Wi-Fi (free in lobby). *In room:* A/C, TV, hair dryer, Internet (free), minibar.

MODERATE

Ocean Reef Yacht Club & Resort ★   Opening onto a marina and the water, this tropically furnished resort lies half a mile from a good beach and a 10-minute drive from Port Lucaya. It caters mainly to yachties but welcomes all vacationers to its individually owned one-, two-, and three-bedroom town houses and suites, which are rented out when the owners are away. Rental units come in various shapes and sizes, the least expensive being the narrow but comfortable efficiencies. Some units have bathrooms with Jacuzzis. Three meals a day are served at the outdoor Groupers Bar & Grill, where the namesake grouper and Bahamian lobster are specialties.

Royal Palm Way, Port Lucaya, Grand Bahama, The Bahamas. www.oryc.com. ℂ **242/373-4661.** Fax 242/373-8261. 64 units. Winter $145–$160 double, $190–$230 2-bedroom apt for 4; off-season $130–$140 double, $165–$175 2-bedroom apt for 4. MC, V. **Amenities:** Restaurant; bar; bikes; 2 outdoor pools; dive shop. *In room:* A/C, TV, kitchen or kitchenette, Wi-Fi (free).

Taíno Beach
MODERATE
Taíno Beach Resort ★ ☺ This hotel lies across a saltwater canal from the grounds of Radisson Grand Lucayan. It's also adjacent to Taíno Beach, the sister shore of the better-known Lucayan Beach. Enveloped by semitropical gardens, but not as posh as the Radisson, it dates back to 1995, when construction began on what evolved into a three-phase development. All units are in coral-or blue-painted concrete buildings and range from efficiencies, studios, and one-bedroom suites up to elaborate villas and penthouses. The rooms are spacious, well furnished, and nicely maintained. The quality, size, and amenities of your accommodations depend on how much you want to pay. Penthouses (on the fourth floor) are multilevel studios with their own deck and private pool. The hotel's hourly ferry service ($2.50 per person each way, free for children 2 and under) makes frequent trips across the canal to a pier very close to the Radisson Grand Lucayan. From there, the restaurants, shops, and bars of the Port Lucaya Marketplace are within a 10-minute walk.

Jolly Roger Dr., Taíno Beach, Lucaya, Grand Bahama, The Bahamas. www.tainobeach.com. ℂ **888/311-7945** or 242/373-4682. Fax 242/373-4421. 157 units. Year-round $150 efficiency; $200 studio (shower only); $220 penthouse for four. Children 12 and under stay free in parent's room. AE, MC, V. **Amenities:** Restaurant; bar; babysitting; outdoor pool; tennis court; watersports equipment/rentals. *In room:* A/C, TV, hair dryer, Wi-Fi (free).

INEXPENSIVE
Flamingo Bay Hotel & Marina This hotel is set back from the water, about a 5-minute walk from a highly appealing length of white sand. Built of painted concrete, with three stories, it offers midsize, unpretentious, and uncomplicated bedrooms that are furnished in a Caribbean motif. Each has a well-maintained bathroom and such extras as a microwave and toaster. From a nearby 20-slip marina, frequent ferry service ($2.50 per person each way, free for children 2 and under) takes guests across a narrow saltwater canal to a pier very close to the Radisson Grand Lucayan, which is a short walk from Port Lucaya Marketplace.

Jolly Roger Dr., Taíno Beach, Lucaya, Grand Bahama, The Bahamas. www.flamingobaymarina.com. ℂ **800/824-6623** or 242/373-5640. Fax 242/373-4421. 58 units. Year-round $90–$150 double. Children 12 and under stay free in parent's room. AE, DISC, MC, V. **Amenities:** W-Fi (free in lobby). *In room:* A/C, TV, hair dryer, kitchenette.

Elsewhere on Grand Bahama
EXPENSIVE
Old Bahama Bay Resort and Yacht Harbour ★★ One of the most dramatic real-estate developments in The Bahamas lies at this outpost on the island's extreme western tip. Built on a site that in the early 1980s was the setting for the unsuccessful Jack Tar Village, the project centers around a cluster of upscale hotel units, a state-of-the-art 72-slip marina, and a palm-flanked beach. Accommodations

ESPECIALLY FUN PLACES FOR kids

The Dolphin Experience, at the Underwater Explorer Society (UNEXSO; ✆ **800/992-3483** or 242/373-1244), a short walk from the Radisson Grand Lucayan, offers child-friendly up-front-and-close ocean and marine experiences that appeal to children, teenagers, and grown-ups. The most visible of these involves an opportunity for swimming nose-to-nose with a colony of friendly dolphins. For more information see p. 135.

Viva Wyndham Fortuna Beach This all-inclusive beachfront hotel (below), a 10-minute drive east of Port Lucaya (making it the island's most easterly resort), maintains its Kid's Club exclusively for children ages 2 to 11. It provides sports, games, and lessons throughout the day, under the supervision of trained staff members who know when to get parents involved and when to let them slip away for pursuits of their own.

are situated in nine two-story beach houses, each with four to six units. The spacious and breezy living quarters are outfitted in a colonial Caribbean style with a tropical country-club feel. Bathrooms are sheathed in marble. A pair of restaurants serve well prepared Bahamian and international dishes.

The resort encompasses much more than just hotel units. Its owners envision it as an entire village-in-the-making, relentlessly upscale and dotted with celebrity references. Building sites, some of them sold already, begin at around $300,000 each.

Bayshore Rd., West End, Grand Bahama, The Bahamas. www.oldbahamabay.com. ✆ **888/800-8959** in the U.S., or 242/350-6500. Fax 242/350-6565. 73 units. Winter $320–$455 suite, from $1,024 2-bedroom suite; off-season $245–$330 suite, $788–$1,024 2-bedroom suite. Breakfast and dinner $115 per person extra per day. AE, MC, V. **Amenities:** 2 restaurants; 2 bars; babysitting; exercise room; outdoor pool; room service; watersports equipment/rentals. *In room:* A/C, TV/DVD, CD player, CD library, hair dryer, kitchenette, Wi-Fi (free).

Viva Wyndham Fortuna Beach ★ ☺ The easternmost resort on Grand Bahama Island has some visitors arguing that the beachfront here is even better than the more extensively developed strands at Port Lucaya. (The pool, however, packs a lot less drama than those at the Radisson Grand Lucayan.) Established in 1993, this cost-conscious all-inclusive resort lies 9.5km (6 miles) east of the International Bazaar along the island's southern coast, amid an isolated landscape of casuarinas and scrubland. The sprawling 10-hectare (25-acre) compound of remote and breezy beachfront property is loaded with sports activities that are included in your room rate (as are all meals and drinks). Stylish, comfortably furnished bedrooms lie in a colorful group of two-story outbuildings; some units are timeshares that are added to the resort's rental pool when they're not occupied. Most rooms have a private balcony, and about three-quarters have ocean views; the others overlook the surrounding scrublands.

In addition to an ongoing series of all-you-can-eat buffet feasts, you'll find Italian and Asian restaurants with a la carte dining. Know in advance that if you stay here, you'll be far from Port Lucaya (though a shuttle bus brings guests to the International Bazaar in downtown Freeport twice each day). For clients who appreciate the all-inclusive format—where there's not a lot of incentive for straying very far from the property—it's a worthwhile choice. Note, however, that singles pay 40% more than the per-person double-occupancy rate.

1 Doubloon Rd. (at Churchill Dr.), Freeport, Grand Bahama, The Bahamas. www.wyndham.com. ℭ **877/999-3223** or 242/373-4000. Fax 242/373-5555. 276 units. Year-round $208–$416 double. Extra person $90. Rates are all-inclusive. AE, DC, MC, V. **Amenities:** 3 restaurants; 3 bars; babysitting; kids' club; exercise room; Jacuzzi; outdoor pool; watersports equipment/rentals; Wi-Fi ($15 in lobby). *In room:* A/C, TV, fridge, hair dryer.

MODERATE

Bell Channel Inn Hotel   Set close enough to Port Lucaya for convenient access to its restaurants and bar options, this is a sprawling, pink-sided, two-story motel-like building. Its rooms evoke an unpretentious, predictably decorated modern inn in Florida, and a somewhat run-down allegiance to fun-in-the-sun motif of Grand Bahama Island in the 1980s. Management provides a free shuttle service several times a day to the beach near the Island Seas Hotel.

Kings Rd, Grand Bahama Island, The Bahamas. www.bellchannelinn.com. ℭ **242/373-1053**. 32 units. Year-round $85 double. AE, MC, V. **Amenities:** Restaurant; bar; pool; watersports equipment/rentals. *In room:* A/C, TV, refrigerator, Wi-Fi (free).

Bishop's Beach Club   This simple inn, set within a one-story white-with-green-trim concrete building beside the beach, is one of the most visible landmarks within the otherwise very sleepy hamlet of High Rock, on the island's sparsely populated East End. One of the "resort's" best features is a wide veranda running the length of the building, a vantage point for watching the sea. Don't expect luxury—it simply isn't part of this stripped-down place's virtues. Bedrooms are reasonably large and immaculately maintained, with much use made of white tile. What you get is hands-on contact with the local community as represented by Ruben ("Bishop") Roberts, and a venue so isolated that you really will get a sense of being very very far from your traditional haunts and venues. Bonefishing expeditions can be arranged on-site.

High Rock, East End, Grand Bahamas, The Bahamas. www.bishopsresort.net. ℭ **242/353-5485**. Fax 242/353-4417. 7 units. Year-round $100 double. MC, V. **Amenities:** Restaurant; bar. *In room:* A/C, TV' no phone.

Paradise Cove Beach Resort ★ 🎁   This lies near the secluded beach of Paradise Cove, just a 15-minute drive from Freeport's International Airport, and a 20-minute drive from Grand Bahama's extreme western tip. Snorkelers, along with seekers of tranquility, will like the resort's remote location. If you're trying to avoid nightlife, and most contact with other people, this might be the retreat for you. Each cottage comes with a full kitchen and a large screened-in porch, and is built on stilts rising above the beach, where you can swim, snorkel, and kayak. Guests gather at the Red Bar for tropical drinks, a limited menu, conch burgers, and one of the island's best piña coladas.

Deadman's Reef, Grand Bahama, The Bahamas. www.deadmansreef.com. ℭ **242/349-2677**. 2 cottages. Year-round $175 1-bedroom; $225 2-bedrooms. AE, MC, V. **Amenities:** Bar; watersports equipment/rentals. *In room:* TV, kitchen.

Sunrise Resort & Marina   Set within a network of inland canals, a 15-minute drive from the shops and restaurants of Port Lucaya, this resort, built in 1991, occupies an L-shaped, two-story, coral-colored building that resembles the kind of low-slung motel you might have expected near the seacoast in Florida. Each unit has tile floors, a color scheme of turquoise and coral, and a view of the resort's 70-slip marina or of the canals that flank it on either side. About half of this resort's clientele arrive from the US mainland aboard private sail or motorcraft, which they moor at the resort's marina during their time (sometimes extended) on shore. There's a restaurant within a cone-shaped building, and a sports bar with some big-screen TVs, and the beach is within a 5-minute bicycle ride.

208 Kelly Court at Knotts Blvd, Grand Bahama, The Bahamas. www.sunriseresortandmarina.com ✆ **800/932-4959** or 242/352-6834. Fax 242/352-6835. 30 units. Winter $135 double, $210 suite; off-season $115 double, $210 suite. AE, MC, V. **Amenities:** Restaurant; sports bar; exercise room; pool; free use of bicycles; snorkeling and fishing gear; free kayaks and paddle boats. *In room:* A/C, refrigerator, hairdryer, Wi-Fi (free).

WHERE TO EAT

Foodies will find that the cuisine on Grand Bahama doesn't match the more refined fare served at dozens of places on New Providence (Nassau/Paradise Island). However, a few places here do specialize in fine dining; the others get by with rather standard food. The good news is that the dining scene is more affordable here.

Freeport

EXPENSIVE

Ruby Swiss European Restaurant ★★ CONTINENTAL   The dishes you may remember from that European vacation are served here, without losing too much flavor in crossing the Atlantic. We're talking Wiener schnitzel, veal cutlets, salads, and that retro favorite of the '50s, lobster Thermidor. Some of the best and freshest seafood is also featured here, along with affordably priced vintages. Ruby Swiss is also a worthwhile place for a snack after midnight, when you might be in the mood for a burger or Southern fried chicken. Live dinner music is sometimes featured.

Atlantic Way, off W. Sunrise Hwy. ✆ **242/352-8507.** Reservations recommended. Main courses $13–$48. AE, DISC, MC, V. Mon–Fri 11am–2am; Sat 6pm–4am.

INEXPENSIVE

Becky's Restaurant BAHAMIAN/AMERICAN   Near a busy landlocked traffic artery midway between Port Lucaya and downtown Freeport, this unpretentious yellow-and-white restaurant serves authentic Bahamian cuisine prepared in the time-tested style of the Out Islands, offering a welcome dose of down-to-earth, non-casino reality to locals and visitors who appreciate more modest lifestyles. Breakfasts, served all day, can be either all-American or Bahamian. Also popular are the minced lobster, curried mutton, fish platters, baked or curried chicken, and conch salads. Stick to the local specialties rather than the lackluster American dishes.

E. Sunrise Hwy. and E. Beach Dr. ✆ **242/352-5247.** Breakfast items $5–$12; main courses $10–$27. AE, MC, V. Daily 7am–8pm.

Geneva's BAHAMIAN/SEAFOOD   To eat where the locals eat, head for this unpretentious spot, where food is made the old-fashioned way. This restaurant is one of the best places to sample conch, which has fed and nourished Bahamians for centuries. The Monroe family will prepare it for you stewed, cracked, or fried, or as part of a savory conch chowder that makes an excellent starter. Grouper also looms large, prepared in every imaginable way. The bartender will get you in a good mood with a rum-laced Bahama Mama.

Kipling Lane and E. Mall Dr., at W. Sunrise Hwy. ✆ **242/352-5085.** Lunch sandwiches and platters $10–$15; dinner main courses $12–$28. DISC, MC, V. Daily 7am–11pm.

Pepper Pot BAHAMIAN   The Pepper Pot might be the only place on Grand Bahama that focuses exclusively on Bahamian-style takeout. It's popular all day, but it's especially mobbed on weekends after midnight, when clubbers descend to squelch their after-disco munchies. (It's the only 24-hr. eatery we know of on the island.) Don't expect glamour, as it's in a cramped, ordinary-looking building within a shopping center a 5-minute drive east of the International Bazaar. Order takeout portions of the island's best guava duff (a Bahamian dessert that resembles a jelly roll), as well as pork chops, fish dishes (usually deep-fried), chicken souse (an acquired taste), sandwiches, and an array of daily specials.

E. Sunrise Hwy. and Coral Rd. ℂ **242/373-7655.** Breakfast items $4–$8; main courses $9–$21; vegetarian plates $8–$14. No credit cards. Daily 24 hr.

Grand Lucayan Resort & Taíno Beach

EXPENSIVE

Iries ★ CARIBBEAN   Configured as a Caribbean-themed restaurant within the Radisson Grand Lucayan Resort, this restaurant shows what a team of food and beverage experts can do when they work to develop Caribbean tradition alongside modern marketing methods. The result looks like the dining room of a colonial Jamaican manor house. Decor includes replicas of pineapples (the region's traditional symbol of hospitality), Rastafarian paintings, and elaborately carved mahogany furniture similar to what might have graced the home of a 19th-century Caribbean planter. It's permeated by a sense of spaciousness and old-fashioned dignity and restraint. Menu items include cracked conch with spicy sauce and sweet potato wedges, grilled sirloin steak with cumin and thyme, blackened grouper with fire-roasted peppers and pineapple sauce, and tamarind-glazed breast of chicken. On your way in, check out the Bahamian Junkanoo costume on display—it's one of the most elaborate, outrageous, and costly examples of its kind.

In the Radisson Grand Lucayan Resort, Royal Palm Way. ℂ **242/373-1333.** www.grandlucayan. com. Reservations recommended. Main courses $17–$36. AE, MC, V. Sat–Wed noon–3pm and 6–10pm, though hours may vary based on resort occupancy.

MODERATE

China Beach ★ ASIAN FUSION   Within its own stone-and-stucco building on the seafront grounds of the Radisson Grand Lucayan, this restaurant proffers a culinary passport to the Pacific Rim. Exotic delights include the spicy cuisines of Vietnam, Thailand, Korea, Indonesia, and Malaysia. The menu changes monthly, but some dishes appear with regularity. Our favorites are a savory Hong Kong roast duckling and a zesty Thai chicken. The beef marinated in soy sauce is served with fresh spring onion, while the grouper filet appears with ginger and scallions. Other specialties include a seafood teppanyaki and stir-fried conch. The decor is particularly imaginative, with scarlet parasols doubling as chandeliers, and architecture that seems to float above one of the resort's serpentine swimming pools.

Radisson Grand Lucayan Resort, Royal Palm Way. ℂ **242/373-1333.** www.ourlucaya.com. Reservations recommended. Main courses $20–$29. AE, DC, DISC, MC, V. Tues–Sat 6–10pm, though hours may vary based on resort occupancy.

Prop Club Sports Bar and Disco AMERICAN/INTERNATIONAL   This is one of our favorite getaway spots in the Radisson Grand Lucayan Resort compound. The low-slung building is the kind of place that attracts raffish-looking crew members from charter yachts moored nearby. Despite its location on the grounds of an upscale resort, it manages to remain fun, funky, and laid-back—a bar, cafe, disco, dance hall, and pickup joint all rolled into one. The interior evokes a battered airplane hangar where mail planes might have been repaired during World War II; industrial parts such as semi-antique propellers hang from the ceiling. When the weather's right, which it is most of the time, large doors open to bring the outdoors in, and the party overflows onto the beach.

Radisson, at Our Lucaya Resort, Royal Palm Way. ☎ **242/373-1333.** www.grandlucayan.com. Reservations not necessary. Thurs–Sun 7pm–1am. Cover charge $15, free for residents of the Grand Lucaya resort.

Willy Broadleaf ★ INTERNATIONAL   Set on the ground level of the Radisson Grand Lucayan, facing one of its S-shaped swimming pools, this imaginatively decorated restaurant is centered on one of the most lavish buffet breakfasts we've ever seen in The Bahamas. The decor fits the cuisine, with various sections evoking a Mexican courtyard, a marketplace in old Cairo, the dining hall of an Indian maharajah (including tables that are cordoned off with yards of translucent fabric), and an African village. Food stations serve cold and hot breakfast foods—try the omelets, pancakes, and French toast, the best version of which is laced with coconut.

Radisson Grand Lucayan Resort, Royal Palm Way. ☎ **242/373-1333.** www. grandlucayan.com. Reservations not necessary. Breakfast buffet $15 for cold foods, $20 for both hot and cold foods; dinner buffet $34. Sunday brunch buffet $23. AE, DC, DISC, MC, V. Mon–Sat 6:30–11am and 5–10pm. Sunday brunch buffet noon–4pm.

Port Lucaya

EXPENSIVE

Luciano's ★ FRENCH/CONTINENTAL   With its tables usually occupied by local government officials and dealmakers, Luciano's is the *grande dame* of the area's restaurants. Classy and elegant, it's the only place in Port Lucaya offering foie gras, and oysters Rockefeller, all served with a flourish by a formally dressed waitstaff, who, fortunately, have a definite sense of charm and humor. Inside, you'll find a bar and elegantly set tables; additional seating on a breezy upstairs veranda overlooks the marina. For a good opener, opt for the lightly smoked salmon, seafood crepe, or snails in garlic butter. Fresh fish and shellfish are delicately prepared, allowing natural flavor to shine through without heavy sauces. Good examples include broiled Bahamian lobster tail and local grouper topped with toasted almonds and a lemon butter sauce. Steak Diane is one of Luciano's classics, along with a delectable veal medallion sautéed with shrimp and chunks of lobster.

Port Lucaya Marketplace. ☎ **242/373-9100.** www.thebahamasguide.com/lucianos. Reservations required in winter. Main courses $29–$45. AE, MC, V. Daily 5:30–9:45pm (last order).

MODERATE

Giovanni's Cafe ★ ITALIAN/SEAFOOD   Tucked into one of the pedestrian thoroughfares of Port Lucaya Marketplace, this cream-colored clapboard house contains a charming 38-seat Italian trattoria. The chefs serve Italian-influenced preparations of local seafood, highlighted by seafood pasta and a lobster special. Giovanni stamps each dish with his Italian verve and flavor, whether it be Bahamian conch, local seafood, or scampi. Choices showing off his precision and rock-solid technique include sirloin steak with fresh mushrooms, shrimp scampi, and fattening but extremely good spaghetti carbonara.

Port Lucaya Marketplace. ☎ **242/373-9107.** Reservations recommended. Main courses $16–$38. AE, MC, V. Mon–Sat 4–10pm; Sun 5–10pm.

La Dolce Vita ★ ITALIAN   This small, upscale Italian trattoria has modern décor, traditional Italian food, and since 2011 a new location near the Freeport Harbour. Enjoy freshly made pastas on a patio overlooking the marina or in the 44-seat dining room. Start with portobello mushrooms with fresh mozzarella, tomatoes, and a vinaigrette, or perhaps carpaccio with arugula and spices. Homemade ravioli has fillings such as cheese, lobster, or spinach. There's also an excellent squid-ink risotto, a roast pork tenderloin, and a crisp, aromatic rack of lamb.

Freeport Harbour, in the Pier One Building. © **242/373-8450.** Reservations recommended. Main courses $17–$32. AE, MC, V. Daily 5–11pm. Closed Sept.

Mediterranean Restaurant & Bar ("Le Med") ★ 🍴 FRENCH/GREEK/ BAHAMIAN   This is a simpler and more cost-effective version of Luciano's (p. 130), which is under the same management. The decor consists of a hardworking, almost indestructible combination of sand-colored floor tiles and refrigerator cases loaded with pastries and salads. Devoid of linen, the bare tables look like they belong in a coffee shop. Don't let this simplicity fool you: The place serves well-flavored, surprisingly sophisticated food that has attracted its share of celebrities. It's crowded in the morning, when omelets (including a feta-and-spinach Greek version), eggs and bacon, and Bahamian stewed fish and steamed conch are crowd-pleasers. Lunch and dinner feature assorted Greek- and Turkish-style mezes and Iberian-influenced tapas that include marinated octopus and grilled calamari. Crepes come in both sweet and savory varieties. Other tempters include a seafood combo piled high with lobster, shrimp, conch, fish, and mussels; *shashlik* (marinated kabobs redolent with herbs); and braised lamb shank cooked in red wine.

Port Lucaya Marketplace. © **242/374-2804.** Breakfast items $5–$13; crepes $9–$12; main courses $13–$28. AE, DC, MC, V. Daily 8am–10pm.

Pisces ★ SEAFOOD/PIZZA/INTERNATIONAL   This ranks high among our favorites in the Port Lucaya Marketplace—and we're seconded by the locals and sailors who pack it every weekend. The place is outfitted with a quirky mixture of nautical accessories and dark-varnished wood, with a prominent bar where more gossip is exchanged the later it gets. Tabletops contain laminated seashells, fake gold coins, and sand. The charming all-Bahamian staff serves more than 20 different varieties of pizzas, including a version with conch, lobster, shrimp, and chicken, as well as one with Alfredo sauce. Dinners are more elaborate, with a choice of curries of all kinds, fish, shellfish, and several pastas.

Port Lucaya Marketplace. © **242/373-5192.** www.the-bahamas-restaurants.com/pisces. Reservations recommended. Pizzas $13–$30; main courses $10–$37. AE, DISC, MC, V. Mon–Sat 5pm–2am.

Sabor SEAFOOD   Located in the garden of the Pelican Bay hotel, this restaurant opens onto a view of a swimming pool and a panoramic sweep over the yachts in Port Lucaya Marina. Diners peruse the menu as exotic, usually Latino, music fills the night air. This has become a favorite watering hole of local yachties, who sample such appetizers as Cajun shrimp, an array of flatbreads layered with a cheese blend and accompaniments such as slow-roasted pork, herbed chicken, or perhaps a salad of pear, blue cheese, and greens mixed with a sweet nut vinaigrette. If you're here for lunch, Sabor has the best burger menu in town, including one flavored with Cajun spices. The fresh-fish dishes are listed on an oft-changing blackboard, and might include sautéed hog snapper in herb tomato sauce, and a small selection of steaks.

Sunday brunch from noon to 2pm is an event here, featuring three varieties of eggs Benedict.

Pelican Bay at Lucaya, Seahorse Rd., Port Lucaya. (C) **242/373-5588.** www.sabor-bahamas.com. Reservations recommended for dinner. Burgers $13–$15; main courses $16–$29. MC, V. Daily 11:30am–10pm.

INEXPENSIVE

Outrigger's Native Restaurant/White Wave Club BAHAMIAN   Cement-sided and simple with a large deck extending out toward the sea, this restaurant was here long before the Port Lucaya Marketplace, which lies 4 blocks away. It's the domain of Gretchen Wilson, whose kitchens produce a rotating series of lip-smacking dishes such as lobster tails, minced lobster, steamed or cracked conch, pork chops, chicken, fish, and shrimp, usually served with peas 'n' rice and macaroni. Every Wednesday from 5pm to 2am, **Outrigger's Famous Wednesday Night Fish Fry** draws as many as 1,000 diners who line up for platters of fried or steamed fish ($10–$17). A DJ and dancers provide entertainment. Almost as well attended are the Tuesday and Thursday **Bonfire Nights,** when all-you-can-eat barbecue dinners go for $30 per person. You can order drinks at the restaurant, but you might consider stepping into the nearby ramshackle bar called the **White Wave Club,** which serves only drinks. *Note:* If you make reservations for a Bonfire Night through your hotel, you may pay an extra $20.

Smith's Point. (C) **242/373-4811.** Reservations not required. Main courses $10–$16. No credit cards. Sat–Thurs noon–8pm.

Zorba's ⬩ BAHAMIAN/GREEK   Zorba provides some of the best food value at Port Lucaya Marketplace. A narrow veranda overlooks a relatively uninteresting pedestrian alleyway outside, and the blue-and-white Formica-clad interior might remind you of a diner. A TV blasts a Greek-language news broadcast. Big photos of Alan Bates and Anthony Quinn (playing Zorba, get it?) dancing on a beach add a touch of nostalgia for *ouzo* and *retsina.* The cuisine is a quirky mixture of Greek and Bahamian, and if you don't remember exactly what *taramosalata* is, the good-looking Bahamian staff will rattle off the ingredients like Peloponnesian pros. First thing in the morning, you'll see locals standing in line for the Bahamian breakfasts, which include chicken souse, corned beef and grits, and an array of pancakes, waffles, and omelets. Lunch could be a fat gyro, burger, or souvlaki. Dinner can begin with a Greek salad and then move on to moussaka, grilled chicken on a bed of spinach, or any of several pasta dishes. End with baklava, those honey and nut-studded pastries, for a sweet finish. We won't pretend the food here is a substitute for a trip to the Greek isles, but it's satisfying and filling.

Port Lucaya Marketplace. (C) **242/373-6137.** Main courses lunch $7–$15; dinner $12–$29. AE, DISC, MC, V. Daily 7am–10:30pm.

The East End

Bishop's Beach Club BAHAMIAN   If you're heading to the East End to visit Lucayan National Park (p. 139), you might want to make this your luncheon stopover. After you've explored the park, you can drive east for about 6 miles to High Rock. To go to it, just continue east along Queens Highway, the major boulevard. Locals, expats, fishermen, and visitors alike patronize this popular joint, which is known as an authentic eatery serving local recipes based on time-tested favorites.

You can visit for lunch and then hang out to get in some time on the nearby beach. Cracked conch is the chef's specialty and it's a savory choice, though often a bit rubbery. If you're not a conch aficionado, there are other choices, especially barbecued ribs and broiled Bahamian lobster. Peas 'n' rice accompany most dishes. If you're arriving in the East End in the morning, consider a breakfast here—nothing special, just ham (or bacon) and eggs. If you're using a credit card, a $30 minimum is needed.

High Rock, Queens Hwy. © **242/353-5485.** Reservations not needed. Breakfast from $6; main courses $6–$15. MC, V. Daily 9am–7pm.

The West End

Pier One AMERICAN/BAHAMIAN/SEAFOOD   This is a favorite restaurant of visitors because it's close to the cruise-ship dock, and it's also an ideal place to sample some fresh Bahamian seafood. Guests from all over the world choose between picnic tables set out on the veranda, or else they dine inside in a large room decorated with nautical paraphernalia. The owner presents shark feedings at 7, 8, and 9pm, when scraps and meat and fish carcasses are thrown into waters which roil, chillingly, with a school of hungry carnivores. The house specialty is actually baby shark, which is most often served smoked. You can also order it sautéed with garlic; or else stuffed with cheese and fresh crab. A fresh fish of the day, perhaps grouper or snapper, is also featured. For the non-seafood eater, there are juicy steaks and poultry dishes such as chicken curry.

Freeport Harbour. © **242/352-6674.** Reservations not needed. Main courses $17–$26. AE, MC, V. Mon–Sat 11am–10pm; Sun 4–10pm.

BEACHES & OUTDOOR PURSUITS

Hitting the Beach

Grand Bahama Island has enough beaches for everyone. The best ones open onto Northwest Providence Channel at Freeport and sweep eastward for some 97km (60 miles) to encompass Xanadu Beach, Lucayan Beach, Taíno Beach, and others, eventually ending at such remote eastern outposts as Rocky Creek and McLean's Town. Once you leave the Freeport/Lucaya area, you can virtually have your pick of white sandy beaches all the way. When you get past the resorts, you'll see a series of

A Secluded Beach Hideaway

More and more visitors are discovering the secluded beach of **Paradise Cove,** at Deadman's Reef (© **242/349-2677**), just a 15-minute drive from Freeport's Grand Bahama International Airport. This has become an all-around recreation center with snorkeling, swimming, ocean kayaking, fishing, beach bonfires, and much more. The on-site Red Bar is the social center, renting underwater cameras and other items needed for the beach, as well as quenching your thirst with Bahama Mamas and serving food such as conch burgers or lobster with pasta salad.

Once you head east from Port Lucaya and Taíno, you'll discover so many splendid beaches that you'll lose count. Though these beaches do have names—directly east of Taíno is **Churchill's Beach,** followed by **Smith's Point, Fortune Beach,** and **Barbary Beach**—you'll never really know what beach you're on (unless you ask a local) because they're unmarked. If you like seclusion and don't mind the lack of facilities, you'll find a string of local beauties. Fortune Beach is a special gem because of its gorgeous waters and white sands.

secluded beaches used mainly by locals. If you like people, a lot of organized watersports, and easy access to hotel bars and rest rooms, stick to Xanadu, Taíno, and Lucayan beaches.

Xanadu Beach ★★ is one of our favorites, immediately south of Freeport and the site of the famed Xanadu Beach Resort. The 1.6km-long (1-mile) beach may be crowded in winter, but that's because of those gorgeous soft white sands, which open onto tranquil waters. The beach is set against a backdrop of coconut palms and Australian pines. You can hook up here with an assortment of watersports, including snorkeling, boating, jet-skiing, and parasailing.

Immediately east of Xanadu is little **Silver Point Beach,** site of a timeshare complex whose guests ride the waves on water bikes and play volleyball. You'll see horseback riders from Pinetree Stables (p. 137) galloping along the sands here.

Despite the allure of other beaches on Grand Bahama, most visitors go to **Lucayan Beach,** right off Royal Palm Way and immediately east of Silver Point Beach. This is one of the best strands in The Bahamas, with long stretches of white sand. In the vicinity of the Radisson hotels, you'll also encounter a worthy scattering of beach bars. At any of the resorts along this beach, you can hook up with an array of watersports or get a frosty drink from a hotel bar. It's definitely not for those seeking seclusion, but it is a fun beach-party scene.

Immediately to the east of Lucayan Beach, and separated from it by a saltwater canal, **Taíno Beach** is a family favorite and a good place for watersports. This, too, is a fine wide beach of white sands, opening onto usually tranquil waters.

Another choice, not too far east, is **Gold Rock Beach,** a favorite picnic spot for weekending locals; you'll usually have it to yourself on weekdays. A 19km (12-mile) drive from Lucaya, it's at the doorstep of **Lucayan National Park** (p. 139), a 16-hectare (40-acre) park filled with some of the island's longest, widest, and most fabulous secluded beaches.

Biking

A guided bike trip is an ideal way to see parts of Grand Bahama that most visitors miss. You'll start at **Barbary Beach** and pedal a mountain bike along the southern coast parallel to the sands. After stopping for a snack, lunch, and a dip, you'll finally reach **Lucayan National Park,** some 19km (12 miles) away. You can explore the cave in which the natives, centuries before the coming of Columbus, buried their dead. Crabs here occasionally come up through holes in the ground carrying bits of bowls once used by the Lucayans. **Grand Bahama Nature Tours,** also known as Kayak Nature Tours (✆ **866/440-4542** or 242/373-2485; www.grandbahamanaturetours.com), runs these bike trips and transports you home to your hotel by van so you don't exhaust yourself in the heat while cycling back. Other tour options give you more time kayaking or snorkeling. All excursions last 5 to 6 hours and cost $79 for adults, $40 for children 11 and under. Rates include all equipment, sustenance, and round-trip transportation from your hotel.

Boat Cruises

Ocean Wonder, Port Lucaya Dock (© **242/373-5880;** www.bahamasvacation guide.com/reeftours), run by Reef Tours, is a gargantuan 18m (59-ft.) Defender glass-bottom boat. Any tour agent can arrange for you to board this vessel. You'll get a panoramic view of the beautiful underwater life off the coast of Grand Bahama. Cruises depart from Port Lucaya behind the straw market on the bay side at 9:30am, 11:15am, 1:15pm, and 3:15pm, except Friday, when only the earlier two tours are offered. The excursion lasts 1½ hours and costs $30 for adults and $18 for children 6 to 12. During high season in midwinter, make reservations a day or two in advance, as the boat does fill up quickly.

The Dolphin Experience

A pod of bottle-nosed dolphins is involved in a unique dolphin-human familiarization program at the **Dolphin Experience,** located at Underwater Explorer Society (UNEXSO), next to Port Lucaya, opposite the entrance to the Radisson Grand Lucayan (© **800/992-DIVE** [3483] or 242/373-1244; www.unexso.com). This close-encounter program allows participants to observe these intelligent, friendly animals and hear a talk by a member of the animal-care staff. This is the world's largest dolphin facility, so conditions aren't cramped. In addition, the dolphins can swim out to sea, passing through an underwater gate that prevents their natural predators from entering the lagoon; the dolphins later return of their own free will to their protected marine habitat.

Unexso offers three different opportunities for up-close-and-personal encounters with dolphins. Each is inaugurated after a 25-minute ferryboat ride from Port Lucaya, to a spot in the ocean that the dolphin colony (at press time there were 14 members) identifies as its home. Participation in any of the dolphin experiences requires a 20-minute waterborne transit from Unexso to a point off the south shore of Grand Bahama Island. It's recommended that participants in any of the dolphin experiences at Unexso allocate about 3 hours for time which will incorporate transit to and from the dolphin colony, and perhaps some time spent at the organization's burger-and-brew-style restaurant, the Dive-In Pool Bar and Grill, open daily from 8am to 8pm.

Least expensive of these options is the **Dolphin Encounter,** priced at $169 per person. After an introductory lecture, you'll step onto a shallow wading platform to interact with the dolphins. Educational and fun, it's an adventure that's suitable for all ages, and the one we especially recommend for any family with children or members whose swimming skills might not be strong. If you'd rather observe than swim, it's priced at $82 for adults and $50 for kids 4 to 7; children 3 and younger participate free. If you like to document the unusual experience, bring your camera. **Dolphin Encounters** are scheduled three times a day, at 9am, 11am, and 2pm.

Dolphin Swims cost more ($199 per person), but offer a longer direct exposure to the dolphins, usually with participants limited to twelve, with no more than six swimmers in the water with the dolphins at a time. Unexso asks that participants have strong, or at least reasonable, swimming abilities during in-water encounters that usually last around 20 minutes. (If the staff isn't sure of your swimming abilities, they'll ask you wear a flotation vest. They also limit participants not by age, but by height, opting not to include anyone under 4 feet 7" in height.) "Observers," meaning any who opt to remain dry, on deck, and for whatever reason, out of the water, pay $82 per person for either of the dolphin experiences described above. Dolphin Swims in the open ocean are scheduled for departure every Sunday to Friday at 9am; swims in the sheltered lagoon, if business warrants, are scheduled daily at 9am, 11am, and 2pm.

Most expensive of all, and strictly limited only to qualified and registered scuba divers, are **Dolphin Dives,** a 3-hour, one-tank dive that departs every Monday, Wednesday, and Saturday at 9am, if reservations warrant it. Priced at $219 per participant (maximum of six participants), it allows humans to submerge themselves amid a colony of dolphins, who always end up as the mammal with the superior swimming skills. Although Unexso provides the tanks for these dives, all other dive equipment must either be provided by the participant or rented on-site.

Swimming with dolphins has its supporters as well as its highly vocal critics. For insight into the various points of view surrounding this issue, visit the Whale and Dolphin Conservation Society's website at www.wdcs-na.org. For more information about responsible travel in general, check out www.ecotourism.org.

Fishing

In the waters off Grand Bahama, you can fish for barracuda, snapper, grouper, yellowtail, wahoo, and kingfish, along with other denizens of the deep.

Reef Tours, Port Lucaya Dock (© **242/373-5880** or 373-5891; www.bahamas vacationguide.com/reeftours), offers one of the least expensive ways to go deep-sea fishing around Grand Bahama. Adults pay $130 if they fish, $60 if they go along only to watch. Four to six people can charter the entire 13m (43-ft.) craft for $750 per half-day or $1,350 per whole day. The 9.6m (31-ft.) boat can be chartered for $480 per half-day or $850 per full day. Departures for the 4-hour half-day excursions are daily at 8:30am and 1pm, while the 8-hour full-day excursions leave daily at 8:30am. Bait, tackle, and ice are included in the cost.

Golf

Since two of the island's older courses, the Ruby and the Emerald, closed after the hurricane damage of the early millennium, Grand Bahama is not as rich in golf courses as it used to be. But golf on the island recently experienced a resurgence, thanks to the improvements to the courses described below. They're open to the public year-round; their pro shops can rent you clubs.

Fortune Hills Golf & Country Club, Richmond Park, Lucaya (© **242/373-2222**), was originally intended to be an 18-hole course, but the back 9 were never completed. You can replay the front 9 for 18 holes and a total of 6,324m (6,916 yd.) from the blue tees. Par is 72. Greens fees are $50 for 9 holes, $64 for 18; carts are included. Club rental costs $20 for 18 holes, $16 for 9 holes.

The island's best kept and most manicured course is **Lucayan Golf Course,** Lucayan Beach, at the Radisson Lucayan Grand (© **242/373-1333**). Made over after 2004's Hurricane Jeanne, this beautiful course is a traditional golf layout with rows of pine trees separating the fairways. Greens are fast, with a couple of par 5s more than 457m (500 yd.) long, totaling 6,240m (6,824 yd.) from the blue tees and 5,933m (6,488 yd.) from the whites. Par is 72.

THE ULTIMATE IN relaxation

The ideal place to relieve the stresses of everyday life can be found at the Radisson Grand Lucayan's **Senses Spa,** boasting an exercise facility with health checks, personal trainers, and yoga classes. A cafe serves fresh, natural food and elixirs. During one of the signature treatments, the Total Senses Massage, two massage therapists work in sync to relieve your tension. Throughout the Salt Glo body polish treatment, a therapist buffs away dead skin cells and polishes your body with natural, locally derived elements. Note that residents of the Radisson Grand Lucayan can use the health and exercise facilities without charge, but spa, health, massage, and beauty treatments must be scheduled in advance and require additional payment.

Its sibling golf course, with an entirely separate clubhouse and staff, is the slightly older **Reef Golf Course ★★**, Royal Palm Way, near the Radisson Lucayan Grand (✆ **242/373-1333**). Designed by Robert Trent Jones, Jr., who called it "a bit like a Scottish course but a lot warmer," the course boasts 6,328m (6,920 yd.) of links-style playing grounds. It features a wide-open layout without rows of trees to separate its fairways and lots of water traps—you'll find water on 13 of the 18 holes and various types of long grass swaying in the trade winds. Play requires patience and precise shot-making to avoid the numerous lakes.

At either the Lucayan or Reef courses, guests at the Radisson hotels, with which the courses are associated, pay between $75 and $120, depending on the time of day, for 18 holes. The 9-hole special goes for $55. Nonguests are charged between $85 and $130 for 18 holes, $65 for 9 holes. Rates include use of an electric-powered golf cart.

Horseback Riding

Pinetree Stables, North Beachway Drive, Freeport (✆ **242/373-3600** or 305/433-4809; www.pinetree-stables.com), has the country's best and—with a boarded inventory of more than 50 horses—biggest riding stables, superior to rivals on New Providence Island (Nassau). Pinetree offers trail rides to the beach Tuesday through Sunday year-round at 9 and 11:30am. The cost is $85 per person for a 2-hour trail ride. Children 8 and under are not allowed. The maximum weight limit for riders is 91kg (200 lb.).

Sea Kayaking

To explore the waters off the island's north shore, call **Grand Bahama Nature Tours** (✆ **866/440-4542** or 242/373-2485; www.grandbahamanaturetours.com) and go on a 6-hour kayak excursion through the mangroves, where you can see wildlife as you paddle along. The cost is $89 for adults and $45 for children 11 and under, with lunch included. Double kayaks are used on these jaunts, and children must be at least 3 years old. For the same price, you can take half-day kayak and snorkeling tour, an experience which includes a 30-minute kayak trip to an offshore island, with lots of snorkeling included along with lunch. Call ahead to book reservations for either of these tours. A van will pick you up at your hotel between 9 and 10am and deliver you back at the end of the tour, usually sometime between 3 and 4pm. A popular variation on this tour, which operates during the same hours and at the same prices, includes more time devoted to snorkeling above a series of shallow offshore reefs and slightly less time allocated to kayaking.

Snorkeling & Scuba Diving

Though there's fine snorkeling along the shore, you should book a snorkeling cruise aboard one of the catamarans to see the most stunning reefs. **Reef Tours** (© 242/373-5880; www.bahamasvacationguide.com/reeftours) offers highly recommended snorkeling tours. Lasting just under 2 hours each, they depart from Port Lucaya thrice daily (10am, 12:30pm, and 2:30pm). Tours are priced at $35 for adults and $18 for children 6 to 12, with all equipment included. Another option is a 3-hour sail-and-snorkel-tour that departs daily at 9:30am and 1:30pm; it's priced at $45 for adults and $25 for children 6 to 12.

Serious divers are attracted to Grand Bahama sites like the **Wall,** the **Caves** (one of the most interesting of which is **Ben's Cavern**), **Treasure Reef,** and the most evocative of all, **Theo's Wreck ★★**, a freighter that was deliberately sunk off Freeport to attract marine life. Today it teems with everything from horse-eyed jacks to moray eels. Other top locales include **Spit City, Ben Blue Hole, Pygmy Caves, Gold Rock, Silver Point Reef,** and the **Rose Garden.**

One of the premier dive outfitters in the Caribbean, **Underwater Explorer Society (UNEXSO) ★★★** (© 800/992-DIVE [3483] or 242/373-1244; www.unexso.com) offers seven dive trips daily, including reef trips, shark dives, wreck dives, and night dives. Divers can even meet dolphins in the open ocean here—a rare experience offered by very few facilities in the world (see "The Dolphin Experience," p. 135).

UNEXSO also has a popular 3-hour learn-to-dive course, the **Mini-B Pool and Reef Adventure,** offered daily. Over the outfitter's 30-year history, more than 50,000 people have successfully completed either this course or its similar predecessors. For $109, students learn the basics in UNEXSO's training pools and dive the beautiful shallow reef with an instructor.

Tennis

The island's best tennis facilities are part of the **Ace Tennis Center,** at the Radisson Grand Lucayan (© 242/350-5294), where four tennis courts feature different playing surfaces. They include a grass court ($100 per hour) that resembles that of Wimbledon, a clay surface ($50 per hour) like that of the French Open, a Rebound Ace rubber surface that's equivalent to the norm at the Australian Open ($35 per hour), and a hard DecoTurf ($25 per hour) that's similar to the surface at the U.S. Open. Advance reservations are necessary, and there is no discount of any kind for resort guests. A resident pro offers individual 1-hour tennis lessons for $90 per person, or $130 for a couple.

Watersports in General

Ocean Motion Watersports Ltd., Sea Horse Lane, Lucayan Beach (© 242/374-2425; www.oceanmotionbahamas.com), is one of the island's largest watersports companies. It offers a wide variety of activities daily from 9am to 5pm, weather permitting, including snorkeling, parasailing, Hobie Cats, banana boating, water-skiing, jet skis, windsurfing, and other activities. **Parasailing,** for example, costs $70 per person for 5 to 7 minutes in the air. **Snorkeling trips** cost $35 for adults, $18 for kids 11 and under, for 1½ hours. **Water-skiing** goes for $40 per 3.2km (2-mile) pull, $60 for a 30-minute lesson. **Hobie Cats** are $50 for the 4.2m (14 ft.), $75 for the 4.8m (16 ft.), and $30 for a lesson. **Windsurfing** costs $30 per hour, $100 for a 2-hour lesson. **Kayaking** costs $20 for a single kayak, $25 for a double. The **water trampoline** is $20 for a full day, $10 for a half-day. **Banana boating** goes for $15 per person for a 3.2km (2-mile) ride along a white-sand beach. Call for reservations, especially for windsurfing.

A worthy competitor is **Lucaya Watersports,** Taíno Beach (© 242/373-6375), which also offers options for fun in the surf, including **WaveRunners,** which cost $70 per 30 minutes; **double kayaks,** which are $20 per hour for two passengers; and **paddle boats,** which hold four people and go for $20 per hour. The **sunset cruises**—a 2-hour sailboat ride offered every Wednesday between 5 and 7pm—are especially popular and cost $50 per person. Snorkeling tours cost $40 for adults, and $25 for children under 12, and a 90-minute ride on a glass-bottom boat with underwater panoramas costs $35 for adults and $12 for children under 12.

SEEING THE SIGHTS

Several informative tours of Grand Bahama Island are available. One reliable company is **H. Forbes Charter Services Ltd.,** West Sunrise Highway, Freeport (© 242/352-9311; www.forbescharter.com). From its headquarters in the International Bazaar, this company operates half- and full-day bus tours. The most popular option is the half-day Super Combination Tour, priced at $35 per adult and $25 per child age 5 to 12. It includes drive-through tours of residential areas and the island's commercial center, stops at the island's deep-water harbor, shopping, and a visit to a wholesale liquor store. Departures are Monday through Saturday at 9am and 1pm; the tour lasts 3½ hours. Full-day tours, conducted whenever business warrants, last from 9am to 3:30pm. In addition to everything included in the half-day tours, they bring participants in a bus or van, with guided commentary, all the way to the Caves, near Grand Bahama Island's easternmost tip, for $45 per adult, $30 per child.

See also the "Beaches & Outdoor Pursuits" section for details on UNEXSO's Dolphin Experience (p. 135), as well as the "Shopping" section, below, for descriptions of the International Bazaar and the Port Lucaya Marketplace.

Garden of the Groves ★★★ ☺ This 5-hectare (12-acre) botanical garden, filled with waterfalls, ponds, and fountains, is a place of enchantment. Destroyed by the hurricanes of 2004 and 2005, it has been rebuilt by the Grand Bahama Port Authority. Today it is filled with some 10,000 species of plants, including orchids. The park is also a birdwatcher's paradise. In addition to the flora and fauna, there is a petting zoo that's home to pot-belly pigs and pygmy goats. Other features include a children's playground and an arts and crafts village. Nature trails cut through the grounds, where you can see a hanging garden, a bougainvillea walk, a banana plantation, and even a tilapia pond. Guides are available to take you on tours, and food and drink are sold at an on-site cafe.

Midshipman Rd. and Magellan Dr., 11km (7 miles) east of International Bazaar. © **242/374-7778.** www.thegardenofthegroves.com. Admission $15 adults, $10 children 4–12. Daily 9am–5pm.

Lucayan National Park This 16-hectare (40-acre) park is filled with mangrove, pine, and palm trees. It also contains one of the island's loveliest, most secluded beaches—a long, wide, dune-covered stretch reached by following a wooden pathway that winds through the trees. Bring snorkeling gear with which to glimpse the colorful creatures living beneath the turquoise waters of the offshore coral reef. As you wander through the park, you'll cross Gold Rock Creek, fed by a spring from what is said to be the world's largest underground freshwater cavern system. There are 36,000 entrances to the caves, some only a few feet deep. You can explore two of the caves because they became exposed when a portion of ground collapsed. The pools in them (accessible via spiral wooden steps) are composed of 2m (6½ ft.) of fresh water atop a heavier layer of saltwater.

The freshwater springs once lured native Lucayans, those Arawak-connected tribes who lived on the island and depended on fishing for their livelihood. They would come inland to get fresh water for their habitats on the beach. Lucayan bones and artifacts, such as pottery, have been found in the caves, as well as on the beaches.

Settlers Way, eastern end of E. Sunrise Hwy. ℂ **242/352-5438.** Admission $3; tickets available only at the Rand Nature Centre (see below). Daily 9am–5pm. Drive east along Midshipman Rd., passing Sharp Rock Point and Gold Rock.

Rand Nature Centre This 40-hectare (99-acre) pineland sanctuary, located 3km (1¾ miles) east of Freeport's center, is the regional headquarters of The Bahamas National Trust, a nonprofit conservation organization. Nature trails highlight native flora, including bush medicine plants, and provide ample opportunities for seeing the wild birds that abound here. As you stroll, keep your eyes peeled for the lush blooms of tropical orchids or the brilliant flash of green and red feathers in the trees. You can join a bird-watching tour on the first Saturday of every month at 8am. Other highlights include native animal displays, an education center, and a gift shop selling nature books and souvenirs.

E. Settlers Way. ℂ **242/352-5438.** Admission $5 adults, $3 children 5–12. Mon–Fri 9am–5pm.

SHOPPING

Shopping hours in Freeport/Lucaya are generally Monday through Saturday from 9am to 6pm. However, in the International Bazaar, hours vary widely, with shops usually closing a bit earlier in the day.

Port Lucaya Marketplace

Port Lucaya and its Marketplace took precedence over the International Bazaar (described below) in the mid-1990s, when it became clear that the future of merchandising on Grand Bahama had shifted. Today, Port Lucaya Marketplace on Seahorse Road rocks and rolls with a spankingly well-maintained facility set within a shopping, dining, and marina complex on 2.4 hectares (6 acres) of low-lying seafront land. Regular free entertainment, such as steel-drum bands and strolling musicians, as well as recorded music that plays throughout the evening hours, adds to a festival atmosphere.

The complex emulates the 19th-century clapboard-sided construction style of the Old Bahamas, all within a short walk of the island's most desirable hotel accommodations, including the Radisson Grand Lucayan. The development arose on the site of a former Bahamian straw market. Today, in addition to dozens of restaurants and upscale shops, it incorporates rows of brightly painted huts from which local merchants sell handicrafts and souvenirs.

The waterfront location is a distinct advantage. Lots of the business that fuels this place derives from the expensive yachts and motor craft that tie up at the marina here. Most of those watercraft are owned by Floridians. You might get the sense that many of them have just arrived from the U.S. mainland, disgorging their passengers out onto the docks here.

Below are the most recommended shops at Port Lucaya Marketplace:

Animale Trendy fashionistas would define this as a hot boutique featuring clingy, sophisticated tropical looks. Come here for long cotton dresses that make the female form look more provocative than usual, accompanied by the kind of accessories—oversized straw hats, chunky necklaces, animal-print scarves—that emphasize the feline, the *animale,* and perhaps, the seductress. ✆ **242/374-2066.**

Bandolera The staff can be rather haughty here, but despite its drawbacks, the store carries a collection of chic women's clothing that's many cuts above the T-shirts and tank tops that are the norm for many of its competitors. ✆ **242/373-7691.**

Colombian Emeralds This branch of the world's foremost emerald jeweler offers a wide array of precious gemstone jewelry and one of the island's best watch collections. Careful shoppers can get significant savings over U.S. prices. The outlet offers certified appraisals and free 90-day insurance. ✆ **242/373-8400.**

Flovin Gallery II This branch of the gallery located in the International Bazaar sells a collection of oil paintings by Bahamian and international artists, along with lithographs and posters. In its limited field, it's the best in the business. Also for sale here are a number of gift items, such as handmade Bahamian dolls, decorated corals, and Christmas ornaments. ✆ **242/373-8388.**

UNEXSO Dive Shop The nation's premier dive shop sells everything related to the water—swimsuits, wet suits, underwater cameras, video equipment, shades, hats, souvenirs, and state-of-the-art dive equipment. ✆ **800/992-3483** or 242/373-1244.

International Bazaar

The older and less glamorous of Grand Bahama Island's two main shopping venues, the International Bazaar has steadily declined since the collapse of the mega-resort Crowne Plaza, immediately next door. Originally conceived as a warren of alleyways loaded with upscale, tax-free boutiques, and still plugging away valiantly at its location at East Mall Drive and East Sunrise Highway, it encompasses 4 hectares (10 acres) in the heart of Freeport.

It's currently a pale shadow of what it was during its peak in the mid-1980s, when it boasted 130 purveyors of luxury goods, when the Marketplace at Port Lucaya was still a dream, and when busloads of cruise-ship passengers would be unloaded in front of its gates at regular intervals. With many shops permanently closed and cracks in its masonry, its aggressively touted role as an "international" venue seems a bit theme-driven and tired. Even worse for the retailers here, its rising competitor, the Port Lucaya Marketplace, is looking better every day.

Buses at the entrance of the complex aren't numbered, but those marked INTER-NATIONAL BAZAAR will take you right to the entrance at Torii Gate on West Sunrise Highway. The fare is $1.25. Visitors walk through this much-photographed gate, a Japanese symbol of welcome, into a miniature World's Fair setting (think of it as a kitschy and somewhat run-down version of Epcot). The bazaar blends architecture and cultures from some 25 countries, each re-created with cobblestones, narrow alleys, and a layout that evokes a somewhat dusty casbah in North Africa.

In the approximately 65 shops that remain in business today, you might find exotic objects that are both unique and a bargain, as well as many more ordinary-looking shops catering to local residents of Freeport with everyday household goods, shoes, housewares, and clothing for adults and children. You'll also see African handicrafts, Chinese jade, British china, Swiss watches, Irish linens, and Colombian emeralds. Many of the enterprises represented here also maintain somewhat more upscale branches within the Port Lucaya Marketplace. Various sections evoke the architecture of the Ginza in Tokyo, with merchandise—electronic goods, art objects, luxury products—from Asia. Other subdivisions suggest the Left Bank of Paris, various regions of India and Africa, Latin America, and Spain.

Some merchants claim their prices are 40% lower than comparable costs in the U.S., but don't count on that. If you're contemplating a big purchase, it's best to compare prices before you leave home. Most merchants can ship your purchases back home at relatively reasonable rates.

A **straw market** next door to the International Bazaar contains items with that special Bahamian touch—colorful baskets, hats, handbags, placemats, and an endless array of T-shirts, some of which make worthwhile gifts. Be aware that some items sold here are actually made in Asia, and expect goodly amounts of the tacky and tasteless.

Below are the best shops that remain in the bazaar:

Flovin Gallery   This gallery sells original Bahamian and international art, frames, lithographs, posters, decorated coral, and Bahamian-made Christmas ornaments. It also offers handmade Bahamian dolls, coral jewelry, and other gift items. Another branch is at the Port Lucaya Marketplace. © **242/352-7564.**

Unusual Centre   Where else can you get an array of items made of walrus skin or peacock feathers? There's another branch at the Port Lucaya Marketplace (© **242/373-7333**).

GRAND BAHAMA AFTER DARK

Many resorts stage entertainment at night, and these shows are open to the general public.

The Club & Bar Scene

Located in the center of Port Lucaya Marketplace, **Count Basie Square** contains a vine-covered bandstand where the island's best live music is performed several nights a week, usually beginning around 7:30 or 8pm. And it's free! The square honors the "Count," who used to have a grand home on Grand Bahama. Steel bands, small Junkanoo groups, even gospel singers from a local church are likely to be heard here, their voices or music wafting across the marina and the nearby boardwalk and wharves. Sip a beer or a tropical rum concoction while tapping your feet.

Club Amnesia   This is one of the most popular discos and pickup joints on Grand Bahama, a local spot that seems a world away from the somewhat sanitized version of nightlife at the island's tourist hotels. Positioned across the street from the Best Western Castaways Resort, it features an interior outfitted with big mirrors, strobe lights, and psychedelic Junkanoo colors. Recorded music grooves and grinds, and live bands are often imported either from the mainland of Florida or from nearby Caribbean islands. Crowds range in age from 18 to 35, and the cover charge, depending on who's playing that night, is from $10 to $24 per person (concerts cost up to $50 per ticket). Open nights vary with the season, but it's a good bet that the place is

Bahamian Theater

Instead of one of those Las Vegas–style leggy-showgirl revues, call the 450-seat **Regency Theater,** West Sunrise Highway ((*C*) **242/352-5533;** www.regency theatregbi.com), and ask what performance is scheduled. This is the home of two nonprofit companies, the Freeport Players' Guild and the Grand Bahama Players. The season runs from September to June, and you're likely to see reprises of such Broadway and London blockbusters as *Mamma Mia!,* as well as contemporary works by Bahamian and Caribbean playwrights. Some very intriguing shows are likely to be staged every year by both groups, which are equally talented. Tickets cost $10 to $40.

operating Thursday through Saturday from 8:30pm until around 2am. E. Mall Dr. (*C*) **242/351-2582.**

Margaritavilla Sand Bar   Arguably the hottest bar on the island is this lively "jump-up" place opening onto an isolated stretch of Mather Town Beach, about a 15-minute drive southeast of Lucaya. It's really a one-room sand-floor shack, but a lot of fun. Before this bar opened, this part of Grand Bahama used to be relatively sleepy. No more. A weekly bonfire cookout is staged Tuesday night from 6:30 to 9:30pm, with fish or steak on the grill and a DJ keeping things lively. Main courses cost $10 to $16 if you'd like to stick around to eat. The place rocks on Wednesday night with younger Bahamians; Sunday is for an older crowd that prefers sing-alongs. The bar swings open at 11am. As for closing times, the owner, Jinx Knowles, says it "might be 7 at night if it's quiet or 7 in the morning if it's jumpin'." Millionaire's Row, Mather Town Beach. (*C*) **242/373-4525.**

Prop Club   Previously recommended within the section devoted to the Radisson Grand Lucayan, this sports bar and dance club flourishes as a singles venue that rocks at high intensity, fueled by high-octane cocktails. A lot happens here, including occasional bouts of karaoke, cultural showcasing of emerging Bahamian and Caribbean bands, and both Junkanoo and retro-disco revival nights, depending on the season. The DJ arrives at 9pm every Friday and Saturday night, and during evenings before national holidays throughout the year. In the Radisson Grand Lucaya Resort, Royal Palm Way. (*C*) **242/373-1333.** Entrance for non-residents of the Radisson, $15.

Rooster's Bar   This is a local watering hole known to virtually every hotel and casino employee on Grand Bahama Island, a joint where lots of people seem to have known one another for a long time. It can be fun, despite its remote location on the pier in an industrial-looking setting about a 15-minute drive west from Port Lucaya. We especially recommend it as a local diversion every Friday and Saturday night from 7pm till closing (2am), when there's live music and sense of conviviality, along with a simple menu of Bahamian platters (conch burgers, hamburgers, roast chicken) available. At Eight Mile Rock, on the coastal road within a 15-minute drive west from Port Lucaya. No phone.

A SIDE TRIP TO WEST END

If you crave a refreshing escape from the plush hotels of Freeport/Lucaya, head to West End, 45km (28 miles) from Freeport. At this old fishing village, and along the scrub-flanked coastal road that leads to it, you'll get glimpses of how things used to be before tour groups began descending on Grand Bahama Island.

To reach West End, head north along Queen's Highway, going through Eight Mile Rock, to the northernmost point of the island.

A lot of the old village buildings had become seriously dilapidated even before the destructive hurricanes of 2004 and 2005, but those that remain hint at long-ago legends and charm. From about 1920 to 1933, when Prohibition rather unsuccessfully held America in its grip, the docks buzzed with activity day and night. West End was (and is) so close to the U.S. mainland that rum-running became a lucrative business, with booze flowing out of West End by day and into Florida by night. No surprise, then, that Al Capone was supposedly a frequent visitor here.

Villages along the way to West End have colorful names like **Hawksbill Creek.** For a glimpse of local life, try to visit the **fish market** along the harbor. You'll pass some thriving harbor areas, too, but the vessels you'll see will be oil tankers, not rumrunners. Don't expect too many historic buildings en route.

Eight Mile Rock is a hamlet of mostly ramshackle houses that stretches along both sides of the road. At **West End,** you come to an abrupt stop. By far the most compelling developments here are associated with **Old Bahama Bay** (p. 125), a good spot for a meal, a drink, and a look at what might one day become one of the most important real-estate developments in The Bahamas.

BIMINI, THE BERRY ISLANDS & ANDROS

I n this chapter, we begin a journey through the Out Islands—a very different place from the major tourist developments of Nassau, Cable Beach, Paradise Island, and Freeport/Lucaya.

Bimini, the Berry Islands, and Andros are each unique. Bimini is famous and overrun with tourists, particularly in summer, but visitors will have the Berry Islands practically to themselves. These two island chains to the north and west of Nassau could be called the "westerly islands" because they, along with Grand Bahama, lie at the northwestern fringe of The Bahamas. They are the closest islands to Florida.

In contrast, much larger Andros is southwest of Nassau and is, in many ways, the most fascinating place in The Bahamas. The story goes that mysterious creatures once inhabited this series of islands laced with creeks and dense forests.

Each of the three island chains attracts a different type of visitor. **Bimini,** just 81km (50 miles) off Florida's east coast, and the setting for Hemingway's *Islands in the Stream,* lures big-game fishermen, yachters from Miami, and drug dealers from elsewhere in Florida. (The proximity to the U.S. mainland helps make drug smuggling big business here.) Bimini is home to world-famous sportfishing, excellent yachting and cruising, and some good scuba diving. Anglers will find seas swarming with tuna, dolphinfish, amberjack, white and blue marlin, swordfish, barracuda, and shark, along with many other varieties. Bonefish are also plentiful around the flats off the coast of Alice Town, the capital, but the blue marlin is the prize—Bahamians think so highly of this fish that they even put it on their $100 bill. Scuba divers can see black-coral trees over the Bimini Wall and reefs off Victory Cay.

The **Berry Islands** might attract the weary Bill Gates or Steve Forbes types. They also draw fishermen, but this string of islands, which has only 700 residents, is mainly for escapists—*rich* escapists. The islands' very limited accommodations (some of which used to be private clubs) lie near the Tongue of the Ocean, home of the big-game fish.

Andros, the nation's largest island, is largely uninhabited. If The Bahamas still has an unexplored wilderness, this is it. The island's forest and mangrove swamps are home to a wide variety of birds and animals, including the Bahamian boa constrictor and the 2m-long (6½-ft.) iguana. The Bahamian national bird, the West Indian flamingo, can also be spotted during migration in late spring and summer. The waters off Andros are home to a wondrous barrier reef, the third largest in the world and a diver's dream. The reef plunges 167km (104 miles) to a narrow drop-off known as the Tongue of the Ocean.

Andros's mysterious blue holes, another diver's delight, are formed when subterranean caves fill with seawater, causing the ceiling to collapse and expose clear, deep pools. Few come here anymore looking for Sir Henry Morgan's pirate treasure, said to be buried in one of the caves off Morgan's Bluff on the north tip of the island. But Andros does attract anglers, mostly because it is known for its world-class fishing.

BIMINI ★

Bimini is still known as the big-game fishing capital of the world, and fishermen come here throughout the year to fish in flats, on reefs, and in streams. Ernest Hemingway came to write and fish. It was here that he wrote much of *To Have and Have Not,* and his novel *Islands in the Stream* put Bimini and its residents (known as "Biminites") on the map. Regrettably, fishing isn't what it used to be in Papa's day, and such species as marlin, swordfish, and tuna have been dangerously overfished.

Located 81km (50 miles) east of Miami, Bimini consists of a number of islands, islets, and cays, including North and South Bimini, the main tourist areas. You'll most often encounter the name "Bimini," but it is more proper to say "The Biminis," since North Bimini and South Bimini are two distinct islands, separated by a narrow ocean passage. Ferries shuttle between the two. The majority of the region's development has taken place on North Bimini, mostly in **Alice Town.** North Bimini's western side is a long stretch of lovely beachfront.

Off North Bimini, in 9m (30 ft.) of water, are some large hewn-stone formations that some people say came from the lost continent of Atlantis. Divers find the reefs laced with conch, lobster, coral, and many tropical fish.

Bimini's location off the Florida coast is where the Gulf Stream meets the Bahama Banks. This fact has made Bimini a favorite cruising ground for America's yachting set, who follow the channel between North and South Bimini into a spacious, sheltered harbor, where they can stock up on food, drink, fuel, and supplies at well-equipped marinas. From here, they can set off to cruise the cays that begin south of South Bimini. Each has its own special appeal, beginning with Turtle Rocks and stretching to South Cat Cay (the latter of which is uninhabited). Along the way, you'll pass Holm Cay, Gun Cay, and North Cat Cay.

Hook-shaped North Bimini is 12km (7½ miles) long and, combined with South Bimini, it makes up a landmass of only 23 sq. km (9 sq. miles). That's why Alice Town looks so crowded. Another reason is that much of Bimini is privately owned; despite pressure from the Bahamian government, the landholders have not sold their acreage, and Bimini can't "spread out" until they do. At Alice Town, the land is so narrow that you can walk "from sea to shining sea" in just a short time. Most of Bimini's population of some 1,700 people lives in Alice Town; other hamlets include Bailey Town and Porgy Bay.

Although winter is usually high season in The Bahamas, summertime visitors flock to Bimini's calmer waters, which are better for fishing. Winter, especially from mid-December to mid-March, is quieter, and Bimini has never tried to develop a resort structure that would attract more winter visitors.

If you go to Bimini, you'll hear a lot of people mention **Cat Cay** (not to be confused with Cat Island in the Southern Bahamas). You can stay overnight at Cat Cay's

marina, which lies 13km (8 miles) off South Bimini; transient slips are available. The island is the domain of **Cat Cay Yacht Club** (© **934/359-9575** or 242/347-3565; www.catcayachtclub.com), whose nonrefundable initiation fee is a cool $25,000. This rigorously private island—attracting titans of industry and famous families—is for the exclusive use of Cat Cay Yacht Club members and their guests. At their leisure, they can enjoy the golf course, tennis courts, a large marina, white-sand beaches, and club facilities such as restaurants and bars. Many wealthy Americans have homes on the island, which also has a private airstrip. Most of the rank-and-file workers on Cat Cay live on-island, commuting back to either of the Biminis at weekly intervals, usually by chartered boats.

Bimini Essentials
GETTING THERE
Note: For non-Bahamians, a passport is required for entry to Bimini and an outbound (return) ticket must also be presented to Bahamian Customs before you will be permitted entry. If you're flying from the U.S., you must have a valid passport.

BY PLANE   The island's only airstrip is at the southern tip of South Bimini, a time-consuming transfer and ferryboat ride away from Alice Town on North Bimini, where most of the archipelago's hotels and yacht facilities are.

From Fort Lauderdale, **Continental** (© **800/231-0856;** www.continental.com) flies in twice daily. **Regional Air** (© **800/598-8660;** www.goregionalair.com) flies in between once and twice a day from Freeport, depending on the day of the week, Finally, **Western Air** (© **242/377-2222;** www.westernairbahamas.com) wings in from Nassau's domestic air terminal to South Bimini. Relatively new to the scene are the seaplane services of **Tropic Seaways** (© **863/307-1657;** www.flytropic.com), which flies 7- or 9-seater planes in from both Miami and Fort Lauderdale, depending on the schedule. Unlike conventional flights coming into Bimini, which land on the above-mentioned airstrip on the south end of South Bimini, this outfit's airplanes land in open water offshore from Alice Town, closer to the population center and in most cases, the hotels.

BY BOAT   In the old days, the way to get from Nassau to Bimini was by slow-moving boat. You can still do it, but it'll take you 12 hours on the MV **Sherice M,** which leaves from Potter's Cay Dock in Nassau and stops at Cat Cay before eventually reaching Bimini. The vessel leaves Nassau on alternate Thursdays at 2pm. For details about departures, call the dock master at Nassau's **Potter's Cay Dock** at © **242/393-1064.**

GETTING AROUND

If you arrive at the small airport on South Bimini, you'll need to pay a combined fee of $5 for a taxi transfer and ferry ride to Alice Town, on North Bimini.

You won't need a car on Bimini—and you won't find a car-rental agency here. Most people walk to where they want to go (though your hotel may be able to arrange a minibus tour or rent you a bike or golf cart). The walk runs up and down **King's Highway,** which has no sidewalks. It's so narrow that two automobiles have a tough time squeezing by. Be careful walking along this highway, especially at night, when drivers might not see you.

This road, lined with low-rise buildings, splits Alice Town on North Bimini. If you're the beachcombing type, stick to the side bordering the Gulf Stream so that you can find the best beaches. The harborside contains a handful of inns (most of which are reviewed in this chapter), along with marinas and docks where supplies are unloaded. You'll see many Floridians arriving on yachts.

VISITOR INFORMATION

The Bahamas Ministry of Tourism maintains a branch office at Bimini's George Weech Building, King's Highway, Alice Town (© **242/347-3529;** www.bahamas.gov. bs). It's open Monday to Friday 9am to 5pm.

[FastFACTS] BIMINI

ATMs   You'll find an ATM at the **Royal Bank of Canada,** in Alice Town (© **242/ 347-3031;** www.rbcroyal bank.com). The bank is open Monday through Thursday from 9:30am to 3pm, Friday from 9:30am to 4:30pm.

Clothing   If you're going to Bimini in winter, take along a windbreaker for those occasional chilly nights.

Customs & Immigration   The office of **Customs** (© **242/347-3100) and Immigration** (© **242/ 347-3446)** is in Alice Town It consists of one Immigration officer and one

Customs official. If you're flying from the U.S., you must carry a valid passport and fill out a Bahamian Immigration Card.

Drugs The rumrunners of the Prohibition era have now given way to those smuggling illegal drugs into the U.S. from The Bahamas. Because of its proximity to the mainland, Bimini, as is no secret to anyone, is now a major drop-off point for drugs, many originating from Colombia. If not intercepted by the U.S. Coast Guard, these drugs find their way to Florida and eventually to the rest of the United States.

Both buying and selling illegal drugs, such as cocaine and marijuana, is an extremely risky business in The Bahamas. You may be approached by dealers on Bimini, some of whom are actually undercover agents. If caught with illegal drugs, you face immediate imprisonment.

Emergencies To call the police or report a fire, dial ✆ **919.**

Medical Care Nurses, a doctor, and a dentist are on the island, as is the **North Bimini Public Clinic** (✆ **242/347-2210**). However, for serious medical emergencies, patients are usually airlifted to either Miami or Nassau. Helicopters can land in the well-lit baseball field on North Bimini.

Where to Stay

Accommodations in Bimini are extremely limited, and it's almost impossible to get a room during one of the big fishing tournaments unless you've reserved way in advance. Inns are cozy and simple; many are owned and operated by a family (chances are, your innkeeper's surname will be Brown). Furnishings are often time-worn, the paint chipped. No one puts on airs here; the dress code, even in the evening, is very simple and relaxed. From wherever you're staying in Alice Town, it's usually easy to walk to another hotel for dinner or drinks.

Bimini Bay Resort & Marina ★★ Incorporated into the Rockresorts chain in 2010, this is Bimini's best-accessorized, most modern, and most comprehensive luxury resort, despite the fact that its widely publicized amplifications are not progressing as quickly as originally intended. When it settles in and realizes all its goals—one of them being to have 1,700 rooms by 2016, as well as a spa and a state-of-the-art casino—it should evolve into the finest and most luxurious resort Bimini has ever seen. Know in advance that there's a lot here, with style and verve that's not easily replicated anywhere else on Bimini.

Despite the slow pace of improvements, life here is as upscale as anything you're likely to find on Bimini, with an aura that's akin to residing in a tropical condo, with rattan furnishings, Bahamian art, contemporary kitchenettes, and a reasonably attentive staff. Bedrooms open onto views of either the Atlantic or the bay. There's a lot of emphasis on this resort's marina. With almost 800 slips, and aggressive plans for enlargement, it's popular with boat owners who prefer their accommodations very close to the moorings for their yachts.

King's Hwy. (north of Bailey Town), Bimini, The Bahamas. www.biminibayresort.com. ✆ **866/344-8759** or 242/347-2900. Fax 242/347-2312. 338 units, about 270 of which are within the rental pool. Year-round $199–$250 double; $230–$325 1-bedroom unit; $230–$410 2-bedroom unit; $500–$1,100 3-bedroom unit. AE, MC, V. **Amenities:** 2 restaurants; 2 bars; bikes; outdoor pool. *In room:* A/C, TV, kitchen, Wi-Fi (free).

Bimini Big Game Fishing Club-A Guy Harvey Outpost Resort ★★ Originally conceived as a dining club in 1936, this legendary resort was enlarged a decade later into a sports and fishing resort for fans of big-game (especially marlin) fishing and the exploits and lifestyle example set by "Papa Ernesto" (Hemingway). It went out of business in 2009, thanks to mismanagement and the global recession. In 2010, after expensive ($3.5 million) renovations, and upgrades to its 75-slip marina, it reopened under the watchful eye of the Guy Harvey group. Harvey, the German-born, Scotland-educated, Jamaica-linked gamefishing entrepreneur, spent part of his youth sketching and painting the seascapes around Bimini, illustrating scenes from the life of Hemingway, and perfecting his knowledge of the local gamefishing scene. Since its re-opening, the resort combines a focus on eco-system education programs for both local residents and paying guests, with a sense of holiday relaxation and fun. Set in the "downtown" heart of Alice Town, the resort is in a dock-fronting venue that focuses on sports venues, deep sea fishing charters, and bonefishing lore and legend. As its name implies, many of its guests are here for gamefishing as part of waterborne expeditions arranged in advance, sometimes as part of package deals, by the hotel's Florida-based management office. Accommodations are cheerfully masculine in their decor, uncluttered and comfortable, with references to the hard-drinking glory days (the 1950 and 60s) of Bimini and to the celebrities who originally made the place famous.

Alice Town, Bimini, The Bahamas. www.biggameclubbimini.com. ✆ **800/867-4764,** 954/763-6025, or 242/347-3391. 51 units. High Season $189 double, $229–$350 studio cottage or penthouse; Off-season $159 double, $209–$350 studio cottage or penthouse. AE, MC, V. **Amenities:** Restaurant; bar; marina; pool. In room: A/C, TV, fridge (in studios and penthouse units), microwave, wet bar, Wi-Fi (free).

Bimini Blue Water Resort ★ 📷

This is essentially a raffish resort complex marketing itself principally to sportfishermen, with complete dockside services and 32 modern slips—one of the country's finest places of its kind. The main building, which contains its bar, restaurant, and reception facilities, is a white-frame, waterfront Bahamian guesthouse, the **Anchorage,** where Michael Lerner, the noted fisherman, used to live. It's at the top of the hill, with views looking out to the ocean (see "Where to Eat," below). The midsize bedrooms contain double beds, white furniture, wood-paneled walls, and picture-window doors that lead to private balconies. The Marlin Cottage, although much altered, and today accessorized as a three-bedroom, three-bathroom rental unit with a kitchen and two porches, was one of Hemingway's retreats in the 1930s. He used it as a main setting in *Islands in the Stream.*

King's Hwy., Alice Town, Bimini, The Bahamas. ✆ **242/347-3166.** Fax 242/347-3293. 12 units. Year-round $116 double; $348 three-bedroom Marlin cottage. MC, V. **Amenities:** Restaurant; bar; outdoor pool; Wi-Fi ($10 one-time fee, valid for the duration of your stay). In room: A/C, TV, fridge.

Bimini Sands Resort & Marina ★ ☺

Lying directly on a good sandy beach on South Bimini, this coffee-colored condo complex features rooms that open onto views of either its marina or the Straits of Florida. Families will find these accommodations rather luxurious, with one- and two-bedroom condos that are spacious and well furnished. The living rooms are artfully decorated, and the kitchens are very modern and fully equipped (including a washer/dryer). You're a bit isolated down in South Bimini, but most people come here to escape from civilization, enjoying the full-service deep-water marina adjacent and restaurants that to an increasing degree are becoming dining destinations in their own right. When the business is brisk and occupancy is high, there's usually a Bahamian Customs officer on-site, allowing easy access for anyone arriving by boat.

Bimini Sands Beach, Bimini, The Bahamas. www.biminisands.com. ✆ **242/347-3500.** Fax 242/347-3501 21 units. Year-round $260–$335 1-bedroom unit; $385–$450 2-bedroom unit. AE, MC, V.

Amenities: 2 restaurants; 2 bars; bikes; 2 outdoor pools; tennis court; Wi-Fi (free). *In room:* A/C, TV, kitchen.

Sea Crest Hotel & Marina ☺ Built in 1981 and upgraded every year since, this property lies right on the main highway of North Bimini in the commercial heart of Alice Town. Rooms in the three-story hotel, which looks like a motel, are best on the third floor thanks to their ocean or bay views. Additional units lie within an apartment complex adjacent to the marina. Many units are small, with rather cramped bathrooms (though each does have a shower stall), but they're comfortably furnished in a simple, traditional way and they open onto small balconies. Much better, larger, and more comfortable are the units in the newer apartment-style building beside the marina. Since the location is right in the heart of Alice Town, you can generally walk wherever you want to go. There's a pleasant on-site restaurant, Captain Bob's, which is open only for breakfast and lunch. The Sea Crest is a family favorite; it's also popular with the boating crowd because it offers an 18-berth marina.

King's Hwy., Alice Town, Bimini, The Bahamas. www.seacrestbimini.com. ℂ **242/347-3071.** Fax 242/347-3495. 26 units. Year-round $99–$135 double; $230 2-bedroom suite; $329 3-bedroom suite. Extra person $15. Children 12 and under stay free in parent's room. MC, V. **Amenities:** Restaurant (breakfast and lunch only); marina; Wi-Fi (free in lobby). *In room:* A/C, TV, fridge, no phone.

Where to Eat

Anchorage Dining Room SEAFOOD/BAHAMIAN/AMERICAN This dining room overlooks Alice Town's harbor; you can see the ocean through picture windows. The modern, paneled room is filled with captain's chairs and unpretentious, Formica-clad tables. You might begin your dinner with conch chowder and then follow with one of the tempting seafood dishes, including spiny broiled lobster, many variations of grouper, or perhaps cracked conch. The kitchen also makes a good fried Bahamian chicken and a tender New York sirloin. The cooking is straightforward and reliable, and never pretends to be more than just that.

Bimini Blue Water Resort, King's Hwy., Alice Town. ℂ **242/347-3166.** Reservations not necessary. Main courses $15–$31. AE, MC, V. Wed–Mon 6–10pm.

The Beach Club Restaurant INTERNATIONAL/SUSHI Set near the southern tip of North Bimini, within the also-recommended Bimini Sands Resort (see above), this is a destination dining venue that attracts residents and yacht owners from all parts of the island. More stylish and "urban" in its culinary venue than many of its competitors, it's set on a deck overlooking the ocean, with either air conditioned (inside) or outdoor dining. Breakfast and dinner are informal affairs served within The Petite Conch, a cheerful daytime eatery nearby. Evening meals, which are usually preceded with drinks, sometimes extensive, are more elaborate, more "fussed over," and more formal. Menu items include fresh local and imported sushi and sashimi, many variations of snapper, grouper, and tuna, prepared in ways that reflect big-city tastes from places like Miami and New York, and such main courses as filets of veal in hoisin-raisin sauce or chicken cutlets with white wine, lemons, and capers.

In the Bimini Sands Resort, Bimini Sands Beach. ℂ **242/347-5000.** Reservations recommended for dinner. Lunch main course $14–$28; dinner main courses $25–$50. AE, MC, V. Daily 7:30am–3pm (in La Petite Conch); and daily 3–10:30pm (in the Beach Club). The bar remains open nightly till 2am.

Sabor ★ FRENCH/MEDITERRANEAN This is one of Bimini's best restaurants, a reliable, long-standing staple, standing on the grounds of the Bimini Bay Resort

(p. 149). The dining venue is divided between a covered outdoor veranda with views of the sea and an enclosed, air-conditioned dining room with big windows. The dishes are inspired, including first-rate versions of fresh seviche, a Spanish-style paella, hummus platters, yucca fritters, and, most definitely, the grilled catch of the day. Such fish as grouper or wahoo might come flavored with sesame seeds and glazed with pineapple if you so prefer. Cracked conch and fresh crab also appear regularly on the menu.

In Bimini Bay Resort, King's Hwy., North Bimini. (C) **242/347-2900.** Reservations not necessary. Main courses $20–$35. AE, DISC, MC, V. Daily 6–10pm. Closed Mon–Wed in summer.

Beaches & Outdoor Pursuits
HITTING THE BEACH
Bimini's beaches are all clearly marked and signposted from the highways. The one closest to Alice Town, **Radio Beach,** is the only one on Bimini with toilets, vendors, and snack bars. It's set adjacent to Alice Town's piers and wharves; consequently, it's the island's most popular and crowded beach.

About 3km (1¾ miles) north of Alice Town, facing west, is **Spook Hill Beach.** Both it and its cousin, **Bimini Bay Beach,** about 4km (2½ miles) north of Alice Town, offer sparser crowds, worthy snorkeling, and lots of sunshine. Both are sandy-bottomed and comfortable on your feet. Many local residents prefer Bimini Bay Beach, which is wider than any other on the island.

On South Bimini, the two favorites are the west-facing **Bimini Sands Beach,** a sandy-bottomed stretch that's immediately south of the channel separating North from South Bimini; and **Bimini Reef Club Beach,** south of the airport, where offshore snorkeling is especially worthwhile, thanks to very clear waters.

Fishing
Ernest Hemingway made fishing here famous, but Zane Grey came this way, too, as did Howard Hughes. Richard Nixon used to fish here aboard the posh cruiser of his entrepreneurial friend Charles "Bebe" Rebozo. In Hemingway's wake, fishermen still flock to cast lines in the Gulf Stream and the Bahama Banks.

Of course, everyone's still after the big one, and a lot of world records have been set in this area for marlin, sailfish, swordfish, wahoo, grouper, and tuna. But these fish are becoming evasive, and their dwindling numbers are edging them close to extinction. Fishing folk can spin cast for panfish, boat snapper, yellowtail, and kingfish. Many experts consider stalking bonefish, long a pursuit of baseball great Ted Williams, the sport's toughest challenge.

Five charter boats are available in Bimini for big-game and little-game fishing, with some center-console boats rented for both bottom and reef angling. At least eight bonefishing guides are available, and experienced anglers who have made repeated visits to Bimini know the particular skills of each of these men who will take you for a half-day or full day of "fishing in the flats," a local term for bonefishing in the sea-level waterways and estuaries that cut into the island. Most skiffs hold two anglers, and part of the fun in hiring a local guide is to hear his fish tales and other island lore. If a guide tells you that 7.25kg (16-lb.) bonefish have turned up, he may not be exaggerating—catches that large have really been documented.

Reef and bottom-fishing around Bimini are easier than bonefishing and can be more productive. Numerous species of snapper and grouper can be found, as well as amberjack. This is the simplest and least expensive boat-fishing experience because

A major attraction for both snorkelers and divers, not to mention rainbow-hued fish, is the wreck of a ship called **Sapona,** which has lain hard aground in 4.5m (15 ft.) of water between South Bimini and Cat Cay ever since it was blown here by a hurricane in 1929. In the heyday of the Roaring Twenties, the ship, which was commissioned by Henry Ford, served as a private club and speak-easy. You'll have to take a boat to reach the site, which is shallow enough that even snorkelers can see it. Local dive operators generally include the site in their repertoire.

you need only a local guide, a little boat, tackle, and a lot of bait. Sometimes you can negotiate to go bottom-fishing with a Bahamian, but chances are, he'll ask you to pay for the boat fuel. That night, back at your inn, the cook will serve you the red snapper or grouper you caught that day.

Most hotel owners will tell you to bring your own fishing gear. A couple of small shops do sell some items, but you'd better bring major equipment with you if you're really serious. Bait, of course, can be purchased locally.

SNORKELING & SCUBA DIVING

Explore the black-coral gardens and reefs here, plus wrecks, blue holes, and a mysterious stone formation on the bottom of the sea that some claim is part of the lost continent of Atlantis (it's 457m/1,499 ft. offshore in Bimini Bay, under about 6m/20 ft. of water). Bimini waters are known for a breathtaking drop-off at the rim of the continental shelf, an underwater mountain that plunges 600m (1,969 ft.) down.

The finest and most experienced outfitter, **Bimini Undersea at Bimini Bay** (② **242/347-4990;** www.biminiundersea.com), was founded a quarter-century ago by local dive legends Bill and Nowdla Keefe, who, in 2011, left the place in capable hands after their departure for new business developments in the waters off Fiji. Scuba enthusiasts pay $59 for a one-tank dive, $110 for a two-tank dive. Snorkelers are charged $39 for a single trip, including use of mask and fins. All-inclusive dive packages are also available. For reservations, call ② **800/348-4644** or 305/653-5572.

Bimini Undersea also gives you the chance to swim with dolphins in the wild two or three times a week, depending on demand. Most excursions take from 3 to 4 hours and cost $129 for adults and $99 for kids 12 and under. Before you go, though, know that this activity has its critics. To learn more about that controversy, visit the Whale and Dolphin Conservation Society's website at www.wdcs.org.

Exploring Bimini

At North Bimini's southern tip, ramshackle **Alice Town** is all that many visitors ever see of the islands, since it's where the major hotels are. You can see the whole town in an hour or two.

As you're exploring the island, you may want to stop off at the **Bimini Crafts Center,** next door to the Bahamas Customs Building, where you'll usually find 17 vendors. Strike up a conversation with some islanders, and perhaps pick up a souvenir or two.

If you're curious, drop into the little **Bimini Museum,** on King's Highway (② **242/347-3038**), a sort of grab bag of mementos left behind by visiting celebrities.

Myths of Bimini

These islands have long been shrouded in myths, none more far-fetched than the one claiming that the lost continent of **Atlantis** lies off North Bimini's shore. This legend grew because of the weirdly shaped rock formations that lie submerged in about 6m (20 ft.) of water near the coast. Pilots flying over North Bimini have reported what they envisioned as an undersea "lost highway." This myth continues, attracting many scuba divers interested in exploring these rocks.

Ponce de León came to South Bimini looking for that celebrated **Fountain of Youth.** He never found it, but people still come here to search. In the late 19th century, a Christian sect reportedly came here to take the waters—supposedly a bubbling fountain or spring. If you arrive on South Bimini and seem interested enough, a local guide will be happy to show you (for a fee) "the exact spot" where the Fountain of Youth once bubbled.

The museum owns the 1964 immigration card of Martin Luther King, Jr., a domino set left by frequent visitor Adam Clayton Powell (the former New York congressman), and Ernest Hemingway's fishing log and vintage fishing films. Also on exhibit are island artifacts such as rum kegs. The location, in a two-story 1920s house, is a 4-minute walk from the seaplane ramp. The museum is open Monday through Saturday from 9am to 7pm, Sunday from noon to 9pm. Admission is free, but donations are appreciated.

Queen's Highway runs up North Bimini's western side, and as you head north along it, you'll see that it's lined with beautiful beachfront. **King's Highway** runs through Alice Town and continues north. It's bordered by houses painted gold, lime, buttercup yellow, and a pink that gleams in the bright sunshine.

At some point, you may notice the ruins of Bimini's first hotel, **Bimini Bay Rod & Gun Club,** sitting unfinished on its own beach. Built in the early 1920s, it flourished until a hurricane wiped it out later that decade. It was never rebuilt, though developers once made an attempt.

To explore **South Bimini,** hire a taxi for about $6 per person to see the island's limited attractions, which, at least to our knowledge, do not include Ponce de León's legendary Fountain of Youth. There's not a lot to see, but you're likely to hear tall tales worth the cab fare. You can also stop off at some lovely, uncrowded beaches.

Bimini After Dark

In Bimini, you can dance to a Goombay drumbeat or try to find some disco music. Most people have a leisurely dinner, drink (a lot) in one of the local watering holes, and go back to their hotel rooms by midnight so they can get up early to continue pursuing the elusive "big one" the next morning. Every bar in Alice Town is likely to claim that it was Hemingway's favorite. He did hit quite a few of them, in fact. There's rarely a cover charge anywhere unless some special entertainment is being offered.

Everybody eventually makes his or her way to the **End of the World Bar** (no phone), on King's Highway in Alice Town. When you get here, you may think you're in the wrong place—it's just a waterfront shack with simple takeout food, sawdust or sand on the floor and graffiti everywhere. The late New York congressman Adam

Clayton Powell put this bar on the map in the 1960s. Between stints in Washington, battling Congress, and in New York, preaching at Harlem's Abyssinian Baptist Church, the controversial politician could be found sitting here. While the bar doesn't attract the media attention it did in Powell's heyday, it's still a local favorite. Open daily from around noon to 1am (till 3am on Friday and Saturday).

THE BERRY ISLANDS ★

A dangling chain of cays and islets on the eastern edge of the Great Bahama Bank, the unspoiled and serene Berry Islands begin 56km (35 miles) northwest of New Providence (Nassau), 242km (150 miles) east of Miami. This 30-island archipelago is known to sailors, fishermen, yachtspeople, Jack Nicklaus, and a Rockefeller or two, as well as to devoted beachcombers who love its pristine sands.

As a fishing center, the Berry Islands are second only to Bimini. At the tip of the Tongue of the Ocean (aka TOTO), it has world record–setting big-game fish and endless flats where bonefish congregate. In the "Berries," you can find your own tropical paradise islet and enjoy—sans wardrobe—totally isolated white-sand beaches and palm-fringed shores. Some of the best shell-collecting spots in The Bahamas are on the Berry Islands' beaches and in their shallow-water flats.

The main islands are, from north to south, Great Stirrup Cay, Cistern Cay, Great Harbour Cay, Anderson Cay, Haines Cay, Hoffmans Cay, Bond's Cay, Sandy Cay, Whale Cay, and Chub Cay. One of the very small cays, north of Frazey's Hog Cay and Whale Cay, has, in our opinion, the most unappetizing name: Cockroach Cay.

The largest island is **Great Harbour Cay,** which sprawls over 1,520 hectares (3,756 acres) of sand, rock, and scrub. It's a multimillion-dollar resort for jet setters who occupy waterfront town houses and villas. Brigitte Bardot and many other stars have all romped on its 12km (7½ miles) of almost solitary beachfront.

Bond's Cay, a bird sanctuary in the south, and tiny Frazer's Hog Cay (stock is still raised here) are both privately owned. An English company used to operate a coconut and sisal plantation on Whale Cay, also near the southern tip. Sponge fishermen and their families inhabit some of the islands.

Berry Islands Essentials

GETTING THERE Great Harbour Cay is an official point of entry for The Bahamas if you're flying from a foreign territory such as the U.S. During many times of the year, you can get here only via charter flights from South Florida, making these some of the most inconvenient islands to reach in all of The Bahamas.

At presstime for this edition, the most popular scheduled air service into the Berry Islands was via **Flamingo Air** (© 242/367-8021; www.flamingoairbah.com) which flies every Friday and Sunday from Freeport for around $90 per adult each way, $55 for children under 12. **Island Express** (© 954/359-0380) can be persuaded to operate a charter flight from Fort Lauderdale, to either Great Harbour Cay or Chub Cay at prices you'll negotiate and which vary, depending on circumstances and the availability of an available aircraft. **Tropic Air Charters** (© 954/267-0707; www.tropicaircharters.com) will charter a flight from Fort Lauderdale to Great Harbour Cay. Most visitors arrive by boat. If you're contemplating the mail-boat sea-voyage route, the **MV *Captain Gurthdean*** leaves Potter's Cay Dock in Nassau every Tuesday at 7pm, heading for the Berry Islands. For up-to-date departure details, call the dock master at Nassau's **Potter's Cay Dock** at © 242/393-1064.

[FastFACTS] THE BERRY ISLANDS

The **Great Harbour Cay Medical Clinic** is at Bullock's Harbour on Great Harbour Cay (© 242/367-8400). The **police station** is also at Bullock's Harbour (© 242/367-8344 or 367-8104).

Great Harbour Cay

An estimated 700 residents live on Great Harbour Cay, making it the most populated island of the Berry chain. Its main settlement is **Bullock's Harbour,** which might be called the capital of the Berry Islands. The cay is about 2.5km (1½ miles) wide and some 13km (8 miles) long. A grocery store and some restaurants are about all you'll find in town. Most visitors arrive to stay at **Great Harbour Inn** (see below).

Great Harbour Cay lies between Grand Bahama and New Providence. It's 97km (60 miles) northwest of Nassau and 242km (150 miles) east of Miami, about an hour away from Miami by plane or a half-day by powerboat. Unlike most islands in The Bahamas, the island isn't flat, but is composed of rolling hills. Most of the non-Bahamians associated with Great Harbour Cay get involved in one way or another with the island's marina (© 242/367-8123), usually for the mooring and maintenance of their boat.

Deep-sea fishing possibilities abound here, with billfish, dolphinfish, king mackerel, and wahoo. Light-tackle bottom-fishing is also good; you can net yellowtail, snapper, barracuda, triggerfish, and plenty of grouper. Bonefishing here is among the best in the world. Great Harbour Cay's marina is an excellent facility, with some 80 slips and all the amenities. Some of Florida's fanciest yachts pull in here.

When you tire of fishing, relax on 13km (8 miles) of gorgeous beaches, play the 9-hole golf course designed by Joe Lee, or try your backhand on one of four clay tennis courts.

WHERE TO STAY

Most visitors who come to this island make arrangements to rent a private house, condo, or apartment for a week or so. The Berry Island's busiest rental agent is **Tat's Rental** at Beach Villas, Great Harbour Cay (© 242/464-4361). Most of its

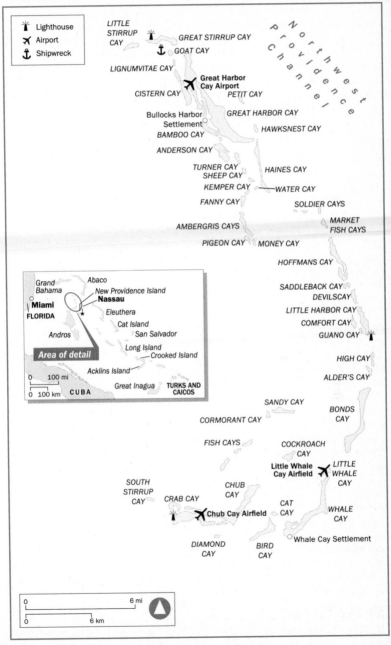

negotiations are rentals for two occupants at a time, although arrangements can be made for up to eight guests. Those who want convenience prefer accommodations in a spacious town house right at the marina, with the dock underneath. All rentals are air-conditioned, and include a fully equipped kitchen. Beach villas are rented along a 13km-long (8-mile) strip of white sands to the east of the airport. If you rent accommodations through Tat's, you're welcomed at the airport when you check in and taken to your rental. Don't expect such conveniences as phones or Internet service, however. Beach Villas lies just northeast of the airport.

WHERE TO EAT

Coolie Mae's ★ 🎁BAHAMIAN   On the north side of the marina, all of the visiting yachties, local islanders, and transplanted statesiders hail Mae for serving well-prepared Bahamian food consistently and well, through Chub Cay's many economic ups and downs. We go for her conch salad, conch fritters, or her fried conch, but you can also enjoy her pan-fried grouper. Broiled lobster appears at certain times, and you can always order pork chops and steaks shipped in from Florida. All of the main platters are served with macaroni and cheese or else peas 'n' rice. The paintings decorating the walls are by island artists.

Bullock's Harbour. ✆ **242/367-8730.** Reservations not necessary. Main courses $14–$22. No credit cards. Mon–Sat noon–9pm.

Chub Cay

Named after a species of fish that thrives in nearby waters, Chub Cay is well known to sportfishing enthusiasts. A self-contained hideaway with a devoted clientele, it's the southernmost of the Berry Islands, separating the Florida mainland from Nassau's commercial frenzy.

Chub Cay's development began in the late 1950s as a strictly private (and rather spartan) enclave of a group of Texas-based anglers and investors. It was originally uninhabited, but over the years, a staff was imported, dormitory-style housing was built, and Chub Cay's most famous man-made feature (its state-of-the-art 90-slip marina) was constructed in the 392-hectare (969-acre) island's sheltered lagoon.

Chub Cay is today a tranquil, scrub-covered sand spit with awesome amounts of marine hardware, a dozen posh private homes, the marina, and a complex of buildings devoted to the **Chub Cay Resort & Marina** (www.chubcay.com; p. 159). At press-time for this edition, Chub Cay was in receivership and awaiting an acquisition by new owners, the identity and intentions of whom hadn't been fully established. But despite the approaching bankruptcy of its present owners, it still accepts room reservations and overnight guests, even though service and amenities may not be as well-orchestrated or as well-maintained as you might have hoped for.

On the island are a liquor store and a yachters' commissary, as well as a marine-supply store and a concrete runway for landing anything up to and including a Boeing 737. Most visitors reach Chub Cay by private yacht from Florida, but if you prefer to charter your fishing craft on Chub Cay, you'll find a miniature armada of suitable craft at your disposal.

The water temperature around Chub Cay averages a warm 81° to 84°F (27°–29°C) year-round, even at relatively deep depths. There's only a small tidal change and, under normal conditions, no swell or noticeable current in offshore waters. The incredibly clear waters make for great snorkeling.

WHERE TO STAY & EAT
Chub Cay Resort & Marina ★   Despite its status, at least at presstime for this edition, as a property in receivership, some of Florida's most impressive yachts still pull into the 110-slip marina, where Immigration services are available, as is fuel. Sportsmen from the East Coast visit here because of the resort's location at the Tongue of the Ocean and the Great Bahama Bank, lying at the archipelago's southernmost tip near sandy beaches. On the property's grounds are a clubhouse, a restaurant, a tiki bar, and facilities for the mooring and maintenance of upscale yachts. Guests can stay in villas or marina-fronting town houses—villas include two-, three-, four-, and five-bedroom homes built in authentic British colonial style.

There's a restaurant, the **Harbour House,** with its own bar, and the **Hilltop Bar,** which sits at the island's highest elevation. The latter has pool tables and a TV for sports broadcasts. Main courses at Harbour House cost $14 to $35.

Chub Cay, Berry Islands, The Bahamas. www.chubcay.com. **©** **954/634-7496** or 242/325-1490. 16 units. Year-round $125 double; $500–$700 2-bedroom villa; $945 3-bedroom villa. AE, MC, V. **Amenities:** Restaurant; bar; tennis court; Wi-Fi (free). *In room:* A/C, TV/DVD, hair dryer, kitchenette (in some), no phone.

ANDROS ★★

The largest island in The Bahamas, Andros is an excellent budget destination. One of the Western Hemisphere's biggest unexplored tracts of land is still quite mysterious. Mostly flat, its 5,957 sq. km (2,300 sq. miles) are riddled with lakes and creeks, and most of the local residents—who still indulge in fire dances and go on wild boar hunts on occasion—live along the shore.

Andros is 161km (100 miles) long and 64km (40 miles) wide. Its interior consists of a dense tropical forest, truly rugged bush, and many mangroves. The marshy and relatively uninhabited west coast is called "the Mud," and the east coast is paralleled for 193km (120 miles) by the world's third-largest underwater barrier reef, which drops more than 167km (104 miles) into the Tongue of the Ocean, or TOTO. On the eastern shore, this "tongue" is 229km (142 miles) long and 1,000 fathoms (1.8km/1 mile) deep.

Lying 274km (170 miles) southeast of Miami and 48km (30 miles) west of Nassau, Andros actually comprises three major land areas: North Andros, Central Andros, and South Andros. In spite of its size, Andros is very thinly populated (its residents number only around 5,000), although the tourist population swells it a bit. The temperature range here averages from 72° to 84°F (22°–29°C).

You won't find the western side of Andros written about much in yachting guides—tricky shoals render it almost unapproachable by boat. The east coast, however, offers kilometers of unspoiled beaches and is studded with little villages. Lodgings that range from simple guest cottages to dive resorts to fishing camps have been built here. "Creeks" (we'd call them rivers) intersect the island at its midpoint. Also called "bights," they range in length from 8 to 40km (5–25 miles) and are dotted with tiny cays and islets.

The fishing potential at Andros is famous, spawning records for blue marlin catches. Divers and snorkelers find that the coral reefs here are among the earth's most beautiful, and everyone loves the pristine beaches.

Warning: Be sure to bring along plenty of mosquito repellent.

IN SEARCH OF THE chickcharnies

One of the legends of Andros Island is that aborigines live in the interior. These were thought to be a lost tribe of native Arawaks—remnants of the archipelago's original inhabitants, who were exterminated by the Spanish centuries ago. However, low-flying planes, looking for evidence of human settlements, have not turned up any indication to support this far-fetched assertion. But who can dispute that *chickcharnies* (red-eyed Bahamian elves with three toes, feathers, and beards) live on the island? Even the demise of Neville Chamberlain's ill-fated sisal plantation was blamed on these mischievous devils.

The *chickcharnie* once struck terror into the hearts of the superstitious islanders. They were supposed to live in the depths of the Androsian wilderness, making their nests in the tops of two intertwined palm trees. Tales are told of how many a woodsman in the old days endured hardship and misery because he thoughtlessly felled the trees that served as stilts for a *chickcharnie* nest. Like the leprechauns of Ireland, the *chickcharnies* belong solely to Andros. They are the Bahamian version of the elves, goblins, fairies, and duppies of other lands. Children may be threatened with them if they fail to behave, and business or domestic calamity is immediately attributed to their malevolent activities.

The origin of the legend is shrouded in mystery. One story has it that the tales began in the late 19th century when a Nassau hunting enthusiast who wanted to protect his duck-hunting grounds in Andros invented the malicious elves to frighten off unwanted interlopers. Another has it that the myth was brought to The Bahamas by bands of Seminoles fleeing Florida in the early 1880s to escape the depredations of white settlers. Some of the Seminoles settled on the northern tip of Andros. But the most probable explanation is one that traces the *chickcharnie* to a once-living creature—an extinct .9m-high (3-ft.) flightless barn owl *(Tyto pollens)*—that used to inhabit The Bahamas and West Indies.

According to The Bahamas National Trust, the local conservation authority, such a bird, "screeching, hissing and clacking its bills in characteristic barn owl fashion, hopping onto its victims or pouncing on them from low tree limbs, would have been a memorable sight. And a frightening one."

The species may have survived here into historical times, and Andros, being the largest Bahamian landmass, was probably able to sustain *Tyto pollens* longer than the smaller islands. It is probable that the early settlers on Andros encountered such beasts, and it's possible that *Tyto pollens* was the inspiration for the *Chickcharnie*. In any event, *Chickcharnie* tales are still told in Andros, and there is no doubt that they will live on as a fascinating part of The Bahamas' cultural legacy.

Andros Essentials

GETTING THERE

BY PLANE Reaching Andros is not too difficult, but selecting which of the island's four airports is closest and most accessible to your final destination is crucial. Landing strips suitable for the single-engine airplanes that service the island include **Andros Town** (ASD; © **242/329-4000**), also known as Fresh Creek, in the north/central part of the island; **Mangrove Cay,** also known as the Clarence Bain Airport (MVE; © **242/369-0003**), in the south-central part of Andros; **Congo Town** (TZN;

Morgan's Bluff

To the Bimini Islands

To the Berry Islands

Nicholl's Town

Lowe Sound

Conch Sound

San Andros

Mastic Point

San Andros Airport

NORTH ANDROS

Tongue of the Ocean

BARRIER REEF

Staniard Creek

Coakley Town (Fresh Creek)

Andros Town

Williams Island

ANDROS

Andros Town Airport

CENTRAL ANDROS

Cargill Creek

Behring Point

North Bight

Moxey Town

Middle Bight

Clarence A. Bain Airport

Drigg's Hill

Mangrove Cay

Congo Town

Alcorine Cay

Congo Town Airport

South Bight

SOUTH ANDROS

Scuba diving

Shipwreck

Reef

Airport

0   10 mi
0   10 km

Abaco

Miami

Grand Bahama

New Providence Island

FLORIDA

Eleuthera

Nassau

Cat Island

Andros

San Salvador

Great Exuma

Long Island

Crooked Island

Acklins Island

0   100 mi
0   100 km

CUBA

Great Inagua

TURKS AND CAICOS

$\textcircled{\textsmaller{C}}$ 242/369-2222) the island's most southerly airport; and **San Andros** (SAQ; $\textcircled{\textsmaller{C}}$ 242/329-2278), also known as North Andros, near the island's northernmost tip.

Continental Connection (operated by Gulfstream Airlines; $\textcircled{\textsmaller{C}}$ 800/231-0856) operates two flights a week from Fort Lauderdale to Andros Town; **LeAir Charters** ($\textcircled{\textsmaller{C}}$ 242/377-2356; www.leaircharters.com) operates flights from Nassau to Andros Town twice a day, in planes holding up to 19 passengers, every day except Monday, a 10-minute flight priced at around $100 round-trip. LeAir then continues on to Mangrove Cay for an additional fee of $20 per person. **Western Air** ($\textcircled{\textsmaller{C}}$ 242/377-2222; www.westernairbahamas.com) has twice-daily 15-minute flights from Nassau to the Andros Town Airport, priced at $100 round-trip, per adult. Those flights then continue on to Congo Town on South Andros. **Regional Air** ($\textcircled{\textsmaller{C}}$ 242/351-5614; www.go regionalair.com) flies from Freeport to San Andros airport every Friday and Sunday.

Make sure you know where you're going in Andros. For example, if you land at Congo Town on South Andros and you've booked a hotel in Nicholl's Town, you'll find connections nearly impossible at times (involving both ferryboats and a rough haul across a bad highway).

Andros's few available **taxis** know when the planes from Nassau land and drive out to the airports, hoping to pick up business. Taxis are most often shared, and a typical fare from Andros Town Airport to Small Hope Bay Lodge is about $26.

BY BOAT   Many locals, along with a few adventurous visitors, use **mail boats** to get to Andros; the trip takes 5 to 7 hours across beautiful waters. North Andros is served by the **MV Lady Rosalind,** which departs Potter's Cay Dock in Nassau heading for Morgan's Bluff, Mastic Point, and Nicholl's Town on Wednesday, returning to Nassau on Tuesday. The **MV Captain Moxey** departs Nassau on Monday, calling at Long Bay Cays, Kemp's Bay, and the Bluff on South Andros; it heads back to Nassau on Wednesday. The **MV Lady Katrina** departs Nassau Thursday night for a 5½-hour trip to Mangrove Cay and Lisbon Creek, sailing back to Nassau on Monday afternoon. Finally, MV Lady D departs from Nassau at weekly, oft-changing intervals, stopping at least four points on Andros before returning to Nassau. For details about sailing, the highly variable schedules, and costs, contact the dock master at Nassau's **Potter's Cay Dock** at $\textcircled{\textsmaller{C}}$ 242/393-1064.

A more luxurious way to go over the waters is aboard the **Sea Link** or **Sea Wind,** operated by **Bahamas Ferries** ($\textcircled{\textsmaller{C}}$ 242/323-2166; www.bahamasferries.com). The Sea Link carries 250 passengers, while the Sea Wind seats 180, with another 100 seats available on the open-air deck of each vessel. Trip time varies depending on where you dock on Andros: From Nassau to Fresh Creek, it takes 1 hour and 45 minutes; from Nassau to Driggs Hill, however, it takes 2½ hours.

ISLAND LAYOUT

Chances are, your hotel will be in either Andros Town (Central Andros) or Nicholl's Town (North Andros).

North Andros is the most developed of the major Andros islands. At its northern end, **Nicholl's Town** is a colorful old settlement with some 600 people and several places that serve local foods. Most visitors come to Nicholl's Town to buy supplies at its shopping complex. North of Nicholl's Town is **Morgan's Bluff,** namesake of Sir Henry Morgan, a pirate later knighted by the British monarch. Directly to the south of Nicholl's Town is **Mastic Point,** which was founded in 1781. If you ask around, you'll be shown to a couple of concrete-sided dives that serve up spareribs and Goombay music.

In **Central Andros,** about 47km (29 miles) south of Nicholl's Town, is **Andros Town,** with its abandoned docks. Most visitors come to Andros Town to stay at **Small Hope Bay Lodge** (p. 166) or to avail themselves of its facilities. The biggest retail industry, **Androsia batik,** is based in the area, too (p. 171). The scuba diving—minutes away on the barrier reef—is what lures most visitors to this tiny place; others come here just for the shelling. On the opposite side of the water is **Coakley Town.** If you're driving, before you get to Andros Town, you may want to stop to spend some restful hours on the beach at **Staniard Creek,** another old settlement that feels like it drifted over from the South Seas.

Moving south from Andros Town, this part of Andros is the least developed and is studded with hundreds upon hundreds of palm trees. The Queen's Highway runs along the eastern coastline, but the only thing about this road that's regal is its name. In some 7km (4⅓ miles), you can see practically the whole island. It's truly sleepy, and for that very reason, many people come here to get away from it all. You won't find much in the way of accommodations—but you will find some places to crash (they're listed below).

The third and last major land area, **South Andros,** is the home of the wonderfully named **Congo Town,** where life proceeds at a snail's pace. The Queen's Highway, partially lined with pink-and-white conch shells, runs for about 40km (25 miles) or so. The island, as yet undiscovered, has some of the best beaches in The Bahamas, and you can enjoy them almost by yourself.

Another tiny island, undeveloped **Mangrove Cay,** in south-central Andros, is an escapist's dream, attracting naturalists and anglers, as well as a few divers. It's separated from Andros's northern and southern sections by bights (inland waterways). The settlements here got electricity and a paved road only in 1989. Mangrove Cay's best place for snorkeling and diving is **Victoria Point Blue Hole** (any local can point you there). Another village (don't blink as you pass through or you'll miss it) is **Moxey Town,** where you're likely to see fishermen unloading conch from fishing boats. Ferries, operated for free by the Bahamian government, ply back and forth over the waters separating Mangrove Cay from South Andros. At the end of the road in North Andros, private arrangements can be made to have a boat take you to Mangrove Cay.

GETTING AROUND

Transportation can be a big problem on Andros. If you have to go somewhere, try to use one of the local **taxis,** though this can be a pricey undertaking.

The few **rental cars** available are in North and Central Andros. These are scarce, owing to the high costs of shipping cars here. The weather also takes a great toll on the cars that are brought in (salty air erodes metal), so no U.S. car-rental agencies are represented. Your best bet is to ask at your hotel to see what's available. In many cases, a car will be procured for your rental use from the driveway of a local resident.

Anyway, it's not really recommended that you drive on Andros because roads are mainly unpaved and in bad condition, and gas stations are hard to find. Outlets for car rentals come and go faster than anybody can count. Renting a car is less formal, and less organized, than you might be used to.

The concierge at Andros's most upscale hotel, Kamaleme Cay, will arrange a cab or a rental car for you, but frankly, it's all word of mouth and terribly unlicensed and informal, with no options for purchase of additional insurance. Taxi drivers and owners of a handful of battered cars that can be rented will be at the airport in time for the landing of most major flights. You can negotiate a car rental on site or—perhaps more safely and conveniently—you can hire one of the local taxis to take you around. Rates run between $85 and $110 per day, plus gas. Be warned that sign postings and road conditions are horrible, but it's hard to get lost because the only road is the north-south, much-rutted thoroughfare known as Queen's Highway.

You may want to rent a **bicycle,** but you'll experience the same bad roads you would in a rental car. Guests of Small Hope Bay Lodge, Chickcharnie, and Mangrove Cay Inn can rent bikes at their hotels.

VISITOR INFORMATION

The Bahamas Ministry of Tourism maintains a branch office on Lighthouse Street in Andros Town (© **242/368-2286**). It's open Monday through Friday 9am to 5pm.

[FastFACTS] ANDROS

ATMs   Banks and ATMs are rare on Andros. There's one bank with an ATM on North Andros, **Scotiabank,** in Nicholl's Town (© **242/329-2700**), and another with an ATM, **The Royal Bank of Canada** (© **242/368-2072**), in the hamlet of Fresh Creek, in north-central Andros, near Mangrove Cay. Both banks are open Monday through Thursday from 9:30am to 3pm, Friday from 9:30am to 4:30pm.

Emergencies   To reach the police, call © **919** from anywhere on Andros Island.

Medical Care   Government-run medical clinics are at Nicholl's Town on North Andros (© **242/329-2055**), at Mangrove Cay on Central Andros (© **242/369-0089**), at Kemp's Bay on South Andros (© **242/369-4849**), and at Fresh Creek, in central Andros (© **242/368-2012**).

Post Office   The island's post office is in Nicholl's Town (© **242/329-2034**), on North Andros. Hours are Monday through Friday from 9am to 4:30pm. Each little village on Andros has a store that serves as a post office, and hotel front desks can also sell Bahamian stamps. Make sure to mark cards and letters as airmail—otherwise, you'll return home before they do.

Where to Stay

Note: At those hotels listed below that have no phones in the guest rooms, phone service is available only at the front desk.

NICHOLL'S TOWN

Conch Sound Resort Inn   It's little more than a basic motel, but bonefishermen and divers seek it out. A 12-minute walk will bring you to a good beach. The location is northeast of Nicholl's Town on the way to Conch Sound. You have a choice of large, simply furnished, and rather basic bedrooms, furnished with dark-wood pieces and handmade quilts, or else you can book one of the two-bedroom suites, each with a kitchenette. Basic Bahamian fare, mostly fish, is served in the little on-site restaurant, which also attracts the locals.

Conch Sound Hwy. (btw. Nicholl's Town and Conch Sound), Andros, The Bahamas. © **242/329-2060.** Fax 242/329-2338. 10 units. $98 double. MC, V. **Amenities:** Restaurant; bar; Internet (free). *In room:* A/C, TV.

STANIARD CREEK

Kamalame Cay ★★★ 🛏   In 1995, a group of international investors created one of the most exclusive resorts in the Out Islands from the scrub-covered 38-hectare

(94-acre) landscape of a private cay off the east coast of Andros Island. Since then, it has discreetly attracted a clientele of banking moguls and financial wizards from Europe and North America, all of whom come for the superb service, escapist charm, 5km (3 miles) of beaches, and waterborne adventures that are among the best of their kind in The Bahamas. A staff of 30 to 50, some of whom were brought in from other parts of The Bahamas, includes six full-time gardeners, an army of chambermaids and cooks, and a sporting-adventure staff that's ready, willing, and able to bring groups of urban refugees out for scuba, windsurfing, and snorkeling, plus deep-sea and bone-fishing excursions above one of the world's largest barrier reefs.

Accommodations include a few smaller rooms, tasteful and very comfortable, next to the marina. More opulent are the cottages and suites, all of which lie adjacent to the beach; these are mainly crafted from local coral stone, cedar shingles, tropical-wood timbers, tiles, and, in some cases, thatch. Each is outfitted in a breezy but stylish tropical motif that evokes a decorator's journal. The food is superb, focusing on fresh fish, lobster, local soups, homemade breads, and surprisingly good wines.

Staniard Creek, Andros, The Bahamas. www.kamalame.com. ☎ **800/790-7971** or 876/632-3213. Winter $407 double, $775–$980 suite, $1,085 1-bedroom villa, $2,325–$2,550 2-bedroom villa; off-season $407 double, $615–$785 suite, $870 1-bedroom villa, $1,845 2-bedroom villa. Rates are all-inclusive, including a boat ride from Kamalame Cay. Discounts available June–Oct. MC, V. **Amenities:** Restaurant; bar; babysitting; outdoor pool; spa, tennis court (lit for night play); water-sports equipment/rentals; Wi-Fi (free). *In room:* A/C, CD player, hair dryer, minibar, no phone.

Love at First Sight   This little inn is for serious fishermen, who are attracted to its location at the mouth of Stafford Creek. It may not be love at first sight when you see the place, but anglers find it suits the bill, especially if they want to spend most of the day in the vast bonefish flats of North Andros. When you come back in the late afternoon, a cold beer awaits, along with some rum punches and delectable locally caught seafood. When you tire of fishing, you can dive along the coral reefs, bird-watch in the wetlands, or kayak to explore Stafford Creek—or just hang out by the pool. The rooms are utterly basic, like those of a roadside motel.

Stafford Creek, Andros, The Bahamas. www.loveatfirstsights.com. ☎ **242/368-6082.** Fax 242/368-6083. 10 units. Year-round $117 double. MC, V. **Amenities:** Restaurant; bar; outdoor pool; Wi-Fi (free). *In room:* Ceiling fan, fridge, no phone.

ANDROS TOWN/FRESH CREEK

Andros Lighthouse Yacht Club & Marina   Situated at the mouth of Fresh Creek with a 31-slip marina, this raffish, comfortably battered hotel/boat repair complex is a favorite of the yachting crowd. Accommodations include comfortably furnished rooms and villas, each with a decor enhanced by Caribbean fabrics and ceiling fans. The standard rooms have pool or harbor views, while the villas open onto private patios or balconies. A good on-site restaurant serves Bahamian and American dishes. Thanks to the hotel's location near one of the world's largest barrier reefs and the deep Tongue of the Ocean, it attracts scuba divers, snorkelers, and fishermen, who make ample use of the beach and the offshore waters. Fishing charters are readily available, and scuba diving and snorkeling can easily be arranged through the hotel. Ask about package rates, which include airport pickup.

Andros Town, Andros, The Bahamas. www.androslighthouse.com. ☎ **242/368-2305.** Fax 242/368-2300. 20 units. Winter $120–$145 double, $150–$170 villa; off-season $120–$130 double, from $145 villa. MAP (breakfast and dinner) $40 per person. Dive packages available. Children 12 and under stay free in parent's room. AE, DISC, MC, V. **Amenities:** Restaurant; 2 bars; outdoor pool; room service; 2 tennis courts (lit for night play); Wi-Fi (free in lobby). *In room:* A/C, TV, fridge, hair dryer (in some), kitchenette.

Small Hope Bay Lodge ★★ ☺ This is the premier diving and fishing resort of Andros, and one of the best in the entire country, with a beach right at its doorstep, and family-friendly management that grew from a corps of relatives associated with the resort's since-deceased founder, Canadian-born Dick Birch. The resort's name comes from a prediction (so far, accurate) made by a pirate named Henry Morgan, who claimed there was "small hope" of anyone finding the treasure he'd buried on Andros. The resort is an intimate cottage colony where tall coconut palms line a lovely beach and a laid-back atmosphere always prevails. And because this place is all-inclusive, your rate includes all accommodations, meals, drinks, taxes, service charges, airport transfers, and even the use of kayaks, windsurfers, and other boats, as well as bicycles and scuba lessons.

The large cabins, cooled by ceiling fans, are made of coral rock and Andros pine, and are decorated with Androsia batik fabrics. Honeymooners like to order breakfast to be served in their waterbed. For groups of three or more, the resort has a limited number of family cottages, featuring two separate bedrooms connected by a bathroom. Single travelers have a choice of staying in one of the two rooms in a family cottage and sharing the bathroom (thereby avoiding a surcharge) or paying extra for regular accommodations with a private bathroom.

For conversation and meals, guests congregate in a spacious living and dining room. Food here is wholesome, plentiful, and good—including island favorites such as conch chowder, lobster, and hot johnnycake. The chef will even cook your catch for you or make you a picnic lunch. Generally, though, lunch is a buffet, while dinner brings a choice of seafood and meat every night. Children 10 and under dine in the games room. The bar is an old boat, the *Panacea*, and drinks are offered on a rambling patio built out over the sea. Nightlife is spontaneous, with dancing in the lounge or on the patio. This place is informal: Definitely do not wear a tie at dinner.

Diving is the lodge's specialty. The owners have been diving for more than 3 decades, and their well-respected dive shop has sufficient equipment, boats, and flexibility to give guests any diving experience they want, including a course for beginners. If you'd rather fish, the lodge can hook you up with an expert guide.

Fresh Creek, Andros, The Bahamas. www.smallhope.com. © **800/223-6961** in the U.S. and Canada, or 242/368-2014. Fax 242/368-2015. 21 units. Winter $285 per adult; off-season $260 per adult; year-round $95 per child 2–7, $130 ages 8–12. Rates include tax, all meals, drinks, tips, airport transfers, and most activities. Dive packages available. AE, MC, V. The lodge is a 10-minute taxi ride from Andros Town Airport. **Amenities:** Restaurant; bar; babysitting; children's programs; Internet (free in office); Jacuzzi. *In room:* A/C (in some), ceiling fan, no phone.

CARGILL CREEK

Andros Island Bonefish Club ★ 🏛 If Hemingway were around today and wanted to go bonefishing, we'd invite him here. The club is the domain of Captain Rupert Leadon, who knows more fishing stories than anybody else in Andros. His rustic lodge lies at the confluence of Cargill Creek, the Atlantic Ocean, and North Bight's eastern end. It fronts a small protected creek, a short distance from a wadeable flat, and fishing boats can dock directly in front of the property. Constructed in 1988, this is a modern but rather bare-bones facility that draws more repeat guests than any other hostelry in The Bahamas. Eighteen more rooms were added to the complex when the Bonefish Club merged with the nearby Creekside Lodge in 2003. More than two dozen fishermen can stay here at a time in rooms with queen-size beds, ample dresser and closet space, and ceiling fans. In the dining room, guests sit at communal tables and dig into hearty and plentiful food, with an emphasis on fresh seafood such as Bahamian lobster and conch.

Cargill Creek, Andros, The Bahamas. www.androsbonefishing.com. © **242/368-5167.** Fax 242/368-5397. 29 units. Year-round $1,235 per person, double occupancy, for 3 nights and 2 days of fishing. Rates include tax, all meals, all-day fishing w/boat and guide, and transportation to and from Andros Town. Room only $225 per person. MC, V. **Amenities:** Restaurant; bar; babysitting; Internet (free in office); outdoor pool. *In room:* A/C, ceiling fan, fridge.

MANGROVE CAY

Mangrove Cay Inn This pleasant, well-managed inn belongs to a native son, Elliott Greene, who returned with his wife, Pat, after years of cold-weather life in Syracuse, New York. It's a short walk from the center of Grant's, Mangrove Cay's third-largest village (Moxey Town and Burnt Rock, though tiny, are still larger). Positioned amid scrubland near the island's eastern edge, about a third of the way up the length of Andros island, the hotel was built in the early 1990s, 2 years after the inn was established as an easygoing and affable restaurant. Accommodations have cozy but unpretentious furnishings.

Separated from Grant's Beach by a brackish lake that's stocked with fish, the inn has a mysterious blue hole positioned beside the path connecting the hotel to the beach (see "Snorkeling & Scuba Diving," below, for more on blue holes). How do guests spend their time here? Sitting on a veranda that runs the length of the building and overlooks the water, riding one of the bicycles that the hotel rents for around $10 per day, snorkeling with the hotel's equipment on the outlying reef (waters offshore are particularly rich in natural sponges and spiny Caribbean lobster), hiking, hill climbing, and looking for chickcharnies (mythical red-eyed, three-toed, birdlike creatures). For fishing excursions, the Greenes can hire a local guide for a full-day outing (about $300 per day for up to four).

The wing that contains the bedrooms is attached to a restaurant that serves Bahamian and American food, with specialties of cracked conch, grilled grouper and snapper, burgers, and steaks.

Grant's, Mangrove Cay, Andros, The Bahamas. www.mangrovecayinn.net. © **242/369-0069.** Fax 242/369-0014. 14 units. Year-round $140 double, $200 1-bedroom cottage, $335 3-bedroom cottage. No credit cards. **Amenities:** Restaurant; bar; bikes; Wi-Fi (free in lobby). *In room:* A/C, TV (in some), hair dryer, kitchen (in some), no phone.

Seascape Inn ★ 🛏 Joan and Mickey McGowan are some of the most welcoming innkeepers in the Andros chain. They took several cottages with private decks opening onto the ocean and turned them into secluded retreats for discerning guests. The cabins here are handsomely furnished with handmade mahogany pieces and original Bahamian art. All are spacious and well maintained, with tidy bathrooms. Included in the price is one of the best breakfasts you'll get on Andros: Joan is an excellent baker, turning out such early morning delights as banana bread. Fellow guests meet in the elevated dining room to enjoy excellent American and Bahamian cuisine. The McGowans will arrange scuba diving and snorkeling trips, if you wish.

Mangrove Cay, Andros, The Bahamas. www.seascapeinn.com. ©/fax **242/369-0342.** 5 cottages. Year-round $159–$175 double. Rates include breakfast and use of kayaks and bikes. AE, MC, V. **Amenities:** Restaurant; bar; bikes; kayaks; watersports equipment/rentals. *In room:* Ceiling fan, no phone, Wi-Fi (free).

SOUTH ANDROS

Tiamo ★ 🛏 One of the most ecologically aware places in the entire Bahamas, with a high percentage of repeat bookings, especially during its busiest season (March and early April), this lodge was built in stages between 1999 and 2003. It's nestled on 5 hectares (12 acres) of land that's studded with unusually large trees, directly beside the bight (inland waterway) that runs along the midsection of Andros. About a third of the guests here come to fish; a boat rental (without fishing equipment included) goes for $425 per day. Accommodations are within wood-framed, plank-sided bungalows, each with a screened-in wraparound porch, a sense of privacy, and a handful of "rustically elegant" amenities that are limited by the resort's eco-sensitive nature. This lack of plush hugely appeals to the nature-loving clients who come here. Days are spent reading, swimming off the white-sand beach that flanks one side of the resort, and generally reflecting on life. It's strongly advised that you bring company to this place, since many of the activities are engineered for couples.

Drigg's Hill, South Bight, Andros, The Bahamas. www.tiamoresorts.com. © **242/369-2330.** 10 units. Year round $895–$1,200 double. Rates include meals, airport transfers, and almost all activities. AE, DISC, MC, V. Closed: Late August to early October. **Amenities:** Restaurant; bar; kayaking; snorkeling; Wi-Fi (free in library). *In room:* No phone.

Where to Eat

Andros follows the rest of The Bahamas in its cuisine. Conch, in its many variations, is the staple of most diets, along with heaping portions of peas 'n' rice, johnnycake, and pig or chicken souse.

If you're touring the island during the day, you'll come across some local spots that serve food. If business has been slow at any of these little places, however, there might be nothing on the stove.

On Mangrove Cay, try **Dianne Cash's Total Experience,** Main Road (© **242/ 369-0430**), where you can sample Dianne's version of baked crab backs served with peas 'n' rice. Don't plan on dropping by without some kind of advance notification, though.

Barefoot Bar and Grill INTERNATIONAL   They only cater to guests of the small resort (the also-recommended 5-unit Seascape Inn) that contains it, unless you reserve in advance. Why? The New York City-derived owners, Mickey and Joan McGowan, endeavor to provide fresh-baked crumb cakes, scones, muffins, bread, and desserts every day, and stockpiling restaurant ingredients on a place as remote as Andros Island has its challenges. You'll dine on an enclosed deck overlooking the beach, with a menu that focuses on staples such as chicken in white wine and caper sauce; barbecued spare ribs, roasted loin of pork, and broiled or stuffed fresh grouper.

In Swains, Mangrove Cay. © **242/369-0342.** www.seascapeinn.com. Reservations required. Lunch main courses $11–$20, dinner main courses $15–$25. No credit cards. Daily, assuming diners reserve before 10:30am on the day of their arrival, noon–2:30pm and 6:30–8pm. Closed: July.

Kristina's BAHAMIAN   Many members of this restaurant's hardworking staff, including its manager, Mario, seem to be related to a local matriarch named Catharine Saunders, who named the place after one of her daughters. It occupies a simple, angular building beside the highway, adjacent to a nondescript shopping center, 2½ miles north of the Andros Town Airport. Menu items include a comprehensive roster of Bahamian staples, including conch fritters, cracked conch, fish fingers, pork or lamb chops, and whole baked fish, the catch of the day.

In Fresh Creek, 2½ miles north of the Andros Town Airport. © **242/368-2182.** Reservations not required. Lunch main courses $7–$12; dinner main courses $12–$16. AE, MC, V. Mon–Tues 6:30am–5pm and Wed–Sat 6:30am–9pm.

Saving Andros for Future Generations

The **Andros Conservancy and Trust** (© **242/368-2882;** www.ancat.net) might be called the guardian angel of Andros. Headquartered in Fresh Creek, this non-governmental organization was created to preserve and enhance the island's natural assets. In 2002, The Bahamas National Trust began to take on its concerns. Today, nearly 120,000 hectares (296,526 acres) of Andros have been preserved as wetlands, reefs, and marine-replenishment zones—doubling the size of the country's national park system.

All this development falls under the general authority of the **Central Andros National Park ★★★**. A great deal of self-policing is involved, with bonefisher-men keeping watch over the flats, crab-bers protecting local breeding grounds, and divers helping to preserve the reefs. This park is only just emerging, so there are no organized tours, no guides, no nature walks—yet. It is still a national park in the making.

Beaches & Outdoor Pursuits

Golf and tennis fans should go elsewhere, but if you're seeking some of the best bonefishing and scuba diving in The Bahamas, head to Andros.

HITTING THE BEACH

The eastern shore of Andros, stretching for some 161km (100 miles), is an almost uninterrupted palm grove opening onto beaches of white or beige sand. Several dozen access points lead to the beach along this shore. The roads are unmarked but clearly visible, and the clear, warm waters offshore are great for snorkeling.

FISHING ★★★

Andros is often called the bonefishing capital of the world, and the epicenter of this activity is at **Lowe Sound,** a tiny one-road hamlet that's 6.5km (4 miles) north of Nicholl's Town. Anglers come here to hire bonefish guides. **Cargill Creek** is one of the island's best places for bonefishing; nearby, anglers explore the flats in and around the bights of Andros. Some excellent ones, where you can wade in your boots, lie only 68 to 113m (223–371 ft.) offshore.

Whether you're staying in North, Central, or South Andros, someone at your hotel can arrange a fishing expedition with one of the many local guides or charter companies. In particular, **Small Hope Bay Lodge,** in Andros Town (© **242/368-2014**), is known for arranging superb fishing expeditions for both guests and nonguests. It also offers fly-, reef-, and deep-sea fishing; tackle and bait are provided.

SNORKELING & SCUBA DIVING

Divers from all over the world come to explore the **Andros Barrier Reef ★★★**, which runs parallel to the island's eastern shore. It's one of the world's largest reefs, and unlike Australia's Great Barrier Reef, which is kilometers off the mainland, the barrier reef here is easily accessible, beginning just a few hundred yards offshore.

One side of the reef is a peaceful haven for snorkelers and novice divers. The fish are mostly tame here. A grouper will often eat from your hand, but don't try it with a moray eel. The water on this side is from 2.5 to 4.5m (8¼–15 ft.) deep.

The Bahamian Loch Ness Monster

When the Atlantic Undersea Test and Evaluation Center (AUTEC) first opened, Androsians predicted that the naval researchers would find **"Lusca."** Like the Loch Ness Monster, Lusca had reportedly been sighted by dozens of locals.

The elusive sea serpent was accused of sucking sailors and their vessels into the dangerous blue holes around the island's coastline, but no one has captured the beast yet.

On the reef's other side, it's a different story. The water plunges to a depth of 167km (104 miles) into the awesome **Tongue of the Ocean (TOTO)** ★★★. One diver claimed that, as adventures go, diving here was tantamount to flying to the moon.

Myriad multicolored forms of marine life thrive on the reef, attracting nature lovers from all over the world. The weirdly shaped coral formations alone are worth the trip. This is a living, breathing garden of the sea, and its caves feel like cathedrals.

For many years, the U.S. Navy has conducted research at a station on TOTO's edge. The **Atlantic Undersea Test and Evaluation Center** (AUTEC; ✆ 242/ 368-2188), as the station is called, is devoted to underwater weapons and antisubmarine technologies. It's based at Andros Town and is a joint U.S. and British undertaking.

Among other claims to fame, Andros is known for its **blue holes,** which drop into the brine. Essentially, these are narrow, circular pits that plunge as far as 60m (197 ft.) straight down through rock and coral into murky, difficult-to-explore depths. Most of them begin below sea level, though others appear unexpectedly—and dangerously—in the center of the island, usually with warning signs placed around the perimeter. Scattered at various points along the coast, you can get to them either in rented boats or as part of a guided trip. The most celebrated one is **Uncle Charlie's Blue Hole,** mysterious, fathomless, and publicized by the legendary underwater explorer Jacques Cousteau.

The other blue holes are almost as incredible. **Benjamin's Blue Hole** ★ is named after George Benjamin, its discoverer. In 1967, he found stalactites and stalagmites 360m (1,181 ft.) below sea level. What was remarkable about this discovery is that stalactites and stalagmites are not created underwater. This has led to much speculation that The Bahamas are actually mountaintops and all that remains of a mysterious continent that has long since sunk beneath the sea (perhaps Atlantis?). Most of the blue holes, like most of the island's surface, remain unexplored. Tour boats leaving from Small Hope Bay Lodge will take you to them.

For good snorkeling, head a few kilometers north of Nicholl's Town, where you'll find a crescent-shaped beach, along with a headland, called **Morgan's Bluff,** honoring the notorious old pirate. If you're not a diver and can't go out to the Andros Barrier Reef, you can do the second-best thing and snorkel near a series of reefs known as the **Three Sisters.** Sometimes, if the waters haven't turned suddenly murky, you can see all the way to the sandy bottom. The outcroppings of elkhorn coral are especially dramatic.

Since **Mangrove Cay** is underdeveloped, rely on the snorkeling advice and gear rentals you'll get from the dive shop at **Seascape Inn** (✆ 242/369-0342; www.sea scapeinn.com). A two-tank dive costs $125 for hotel guests; nonguests are not served.

Small Hope Bay Lodge (p. 166) lies not far from the barrier reef, with its still-unexplored caves and ledges. A staff of trained dive instructors at the lodge caters to both beginners and experienced divers. Snorkeling expeditions can be arranged, as well as scuba outings (visibility underwater exceeds 30m/98 ft. on most days, with water temperatures 72°–84°F/22°–29°C). You can also rent gear here. To stay at the all-inclusive hotel for 7 nights and 8 days (rates include meals, tips, taxes, airport transfers, and three dives per day), you'll pay around $2,400 to $2,600 per person, with reduced rates of $1,300 for children. All guests are allowed, at no extra cost, to use the beachside hot tub and the sailboats, windsurfers, and bicycles.

Exploring Andros

Andros is largely unexplored, and for good reason—getting around takes some effort. With the exception of the main arteries, the few roads that exist are badly maintained and full of potholes. Sometimes you're a long way between villages. If your car breaks down, all you can do is wait and hope that someone comes along to give you a ride to the next place, where you'll hope to find a skilled mechanic. If you're heading out on your own, make sure you have a full tank of gas—service stations are few and far between.

At present, not all of Andros can be explored by car. We hope that as the island develops, roads will be constructed so that it will be easier to get around. Most of the driving and exploring is currently confined to North Andros; even there, roads go only along the eastern sector past Nicholl's Town, Morgan's Bluff, and San Andros.

Bird-watchers are attracted to Andros for its varied avian population. In the dense forests, in trees such as lignum vitae, mahogany, Madeira, horseflesh, and pine, dwell many **birds,** including parrots, doves, marsh hens, and whistling ducks.

Botanists are lured by the **wildflowers** of Andros. Some 40 to 50 species of wild orchid are said to thrive here, some of which can be found nowhere else. New discoveries are always being made, as more botanists study the land's rich vegetation.

If you're driving on Central or South Andros, you must stay on the rough **Queen's Highway.** The road in the south is paved and better than the one in Central Andros, which should be traveled only for emergency purposes or by a local.

In Andros Town, on Androsia Street next to the Lighthouse Club, you can visit the workshop where **Androsia Batik** (✆ **242/368-2020;** www.androsia.com) is made. These are the same textiles sold in the shops of Nassau and other towns. Here, artisans create designs using hot wax on fine cotton and silk fabrics. The fabrics are then crafted into island-style wear, including blouses, skirts, caftans, shirts, and accessories. All are hand-painted and hand-signed, and the resort wear comes in dazzling red, blue, purple, green, and earth tones. You can visit the factory and its sales room Monday through Friday from 8am to 5pm, Saturday from 9am to 2pm.

Morgan's Bluff, at the tip of North Andros, lures people hoping to strike it rich. The pirate Sir Henry Morgan supposedly buried a vast treasure here, but it has eluded discovery to this day, though many have searched.

Located off the northwestern coast of Andros, **Red Bay Village** is the type of place that continues to make these islands seem mysterious. In the 1840s, Seminoles and people of African descent escaping slavery in Florida fled to Andros and, miraculously, remained hidden until about 50 years ago, when an explorer "discovered" their descendants, who remain a very small, virtually self-sufficient tribe, living just as the Seminoles did in the Florida Everglades some 2 centuries ago. You should be polite and ask permission before indiscriminately photographing them. Red Bay Village is

What Would Tennessee Have Thought?

One custom in Andros recalls the Tennessee Williams drama *Suddenly, Last Summer:* catching **land crabs,** which leave their burrows and march relentlessly to the sea to lay their eggs. The annual ritual occurs between May and September. However, many of the hapless crabs will never have offspring, since both visitors and Androsians walk along the beach with baskets and capture the crustaceans before they reach the sea. Later, they get cleaned, stuffed, and baked for dinner.

connected by a causeway to the mainland, and tourists can get here by road from Nicholl's Town and San Andros

Andros After Dark

The Point, outside Congo Town (© **242/369-4977**), is one of the genuinely popular hangout venues of the South Andros area. Native-born son George Farrington settled here after a decades-long career in a New York bank. When he couldn't find a place to get a good steak, an aged rum, a vintage bottle of wine, and a decent cigar, he decided to open this bar, where food is an afterthought (if it's available at all) to live dialogue from a companionable mix of local residents and holidaymaking fishermen. Sometimes George brings in a rake 'n scrape (folk music) band or a Junkanoo troupe to entertain his clients. It's open most days from 5pm till around midnight, depending on business.

THE ABACOS

Called the "top of The Bahamas," the Abacos comprise the northernmost portion of the nation. This boomerang-shaped mini-archipelago is 209km (130 miles) long and consists of Great Abaco and Little Abaco, as well as a sprinkling of cays. The islands are about 322km (200 miles) east of Miami and 121km (75 miles) north of Nassau.

People come here mainly to explore the outdoors. The **sailing ★★** and **fishing ★★** are spectacular, and the **diving** is excellent, too. There are also many lovely, uncrowded beaches. The Abacos are definitely a world apart from the glitzy pleasures of Freeport/Lucaya, Nassau, and Paradise Island.

Many residents descend from Loyalists who left New England after the American Revolution. Against a backdrop of sugar-white beaches and turquoise water, their pastel-colored clapboard houses and white picket fences retain the Cape Cod architectural style of the area's first settlements. One brightly painted sign in Hope Town says it all: SLOW DOWN. YOU'RE IN HOPE TOWN. The same could be said for all the Abacos.

The weather is warmer here than in southern Florida, but if you visit in January or February, remember that you're not guaranteed beach weather every day—it can get chilly at times, and when winter squalls hit, temperatures can drop to the high 40s (high single digits Celsius) in severe cases. Spring in the Abacos, however, is one of the most glorious and balmy seasons in all the islands. In summer, it gets very hot around noon, but if you act as the islanders do and find a shady spot in which to escape the broiling sun, the trade winds will cool you off.

Some yachters call the Abacos the world's most beautiful cruising grounds. Excellent marine facilities, with fishing guides and boat rentals, are available here; in fact, Marsh Harbour is the bareboat-charter center of the northern Bahamas. Here you can rent a small boat, pack a picnic, and head for one of many uninhabited cays just big enough for two.

Anglers from all over the world come to catch blue marlin, kingfish, dolphinfish, yellowfin tuna, sailfish, wahoo, amberjack, and grouper. Fishing tournaments abound at Walker's Cay.

Finally, scuba divers can plumb the depths to discover caverns, inland blue holes, coral reefs, and underwater gardens, along with marine preserves and long-ago shipwrecks. Some scuba centers offer night dives.

ABACOS ESSENTIALS
GETTING THERE
BY PLANE   There are three airports in the Abacos: **Marsh Harbour** (the major one, on Great Abaco Island), **Treasure Cay,** and **Walker's**

Cay. The official points of entry by water are at Marsh Harbour, Treasure Cay, Walker's Cay, and Green Turtle Cay (New Plymouth). The latter doesn't have an airstrip, but yachters can clear Customs and Immigration there.

Many visitors arrive from Nassau or Miami on **Bahamasair** (© **800/222-4262** or 242/377-8451; www.bahamasair.com). Flight schedules change frequently, but usually include two daily flights out of Nassau (and in some seasons, three flights a day on Friday and Sunday) going first to Marsh Harbour and then on to Treasure Cay. From West Palm Beach, there's often a direct morning flight to Marsh Harbour and Treasure Cay.

Other connections include **American Eagle** (© **800/433-7300** or 242/367-2231; www.aa.com), with flights from Miami to Marsh Harbour once daily, and **Continental Connection** (© **800/231-0856;** 242/367-3415 in Marsh Harbour, 242/365-8615 in Treasure Cay; www.continental.com), which flies to Marsh Harbour and Treasure Cay two to three times daily from several Florida locales. A smaller carrier is **Twin Air** (© **954/359-8266;** www.flytwinair.com), flying from Fort Lauderdale to Treasure Cay, depending on the season, either two or three times a week.

BY BOAT   The mail boat **MV *Legacy*** sails on Tuesday from Nassau to Hope Town, Marsh Harbour, Turtle Cay, and Green Turtle Cay. It returns to Nassau on Friday. Trip time is 12 hours. For details on sailings (subject to change) and costs, contact the dock master at Nassau's **Potter's Cay Dock** at © **242/393-1064.**

Bahamas Ferries (© **242/323-2166;** www.bahamasferries.com) operates a direct service from Nassau aboard the ***Sea Wind.*** A round-trip passage costs $125 for adults and $85 for children. The trip from Nassau to Sandy Point in the Abacos takes about 3 hours. Call for bookings and more information.

GETTING AROUND

BY TAXI   Unmetered taxis, which you often have to share with other passengers, meet all arriving flights. They will take you to your hotel if it's on the Abaco "mainland"; otherwise, they will deposit you at a dock where you can hop aboard a water taxi to one of the neighboring islands. For more on accessing each island within the Abaco archipelago, refer to this chapter's introductions to Elbow Cay (p. 183), Man-O-War Cay (p. 189), Great Guana Cay (p. 190), Treasure Cay (p. 192), Green Turtle Cay (p. 195), and Spanish Cay (p. 202).

BY FERRY   Mostly, you'll get around on **Albury's Ferry Service** (© **242/367-0290;** www.alburysferry.com), which provides ferry connections between its headquarters in Marsh Harbour and both Elbow Cay (Hope Town) and Man-O-War Cay, and Guana Cay, a trip of between 20 and 30 minutes to any of them. The one-way fare from Marsh Harbour to any of those points is $17 for adults, half-price for children 6 to 11, and free for kids 5 and under. The point of departure for these ferryboat transits is the Albury Ferryboat Docks, close to the Marsh Harbour Airport. They lie within a 10-minute cab ride, priced at $15 for two passengers, plus $3 for each additional passenger.

Ferries also travel from Great Abaco Island to Green Turtle Cay, but those docks are a 35-minute, $80 cab ride (for up to four passengers) from Marsh Harbour Airport. If your final destination is Green Turtle Cay, it's better to fly into the Treasure Cay airport than the Marsh Harbour Airport. From Treasure Cay, it's a shorter (and cheaper) taxi ride to the appropriate ferryboat docks.

MARSH HARBOUR (GREAT ABACO ISLAND)

The largest town in the Abacos, and the third largest in The Bahamas, Marsh Harbour lies on Great Abaco Island and is the major gateway to this island group.

Marsh Harbour is also a shipbuilding center, but tourism accounts for most of its revenues. A number of good inns are located here. Although the town doesn't have the quaint New England charm of either New Plymouth or Hope Town, it does have a shopping center and various other facilities not found in many Out Island settlements. Good water-taxi connections, too, make this a popular place from which to explore offshore cays, including Man-O-War and Elbow. Several hotels will rent you a bike if you want to pedal around town.

Marsh Harbour Essentials

GETTING THERE   See "Abacos Essentials," above. Marsh Harbour is the most easily accessible point in the Abacos from the U.S. mainland, served by daily flights from Florida.

GETTING AROUND   You won't need a car to get around town, but if you want to explore the rest of Great Abaco Island, you can rent one for $70 to $95 per day or $350 to $400 per week (be prepared for bad roads, though). Call **A & P Rentals,** Marsh Harbour (© **242/367-2655;** www.aandpautorentals.com), to find out whether any vehicles are available. **Rental Wheels,** in Abaco, Marsh Harbour (© **242/367-4643;** www.rentalwheels.com), rents bicycles for $10 per day or $45 per week; mopeds go for $45 per day or $200 per week. Other local outlets for equivalently priced car rentals include **Bargain Car Rentals** (© **242/367-0500**) and **Sea Star Car Rentals** (© **242/367-4887**).

VISITOR INFORMATION   The **Abaco Tourist Office,** on Queen Elizabeth Drive, in the commercial heart of town (© **242/367-3067**), is open Monday through Friday from 9am to 5pm.

[FastFACTS] MARSH HARBOUR ISLAND

The **First Caribbean International Bank** is on Don MacKay Boulevard (© **242/367-2152;** www.firstcaribbeanbank.com), where you'll also find several other banks, including the **Royal Bank of Canada** (© **242/367-2420**) and **Scotiabank** (© **242/367-2142**), as well as a **post office** (© **242/367-2157**). For medication, go to the **Chemist Shop Pharmacy,** Don MacKay Boulevard (© **242/367-3106**), open Monday through Saturday from 8:30am to 5:30pm. Dial © **911** if you need the **police.**

SPECIAL EVENTS   In July, Marsh Harbour hosts **Regatta Time in Abaco,** the premier yachting event in the Abacos, attracting sailboats and their crews from around the world. Many of the yachters stay at the Green Turtle Club (p. 197). For registration forms and information, call Ruth Saunders (© **242/367-3202**) or check out www.regattatimeinabaco.com.

Where to Stay

Abaco Beach Resort & Boat Harbour ★ This beachfront resort—Marsh Harbour's biggest and best—is a good choice, especially if you're serious about diving or fishing. Extending over sprawling acreage at the edge of town and fronting a small, lovely beach, it's a business with several different faces: the hotel, with handsomely furnished rooms that overlook the Sea of Abaco; the well-managed restaurant and bar; the Boat Harbour Marina, which has slips for 180 boats and full docking facilities; and a full-fledged dive shop. The on-site **Angler's Restaurant** (see "Where to Eat," below) offers one of Marsh Harbour's best dining experiences. A swim-up bar and a beachfront bar serve snacks and grog. *Tip:* To reach the resort from Marsh Harbour Airport, 6.5km (4 miles) away, take a taxi—but be sure to agree on the price first with the driver (expect to pay around $17).

Marsh Harbour, Abaco, The Bahamas. www.abacobeachresort.com. © **800/468-4799** in the U.S., or 242/367-2158. Fax 242/367-4154. 82 units. Year-round $290–$435 double; from $570 suite. AE, DISC, MC, V. **Amenities:** Restaurant; 2 bars; bikes; exercise room; 2 outdoor pools; 2 tennis courts (lit for night play); watersports equipment/rentals. *In room:* A/C, TV, hair dryer, kitchen (in some), minibar, Wi-Fi (free).

Conch Inn Hotel & Marina At the harbor's southeastern edge, this is a casual one-story hotel leased on a long-term basis by one of the world's largest yacht-chartering companies, the Moorings. A number of small, sandy beaches are within walking distance. Its unpretentious motel-style bedrooms are midsize, each with two double beds (rollaways are available for extra occupants). Bathrooms are small but neatly kept. All units overlook the yachts bobbing in the nearby marina. On the premises is a pool fringed with palm trees, and nearby is a branch of the Dive Abaco scuba facility. The on-site restaurant and bar, called **Curly Tails** (see "Where to Eat," below), is independently managed and serves standard, recommendable fare.

E. Bay St., Marsh Harbour, Abaco, The Bahamas. www.conchinn.com. © **242/367-4000.** Fax 242/367-4004. 9 units. Feb–July $160 double; Aug–Jan $120 double. Extra person $20. AE, MC, V. **Amenities:** Restaurant; bar; outdoor pool. *In room:* A/C, TV, fridge.

Lofty Fig Villas This family-owned bungalow colony, across from the Conch Inn, overlooks the harbor. It doesn't have the services of a full-fledged resort, but it's good for families and self-sufficient types. Built in 1970, it consists of three single-story structures, each painted in tones of aqua and yellow, standing in a tropical landscape with a freshwater pool and a gazebo where you can barbecue. Rooms each contain one queen-size bed, a queen-size sleeper sofa, a dining area, a kitchen, a private screened-in porch, and a fully tiled bathroom with a shower stall. Maid service is provided Monday through Saturday.

You're about a 10-minute walk from a supermarket and shops; restaurants and bars sit just across the street. Marinas, a dive shop, and boat rentals are also close at hand. From here, you can walk, bike, or drive 1.5km (1 mile) east to a point near the ferry docks for access to a sandy beach and a snorkeling site, or you can take a ferry to Guana Cay for your day at the beach.

Marsh Harbour, Abaco, The Bahamas. www.loftyfig.com. © **242/367-2681.** 6 units. Dec 15–Sept 15 $170 double, extra person $20; Sept 16–Dec 14 $135 double, extra person $10. DISC, MC, V. **Amenities:** Outdoor pool. *In room:* A/C, TV, hair dryer, no phone, Wi-Fi (free).

Pelican Beach Villas ★   On a private peninsula near Marsh Harbour, this cottage colony gives you a choice of colors for your villa: robin's egg blue, sunflower yellow, rosy pink, or even turtle green. The complex opens onto a private beach, and there is some of the best snorkeling on the island at nearby Mermaid Reef. The spacious cottages are furnished in a Caribbean motif, with rattan pieces resting on porcelain tile floors. You can purchase supplies at the Marsh Harbour Marina and prepare meals in your own small kitchen. Picnic tables are placed outside, and coin-operated washers and dryers are available. Within walking distance are boat rentals, dive shops, and restaurants.

Northwest of Marsh Harbour Marina, The Bahamas. www.pelicanbeachvillas.com. © **877/326-3180** or 242/367-3600. 7 cottages. Year-round $175–$275 double; $375 for up to six people. AE, MC, V. *In room:* A/C, TV, kitchen, Wi-Fi (free).

Where to Eat

If you'd like to go really casual, try **Island Bakery,** on Don MacKay Boulevard (© **242/367-2129**), which has the island's best Bahamian bread and cinnamon rolls, often emerging fresh from the oven. You might even pick up the makings for a picnic. It's open Monday through Saturday from 7am to 6pm.

Angler's Restaurant ★ BAHAMIAN/INTERNATIONAL   At the Boat Harbour, overlooking the Sea of Abaco, this is the main restaurant of the town's major resort (p. 177). The interior features a nautical theme and Bahamian decor. Dock pilings rise from the water within steps of your table, yachts and fishing boats come and go, and the whole place is open and airy. The menu changes daily, but there's always fresh seafood, which the chef prepares with finesse, plus a well-chosen selection of meat dishes. Begin with crab cakes served with a Caribbean salsa and garnished with mesclun greens, or perhaps the sesame-encrusted tuna steak with sweet soy sauce. Main dishes dance with flavor, especially the cracked conch marinated in a coconut-lime sauce.

Abaco Beach Resort & Boat Harbour. © **242/367-2158.** www.abacobeachresort.com. Reservations recommended for dinner. Main courses $19–$44. AE, DISC, MC, V. Wed–Mon 11:30am–3pm and 6–10pm.

Curly Tails Restaurant & Bar BAHAMIAN   Adjacent to the Conch Inn and the Moorings facilities, this eatery attracts a lot of yachties and visiting pro athletes. The cooks use local ingredients, such as freshly caught grouper and snapper, whenever they can. They also know every conceivable way to prepare conch. The regulars don't even have to consult the menu; they just ask, "What's good?" Fish and seafood are always available; diners also look for daily specials, such as curried or steamed chicken. If you're frittering away a few hours, drop in for either a Conch Crawl, a potent rum-based drink made with secret ingredients, or a "curlytail martini" garnished with (guess what?) shrimp. The bar, set beneath an octagonal gazebo near the piers, is a fine place to meet people.

Conch Inn Hotel & Marina (The Moorings), E. Bay St. © **242/367-4444.** www.conchinn.com. Reservations not needed. Main courses $22–$50. MC, V. Daily 7am–10pm.

Jib Room BAHAMIAN/AMERICAN   This funky restaurant and bar is a hangout for locals and boat owners who savor its welcoming spirit. If you want the house-special cocktail, a Bilge Burner, get ready for a head-spinning combination of apricot brandy, rum, coconut juice, and Kahlúa. Saturday night brings Jib's steak barbecue, when as many as 300 1-pound New York strip steaks are brought out. The only other night dinner is served is Wednesday, when grilled baby back ribs might be the featured dish. Other choices include a seafood platter, grilled chicken, and broiled lobster—and yes, you've probably had it all before in better versions, but the dishes are prepared well enough. Go for the convivial atmosphere rather than the food.

Marsh Harbour Marina, Pelican Shores. 📞 **242/367-2700.** www.jibroom.com. Reservations required for dinner. Lunch platters $9–$15; fixed-price dinners $22–$30. MC, V. Wed–Sat noon–2:30pm; Wed and Sat 7–11pm.

Mangoes Restaurant ★ BAHAMIAN/INTERNATIONAL   Near the harbor in one of the town's most distinctive buildings, Mangoes is the best, and certainly the most popular, restaurant on the island, attracting both yachties and locals. It boasts a cedar-topped bar and a cathedral ceiling that soars above a deck jutting over the water. Chefs seem to try a little harder here, offering a typical menu along with a hint of island spirit. Grilled grouper gets dressed up a bit with almonds and lime-flavored butter, wild salmon gets a dressing of dill-flavored mustard sauce, and cracked conch makes an appearance on the menu as well. Your best bet, as in nearly all Bahamian restaurants, is usually the fresh catch of the day. At lunch, you can sample the restaurant's locally famous conch burger or an array of hero sandwiches.

Front St. 📞 **242/367-2366.** www.mangoesmarina.com. Reservations recommended. Main courses $11–$20 lunch; $25–$48 dinner. MC, V. Mon–Sat 11:30am–2:30pm; daily 6:30–10pm.

Snappas Bar & Grill BAHAMIAN   At the Harbour View Marina, this bar and tavern with its open-air waterside deck attracts yachties and also owners of small boats. It's one of the best places to hang out in Marsh Harbour when the sun goes down. Party time with live music is on Friday and Saturday nights when both locals and visitors fill up the joint. Happy hour is daily from 5 to 7pm.

For lunch, the best sandwiches on island are served here, along with freshly made salads, burgers, and seafood. Try the 8-ounce Black Angus burger or the catch of the day which might be mahimahi or sushi tuna. All dinners are served with baked potato and a Caesar salad, and the food is cooked to order. The fish dinner can either be grilled or blackened. The most expensive item on the menu is surf & turf, a 10-ounce steak and an 8-ounce crawfish tail. A real Bahamian dish, conch steak wrapped in foil and grilled, is featured most nights, depending on the catch.

Harbour View Marina, Bay St. 📞 **242/367-2278.** www.snappasbar.com. Reservations not needed. Lunches from $15; dinner main courses $20–$52. MC, V. Daily 11am–4pm and 5–10pm.

Wally's BAHAMIAN/INTERNATIONAL   Across the street from the water, this eatery occupies a tidy pink colonial-style villa on a hibiscus-dotted lawn. It's got an outdoor terrace, a boutique, and an indoor bar and dining area filled with Haitian paintings. The drink of the house is Wally's Special, which contains four kinds of rum and a medley of fruit juices. The chef prepares the island's best Bahamian cracked conch, as well as tender filet mignon, lamb chops, fried chicken, and excellent variations of grouper, either fried, grilled, blackened, or smothered in a tomato/onion sauce. Main dishes come with a generous portion of vegetables or salad and your choice of rice or potatoes. The place really shines at lunchtime, when things get very busy as hungry diners devour dolphinfish burgers, several kinds of chicken platters, and some well-stuffed sandwiches. Live music performances take place on Wednesday and Saturday nights.

E. Bay St. 📞 **242/367-2074.** Reservations recommended for dinner. Lunch sandwiches and platters $12–$20; dinner main courses $19–$40. AE, DISC, MC, V. Tues–Sat 11:30am–3pm and 6–9pm. Closed 8 weeks Sept–Oct.

Beaches & Outdoor Pursuits

Whatever sport you want to pursue—whether it be **snorkeling** or **fishing**—Marsh Harbour's innkeepers can set you up with the right people and equipment. You can also take the ferry over to Hope Town (on Elbow Cay) and check out the facilities and outfitters there.

Of the major Out Islands towns, Marsh Harbour has some of the least appealing shores. You can try one of three private beaches, but none is very enticing, and none really wants outsiders. The easiest to get into is at Abaco Beach Resort, but it's small, not fabulous, and, again, private. Buy a drink for a local at the hotel bar, and you're in, but that, at best, is a somewhat uncomfortable arrangement.

To compensate, beach seekers head south of Marsh Harbour. Once south of Little Harbour, after 15 to 20 minutes of driving, lots of good options begin to appear. The beaches near the hamlet of **Casuarina Point** benefit from some battered, all-Bahamian restaurants in the vicinity.

Some **swimmers** heading south from Marsh Harbour make it a point to go eastward from the main highway whenever an offshoot road appears, usually at points south of Little Harbour.

None of the beaches on Great Abaco Island has facilities or lifeguards. Guard your valuables and stay alert.

BOAT CHARTERS

The **Moorings** (© 888/952-8420 or 242/367-4000; www.moorings.com) is one of the world's leading charter sailboat and powerboat outfitters. It operates from a perch behind the Conch Inn Hotel & Marina, overlooking intersecting piers and wharves—at least 40 berths—where upscale watercraft are tied up (many of them for rent). With one of its vessels, you can enjoy short sails between the islands, stopping at white-sand beaches and snug anchorages. Yacht rentals generally range from as low as $190 per day to as much as $1,600 per day, depending on the craft and the season, with a skipper costing another $190 per day, and an onboard cook (if you want one) for an additional $175 per day. Onboard provisions cost extra.

For the more casual boater, **Sea Horse Boat Rentals,** at Abaco Beach Resort & Boat Harbour (© 242/367-5460; www.seahorseboatrentals.com), offers some of the best rentals. A 5.1m (17-ft.) Boston Whaler goes for $165 per day, while a 7.8 m (26-foot) 250-horsepower Paramount costs $305 per day. Other vessels are for rent, too, and all boats are equipped with coolers, a compass, a swimming platform, life jackets, a paddle, docking lines, and other equipment. Sea Horse is open daily from 8am to 5pm.

SNORKELING & SCUBA DIVING

The strangest dive site of all is the **Abacos Train Wreck,** 4.5 to 6m (15–20 ft.) deep. This unusual wreck consists of two locomotives lying on their sides. During the U.S. Civil War, they were reportedly part of a Union train captured by Confederate troops and then sold to Cuba. The barge transporting the train ran aground on the reef during a storm in 1865. Enough of the train still exists to make it an interesting shore dive. Another nearby wreck, the *Adirondack,* lies in shallow water some 3 to 7.5m (9¾–25 ft.) deep. Many divers come here to explore the government-protected **Sea Preserve and Fowl Cay Land,** which teems with multicolored sea life in shallow reefs.

The best place to snorkel is **Mermaid Reef and Beach,** with its colorful reef, moray eels, and a plethora of beautiful rainbow-hued fish. The reef and beach lie on

Pelican Shores, the northernmost edge of the Marsh Harbour waterfront directly west of the Marsh Harbour Marina. From the center of Marsh Harbour at East Bay Street, walk east along the harbor, and then head northwest until you reach the marina. Once there, continue walking west to Pelican Shores across the stretch of scrub and sand until you reach Mermaid Reef, where you can enjoy the beach or snorkel in the clear waters. **Sea Horse Boat Rentals,** at Abaco Beach Resort & Boat Harbour (© **242/367-5460**), rents snorkel gear.

Scuba divers should check out the nearby **Pelican Cays Land and Sea Park ★**. You won't find any organized excursions here, but Dive Abaco (see below) is the best source of information and might arrange a trip for you. You can also drive down to the park by following the road immediately south of Marsh Harbour and then turning east at the sign leading you toward the park. Several small beaches are suitable for swimming. The easiest jumping-off point is at Pelican Harbour.

Dive Abaco, Marsh Harbour (© **800/247-5338** in the U.S., or 242/367-2787; www.diveabaco.com), rents snorkel gear and offers dive trips to tunnels and caverns along the world's third-longest barrier reef. Resort courses for uncertified novice divers are all-inclusive at $195. Two-tank dives for certified divers cost $125, including tanks and weights, and depart daily at 9:30am; afternoon times are dictated by demand. Full P.A.D.I. or N.A.U.I certification costs $650, and requires participation in a 4-to-5-day program that includes classroom instruction, pool training, and four open water dives. Shop hours are daily from 8:30am to 5pm; ask for owner-operator Keith Rogers.

Attractions on Land

Marsh Harbour is the best central point for exploring the nature-created attractions of Great Abaco and Little Abaco.

A fully graded and tarred main highway links all the settlements, with such colorful names as Fire Road, Mango Hill, Red Bays, Snake Cay, Cherokee Sound, and, our favorite, Hole-in-the-Wall, which lies at the "bottom" of Great Abaco.

Driving south for 40km (25 miles) from Marsh Harbour along Great Abaco Highway, you come first to **Cherokee Sound,** set at the end of a jutting peninsula. The 150 residents are descended from Loyalists who fled the mainland U.S. in 1783 to remain faithful to the British Crown. These people faced an inhospitable environment for 2 centuries and have tried to make a living as best they can. The men dive for lobsters or go out at night "sharking" (the sharks' jaws are sold in Marsh Harbour). They also hunt down tiniki crabs, as well as pigeon and wild boar in the remote pinelands of the Abacos.

The unhurried routine around here is in the process of major change. About a decade ago, on scrublands adjacent to Winding Bay, hotel entrepreneur and lifestyle guru Peter de Savary opened one of the most exclusive members-only residence clubs in The Bahamas. Now owned and operated by the Ritz-Carlton Group, **Abaco Club on Winding Bay Ritz Carlton** (www.ritzcarltonclub.com; © **866/605-8681** or 242/367-0077) is deluxe living personified, but only for the super-rich. The first time you stay, a studio-style cabana will cost between $489 and $850 per night as part of a promotional rate, and two- to four-bedroom units will range from $1,200 to $3,500 per night. If you return, however, for a second visit, you'll be expected to pay a hefty membership fee and invest in a fractional ownership share of the Ritz-Carlton Clubs—a kind of ultra-upscale timeshare investment with many complicated ramifications.

Forty-eight kilometers (30 miles) south of Marsh Harbour, to the immediate east of Cherokee Sound, is **Little Harbour,** a circle-shaped cay with a white-sand beach running along most of its waterfront. Here you can visit **Pete Johnston's Foundry** (© **242/577-5487**), the only bronze foundry in The Bahamas. Settling here in 1951, the Johnston family achieved international fame as artists and sculptors. They use an old "lost-wax" method to cast their bronze sculptures, many of which are sold in prestigious art galleries in the U.S.; you can also buy them here. Margot Johnston creates porcelain figurines of island life such as birds, fish, boats, and even fishermen. The Johnstons welcome visitors to their studio daily from 10 to 11am and 2 to 3pm. You can purchase a remarkable book here, *Artist on His Island,* detailing the true-life adventures of Randolph and Margot Johnston, who lived a *Swiss Family Robinson* adventure when they first arrived at Little Harbour with their three sons. Sailing in an old Bahamian schooner, the *Langosta,* they stayed in one of the local caves until they eventually erected a thatched dwelling for themselves.

After a visit to the foundry, stop in for a drink at laid-back **Pete's Pub and Gallery** (© **242/577-5487;** www.petespubandgallery.com), whose decor evokes *Gilligan's Island.* The pub was constructed in part from the timbers of the *Langosta* and opens daily at 11am, staying that way "until everyone leaves at night" (it's closed Sept–Oct). The beer is cold, and the art on the walls is for sale. You can also order lunch here daily, costing around $23. Fresh seafood such as mango-glazed grouper or lemon-pepper mahimahi is served along with burgers. A boar roast happens every Saturday from April through July. In the evening, Pete Johnston might sing a medley of sea chanteys, accompanying himself on his guitar.

After leaving Cherokee Sound and Little Harbour, you can return to Great Abaco Highway, heading south once again to reach the little fishing village of **Casuarina Point,** west of Cherokee Sound, where you'll find a lovely stretch of sand and some jade-colored flats (low-water areas where bonefish are plentiful). If you keep going south, you'll come to **Crossing Rocks,** another little fishing village 64km (40 miles) south of Marsh Harbour. This hamlet, where locals barely eke out a living, takes its name from the isthmus where Great Abaco Island narrows to its thinnest point. It's noted for its kilometer-long (⅔-mile) beach of golden sand.

If you continue traveling south from here, you'll come to a fork in the road. If you take the southern route, you'll be heading toward **Abaco National Park,** also called **Bahamas National Trust Sanctuary** (© **242/367-6310;** www.bnt.bs), and the aptly named **Hole-in-the-Wall,** a poor little hamlet with few settlers; it marks the end of the line for drives along the Abacos. Protected by the government, the 8,296-hectare (20,500-acre) Abaco National Park, established in 1994, sprawls across Grand Abaco Island's southeastern portion. Some 2,023 hectares (4,999 acres) of it is pine forest, with a lot of wetlands that are home to native bird life, including the endangered Bahama parrot. Hardwood forests, sand dunes, and mangrove flats fill the area. Rangers, under the sponsorship of the Bahamas National Trust, lead occasional tours of the sanctuary and protect the area.

Shopping

For women's clothing, check out a locally owned emporium of resort wear, **Island Girl** (© **242/367-0283**), on Main Street, across from the Conch Inn. Almost next door, try **Iggy Biggy** (© **242/367-3596**) for souvenir items. For jewelry and resort wear for men and women, try **Sand Dollar Abaco Gold** (© **242/367-4405**), opposite the entrance to the Abaco Beach Resort. A few steps away, you'll find a local

Off-beat Beach Bar Called One of the World's Best

An off-beat oddity **Cracker P's Bar and Grill** is found at Lubbers Quarters, a small islet measuring 1½×¼ miles in size. There are about 70 private homes on this islet between Marsh Harbour and Elbow Cay. There is no ferry service, and it's reached only by a rented boat or private boat. Mr. and Mrs. Patrick Stewart operate Cracker P's (© **242/366-3139;** www. crackerps.com), named after a Georgia "Cracker," Paul John Simmons, who lived on the island for about 4 decades, after fleeing here when he shot the sheriff in his own state of Georgia. The *Sunday Times* of London named their beach bar one of the best in the world.

At lunch you can order Cracker's grilled conch or burgers and sandwiches, with such side dishes as Grandma's baked beans or grilled veggies. The offerings at dinner are more elaborate including such main dishes as New York strip steak, grilled chicken breast, or the catch of the daily, plus sumptuous desserts made fresh daily. Lunch platters cost from $8 to $11, with main dishes at night ranging from $24 to $38. MasterCard and Visa are accepted. The eatery is open from Christmas to mid-August Wednesday to Sunday (also Tuesday during June and July, their busiest months). Discuss hours for your reservations and transportation when you call the Stewarts to book a table.

branch of the international purveyor of cameras, jewelry, perfume, luggage, and clothing, **John Bull** (© 242/367-2473).

Marsh Harbour After Dark

Opening onto the Sea of Abaco, the **Sand Bar,** at Abaco Beach Resort (© **242/367-2158**), is the most popular gathering spot in town. The yachting crowd, often from Miami, hangs out here, swapping tall sea tales while downing strong rum punches. Another good hangout is **Wally's,** on East Bay Street (© **242/367-2074**), where drinkers enjoy the special punch on an outdoor terrace or inside the cozy bar. On Wednesday and Saturday, live entertainment is often presented. Other nightlife venues include the also-recommended **Snappa's** (p. 179), **Curly Tails** (p. 178), and the **Jib Room** (p. 178), all of which become more convivial for a few hours after about 8pm, especially on Fridays and Saturdays.

ELBOW CAY (HOPE TOWN) ★

Elbow Cay is known for its spectacular beaches. One of the best in The Bahamas, **Tahiti Beach,** lies in splendid isolation at the far end of Elbow Cay, with sparkling waters and powdery white sand. Access is possible only on foot, by riding a rented bicycle across sand and gravel paths from Hope Town, or by private boat.

The cay's largest settlement is **Hope Town,** a scenic little village with a candy-striped 36m (118-ft.) lighthouse—the most photographed attraction in the Out Islands. Hope Town seems frozen in time. Like other offshore cays of the Abacos, it was settled by Loyalists who left the new United States to remain subjects of the British Crown. Its clapboard saltbox cottages are weathered to a silver gray or painted pastel colors, with white picket fences setting them off. The buildings may remind you of New England, but this palm-fringed island has South Seas flavor.

The island is almost free of cars. While exploring Hope Town, you can take one of two roads: "Up Along" or "Down Along," which both run along the water.

Elbow Cay Essentials

GETTING THERE   You can reach Elbow Cay in about 20 minutes via regularly scheduled ferry service from Great Abaco Island's Marsh Harbour. **Albury's Ferry Service** (✆ **242/367-0290;** www.alburysferry.com) makes the trip between six and seven times daily, depending on the season. One-way fare is $17 for adults; a same-day round-trip costs $27. Children 6 to 11 pay half-price.

GETTING AROUND   Many visitors rent **boats** to get around the island, snorkel, fish, and explore nearby cays. But if you're not interested in playing sea captain, you can still move easily around Elbow Cay. Hope Town's quiet, narrow streets are reserved for pedestrians; you can walk to many other parts of tiny Elbow Cay, too. You can't rent a car on the island, but that's not a problem, as Hope Town has banned all motor vehicles. **Bicycles** are available at or near most accommodations, which often loan them out free to guests.

If you'd like a golf cart delivered to your hotel, call **Island Cart Rentals** (✆ **242/366-0448** in the U.S.; www.islandcartrentals.com); these gas or electric carts cost $45 per day or $270 per week. Hotels provide **shuttle vans** to and from town, and some restaurants offer pick-up and drop-off service at dinnertime if you call ahead. **Taxis** meet incoming flights at Marsh Harbour Airport, as well as arriving ferries at the docks. The staff at your hotel can call for one when you need it.

[FastFACTS] ELBOW CAY

The **Hope Town Medical Clinic** (✆ **242/366-0108**) lies at the end of the ferryboat dock, point of arrival for the ferryboats coming in from Marsh Harbour. A local **post office** (✆ **242/366-0098**) is at the head of the upper public dock, but expect mail sent from here to take a long time. Hours are Monday through Friday from 9am to noon and 1 to 5pm.

Where to Stay

Elbow Cay's long, secluded white-sand shores, some backed by dunes, are some of the most stunning in The Bahamas. Though accommodations are located on or near beaches, the strands remain virtually vacant because the hotels are small and few in number.

If you're considering anchoring into Elbow Cay for a week or so, consider one of the rentals at **Hope Town Hideaways,** 1 Purple Porpoise Place (www.hopetown. com; ✆ **242/366-0224**). Staying here is like having your second home in the islands. This is a rental agent with listings for some 75 cottages or private homes and apartments.

Some units come with boat slips, and some also contain private pools. Each rental unit is different, depending on the individual owner's taste. Accommodations for four occupants cost from a minimum of $1,100 per week for the simplest accommodations to $4,500 per week for a more luxurious space. Hope Town Hideaways is the largest rental agency in Elbow Cay.

Abaco Inn ★ 🏠   A sophisticated little hideaway about 3km (1¾ miles) south of Hope Town, Abaco Inn faces a lovely beach on White Sound. An informal barefoot elegance and a welcoming spirit prevail here. The inn is located on Elbow Cay's narrowest section, between the jagged east coast's crashing surf and the sheltered waters of White Sound and the Sea of Abaco to the west. From the cedar-capped gazebo, you can gaze out over the Atlantic's rocky tidal flats. Excellent snorkeling is nearby. The midsize accommodations are arranged in a crescent facing the beach. They're set amid palms and sea grapes, and each has its own hammock placed conveniently close for quiet afternoons of reading or sleeping. Each comfortable unit has a ceiling fan, white-tile floors, sliding-glass doors, and traditional furniture. The luxury villa suites have decks with views. A modern, rambling clubhouse with a fireplace is the social center and the island's most appealing restaurant (p. 186). Shuttle service is available from the airport, and boating and fishing can be arranged through the hotel.

White Sound, Hope Town, Elbow Cay, Abaco, The Bahamas. www.abacoinn.com. © **800/468-8799** in the U.S., or 242/366-0133. Fax 242/366-0113. 22 units. Year-round $130–$195 double, $200–$270 villa for two. Extra persons $50 each. AE, DISC, MC, V. Closed mid-Aug to mid-Nov. **Amenities:** Restaurant; 2 bars; babysitting; bikes; outdoor pool; Wi-Fi (free in bar). *In room:* A/C, hair dryer, no phone.

Hope Town Harbour Lodge ★★

This much-expanded former private home lies near Hope Town's beach and harbor. It was the home of Brigadier Thomas Robbins, a British army officer who constructed the original core as his retirement house in 1948. After suffering damage from Hurricane Floyd in 1999, the property lay dormant until its radical renovation a year later. Hurricane-strength windows and doors were implemented, along with new furnishings. Possibly the best addition was the installation of private balconies in all the rooms in the main building, each opening onto a water view. Boardwalks and artful landscaping added other grace notes. In addition to the lodge rooms, there are six independent cottages, each with terra-cotta tile floors and French doors opening onto private decks, as well as six cabanas. The best way to stay here is to rent the luxurious century-old Butterfly House. See "Where to Eat," below, for a dining review.

Upper Rd., Hope Town, Elbow Cay, Abaco, The Bahamas. www.hopetownlodge.com. © **866/611-9791** or 242/366-0095. Fax 242/366-0286. 28 units. Year-round $155–$195 double; $185–$235 cabana; $235–$335 cottage; $450 for 4 or $625 for 6 in Butterfly House. MC, V. **Amenities:** 2 restaurants; 2 bars; outdoor pool. *In room:* A/C, TV (in Butterfly House only), hair dryer, kitchenette (in some), minibar, no phone, Wi-Fi ($20).

Hope Town Inn and Marina

Acquired and renovated by a new investment group in 2010, this is one of the most tranquil inns anywhere. Because of its isolated position near the lighthouse on the west edge of Hope Town's harbor, the only way to get to this Spanish-style resort is by boat. Once here, you're just a short walk from some lovely beaches. If you bring your own boat, you can moor it at this hotel's marina—but if you just happen to have left your boat at home, call a member of the staff, who will arrange a complimentary waterborne transfer from any nearby coastline. The midsize rooms are set in a two-story, Mediterranean-inspired annex, overlooking a pool and the boats in the harbor. Each contains two double beds, a bathroom with shower, and clean, tasteful decor. At presstime, the restaurant formerly associated with this place was closed, but plans were underway to re-open it, so call to check the status if this is a priority for you.

Western Harbourfront, Hope Town, Elbow Cay, Abaco, The Bahamas. © **850/588-4855** or 242/366-0003. Fax 242/366-0254. 7 units. Year-round $130–$150 double; $140 triple; $150 quad; $180 2-bedroom apt. AE, MC, V. **Amenities:** Outdoor pool. *In room:* A/C, TV, hair dryer, kitchen (in apt), minibar, no phone.

Sea Spray Resort & Marina ★ On 2.4 hectares (6 acres) of grounds, 5.5km (3½ miles) south of Hope Town and near Elbow Cay's southernmost tip, these beachfront villas are managed by Junior Menard, who runs them in a welcoming, personal way. Accommodations are spacious and comfortably furnished, each with a small bathroom. Villas include full kitchens and decks that overlook the water and the boats bobbing within the resort's 60-slip marina. The hardworking staff is happy to share their knowledge of what to see and do around here; you can bike, sail, fish, snorkel, or explore nearby deserted islands.

At Sea Spray's **Helm Bar and Boat House Restaurant,** guests can enjoy well-prepared food at all three mealtimes, accompanied by a view of the surf and a weathered gazebo.

White Sound, Elbow Cay, Abaco, The Bahamas. www.seasprayresort.com. ℂ **717/718-8267** or 242/366-0065. Fax 242/366-0383. 7 units. Year-round $235–$300 1-bedroom unit; $455 2-bedroom unit; $585 3-bedroom unit. AE, MC, V. **Amenities:** Restaurant; bar; outdoor pool; watersports equipment/rentals. *In room:* A/C, TV, kitchen, no phone, Wi-Fi ($15).

Turtle Hill Vacation Villas ★ On the outskirts of Hope Town, a trio of luxury villas (each housing two rental units) lies just steps from a vast beach where sea turtles return to nest. Fruit trees and other tropical foliage make this a secluded getaway. Each of the units can be configured to sleep either four or six occupants, with a queen-size sleeper sofa in the living room, a full bathroom, a well-equipped kitchen, and ceiling fans. Linens are provided, and a Caribbean-style cabana bar with a deck stretching out over the sands of the beach serves drinks and simple platters.

Hope Town (btw. Abaco Sea and Hope Town), Elbow Cay, Abaco, The Bahamas. www.turtlehill. com. ℂ **954/636-6066** in the U.S., or 242/366-0557. Fax 242/366-0557. 6 units. $275–$380 daily for up to 4 guests; $310–$420 for 5–6 guests. AE, DISC, MC, V. **Amenities:** Bar; babysitting; 2 outdoor pools; Wi-Fi (free). *In room:* A/C, TV/VCR, CD player, hair dryer (in some), kitchen, no phone.

Where to Eat

Abaco Inn ★ BAHAMIAN/INTERNATIONAL Flavorful food is served in a breezy, almost elegant waterfront setting here. The chef prepares lunch dishes such as conch chowder, pasta primavera, and salads with delectable homemade dressings featuring tarragon and other herbs. The dinner menu changes frequently but usually offers seafood, vegetarian, and meat dishes, each expertly seasoned and well-prepared. Typical meals are likely to begin with seafood bisque or vichyssoise, followed by coconut grouper (a house specialty), spinach fettuccine Alfredo, roasted lamb with herbs and mint sauce, or, broiled red snapper with a light salsa. The crème brûlée and Key lime, coconut, and chocolate-silk pies are delectable. The inn will send a minivan to pick you up from other parts of the island if you phone in advance.

About 4km (2½ miles) south of Hope Town. ℂ **242/366-0133.** Reservations required for dinner. Lunch sandwiches, salads, and platters $11–$19; dinner main courses $25–$50. AE, DISC, MC, V. Daily 8–10:30am, noon–3pm, and 6:30–9:30pm.

Cap'n Jack's BAHAMIAN Depending on when you come, you may find conch burgers, beef burgers, or crayfish on the menu at this casual alfresco dining spot at the harbor's edge. Any time of year, the grouper and conch are well prepared and are the menu's freshest options. Landlubbers gravitate toward the more routine fried chicken and burgers. The coconut pies, pumpkin rolls, and chocolate-silk pies are justifiably popular dessert choices. Try the bar's version of the omnipresent Goombay

Smash. Come on Wednesday or Friday nights when a local DJ spins music between 8 and 11pm.

On the harbor in Hope Town. 𝓒 **242/366-0247.** Main courses $12–$25. MC, V. Mon–Sat 8:30am– 11pm.

Harbour's Edge ★ BAHAMIAN Hope Town's most popular restaurant is set above the water in a clapboard house. It's the island's lighthearted social center. The bar has an adjacent waterside deck where you can moor if you arrive by boat, as many visitors do. Here and in the dining room, the crackle of VHF radio is always audible, since boat owners and locals often reserve tables over shortwave radio, channel 16. Lunch includes typical yet flavor-filled dishes like hamburgers, club sandwiches, conch fritters, conch chowder, and conch platters. At dinnertime, main course options include generous portions of chicken in white wine with potatoes, Greek or Caesar salad, pan-fried pork chops, filet steaks, char-grilled grouper, stewed fish in coconut milk, and more.

Hope Town, next to the post office. 𝓒 **242/366-0087.** Reservations recommended. Main courses $11–$21 lunch; $17–$45 dinner. MC, V. Restaurant Wed–Mon 11:30am–11pm. Bar Wed–Mon 10am–2am. Closed mid-Sept to mid-Oct.

Hope Town Harbour Lodge ★ BAHAMIAN One of the first lodgings ever built in Hope Town (p. 185), this hotel's dining options are still winning it new friends. At night, romantic couples opt for a table on the cozy terrace with views of the harbor and yachts' lights. Begin the evening with a rum punch at the bar, which also overlooks the water. The menu here is hardly inventive, but it's good, featuring the usual array of chicken, steak, and pork chops. Occasionally, a fisherman will bring in a big marlin that the chef then grills to perfection. Bahamian lobster appears delightfully in a creamy fettuccine, and the local grouper is fashioned into spring rolls served with a mustard-laced chutney. In the main dining area are picture windows, rattan chairs, and nautical prints. During lunch, diners head to the Reef Bar & Grill fronting the water.

Upper Rd., Hope Town. 𝓒 **242/366-0095.** Reservations recommended for dinner. Main courses $11–$16 lunch; $25–$38 dinner. MC, V. Daily 11:30am–3pm and 6:30–8pm.

Beaches & Outdoor Pursuits

In Hope Town, you'll find sandy beaches right at your doorstep, with more beaches only a 15-minute ride south. **Garbanzo Beach,** in the White Sound area, lures many surfers. The waves and breezes make it prime hang-ten territory. If you didn't bring a board, the staff at nearby **Sea Spray Resort** (𝓒 242/366-0065) can help you get one.

Isolated **Tahiti Beach ★★**, at the island's southern end, got its name from its thick wall of palms. At low tide, the shelling can be excellent along this gorgeous curve of sand, and the shallow waters make for good bonefishing, too. Across the way, you can see uninhabited Tilloo Cay and the Atlantic's crashing waves in the distance. Tahiti Beach is about a 10-minute bike ride from Sea Spray and about 20 minutes from Abaco Inn, in the White Sound area. To get here, you have to walk your bike up and down a few small but rocky rises.

Traveling along, you'll pass sea-grape trees, fluffy long-needled pines, and other varied roadside vegetation. Turn left when you come to the first major place to do so (by the white house on the bluff) and then turn right when you see two stone pillars. Go downhill and turn left at the end of the road at the wire fences. Take this path to the end. Walk along the dense palm grove to the beach. Because you're heading for the shore, which is public, ignore the PRIVATE—NO TRESPASSING signs.

Irresistible deserted beaches lie south of Elbow Cay on pencil-thin **Tilloo Cay** and the tiny **Pelican Cays,** excellent targets for a day's sail. The waters here, packed with grouper and conch, are particularly good for fishing and swimming. In **Pelican Cays Land and Sea Park,** one of the most colorful dive sites around is **Sandy Cay Reef.** Line fishing, spear fishing, and shelling, however, are all taboo in this protected area.

About 20 steps south of Hope Town's post office, **Froggies Out Island Adventures,** Harbour Road (© 242/366-0431; www.froggiesabaco.com), is the largest dive outfitter in the Abacos, with three boats (ranging 9–17m/30–56 ft. in length) that owner Theresa Albury uses to take divers to local sites. Certified scuba divers pay $120 for an outing and gear rental. Snorkeling excursions cost $80 for adults and $55 for children.

The ideal way to explore the Abacos is by boat. The waters off the coast of Elbow Cay are popular for boating and fishing—just head to the marina to join the fun. Or you can contact **Island Marine,** Parrot Cay near Hope Town (© 242/366-0282; www.islandmarine.com), to be set up with one of its rentals. You can then cruise to the boat-building settlement of Man-O-War Cay, to artist Pete Johnston's bronze foundry/gallery/pub in Little Harbour (p. 182), and to many uninhabited cays and deserted beaches where you can go shelling, exploring, and picnicking in peace. Small-boat rentals range from a 5.1m (17-ft.) Boston Whaler to a 7m (23-ft.) Man-O-War. Prices run from $125 to $250 per day or $625 to $1,800 per week.

Attractions on Land

No cars are allowed in the heart of **Hope Town,** so bikers and pedestrians have the narrow paved streets, with names like Lovers' Lane, to themselves. As you wander through town, you'll see harborside restaurants and pastel-painted cottages with purple and orange bougainvillea tumbling over stone and picket fences. Amid the usual island fare at the handful of souvenir shops is resort wear made from Androsia batik fabric (see "Shopping," below).

To find out why Malone is such a common surname here, stop by the **Wyannie Malone Museum** (officially open most days 10am–noon, but unofficially open "whenever"). This small collection of island lore is in tribute to the South Carolinian widow and mother of four who founded Hope Town around 1783.

Before Hope Town's red-and-white-striped **lighthouse** was erected in 1838, many locals made a good living luring ships toward shore to be wrecked on the treacherous reefs and rocks, and then turning the salvaged cargo into cash. To protect this livelihood, some people tried in vain to destroy the beacon while it was being built. Today, you can climb to the top of the 36m (118-ft.) tower for panoramic views of the harbor and town. Most weekdays between 10am and 4pm, the lighthouse keeper will be happy to give you a peek. The lighthouse is within walking distance of Club Soleil and Hope Town Hideaways. If you're staying elsewhere, make arrangements through your hotel for a visit.

Shopping

Of course, no one comes to Hope Town just to shop, but once you're here, you might want to pick up a souvenir. The **Ebb Tide Gift Shop** (© 242/366-0088) is the town's best-stocked boutique. It's in an aqua-trimmed white-clapboard house a block from the harbor. Inside, you'll find many imaginative items, including Androsia batiks (p. 171), costume jewelry, T-shirts, original watercolors, and fabrics sold by the yard. Hours are Monday through Saturday from 9am to 5pm.

Elbow Cay After Dark

On Saturday nights, a young party crowd gathers at **Harbour's Edge** (✆ 242/366-0087), a Hope Town bar and restaurant with the island's only pool table. On Monday night, Bahamian barbecues draw many people to **Sea Spray Resort** (✆ 242/366-0065), about 4.8km (3 miles) from Hope Town. The food is good, considering the low prices, and you can hear live music. Other evenings, people hang out at the bars of hotels and restaurants—including **Captain Jack's** (✆ 242/366-0247) especially on Wednesday or Friday night, when there's a DJ—or they turn in early to rest up for yet another day of exploring.

MAN-O-WAR CAY

Visiting Man-O-War Cay is like going back in time. The island has lovely beaches, and many visitors come here to enjoy them—but it's best to leave more daring swimwear at home, as the people who reside on this island are deeply religious and conservative. You won't find any crime—unless you bring it with you. No alcoholic beverages are sold on the island, although you can bring your own supply.

Like New Plymouth on Green Turtle Cay or Hope Town on Elbow Cay, Man-O-War is a Loyalist village, with resemblances to a traditional New England town. The pastel clapboard houses, built by ships' carpenters, are set off by freshly painted white picket fences intertwined with bougainvillea.

The people here are shy, but they do welcome outsiders to their isolated island and are proud of their heritage, which includes a long boat-building tradition. Many locals, especially the old-timers, have known plenty of hard times. Like Key West's Conchs (pronounced "conks"), to whom they're related, these are a tough, insular people who have exhibited a proud independence for many years.

Tourism has only just begun to infiltrate Man-O-War Cay. Because of the relative lack of hotels and restaurants, many visitors come just for the day, often in groups, from Marsh Harbour. If you do stay for a while, stop by the **Man-O-War Marina** (✆ 242/366-6008) to arrange your boat rentals and watersports; there's also a dive shop there.

Getting There & Getting Around

To reach Man-O-War Cay, you must cross the water from Marsh Harbour (Great Abaco Island). **Albury's Ferry Service** (✆ 242/367-3147 in Marsh Harbour, 242/365-6010 in Man-O-War; www.alburysferry.com) leaves from a dock near Abaco Beach Resort. The round-trip same-day fare is $27; one-way fare is $17. Children 6 to 11 pay half-price. The ride takes about 20 minutes.

Except for a few service vehicles, Man-O-War Cay has almost no cars. If you want to explore farther than your feet will carry you, ask around to find out whether one of the locals will rent you a golf cart.

Where to Stay

Schooner's Landing Ocean Club Set in isolation on Man-O-War Cay's northeastern edge, this four-unit apartment complex is the island's only official place to stay. A sea wall separates its lawns and hibiscus shrubs from the crashing surf, so swimmers and snorkelers meander a short distance down to the sands of a nearby beach. Each two-story unit contains a kitchen, ceiling fans, two private bathrooms, a TV, and a summery decor of wicker and rattan furniture. There's no bar or restaurant, but the island's two grocery stores will deliver. Most visitors opt to cook in anyway.

Man-O-War Cay, Abaco, The Bahamas. www.schoonerslanding.com. (C) **242/365-6143.** Year-round $275 per day; $1,850 per week. MC, V. **Amenities:** Outdoor pool; communal outdoor gas-fired grill, watersports (fishing and diving); Wi-Fi (free). *In room:* A/C, TV/VCR, kitchen.

Where to Eat

Bradley's at the Marina 🏛 AMERICAN/BAHAMIAN   The sides of this wooden pavilion are open to the breezes and a view of boats bobbing at the nearby harbor. A crowd of loyal boat owners and local residents is always here, enjoying simple but savory cuisine. At lunchtime, the focus is on such time-favored staples as roasted chicken fingers, grilled fish, burgers, fried conch with peas 'n' rice, and steaks. Evenings, however, many locals arrive for grilled lamb, fish, steaks, or chicken, and on Friday and Saturday nights, the place is practically transformed into a neighbor-hood block party.

Man-O-War Marina. (C) **242/365-6380.** Main courses $11–$22 lunch; $16–$40 dinner. MC, V. Mon–Sat 11am–2:30pm and 5:30–9pm.

Shopping

A most unusual store and studio, **Albury's Sail Shop,** at the eastern end of Man-O-War Marina ((C) 242/365-6014), occupies a house overlooking the water. The floor space is devoted to the manufacture and display of brightly colored canvas garments and accessories. They're made using 8-ounce cotton duck fabric, which once served as sailcloth for the community's boats. When synthetic sails came into vogue, four generations of Albury women put the cloth and their talents to use. Don't stop in without chatting with them. It's open Monday through Saturday from 7am to 5pm.

GREAT GUANA CAY ★

The longest of the Abaco cays, Great Guana, on the chain's east side, stretches 11km (6¾ miles) from tip to tip and lies between Green Turtle and Man-O-War cays. The spectacular beachfront running the length of the cay is one of the loveliest in The Baha-mas. The reef fishing is superb here, and bonefish are plentiful in the shallow bays.

The settlement stretches along the beach at the head of the palm-fringed **Kidd's Cove,** named after the pirate. Ruins of an old **sisal mill** near the western end of the island make for an interesting detour. The island has about 150 residents, most of them descendants of Loyalists who left Virginia and the Carolinas to settle in this remote place, often called "the last spot of land before Africa." The islanders' tradi-tional pursuits include boat-building, carpentry, farming, and fishing.

As in similar settlements in New Plymouth and Man-O-War Cay, houses here resemble those of old New England. It won't take you long to explore the village; it has only two small stores, a one-room schoolhouse, an Anglican church—and that's about it.

Getting There & Getting Around

Albury's Ferry Service ((C) 242/367-0290; www.alburysferry.com) runs between four and five times a day, depending on the season, from Marsh Harbour (Great

Abaco Island) to Great Guana Cay. One-way transit for adults costs $17. A round-trip same-day ticket goes for $27. Children 6 to 11 pay half-price.

Instead of driving on the island, most people get around in small boats. Boats are available to charter for a half-day or full day (or a full month, for that matter). A 7m (23-ft.) sailboat, fully equipped for living and cruising, is also available for charter, and deep-sea fishing trips can be arranged. Two local outfitters willing and able to rent you a watercraft: **Island Marine Boat Rentals** (© 242/366-0282; www.island marine.com), based in Hope Town (Elbow Cay), who rent 5m (16-ft.) Boston Whalers at $125 per day, $100 per day for 3 days, or $625 per week; and **Sea Horse Boat Rentals,** with branches in both Marsh Harbour and Hope Town (© 242/366-0023; www.sea-horse.com) rents 5.4m (18-ft.) Privateers at $190 per day; for rentals of 7 days or more, the cost is $105 per day or $735 for the week. Both establishments are open Monday through Saturday from 8am to 5pm. Island Marine is also open on Sunday from 8am to noon.

Where to Stay

Dolphin Beach Resort ★   Set directly astride one of the best beaches in The Bahamas, a 15-minute walk north of Guana Cay's largest settlement (Guana Village), with miles of powder-soft sand, this resort offers informal but very comfortable lodgings. Four of the units are in the main house and have queen-size beds, ceiling fans, and kitchenettes; three have private screened-in decks with teakwood furniture. The oceanfront cottages (nine in all) also have queen-size beds, ceiling fans, and full-size kitchens with stoves and charcoal grills. Cottages can accommodate between two and four guests each. The showers are outside, but they're secluded and screened off by island flora. The entire place is private, intimate, and laid-back. Nippers, a beachfront bar and grill (see below), is within a 5-minute walk.

Great Guana Cay, Abaco, The Bahamas. www.dolphinbeachresort.com. © **800/222-2646** or 242/365-5137. Fax 242/365-5163. 13 units. Winter $218–$320 double, $390–$436 2-bedroom unit, $380–$435 3-bedroom unit; off-season $147–$245 double, $316–$355 2-bedroom unit, $327–$360 3-bedroom unit. MC, V. Closed Sept to mid-Oct. **Amenities:** Restaurant; bar; Internet (free); outdoor pool; watersports equipment/rentals. *In room:* A/C, TV/VCR, hair dryer, kitchen (in cottages) or kitchenette (in rooms).

Flip Flops on the Beach ★ 🎒   The name alone suggests how laid-back and casual things are at this little colony of upscale one- and two-bedroom cottages. It opens onto one of the best sandy beaches in The Bahamas, stretching for 8km (5 miles). Picnic tables are set out for guests who often lunch here, and there's also a private beach pavilion if you'd like a "sundowner." The well-furnished bungalows are breezily decorated with Bahamian handmade art prints and accented by thoughtful extras such as canvas beach chairs, mahogany four-poster beds, and charcoal grills.

Great Guana Cay, Abaco, The Bahamas. www.flipflopsonthebeach.com. © **242/365-5163.** 4 units. Winter $330 1-bedroom cottage, $400 2-bedroom cottage; off-season $235–$310 1-bedroom cottage, $330–$350 2-bedroom cottage. 3-night minimum stay. MC, V. Closed Sept to mid-Oct. **Amenities:** Access to pool at Dolphin Beach Resort (see above); Wi-Fi (free). *In room:* Ceiling fan, TV, kitchen, no phone.

Where to Eat

Nippers Beach Bar & Grill AMERICAN/BAHAMIAN   For fun on the beach, head for this dive, where visitors hang out with locals. Right on the sand, customers sit in split-level gazebos and take in the most stunning seascape in the Abacos, with a snorkeling reef just 11m (36 ft.) offshore. Burgers, Caesar salads, conch fritters, and well-stuffed sandwiches satisfy lunchtime appetites, and dinners usually feature pasta alfredo, blackened grouper, and rib-eye steaks, but the best time to go is on a Sunday afternoon, for a pig roast attended by up to 1,000 people who gather for food, drinks, and dancing on the beach. The Sunday pig roast lasts from 12:30 to 4:30pm and costs $23. One guest is said to have consumed five "Nipper Trippers"—and lived to tell about it. This is the bartender's specialty, a mix of five rums along with tropical juices. It's lethal.

Great Guana Cay. © **242/365-5111.** www.nippersbar.com. Reservations not necessary. Lunch main courses $11–$20, dinner main courses $30–$32. AE, MC, V. Grill daily 11:30am–10pm; bar 7am–10pm.

TREASURE CAY ★

Treasure Cay now contains one of the most popular and elaborate resorts in the Out Islands. Off Great Abaco's east coast, it boasts not only 5.5km (3½ miles) of spectacular sandy beach, widely recognized as being among the top 10 beaches in The Bahamas, but also one of the finest marinas in the Commonwealth, with complete docking and charter facilities.

Before the tourist complex opened, the cay was virtually undeveloped. As a result, the resort has become the "city," providing its thousands of visitors with everything they need, including medical supplies, grocery items, liquor (naturally), and bank services. But don't count on having these services when you need them. There are no ATMs on the island, and the bank is open only on Tuesday and Thursday—and Thursday is payday on the island, so it's impossibly overcrowded. Medical supplies, even contact-lens solution, aren't available on the weekends. The real-estate office peddles condos, and the builders predict that they will one day reach a capacity of 5,000 owners. They're hoping that many visitors will like Treasure Cay enough to buy into it.

Treasure Cay hosts one of the most popular fishing tournaments in The Bahamas: the **Treasure Cay Billfish Championship** in May. For more information, go to www.bahamasbillfish.com.

Getting There & Getting Around

See "Getting There" under "Abacos Essentials," at the beginning of this chapter, for details on flying to Treasure Cay. Some direct service is available to the island from Florida. You can also fly into Marsh Harbour, on Great Abaco Island, and take a 32km (20-mile) taxi ride north along the paved but bumpy Sherben A. Boothe Highway.

Once you're on the island, renting a car isn't necessary. To get where you're going, you can walk, bike, or take a golf cart or taxi. Some restaurants outside the resort will send a shuttle to pick you up from your hotel. You likely won't need a cab except to get between the airport or ferry dock and your hotel. For details about taxi fares, call the **Treasure Cay Airport Taxi Stand** (© 242/365-8661). The only real reason to rent a car is for the 35-minute drive to Marsh Harbour to catch the ferries to Elbow Cay and Man-O-War Cay. If you decide to do so, **Cornish Car Rental,** at Treasure Cay Airport (© 242/365-8623), charges about $75 to $85 a day.

Wendell's Bicycle Rentals (© 242/365-8687), across from the bank in the Treasure Cay shopping center, rents beach cruisers (single-gear bikes with wide wheels) and mountain bikes for $12 to $17 a day or for $50 per week. Four-seater electric golf carts go for $45 to $50 a day or $265 a week at either Wendell's or **Claridge Golf Carts** (📞 **242/365-8248** or 365-8053), just outside town.

Where to Stay

Note: Rooms can be scarce in May, when the place is packed with anglers trying to achieve fame in the Treasure Cay Billfish Championship.

Bahama Beach Club ★ Lying right off Treasure Cay Beach, this luxurious condo complex, the most idyllic spot in the Abacos for families, maintains elegantly furnished accommodations with two to four bedrooms. Built in 2002, it was expanded in 2007, with ongoing renovations ever since. Although the property has no particularly child-friendly facilities, the multi-bedroom units draw mostly families, who appreciate the amount of space and the well-equipped kitchens for cooking meals. Most of the condos, though individually decorated, are filled with rattan furnishings and bold, colorful fabrics. Each unit opens onto a private patio or balcony overlooking the ocean. Daily housekeeping services are provided, a small grocery store lies within a 5-minute walk, and eateries are nearby. There's also an on-site restaurant, open only 2 nights a week, and only for dinner.

Treasure Cay, Abaco, The Bahamas. www.bahamabeachclub.com. 📞 **800/284-0382** or 242/365-8500. Fax 242/365-8501. 88 condos, 60 of which are available as rentals. Year-round $300–$350 2-bedroom; $350–$400 3-bedroom; $500–$700 4-bedroom. 3-night minimum stay. AE, MC, V. **Amenities:** Restaurant (open only 2 nights a week, dinner only); outdoor pool. *In room:* A/C, TV, kitchen, Wi-Fi (free).

Treasure Cay Beach, Marina, and Golf Resort ★ One of the biggest of the Out Island resorts, this property attracts boaters, golfers, fishermen, and divers, as well as yachties and escapists seeking a remote yet relatively luxurious retreat. The foundation for this resort was laid in 1962, when a group of international investors recognized its potential. The hotel accommodations nestle comfortably amid a larger infrastructure that includes a privately owned 150-slip marina and a scattering of privately owned condominiums and villas, only a few of which are included within the pool of available-for-rent accommodations. Guests can rent electric golf carts (around $35 per day) or bicycles to explore the sprawling compound's far-flung tennis courts and palm and casuarina groves.

Along with architecture that looks like it jumped off the pages of a magazine, the setting here includes tropical plants, a spectacular beachfront, an excellent golf course, and marina facilities. Furnished simply in modern tropical motifs, most accommodations overlook the dozens of sailing craft moored in the marina. The rentals are very attractive, many with full kitchens, plus a midsize bathroom. A restaurant, the **Spinnaker** (see "Where to Eat," below), serves standard fare, while two bars dispense tropical drinks.

Treasure Cay, Abaco, The Bahamas. www.treasurecay.com. 📞 **800/327-1584** or 242/365-8801. 96 units. Mar–Dec $130–$160 double, $250 2-bedroom suite, $390 3-bedroom suite; Jan–Feb $115–$140 double, $220–$300 2-bedroom suite, $350 3-bedroom suite. Extra person $20. Full board $70 per person per day. AE, DISC, MC, V. Closed Sept–Oct. **Amenities:** Restaurant; 2 bars; airport transfers ($30 for 2); golf course; outdoor pool; 6 tennis courts (lit for night play); watersports equipment/rentals; Wi-Fi (free). *In room:* A/C, TV, hair dryer.

Where to Eat

Many vacationers opt to stay in accommodations with full kitchens or kitchenettes. However, if you know you're not going to feel like cooking, consider purchasing your hotel's meal plan or dining at the Spinnaker.

Spinnaker Restaurant & Lounge AMERICAN/BAHAMIAN   Serving reliable seafood, steak, pasta, and Bahamian specialties, this restaurant at the Treasure Cay Hotel Resort (see above) occupies a prime waterside spot. For lunch, the cracked conch makes a good choice. At night, the dinner portions of meat and potatoes or fresh fish (prepared in a variety of ways, from steamed to blackened) are generous. Guests of the Banyan Beach Club, about a half-mile away, usually arrive by golf cart.

Treasure Cay Marina. ✆ **242/365-8801** or 365-8469. Reservations recommended for dinner. Lunch platters $12–$22, dinner main courses $18–$32. MC, V. Daily 7am–10pm. Limited hours in autumn and early winter.

Beaches & Outdoor Pursuits

The beaches here are blissfully tranquil. Watersports in Treasure Cay are lots of fun, especially during the Treasure Cay Billfish Championship each May. And although this area is far less developed than the more popular islands, golfers don't have to head to Nassau or Freeport for a great game. The course here is a big draw.

If you're seeking a beach with some of the softest, whitest sand you can imagine and water in some of the most amazing shades of blue and green, then **Treasure Cay Beach ★★** is it. What's especially alluring is that—unlike eye-catching stretches on busier, more built-up islands—this 5.5km (3½-mile) shore is never crowded.

Treasure Cay Golf Club (✆ **242/475-5515**), designed by Dick Wilson, offers 6,387m (6,985 yd.) of fairways, though it's hardly the best course the famed golf architect ever designed. Greens fees for hotel guests are $60 for 9 holes and $70 for 18 holes; for nonguests, it's $80 for 9 holes and $110 for 18 holes. This is the only golf course in the Abacos, and it lies 1km (⅔ mile) from the center of the resort.

Treasure Cay Marina (✆ **242/365-8250;** www.treasurecay.com) offers full-service facilities for a variety of watersports. Fishing boats with experienced skippers guide anglers to tuna, marlin, wahoo, dolphinfish, barracuda, grouper, yellowtail, and snapper. You can also rent a sailboat, a Hobie Cat, windsurfing boards, and snorkeling gear. The marina provides shower stalls, fish-cleaning facilities, daily laundry service, and water and electricity hookups.

Deep-sea fishing is set up through the marina of the Treasure Cay Hotel Resort (✆ **242/365-8250**), which can also arrange for you to hire a bonefishing guide.

Treasure Divers (✆ **242/365-8571;** www.treasure-divers.com) offers the best snorkeling and diving in the area, with PADI instructors. Their dive boat is the 10m (34-ft.) *Crusader*. This vessel carries you to the best spots in the area for both snorkeling and diving. Divers can also visit the underwater wreck of *San Jacinto,* a steamship freighter that sank in 1865. The cost of any dive is $99 for one tank or $190 for two tanks.

Treasure Cay Beach, Marina, and Golf Resort (www.treasurecay.com; ✆ **242/365-8801**), also offers somewhat battered **tennis courts,** each lit for night play. Three courts have clay surfaces ($16 per hour) and three have hard surfaces ($14 per hour). Check with the hotel to make arrangements.

Treasure Cay After Dark

Fishermen, yachties, and hotel guests head to the **Tipsy Seagull Bar** (✆ **242/365-8801**), which presents live music sometime after 8pm several nights a week in winter, and on Friday and Saturday nights only in the off season. The setting is an A-frame structure beside the beach, and the decor includes lots of nautical memorabilia. When there's a fishing tournament on the island, this bar is jam-packed. Bar patrons can order pizza and lobster from the resort's adjoining Spinnaker restaurant. Happy hour is nightly from 5 to 7pm. It's closed in autumn and early winter.

GREEN TURTLE CAY (NEW PLYMOUTH) ★★

Five kilometers (3 miles) off Great Abaco's east coast, Green Turtle Cay is the archipelago's jewel, a little island with an uneven coastline, deep bays, sounds, and good beaches, one of which stretches for 1,080m (3,543 ft.). You can roam through green forests, gentle hills, and secluded inlets. The island is 5.5km (3½ miles) long and 1km (⅔ mile) across, lying some 274km (170 miles) due east of Palm Beach, Florida.

Water depths seldom exceed 4.5 to 6m (15–20 ft.) around here, and coral gardens teem with colorful sea life, making for fabulous snorkeling. The shells you'll find on

FAR FROM THE MADDING crowd

The settlers of New Plymouth were Loyalists who found their way here from other parts of the Abacos shortly before the end of the 18th century, with some "new" blood thrown in when émigrés from Eleuthera moved to Marsh Harbour and other Abaconian settlements.

The people of New Plymouth today are mostly named Curry, Lowe, Russell, Roberts, and especially Sawyer. Because they all came from the same rootstock—English, Welsh, and Scottish—and because of a long history of intermarriage, many of the faces are amazingly similar: deeply tanned, often freckled skin, blue eyes, and red or blond hair. The people here are friendly but not outgoing, having lived for generations far from the madding crowd.

One morning we spent an hour with a lifelong resident. The next morning, encountering what we took to be the same man on the ferryboat, we resumed our conversation, only to learn we were talking to a different man entirely. "No relation," he said, until chided by a woman passenger, which elicited from him, "Well, I think my mother's cousin did marry . . ."

The insularity of these people has also caused their speech patterns to retain

many facets of those their forebears brought from the mother country, with even a smattering of cockney to flavor it. Many drop their initial letter *h*, using it instead at the beginning of words that start with vowels. You may hear someone ordering "'am" and with it some "heggs." Also, the letter v is often pronounced "w," and vice versa.

Many of the inhabitants of New Plymouth today are engaged in turtling, lobstering, shark fishing, and sponging. New Plymouth is a so-called "sister city" to Key West, Florida, and if you have ever visited there, you'll see startling similarities between the American people of "conch" descent and the Abaconians, even to their wrecking history, fishing industries, and appearance.

A big event in the day-to-day life of the people of New Plymouth is the arrival at the Government Dock of the mail boat from Nassau. People gather there also whenever the ferryboat is arriving or leaving, just to keep tabs on what's going on.

There is no auto traffic in New Plymouth except for a few service vehicles—but who needs a car? You can walk all the way around the village in a fairly brief stroll.

the lovely beaches and offshore sandbars are among the finest in The Bahamas. If you have a boat, you can explore such deserted islands as Fiddle Cay to the north, or No Name Cay and Pelican Cay to the south.

New Plymouth, at the cay's southern tip, is an 18th-century settlement that has the flavor of an old New England sailing port. Much of the original masonry was fashioned from lime that was produced when conch shells were broken up, burned, and sifted for cement (records say that the alkali content was so high that it would burn the masons' hands). Clapboard houses with pretty trimmings line the little town's narrow streets. New Plymouth, which once had a population of 1,800 people, now has 400. Parliament is the village's main street, and you can walk its length in just 10 minutes, passing by only a few clucking hens. Many of the houses have front porches, on which locals sit in the evening to enjoy the breezes.

Green Turtle Cay became known for the skill of its shipbuilders, though the industry, like many others in the area, failed after slaves were emancipated in 1838.

Green Turtle Cay Essentials

GETTING THERE   Fly to **Treasure Cay Airport,** where a taxi will take you to the ferry dock for departures to Green Turtle Cay (New Plymouth). Once at the dock, you may have to wait a while for the ferry. The crossing takes about 15 to 20 minutes, and the boat will take you to the Green Turtle Club, if you're staying there, or otherwise to New Plymouth. This land-and-sea transfer costs $22 per person round-trip.

GETTING AROUND   Though you can walk to many parts of Green Turtle Cay, the most common mode of transportation is by water. Some accommodations provide water transport to town or to weekly hotel parties. Many vacationers rent **boats,** but if you'd rather not, you have other choices for getting around. Most of the island is accessible on foot, and the virtually car-free streets of New Plymouth, the quiet 18th-century village by the sea, are prime walking territory. On Green Turtle Cay, **golf carts** stand in for rental cars. **D & P Rentals,** at Green Turtle Club (© **242/365-4655**), rents theirs for $45 for 8 hours or $55 for 24 hours. You can also get all over the island by **bicycle,** and pedaling is especially scenic in historic New Plymouth.

[FastFACTS] GREEN TURTLE CAY

The local branch of **First Caribbean International Bank** (© **242/365-4144**), which has an ATM, is open only Tuesday and Thursday from 10am to 2pm. You enter Green Turtle Cay's **post office** (© **242/365-4242**), also the site of a **public telephone,** through a pink door on Parliament Street. Its hours are Monday through Friday from 9am to 5pm.

If you need medical attention, visit the **government clinic** (© **242/365-4028**), which is run by a nurse. There's virtually no crime in New Plymouth, so the little stone **jail** here makes visitors chuckle. No one can remember when, if ever, it held a prisoner.

SPECIAL EVENTS   One event that draws visitors in droves is the **Green Turtle Club Fishing Tournament,** held in May. In 1984, the winner hooked a 226kg (498-lb.) blue marlin; it was so heavy that the competing participants from other boats generously climbed aboard the winning craft to help reel the fish in. For more information, contact one of the Bahamian tourist offices or the **Green Turtle Club** (© **866/528-0539** or 242/365-4271; www.greenturtleclub.com), which more or less becomes the tournament's official headquarters each year.

Where to Stay

Barefoot Homes This is the second-largest rental agent for private homes on Green Turtle Cay, attracting the most business, based partly on the personalized attention of its hardworking owner, Ohio-born Robin Phillips. A former owner of the island's most iconic hotel, Bluff House, she now runs an agency where temporary visitors can rent, usually for a minimum of 3 days, any of 15 privately owned homes, many of them within a short walk of the marina facilities at New Plymouth or in the vicinity of Bluff House, which at presstime was partially under renovation. Each of the rentable houses is owned as a supplemental home by (usually off-island) investors, who entrust their buildings to Barefoot Homes as a means of offsetting the costs and as a means of keeping them well-maintained during the periods they spend off-island. Most have tile floors, wicker or at least summer-inspired furnishings, water views, porches or enclosed patios, and fully equipped kitchens. About 60% of the clients of this agency arrive by airplane and rent some kind of watercraft. The others tend to arrive on their own boats from the U.S. or Canadian mainland, using the time onshore to unwind from the cramped quarters of whatever vessel they arrived on. A 3-day minimum rental is enforced, and full catering services are available.

P.O. Box AB-22741, Green Turtle Cay, Abaco, The Bahamas. www.barefoothomesbahamas.com. ℂ **800/717-6309** or 242/577-4092. 15 private homes with between one and four bedrooms. Year-round $165–$240 one-bedroom units for 2; $335–$500 two-bedroom units for 4; $465–$600 3-BR units for 6. AE, DC, MC, V. **Amenities:** Most with kitchens, some with pools. *In room:* A/C, TV/DVD, Wi-Fi (free).

Cocobay Cottages On the north end of Green Turtle Cay, where 150m (492 ft.) of land separate the Atlantic from the Sea of Abaco, this complex of simple cottages opens onto one beach on the island's Atlantic side and another sandy beach on the more tranquil bay. It's ideal for those who don't care about the amenities of a full-service resort and who'd like to anchor in for a while. During the summer months, many residents of Florida arrive by private boat, which you can moor here for free. Otherwise, guests arrive by water taxi from the airport dock. The management welcomes a 75% repeat clientele. Set on 2 hectares (5 acres) dotted with tropical fruit trees, the spacious cottages here, which have improved over the years, feature Caribbean furnishings and refreshing pastel colors. The smallest unit, the honeymoon cottage, sleeps two in one bedroom. The largest accommodation is a two-bedroom, two-bathroom unit, which can comfortably sleep five. It offers a living room, a dining room, and a fully equipped kitchen with microwave. Linens and kitchen utensils are also provided (you can stock up on food at any of New Plymouth's three grocery shops, each about 3 miles away), and air-conditioning, ceiling fans, and trade winds cool the rooms. A 4-night minimum stay is required.

Green Turtle Cay, Abaco, The Bahamas. www.cocobaycottages.com. ℂ **800/752-0166** or 561/202-8149. 6 cottages. Year-round $250–$500 per day; $1,600–$4,500 per week. MC, V. **Amenities:** Exercise room; Wi-Fi (free). *In room:* A/C, hair dryer, kitchen, no phone.

Green Turtle Club Resort & Marina ★★★ An elegant and outstanding place for laid-back luxury, this resort attracts both honeymooners and snorkelers. The excellent full-service on-site marina and dive shop draw serious anglers, boaters, and divers. The waters around the resort are shallow enough to spot schools of fish from the shore—sometimes you'll even see a green turtle paddling above the sandbanks. Spread across 32 hectares (79 acres) of low-lying scrubland, the inn feels very much like a country club. The courteous staff members offer assistance, yet don't intrude on peace or privacy. The resort is the headquarters of the Green Turtle Club Fishing Tournament, a highly visible event held for 3 days every year in May. (For more information, contact the hotel directly.)

Guests are lodged in spacious bungalows (usually two units to a building), set within a gently sloping, carefully landscaped garden. The accommodations are among the region's most upscale and luxurious—think England in the Tropics. Bedrooms boast Sheraton-style mahogany furniture, four-poster beds, French-inspired draperies, oak floors, terra-cotta tiled patios, and wicker or rattan furniture. Villas with kitchens are also available.

The flag-festooned bar is the resort's social center, where there's occasionally live music. There's a vaguely British tone to evenings here, which begin with pre-dinner cocktails beside a roaring fire in the bar's iron stove (in chilly weather only, of course). Everyone then adjourns to the pine-paneled dining room for well-prepared dinners (see "Where to Eat," below). Breakfast and lunch are usually served on the veranda.

Green Turtle Cay, Abaco, The Bahamas. www.greenturtleclub.com. ℰ **800/370-4468** or 242/365-4271. Fax 242/365-4272. 34 units. Year-round $149–$249 double; $259–$469 2-bedroom unit; $319–$569 3-bedroom unit. Children 12 and under stay free in parent's room. Meal plan (breakfast and dinner) $50. AE, MC, V. The resort is closed every year from mid-September to late October. Take a taxi for $8 from Treasure Cay Airport to the ferry dock; transfer to a water taxi to the club for about $17 one-way. **Amenities:** Restaurant; 2 bars; babysitting; bikes; outdoor pool; watersports equipment/rentals; Wi-Fi (free). *In room:* A/C, TV/VCR, movie library, fridge, hair dryer, no phone.

Where to Eat

Green Turtle Club ★ CONTINENTAL If you arrive early on Green Turtle Cay, your day can begin here with breakfast on the covered patio, overlooking the white sandy beach of White Sound Harbour. Feast on morning favorites such as fluffy pancakes, omelets, and French toast made with freshly baked Bahamian bread. Lunch is also served on the covered patio or on an outdoor deck, the menu tempting customers with its homemade soups, fresh salads, well-stuffed sandwiches, and platters of local Abaco seafood. The lobster salad, conch chowder, and cracked conch are the best on the island. At night, the setting becomes more elaborate and a bit more formal, with linen-draped tables and candlelight establishing the mood. You can also dine indoors within a pine-trimmed, high-ceilinged dining room outfitted with Queen Anne furniture. Try such specialties as mango-flavored breast of duck, sesame-crusted snapper with vanilla sauce, or char-grilled mahimahi.

Green Turtle Club. ℰ **242/365-4271.** www.greenturtleclub.com. Reservations required. Breakfast items from $12; lunch items $13–$21; dinner main courses $29–$45. AE, MC, V. Daily 7:15–10:30am, 11:30am–2:45pm, and 7:30pm dinner seating.

The Jolly Roger BAHAMIAN/AMERICAN At presstime, this was the only dining venue available within what was previously known as Bluff House Resort, which was mostly destroyed by a hurricane in 2011. The Jolly Roger occupies a low-slung building adjacent to Bluff House's 38-slip marina, serving a somewhat standardized menu of lunchtime burgers, salads, and platters, and an evening menu of seafood, chicken, and steaks. Grouper comes, depending on the mood of the chef, either blackened, fried, or stewed. Chicken might be served with marsala sauce or a white-wine and lemon-caper butter. Drinks are appropriately stiff and appropriately tropical.

The Marina at Bluff House. ℰ **242/365-4247.** Reservations recommended at dinner. Lunch platters $12–$20; dinner main courses $17–$38. AE, DC, MC, V. Daily 11am–3:30pm and 5–9pm.

Laura's Kitchen BAHAMIAN/AMERICAN   On the town's main street, across from the Albert Lowe Museum, this family-owned spot occupies a well-converted white Bahamian cottage. When she's in town, and when business warrants, Laura Sawyer serves up lunch and dinner amid her simple, homey decor. The menu changes nightly, depending on what's at the market, but she always serves the old reliables her family has eaten for generations: fried grouper, fried chicken, and a tasty cracked conch. The eatery is mainly known for its burgers: fish burgers, conch burgers, hamburgers, cheeseburgers, and bacon-and-cheese burgers.

King St. *℃* **242/365-4287.** Reservations required for dinner. Lunch items $4–$12; dinner main courses $13–$32. MC, V. Mon–Sat 11am–3pm and 6–9pm; Sun 5:30–8pm, with occasional unannounced closings based on the health and schedule of the owners. Closed Sept.

Pineapples Bar & Grill AMERICAN/BAHAMIAN   This is a laid-back, Bahamian-American restaurant spearheaded by a U.S.-derived grandmother named "Babs." Its waterview premises might be a bit more casual and slower than you might have wanted, but you'll find well-prepared platters and flavorful versions of local staples. It's set in the center of New Plymouth, with a deck, a canopy-covered bar, and a small swimming pool overlooking the town and its waterfront. The cook specializes in very fresh fish, prepared any way you specify, conch fritters, fresh salads, and jerk versions of grouper, chicken, and pork. Specialty drinks of the house include Yellow Birds and Pineapple Smashes, which in quantity can be potent indeed. The owners maintain a rentable cottage nearby priced at $120 a night for two, and a larger house on a nearby peninsula, suitable for four occupants, and rentable for $220 a night, with a 3-night minimum rental required.

In "the Other Shore Club," Black Sound, New Plymouth. *℃* **242/365-4039.** Reservations not necessary. Lunch main courses $8–$16; dinner main courses $18–$22. MC, V. Daily 11am–10pm. Closed Sept–Nov.

Plymouth Rock Liquors & Cafe BAHAMIAN/AMERICAN   This place has New Plymouth's best selection of wines and liquors, including at least 60 kinds of rum; it also carries Cuban cigars. Part of its space is set aside for a pleasant and attractive luncheonette run by hardworking co-owners Kathleen and David Bethell. They serve up tasty sandwiches, split-pea soup, beef souse, and cracked conch with cucumber slices and potato salad.

Parliament St. *℃* **242/365-4234.** Sandwiches and platters $6–$14. DISC, MC, V. Cafe Mon–Tues and Thurs–Sat 9am–3:30pm. Liquor store Mon–Thurs 9am–6pm; Fri–Sat 9am–7pm.

The Wrecking Tree BAHAMIAN   Set in the center of town, this eatery lies at the edge of the channel used by watercraft as they approach their docks and moorings. This casual restaurant is named after the very old, much-cropped cedar ("the wrecking tree") which marks the site where whatever was salvaged from 19th-century ships wrecked offshore were laid out for display, inventory, and sale. Tables are placed with views of the water. Platters of simple but well-prepared local food include many kinds of fresh fish, either grilled or fried; conch fritters, conch salad, cracked conch, and fresh salads. Marguerite and Cindy Lavarity are the mother-daughter team who gracefully manage this well-respected local joint.

Bay St., New Plymouth. *℃* **242/365-4263.** Reservations not required. Lunch main courses $5–$13; dinner main courses $14–$19. No credit cards. Mon–Thurs 11am–5pm; Fri–Sat 11am–9pm. Closed late Sept–early Nov.

Beaches & Outdoor Pursuits

About a 10-minute walk from Bluff House and a 5-minute walk from the Green Turtle Club is **Coco Bay ★★**, one of the most beautiful crescents in The Bahamas. Shaded by casuarina pine trees and lapped by lazy waves, this long beach is often empty. The rougher **Ocean Beach,** about a 10-minute stroll from either Bluff House or the Green Turtle Club, is another stunner. Frothy waves thrash the starkly white sand, set off by the Atlantic's intense blue.

For more beach time, you can take a boat trip to one of the nearby uninhabited islands that are ringed with even more pristine sands. On **Manjack Cay,** for example, the expanse of sugar-white sand seems to go on forever, and the shallow water is a brilliant shade of turquoise. There's no regular service from the ferry dock, but you can negotiate with one of the local boatmen. The staff at your hotel will be helpful in this regard.

With one of the world's largest barrier reefs, the Abacos offer some of the best **snorkeling** and **diving** sites in The Bahamas. You can get an eyeful at reefs starting in depths of just 1.5m (5 ft.) and ranging to more than 18m (59 ft.). Like sheets on a clothesline, sprawling schools of fish billow by coral caverns, huge tube and barrel sponges, and fields of elk- and staghorn coral. Sea turtles and large groupers are common sights. In fact, the waters are so clear that you can often see farther than 30m (98 ft.).

If you like small groups and big fun, try **Brendal's Dive Center,** at the Green Turtle Club Marina (✆ **242/365-4411;** www.brendal.com). Whether you're an experienced diver or snorkeler or you're just getting your feet wet, the personal attention makes the difference here. Originally from Acklins, a small Bahamian island to the south, Brendal has more than 20 years of underwater experience. A special treat for snorkelers is the **Wild Dolphin Encounter** ($85 per person), which includes stops at undisturbed islands. This company also rents kayaks ($15 per hour for singles, $25 per hour for doubles, or $199 per week for singles, $250 for doubles).

For a snorkeling adventure, call **Lincoln Jones** at ✆ **242/365-4223,** and he'll arrange everything for you—probably on some deserted beach that only he knows about. Prices are to be negotiated, of course, but a lunch of fresh conch or lobster is a fine addition to any day.

If you've spent enough time sitting on the beach and exploring underwater, it's time to get out *on* the water. From boat rentals to fishing expeditions, Green Turtle Cay offers an array of things to do. Note that reserving a boat when you make your hotel and airline bookings is a good idea, particularly during the busy spring and summer months.

The aforementioned **Brendal's Dive Center,** at the Green Turtle Club Marina (✆ **242/365-4411;** www.brendal.com), can take you on a group sunset sailboat cruise (complete with rum punch) for $85 per person (up to eight passengers).

To rent a speedboat, contact **Donnie's Boat Rentals,** in Black Sound (✆ **242/365-4119;** www.donniesboatrentals.com). Its Whaler and Mako motorboats start at $65 a day for a 4.2m (14-ft.) boat, going up to $110 a day for one that's 7m (23-ft.). Fishermen from all over the world visit Green Turtle Cay in search of yellowfin, dolphinfish, and big-game wahoo, among other catches. If you want to go **deep-sea fishing,** check with the two cousins in the Sawyer family: Referrals are usually made through the **Green Turtle Club** (✆ **242/365-4070**), or you can call directly at ✆ **242/365-2461.**

At press time, the annual **Green Turtle Club Fishing Tournament** (© 800/ **688-4752** or 242/365-4271), after being suspended for several seasons, lived again over 3 days in May of 2012. Plans for 2013 and beyond were still being debated. Call for additional details.

Attractions on Land

Once you've had your fill of Green Turtle Cay's aquatic diversions, you can visit a museum and wander the streets of **New Plymouth,** the historic waterfront village, journeying back in time to the 18th century.

New Plymouth celebrated its bicentennial in 1984 by establishing the **Memorial Sculpture Garden** to honor Loyalists and some of their notable descendants, including Albert Lowe, a pioneer boat-builder and historian, and African-Bahamian Jeanne I. Thompson, the second woman to practice law in The Bahamas. At the memorial, across from New Plymouth Inn on Parliament Street, you can read about some of the Loyalists who came to The Bahamas from New England and the Carolinas. Statues are also dedicated to those people who were enslaved in these islands. This garden is laid out in the pattern of the Union Jack flag.

There isn't much shopping here, but consider a visit to **Ocean Blue Gallery,** adjoining Plymouth Rock Liquors & Cafe on Parliament Street (© 242/365-4234). This two-room outlet has one of the best collections of local artwork in the Abacos, including original sculptures and paintings.

Albert Lowe Museum ★★   More than anything else we've seen in The Bahamas, this museum, set in a beautifully restored Loyalist home, conveys the rawboned and sometimes difficult history of the Out Islands. You could easily spend a couple of hours reading the fine print of the dozens of photographs here, which show the hardship and the valor of citizens who changed industries as often as the economic circumstances of their era dictated.

The caretaker will give you a tour of the stone kitchen, which occupants of the house used as a shelter when a hurricane devastated much of New Plymouth in 1932. Inside the house, a narrow stairway leads to three bedrooms that reveal the simplicity of 18th-century life on Green Turtle Cay. Amid antique settees, irreplaceable photographs, and island artifacts, you'll see a number of handsome ship models, the work of Albert Lowe, for whom the museum was named.

The paintings of Alton Lowe, son of the museum's namesake, are also on display. Cherub-faced and red-haired, Alton is—and has been for a while—one of the best-known painters in The Bahamas. His works are part of collections all over the world; some appear on Bahamian postage stamps, blowups of which are displayed here. Your tour guide might open the house's basement, where some of Alton's paintings are for sale alongside work by other local artists. There's also a garden in the back of the house.

Parliament St. © **242/365-4094.** Admission $5 adults, $3 students, free for children 5 and under. Mon–Sat 9–11:45am and 1–4pm.

Green Turtle Cay After Dark

Ask at your hotel if the local Junkanoo band, the **Gully Roosters,** is playing its reggae- and calypso-inspired sounds. They're the best in the Abacos and often appear at various spots on the island. Also make sure to visit **Miss Emily's Blue Bee Bar** (described in the box below). You might catch a live band, and you'll certainly enjoy

A Toast to Miss Emily

Our favorite bar in the Out Islands is **Miss Emily's Blue Bee Bar,** on Victoria Street in New Plymouth (📞 **242/365-4181**). This simple bar is likely to be the scene of the liveliest party in the Out Islands at any time of day; even normally buttoned-up types find themselves flirting or dancing before long. Until rising waters from the 1999 hurricanes washed some of them away, most of its walls were covered with the business cards of past guests and celebrities. Stop by and see how many replacements have been plastered up.

The Goombay Smash, a specialty here, has been called "Abaco's answer to atomic fission." Its recipe includes proportions of coconut rum, "dirty" rum, apricot brandy, and pineapple juice. Miss Emily (Mrs. Emily Cooper) was a legend in these parts. She's gone now, but her memory lives on: Her daughter, Violet Smith, knows her secret recipe for the Goombay Smash and makes a potent rum punch. Tips go to St. Peter's Anglican Church. No food is served, but the bar is open Monday through Saturday from 11am until late.

a wonderful setting for a drink, in the **Jolly Roger's** bar (p. 198) at the otherwise closed-for-renovation Bluff House and the **Green Turtle Club** (p. 198).

Rooster's Rest Pub (Gilliam's Bay Rd. 📞 **242/365-4066**) is a local dive, located just beyond the edge of town. It abandoned its original self-definition as a down-home restaurant and now focuses exclusively on its role as a bar and pub, where many of the locals gather on weekends to drink, jive, and gossip. If you opt to pop in for a drink, it operates at erratic hours that vary according to national holidays and the mood of its owners. The greatest likelihood of seeing significant numbers of other patrons would happen on weekends, after around 8pm.

An even newer hangout for late-afternoon cocktails and gossip is **Sundowners,** on Parliament Street, near the Albert Lowe Museum (no phone). Don't expect glamor, or anything approaching a fully functional restaurant, although there's a short list of takeaway pizzas and submarine sandwiches. It's open Monday to Saturday from 5 to 10pm, with what sometimes evolves into a mini-flood of business every Friday and Saturday night from both locals and the crews from whatever yacht might be moored at any of the cay's marinas.

A much more upscale bar than Miss Emily's is the **Yacht Club Pub,** at the Green Turtle Club (📞 **242/365-4271**). Along with sailors and fishermen, some of the captains (and owners) of the world's most expensive yachts stop here to enjoy the lively atmosphere and the bartender's special, a Tipsy Turtle, made by the gallon (it's got orange juice, pineapple juice, vodka, coconut rum, banana rum, and grenadine). Appetizers are served nightly from 6:30 to 7:30pm. Live bands perform on Monday, Wednesday, and Friday nights.

SPANISH CAY

Set 19km (12 miles) northwest of Green Turtle Cay, this island—an on-again, off-again darling of several investment consortiums with big plans for it—was named after a pair of Spanish galleons that sank offshore in the 17th century. Originally owned by Queen Elizabeth II, the island was purchased in the 1960s by Texas-based investor (and former owner of the Dallas Cowboys) Clint Murchison. After his death in the early 1980s, two successive Florida conglomerates poured time, money, and landscaping efforts into developing the island as a site for upscale private homes. As of this writing, things are slowly evolving, with hopes that business will pick up and additional units will be marketed, sold and rented. Today, visitors, potential investors, and locals putter along the island's paved roads in electric golf carts.

Most visitors arrive by private boat or chartered aircraft from Fort Lauderdale. You can also fly from West Palm Beach to Treasure Cay on **Bahamasair** (© **242/365-8601;** www.bahamasair.com) and have the resort arrange water transportation. Two daily flights arrive from Nassau as well.

Where to Stay & Eat

Spanish Cay Resort & Marina ★   Renovations and improved transportation have made this isolated property better and more accessible than ever. Accommodations, each a subsection of two-story, white-sided, big-balconied buildings that evoke private homes, come in a variety of sizes, thanks in some cases to doors that open and shut to seal or open separate areas within them. Regardless of their size, most contain a full kitchen, living room/dining room, and a deck or balcony overlooking the marina. A one-bedroom apartment can sleep up to four people; a two-bedroom accommodates as many as six.

Two on-site restaurants, the **Point House,** open daily, and **Wrecker's Bar,** open in high season, serve conch, chicken, fresh fish, steak, and, occasionally, lobster. Dinners are reasonably priced, with dinner main courses going for between $15 and $32 each. You can also get food and drinks at the poolside bar.

Cooper's Town, Abaco, The Bahamas. www.spanishcay.com. © **242/365-0083.** Fax 242/365-0453. 16 units. Winter $215–$275 double, $215–$375 one-bedroom suite; off-season $195–$215 double, $165–$295 one-bedroom suite. Year-round $875 for a 4-BR house, per night, sleeping 8. MC, V. **Amenities:** 2 restaurants; bar; outdoor pool; spa; 4 tennis courts (lit for night play); watersports equipment/rentals; Wi-Fi ($10 in marina). *In room:* A/C, TV, fridge, no phone.

ELEUTHERA

A sort of Bahamian Plymouth Rock, Eleuthera Island (pronounced "E-loo-ther-uh") was the first permanent settlement in The Bahamas, founded in 1648. A search for religious freedom drew the Eleutherian Adventurers from Bermuda here, to the birthplace of The Bahamas. The long, narrow island they discovered and colonized still bears the name Eleuthera—Greek for "freedom." Locals call it Cigatoo.

These adventurers found an island of white- and pink-sand beaches framed by casuarina trees; high, rolling green hills; sea-to-sea views; dramatic cliffs; and sheltered coves—and these beautiful sights are still here, unspoiled, waiting for you to discover them. More than 161km (100 miles) long but a mere 3km (1¼ miles) wide—guaranteeing that you'll never be far from the beach—Eleuthera is about 113km (70 miles) east of Nassau, a 30-minute flight. The population of 12,000 is largely made up of farmers, shopkeepers, and fishermen who live in old villages of pastel-washed cottages. The resorts are built around harbors, and roads run along the coastline, though some of them are inadequately paved.

Eleuthera and its satellite islands, **Spanish Wells** (on St. George's Cay) and **Harbour Island,** offer superb snorkeling and diving amid coral gardens, reefs, drop-offs, and wrecks. Anglers come to Eleuthera for bottom-, bone-, and deep-sea fishing, testing their skill against dolphinfish, wahoo, blue and white marlins, Allison tuna, and amberjacks. Charter boats are available at Powell Point, Rock Sound, Spanish Wells, and Harbour Island. You can also rent Sunfish, sailboats, and Boston Whalers for reef fishing.

Eleuthera rivals the Abacos in popularity among foreign visitors, though boaters are more drawn to the Abacos and the Exumas. Along with the Abacos, Eleuthera has the largest concentration of resort hotels outside of Nassau/Paradise Island and Freeport/Lucaya. It's also got a wealth of sandy beaches.

With the exception of Andros Island (which has four airports), Eleuthera has more airports (three) than any other island in The Bahamas, ensuring that most points along its surface are relatively easy to access. Best of all, it has one long, completely interconnected highway, stretching 177km (110 miles) from the island's northern to southern tip, thereby avoiding the complicated ferryboat crossings that hinder development in, say, Andros and the Abacos. There's not a traffic light anywhere on the island, a fact that makes locals inordinately proud. An offbeat adventure involves driving the island's entire length, along a sometimes bumpy road with nary a dividing line. Everywhere, you'll confront a landscape of rocks, sand, scrub, and sea views.

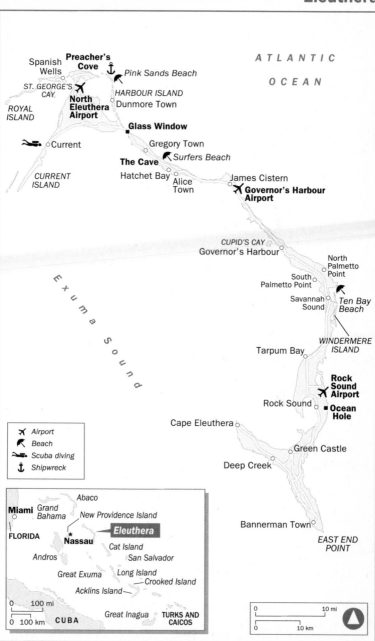

ATLANTIC

OCEAN

Spanish
Wells

**Preacher's
Cove**

Pink Sands Beach

*ST. GEORGE'S
CAY*

**North
Eleuthera
Airport**

HARBOUR ISLAND
Dunmore Town

*ROYAL
ISLAND*

Glass Window

Current

Gregory Town

The Cave

Surfers Beach

*CURRENT
ISLAND*

Hatchet Bay

Alice
Town

James Cistern

**Governor's Harbour
Airport**

CUPID'S CAY
Governor's Harbour

North
Palmetto
Point

South
Palmetto Point

Savannah
Sound

*Ten Bay
Beach*

*WINDERMERE
ISLAND*

Tarpum Bay

**Rock
Sound
Airport**

Rock Sound

**Ocean
Hole**

Cape Eleuthera

Green Castle

Deep Creek

E x u m a

S o u n d

✈ Airport
🏄 Beach
🤿 Scuba diving
⚓ Shipwreck

Abaco

Miami
Grand
Bahama

New Providence Island

Eleuthera

FLORIDA

★
Nassau

Cat Island

Andros

San Salvador

Great Exuma

Long Island

Crooked Island

Acklins Island

0   100 mi

0   100 km   **CUBA**

Great Inagua

**TURKS AND
CAICOS**

Bannerman Town

*EAST END
POINT*

0   10 mi

0   10 km

8

ELEUTHERA   Introduction

205

We love gorgeous **Harbour Island,** with its charming Dunmore Town, even more than New Plymouth or Hope Town in the Abacos; it's almost a Cape Cod in the Tropics. Of the 10 destinations recommended in this chapter, Harbour Island gets our vote as the number-one choice.

Spanish Wells is another small island settlement just off Eleuthera's north end. Spanish galleons put sailors ashore to fill the ships' casks with fresh water after long sea voyages—hence the community's present-day name.

ELEUTHERA ESSENTIALS

GETTING THERE

BY PLANE   Eleuthera has three airports, each of which functions as an official Bahamian port of entry, with Customs and Immigration officials on hand. **North Eleuthera Airport** (© 242/335-1242; www.eleuthera.com), as its name implies, serves the island's northern portion, along with two major towns on offshore cays, Harbour Island and Spanish Wells. **Governor's Harbour Airport** (© 242/332-2321) serves the center of the island, and **Rock Sound Airport** (© 242/334-2177) serves the island's southern tier.

Bahamasair (© 800/222-4262; www.bahamasair.com) provides daily flights between Nassau and the three airports. In addition, several commuter airlines with regularly scheduled service fly in from Florida on either nonstop or one-stop flights. **Continental** (© 800/525-0280; www.continental.com) flies once daily from Miami and twice daily from Fort Lauderdale. Many private planes land on North Eleuthera Airport's 1,350m (4,429-ft.) paved runway.

Other small carriers include **Twin Air** (© 954/359-8266; www.flytwinair.com), flying from Fort Lauderdale three times a week to Rock Sound and Governor's Harbour, and Thursday through Tuesday to North Eleuthera. Also contact **Yellow Air Taxi** (© 888/935-5694 or 242/367-0032; www.flyyellowairtaxi.com) for flight information about charters.

BY FERRYBOAT   The inter-island ferryboats operated by **Bahamas Ferries** (© 242/323-2166 or 242/332-2707; www.bahamasferries.com) launch daily from Potter's Cay, beneath the Paradise Island Bridge, and go to points including Harbour Island, North Eleuthera and, somewhat less frequently, to Governor's Harbour. Round-trip fares are $125 for adults, $85 for children 12 and under.

BY MAIL BOAT   For details on mail-boat sailings, consult the dock master at Nassau's **Potter's Cay Dock** at © 242/393-1064. Weather conditions and the vagaries of the Bahamian postal system sometimes cause these schedules to change. Transit from Nassau to anywhere on Eleuthera costs $60 each way for adults, and $38 for children 12 and under.

Every Monday, the **MV Bahamas Daybreak III** departs Nassau for South Eleuthera, stops at Rock Sound and Governor's Harbour, and then returns to Nassau on Tuesday. On Thursday, it leaves Nassau for the Bluff (a small village in North Eleuthera) and Harbour Island, returning on Sunday.

On Monday and Thursday, the **MV Eleuthera Express** sails from Nassau to Spanish Wells, Governor's Harbour, and Rock Sound, with return trips to Nassau on Sunday and Tuesday.

Every Thursday, the **MV Current Pride** goes from Nassau to both Lower and Upper Bogue on Current Island, and to Hatchet Bay. It returns to Nassau from Current Island every Tuesday.

GETTING AROUND

It's virtually impossible to get lost on Eleuthera—there's only one road that meanders along the entire length of its snake-shaped form, and you'll stray from it only very rarely. You can easily traverse all the settlements—really hamlets, in most cases—on foot. With little traffic on the island, walking is an enjoyable experience here.

Most visitors take a **taxi** only right after arriving at the airport or when they have to return to that airport to go home. Taxis meet all incoming flights and are also available at ferry docks. Because cabbies are independent operators, you can't call one central number. Your hotel staff can summon a taxi for you, but you may have to wait a while, so plan ahead. Know, too, that taxis on Eleuthera are battered and expensive; the cost to haul you and up to two companions, plus your luggage, from North Eleuthera Airport, in Eleuthera's far north, to Cape Eleuthera, near the island's southern tip, is around $180, and it's a long, monotonous ride. As such, we advise you to select the airport on Eleuthera that's the closest, within reason, to wherever you'll be staying.

You won't find any American car-rental agencies on the island. Usually, your hotel can arrange for a **car rental** at prices ranging from $65 to $125 a day. You might end up driving a car that belongs to a local looking for extra cash. The four top contenders for car rentals on Eleuthera include **North Eleuthera Service Station** (𝒞 242/335-1128 or 335-1548), **Hilton Johnson's Car Rentals** (𝒞 242/359-7585 or 335-6241), the **Highway Service Station** in Governor's Harbour (𝒞 242/332-2077) and **Frederick "Fine Threads" Neely Car Rentals 2** (𝒞 242/359-7780), whose owner's nickname was begotten because he wears great clothing.

ROCK SOUND/CAPE ELEUTHERA

Rock Sound, in South Eleuthera, is a small, shady village, the island's main town and once its most exclusive enclave. The downsizing of a major touristic landmark, the Windermere Club, has, at least for now, halted the flow of famous visitors, who once included everybody from Princess Diana to a parade of CEOs. No reopening of that semi-private club is yet in sight, but at least that means that you can have many of South Eleuthera's best beaches practically to yourself.

Rock Sound opens onto Exuma Sound and is south of Tarpum Bay. The town is at least 200 years old and has many old-fashioned homes with picket fences out front. Once notorious for wreckers who lured ships ashore with false beacons, it used to be known as "Wreck Sound."

A "Bottomless Hole" in the Ocean

The **Ocean Hole,** in a sparsely populated neighborhood about 2km (1¼ miles) east of the heart of Rock Sound, is said to be bottomless, though modern depth soundings have defined it as being an astonishing 100 fathoms (about 600 ft.) deep. This saltwater lake, whose waters, through uncharted underground channels, eventually meet the sea, is one of Eleuthera's most ecologically unusual spots. As such, it's closely monitored by geologists, zoologists, and botanists. Many birds and tropical fish can be seen through the greenish filter that seems to hover above the waters here; they seem to like to be photographed—but only if you feed them first.

After leaving Rock Sound, you can head south, perhaps with a detour for a view of the re-inaugurated, all-new **Cotton Bay Club** (see the "Cotton Bay's Comeback" box, below), and continue through the villages of Green Castle and Deep Creek. At this point, take a sharp turn northwest along the only road leading to **Cape Eleuthera.** Locals call this byway Cape Eleuthera Road, though you won't find any markings other than a sign pointing the way. If you continue to follow this route northwest, you'll reach the end of the island chain, jutting out into Exuma Sound.

Rock Sound Essentials

In addition to its airport, Rock Sound has a **shopping center** and a local branch of **Scotiabank** (© 242/334-3620), with an ATM but not a lot else. Many residents who live in South Eleuthera come here to stock up on groceries and supplies.

A doctor and four resident nurses form the staff of **Rock Sound Medical Clinic** (© 242/334-2226). It's open Monday through Friday from 9am to 4pm; outside those hours, the doctor is always available to handle emergencies. If you need the **police,** call © 242/334-2244.

Where to Stay

Powell Pointe at Cape Eleuthera Resort & Yacht Club ★★ ☺   During an earlier incarnation, this resort attracted some major American movers and shakers. Some of the top U.S. golfers played its Bruce Devlin/Bob van Haage 18-hole course, which now, in a much-upgraded format, winds its way along the water. In 2007, the resort was reopened as part of a sweeping real estate development plan that incorporated a roster of ultra-upscale private homes and condos, a hotel, and the most up-to-date and best-accessorized marina on "mainland" Eleuthera. Everything is perched on the tip of a sun-flooded peninsula that juts toward Nassau and the prevailing sea lanes, and it's all flanked by 20 splendid white-sand beaches. Locals claim the deep-sea fishing is as fine as it ever was.

Accommodations are plusher and more state-of-the art than anything else in Eleuthera, easily rivaling the best lodgings on Harbour Island. A string of custom-built two-bedroom apartments lines the edges of the harbor. Each is owned by a different absentee investor but rented out as a hotel lodging. Expect spectacular kitchens with polished-stone countertops, lots of high-tech lighting, convenient washer/dryers, and supremely comfortable furniture. Depending on the floor plan, units are either all on one level or arranged as a duplex. Each has an outdoor balcony that's wide and broad enough for a private reception, and if you're tired of either **Barracuda's Restaurant** (unlikely) or the on-site coffee shop, modeled on a Starbucks, you can have the resort's cooks make you a private dinner within your suite.

Cape Eleuthera, Rock Sound, Eleuthera, The Bahamas. www.capeeleuthera.com. © **888/270-9642** or 242/470-8242. Fax 242/334-8507. 19 town houses. Year-round $275–$450 2-bedroom apt for up to 4 occupants. AE, MC, V. **Amenities:** 2 restaurants; bikes; children's programs; access to nearby golf course; marina; outdoor pool; watersports equipment/rentals. *In room:* A/C, TV/DVD, washer/dryer, kitchen, Wi-Fi ($10 per day).

Where to Eat

Sammy's Place BAHAMIAN   At Eleuthera's southern tip, hot gossip and cheap, juicy burgers make Sammy's a popular hangout—come here for a slice of local life. Sammy's is in a neighborhood that even the owner refers to as "the back side of town." Sammy Culmer (assisted by Margarita, his daughter) serves drinks (including

Cotton Bay's Comeback

In the heyday of Pan American Airlines and its founder, Juan Trippe, **Cotton Bay Club** was the chicest enclave in The Bahamas. Once a household name in the U.S., Trippe was a relatively forgotten figure until his character appeared in *The Aviator,* Martin Scorsese's film about Howard Hughes. Cotton Bay Club was where the who's who of America went barefoot in the sand. But ever since it folded, it has been a ghost of itself, despite its picture-perfect beaches. Change, however, is slowly (very slowly) on the way.

If change comes at all, it will probably revolve around the long-envisioned but long-delayed debut of the **Cotton Bay Villas,** a complex of one-, two-, three-, and four-bedroom hotel villas surrounding a clubhouse. Future plans call for a golf course designed by Robert Trent Jones, Jr., but there's no guarantee that this long-slumbering vision will be up and running anytime during the life of this edition. For more information about the state of construction (or the lack of it) here, go to www.discovercottonbay.com.

Bahama Mamas and rum punches), conch fritters, Creole-style grouper, breaded scallops, pork chops, and lobster. If you drop in before 11am, you might be tempted by the selection of egg dishes.

This is primarily a restaurant and bar, but Sammy does rent four rooms with air-conditioning and cable TV, plus two efficiency cottages containing two bedrooms and a kitchen. The double-occupancy accommodations can be yours for $66 per night; cottages cost $100 per night.

Albury's Lane, Rock Sound ⓒ **242/334-2121.** www.discover-eleuthera-bahamas.com/sammys. html. Breakfast items $5–$12; lunch items $5–$15; dinner main courses $9–$21. No credit cards. Daily 7:30am–10pm.

TARPUM BAY

A good stopover when you're touring the island is Tarpum Bay, a tiny settlement with many pastel-washed, gingerbread-trimmed houses. It's a favorite of artists, who have established a small colony here, complete with galleries and studios. The charming waterfront village, some 15km (9⅓ miles) north of Rock Sound, is good for fishing and has a number of simple, inexpensive guesthouses. **Gaulding's Cay,** north of town, has a lovely beach with great snorkeling.

WINDERMERE ISLAND

Windermere is a very tiny island, connected somewhat haphazardly by ferry to "mainland" Eleuthera. It lies midway between Governor's Harbour and Rock Sound.

Even during its heyday, this enclave of private homes couldn't be more discreet. "We like to keep it quiet around here," a former staffer at the now-closed **Windermere Island Club** once told us. Regrettably, that wasn't always possible for this once-deluxe and snobbish citadel. When Prince Charles first took a pregnant Princess Diana here in the 1980s, she was photographed by the paparazzi in her swimsuit. Much to the club's horror, the picture gained the place worldwide notoriety.

At press time, the hotel once associated with this cluster of private homes was closed, and most of its elegant private homes were occupied only a few weeks per year by their mostly absentee owners, including Mariah Carey. Wracked with inner dissent and an increasing state of disrepair, the property has been the subject of many rumors about a rebirth. Stay tuned for more news about Windermere Island's on-again, off-again re-development plans (future editions of this book will keep you updated).

Meanwhile, if the ferryboat is operational by the time you visit, you can visit this island for its sandy, sheltered beaches and outstanding snorkeling opportunities, even though you'll have to bring your own gear. Be warned that in its present isolated, virtually uninhabited state, absolutely none of the beaches has anything even approaching supervision, so swim and cavort at your own risk. A security gate prevents you from rubber-necking the million-dollar vacation homes of the rich and famous who still occupy retreats here.

PALMETTO POINT

On the east side of Queen's Highway, south of Governor's Harbour, **North Palmetto Point** is a little village where visitors rarely venture, although you can get a simple meal here. This laid-back town will suit you if you want peace and quiet off the beaten track.

Ten Bay Beach ★★ is one of the best beaches in The Bahamas, with sparkling turquoise water and a wide expanse of soft, white sand. The beach is a 10-minute drive south of Palmetto Point and just north of Savannah Sound. There are no facilities, only idyllic isolation.

THE ELEUTHERIAN adventurers

Long before the first English colonists arrived, Eleuthera was inhabited by native Lucayans. However, around the mid-16th century, Spaniards came this way, capturing the peaceable people and shipping them out to the Caribbean as slaves.

Pirates plied the waters off Eleuthera and its adjacent islands, but after the removal of the Lucayans there were no inhabitants here for a century, until Capt. William Sayle led the Eleutherian Adventurers here from Bermuda to start a new life. The founding party consisted of about 70 people. They had a rough time of it. Dangerous reefs on the north coast of the island caused their ship and cargo to be lost. Trapped, they had to live off the land as best they could, initially inhabiting a cave. Many of them nearly starved, but they nevertheless drew up their own constitution, promising justice for all. Help came from Virginia colonists who sent food to the little band of adventurers.

Life on Eleuthera proved too much for many of the founding party, however. Many, including Captain Sayle, later returned to Bermuda. But reinforcements were on the way, both from Bermuda and from England, some bringing slaves with them. A permanent settlement had been founded. Freed slaves also came to this island and established settlements. The next wave of settlers were Loyalists fleeing the new United States to continue living under the British Crown. These settled principally in two offshore cays, Harbour Island and Spanish Wells.

Where to Eat

Mate & Jenny's Pizza Restaurant & Bar BAHAMIAN/AMERICAN This restaurant, known for its conch pizza, has a jukebox and a pool table. It's the most popular local joint, completely modest and unassuming. In addition to pizza, the Bethel family prepares pan-fried grouper, cracked conch, and light meals, including snacks and sandwiches. Lots of folks come here just to drink. Try their Goombay Smash, a Rum Runner, a piña colada, or just a Bahamian Kalik beer.

Off Queen's Hwy., South Palmetto Point. ✆ **242/332-1504.** Pizzas $8–$29; main courses $6–$22. MC, V. Wed–Mon 11am–3pm and 5:30–9pm.

GOVERNOR'S HARBOUR

With a British colonial heritage that goes back at least 300 years, Governor's Harbour is the island's oldest settlement and was reportedly the Eleutherian Adventurers' first landing place. The largest town on Eleuthera after Rock Sound, it lies midway along the 161km-long (100-mile) island. A few of its clapboard-sided houses evoke the gracious elegance of Harbour Island to the north, and the sleepy harborfront carries memories of the town's role as a provider of black pineapple to the supermarkets of England, Canada, and the United States. Today, however, things can get very sleepy indeed here. This is Out Island living at its most peaceful and uneventful.

The town currently has a population of about 1,600, with some bloodlines going back to the original settlers, the Eleutherian Adventurers, and to the Loyalists who followed some 135 years later. A scattering of fine old homes lines the streets uphill from the harbor, amid trailing bougainvillea and coppices of casuarina trees. **James Cistern** is a little hamlet north of the Governor's Harbour Airport.

Governor's Harbour Essentials

GETTING THERE See "Getting There" under "Eleuthera Essentials," at the beginning of this chapter, for details. The town airport is one of the island's major gateways, with daily flights arriving from Nassau and Florida.

VISITOR INFORMATION The friendly and welcoming **Eleuthera Tourist Office** is on Queen's Highway (✆ **242/332-2142;** www.eleuthera.bahamas.com, or www.bahamas.com), in modern, contemporary-looking premises about 2 blocks uphill from the harbor. It's usually open Monday through Friday from 9am to 5pm.

[FastFACTS] GOVERNOR'S HARBOR

If you're staying outside the town in a cottage or apartment, you can find services and supplies in Governor's Harbour or at nearby Palmetto Point.

Governor's Harbour has a branch of **First Caribbean International Bank,** on Queen's Highway (✆ **242/332-2300;** www.firstcaribbeanbank.com), with an ATM dispensing Bahamian (but not U.S.) dollars. Hours are Monday through Friday from 9:30am to 3pm.

Governor's Harbour's Medical Clinic, Queen's Highway (✆ **242/332-2774**), is the island's largest and most comprehensive healthcare facility. It's open Monday through Friday from 9am to 5:30pm and fills prescriptions. The clinic is also the site of a **dental office,** which operates Monday, Tuesday, and Friday from 9am to 1pm; call for an appointment ahead of time.

Check with your hotel for **Internet access,** which is also available on the second floor of Governor's Harbour's **Haynes Library** (© 242/332-2877). The charge is $5 per hour, and the library is open Monday through Friday from 9am to 5pm, Saturday from 10am to 4pm.

If you need the **police,** call © 242/332-2111.

The **post office,** on Haynes Avenue (© 242/332-2060), is open Monday through Friday from 9am to 4:30pm.

Where to Stay

Cocodimama Resort ★   The Junkanoo colors of this upmarket boutique hotel, located 7 miles north of historic Governor's Harbour, will attract your attention to its location at Cocodimama Beach and its celebrated sunsets over the waters of Alabaster Bay. In the colonial main house is a convivial bar and lounge, plus an award-winning restaurant (p. 214). Even if you don't stay here, you may want to patronize the restaurant.

All the large and well-furnished two-story beachfront guest rooms lie in a trio of Bahamian style cottages with covered verandas. The beach is at your door step, and the staff is one of the most helpful on island, arranging boat charters, fishing, all sorts of watersports, even horseback riding and car rentals.

Queen's Hwy., Governor Harbour, Eleuthera, The Bahamas. www.cocodimama.com. © 242/332-3150. Fax 242/332-3155. 9 units. Year-round $195–$228 MC, V. **Amenities:** Restaurant; bar; outdoor pool; room service; watersports equipment/rentals. *In room:* A/C, ceiling fan, TV, Wi-Fi (free).

Duck Inn Cottages and Orchid Gardens ★ 🏠   The accommodations you'll find here are larger, plusher, cozier, more historic, and more charming than what you'd expect in a conventional hotel. All units come with kitchenettes and access to a menagerie of friendly dogs and cats who will, if you're an animal lover, quickly insinuate themselves into your heart. Within a garden surrounded by a high wall, the complex consists of three masonry-sided houses, each built between 90 and 200 years ago, and set almost adjacent to one another, midway up a hillside overlooking the sea. The finest of these is Flora's Cottage, with four bedrooms that can sleep eight comfortably. Nassau-born Johnson "J. J." Duckworth and Katie, his Exuma-born wife, are the resident owners and managers. Much of their time is spent nurturing a sprawling collection of orchids—one of the country's largest—that are cultivated for export to Europe and the U.S.

Queen's Hwy., Governor's Harbour, Eleuthera, The Bahamas. www.duckinncottages.com. © 242/332-2608. Fax 242/332-2160. 3 units. Winter $155 double; off-season $130 double. Year-round $290 Flora's Cottage. AE, DISC, MC, V. **Amenities:** Babysitting; watersports equipment/ rentals. *In room:* A/C, TV, CD player, kitchenette, no phone.

Hut Pointe ★ 🏠   This two-story limestone building has been given a new lease on life and has been recycled into a small boutique hotel with a touch of class. It was designed and built in 1944 by Roland "Pop" Symonette, the first premier of The Bahamas, as his private home. Symonette started out with nothing but became one of the wealthiest of all Bahamians; his face appears on the Bahamian $50 note.

Hut Pointe lies only a short distance from a good beach; perhaps by the time of your arrival a pool will have been installed on the landscaped grounds.

Each spacious unit is a two-bedroom suite containing two tastefully furnished bedrooms, a large living room, and a full service kitchen. The upper floors open onto balconies. The solid stone construction is evident everywhere, along with the vintage handmade Bahamian floor tiles, interior ceilings and roof rafters constructed with

Abaco pine, and mahogany-floored decks. The resort is also eco-friendly, using solar power and rainwater "harvesting." The location is about 10 minutes from the center of Governor's Harbour and 10 minutes from the airport.

Queen's Hwy., Governor's Harbour, Eleuthera, The Bahamas. www.hutpointe.com. ⓒ **760/908-6700.** 7 units. Year-round $200–$255 suite. MC, V. Closed Sept-Oct. *In room:* Ceiling fans, TV/DVD, kitchen, Wi-Fi (free).

Laughing Bird Apartments   Set within a quarter-mile south of Governor's Harbour's public library, across a rarely used road from the beach, the red roof of this apartment complex is the well-maintained domain of Jean Davies and her son Pierre. Originally built in 1989 in a low-slung one-story format, its sightlines to the sea were "improved" in 2011 when Hurricane Irene ripped the tops off many of the trees which had formerly blocked its view. It is clean, decent, and appealingly uncluttered, each unit outfitted with summery furniture and a fully equipped kitchenette.

Haynes Highway East, Governor's Harbour. ⓒ **242/332-2012.** Fax 242/332-2358. 4 apartments. Year round $100 studio for 2; $150 2-bedroom unit for 2–4 occupants. DISC, MC, V. *In room:* A/C, ceiling fan, TV, kitchenette, no phone.

Pineapple Fields ★★ 🛍   Offering some of Eleuthera's most comfortable accommodations, this condominium complex sits across a quiet coastal road from a spectacular sandy beach. Isolated and very quiet, this retreat ranks alongside the (better-accessorized) Powell Pointe at Cape Eleuthera (p. 208) as our favorite resort on "mainland" Eleuthera. Built on the grounds of the once-fabled and very exclusive Potlatch Club, it occupies a meticulously landscaped 32-hectare (79-acre) site on the Atlantic, just minutes south from the center of Governor's Harbour. Accommodations sit within carefully maintained gardens, a very short walk from 305m (1,001 ft.) of beach. All units are spacious, well kept, and furnished in a style you'd expect from an upper-middle-bracket condo complex in Florida. There are also outdoor showers for when you're coming in from the beach, plus a free-form swimming pool. For a review of **Tippy's,** the resort's independently managed bistro, see below. At press time, most, but not all, of the units had been sold to investors who rent them out to visitors.

Banks Rd., Governor's Harbour, Eleuthera, The Bahamas. www.pineapplefields.com. ⓒ **877/677-9539** or 242/332-2221. Fax 242/332-2203. 32 units. Winter $220–$270 1-bedroom unit; $320–$370 2-bedroom unit; off-season $160–$200 1-bedroom unit, $250–$310 2-bedroom unit. 5-night minimum stay required over Christmas, New Year's, and Easter. AE, MC, V. **Amenities:** Restaurant; bar; outdoor pool. *In room:* A/C, TV, kitchen.

Quality Inn Cigatoo 🏊   Built in 1976 and virtually reconstructed in 2000, this low-rise, concrete-sided hotel has a faded style, evoking the kind of motel you might find in a small town somewhere in Florida. It's on the crest of a steep hill overlooking the town, within a 7-minute walk of the beach. The hotel is small-scale, intensely local, and unpretentious. It consists of one two-story central core and three white one-story buildings, with doors to each room painted a different primary color. The buildings are clustered around a swimming pool, the resort's focal point. Management is cordial, albeit a bit blasé. The hotel's restaurant, a fixture in this part of Eleuthera for many years, closed in 2011, but management directs hungry guests to Buccaneer Club (see below), which is under the same management.

Queen's Hwy., Governor's Harbour, Eleuthera, The Bahamas. www.bahamaslocal.com. ⓒ **242/332-3060.** Fax 242/332-3061. 18 units. $134 double. AE, MC, V. **Amenities:** Restaurant; bar; babysitting; outdoor pool; room service. *In room:* A/C, TV, hair dryer, Wi-Fi (free).

Where to Eat

Buccaneer Club BAHAMIAN/CHINESE   A farmhouse from the 1800s atop Buccaneer Hill has been converted into this local restaurant, which has a view and a menu that's about equally divided between Bahamian and Chinese specialties. You can dine al fresco in a flowery setting of bougainvillea and hibiscus shaded by coconut palm. The conch fritters are dependably good, as are any of the stir-fries, the fried chicken, Bahamian style, and most definitely the blackened grouper freshly caught that day. Americans feel at home when they drop in for lunch and order the likes of a BLT, burger, or freshly made salad, as well as crispy French fries or cold beers.

Daily specials are ever changing, but rotisserie chicken always is offered. The catch of the day, which can be prepared according to your specifications, usually turns up with crawfish, conch, and grouper.

Haynes Ave., Governor's Harbour. © **242/332-2000.** Reservations not needed. Main courses $14–$25. DC, MC, V. Daily 7am–9pm.

Cocodimama Restaurant ★★ ITALIAN/SWISS   In this previously recommended hotel (p. 212) has awakened the sleepy tastebuds of Governor's Harbour with its unusual interpretations of traditional Italian food. Opt for a table overlooking the magnificent Cocodimama beach. If you arrive at the end of a day, you'll be treated to a spectacular sunset over the bay. You can select a table either in the colonial main house or else on the outdoor patio.

Some of the finest ingredients are imported from Italy or else the United States. Appetizers include an array of antipasti, including the best Italian cheeses and cold cuts. Pastas are succulent, especially one of the chef's specialties, homemade spaghetti sautéed with calamari and shrimp. Meat, poultry, and salads are well crafted as well. Save room for the chef's special desserts which are changed daily.

In the Cocodimama Resort, Queen's Hwy. © **242/332-3150.** Reservations recommended. Main courses $15–$30. DC, MC, V. Daily 7–10:30am, noon–3pm and 6–10pm.

Lee's Cafe BAHAMIAN   A hardworking local matriarch, Leona Johnson, established this down-home restaurant in 2001 and has conducted a roaring business with local residents ever since. Don't expect an orchestrated decor; you'll enter a long, low, endlessly efficient dining room where the day's specials are written on a large paper pad. If no one appears to take your order, poke your head inside an impossibly small opening for a view of the kitchen, where Leona might be whipping up what we think is the best souse on Eleuthera: Even the Bahamian Minister of Tourism has complimented it and hauled some back to Nassau with him. Other menu items include conch salad, conch fritters, conch burgers with salad, grouper fingers either steamed or grilled, lobster, chicken, steak, and morning omelets. Most diners opt for takeout; a smaller percentage dine in. Leona, incidentally, is related to many dozens of relatives within James Cistern, and at any time during your experience here might greet one or another of them with grandmotherly affection.

Spencer St., James Cistern. © **242/335-6444.** Reservations not needed for dinner. Lunch platters $10–$15; dinner platters $18–$25. No credit cards. Mon–Sat 11:30am–3pm and 6:30–9pm.

Pammy's Takeaway BAHAMIAN   Tile-floored and Formica-clad, this is just a little cubbyhole with a few tables. Lunchtime brings sandwiches and platters of cracked conch, pork chops, and either broiled or fried grouper. Don't expect anything fancy because this definitely isn't. Run by hometown matriarch Pammy Moss, it's a true local joint serving up generous portions of flavor-filled food.

Queen's Hwy. at Gospel Chapel Rd. ⓒ **242/332-2843.** Reservations accepted only for dinner. Breakfast items $4–$8; light lunch $6–$12; main courses $14–$24. No credit cards. Mon–Sat 8am–5pm.

Tippy's Restaurant, Bar & Beach ★★ CONTINENTAL   By anyone's standards, this is the most urbane, international, and sophisticated restaurant on mainland Eleuthera, easily matching the flair of Harbour Island's best restaurants. Incorporating many vaguely Continental touches, it's set within a wood-and-masonry pavilion in an eerily isolated spot uphill from a spectacular beach. Originally established by a culinary team from Austria, it evokes the kind of bistro you'd expect to see in an Austrian ski resort, albeit with a greater emphasis on fresh fish, sea breezes, and touches of island sizzle and spice. Those menu items which aren't recited to you verbally by the staff are recorded on a blackboard. Examples include pistachio-studded pâté, an ultra-fresh version of fish and chips, lobster ravioli, pan-fried grouper, veal chops with a mushroom cream sauce, snapper served either *en papillote* or as part of the above-mentioned fish and chips, seared sesame tuna with papaya chutney, and a roulade of smoked salmon layered with goat cheese.

Across the coastal road from Pineapple Fields. ⓒ **242/332-3331.** Main courses $20–$34. MC, V. Daily noon–2:30pm and 6–10pm.

Hitting the Beach

Near the town center are two beaches known as the **Buccaneer Public Beaches;** they're adjacent, appropriately enough, to the Buccaneer Club, on the island's sheltered western edge, facing Exuma Sound. Snorkeling is good here—it's best where the pale turquoise waters near the coast deepen to a dark blue. Underwater rocks shelter lots of marine flora and fauna. The waves at these beaches are relatively calm.

On Eleuthera's Atlantic (eastern) side, about 1km (⅔ mile) from Governor's Harbour, is a much longer stretch of mostly pale pink sand, similar to what you'll find in Harbour Island. Known locally as **French Leave Beach** (or, less frequently, as the Club Med Public Beach), it's good for bodysurfing and, on days when storms are surging in the Atlantic, even conventional surfing.

Don't expect touristy kiosks selling drinks, snacks, or souvenirs at any of these beaches—everything here is pristine and undeveloped.

Governor's Harbour After Dark

Ronnie's Smoke Shop & Sports Bar, Cupid's Cay (ⓒ **242/332-2307**), is central Eleuthera's busiest and most popular nightspot, drawing folks from miles away. It's adjacent to the cargo depot of Cupid's Cay, in a connected cluster of simple buildings painted in combinations of black with lots of natural-stained wood. Most folks come here just to drink Kalik beer and talk at either of the two bars. But if you want to dance, there's an all-black room just for disco music on Friday nights. You'll also find Eleuthera's only walk-in cigar humidor. If you get hungry, order some barbecue, a pizza, chicken wings, or popcorn. The place is open Monday through Friday from 10am until midnight. On weekends, it often stays open until about 3am.

HATCHET BAY

Forty kilometers (25 miles) north of Governor's Harbour, Hatchet Bay was once known for a British-owned plantation that had 500 head of dairy cattle and thousands of chickens. Today, that plantation is gone, and this is now one of Eleuthera's sleepiest villages, as you'll see if you veer off Queen's Highway onto one of the town's ghostly main streets, Lazy Shore Road or Ocean Drive.

Where to Stay & Eat

Bay Inn Estates Bed and Breakfast   The beaches are a 5-minute walk away, but this simple B&B has many other things going for it. Set in lush landscaping, it offers a series of large bedrooms decorated with traditional mahogany furnishings, although baths are modern. Each unit opens onto a balcony or terrace. On site is an Internet cafe, plus a helpful staff who arranges sightseeing tours, even some good fishing. This building itself is one of the brightest in the area, its clapboard structures painted in lemon yellow, lime green, and flamingo pink. A continental breakfast is offered in an adjoining building and can be taken at an al fresco table set under almond trees.

Queen's Hwy., Hatchet Bay, Eleuthera, The Bahamas. ✆ **242/335-0730.** 14 units. Year-round $150 double. DC, MC, V. **Amenities:** Bike rentals; Internet cafe. *In room:* A/C, TV, Wi-Fi ($8 per hr.).

Rainbow Inn ★   Three kilometers (1¾ miles) south of Alice Town, near a sandy beach, the Rainbow Inn is a venerable survivor in an area where many competitors have failed. Quirky and appealing to guests who return for quiet getaways again and again, it's an isolated collection of seven cedar-sided octagonal bungalows. The accommodations are simple but comfortable, spacious, and tidy. A sandy beach is just steps away.

   One of the most appealing things about the place is its bar and restaurant, which make it a destination for residents far up and down the length of Eleuthera. It's an octagon with a high-beamed ceiling and a thick-topped woodsy-looking bar where guests down daiquiris and piña coladas amid nautical trappings. It has live Bahamian music twice a week and a relatively extensive menu. The owners take pride in the fact that the menu hasn't changed much in 20 years; this suits its loyal fans just fine. Local Bahamian food includes conch chowder, fried conch, fresh fish, and Bahamian lobster. International dishes feature French onion soup, escargot, and steaks, followed by Key lime pie for dessert. Table no. 2, crafted from a triangular teakwood prow of a motor yacht that was wrecked off the coast in the 1970s, is a perpetual favorite.

Governor's Harbour, Eleuthera, The Bahamas. www.rainbowinn.com. ✆/fax **242/335-0294.** 5 units. Winter $155 double; off-season $130 double. Year-round $225 2-bedroom villa; $250 3-bedroom villa. MAP (breakfast and dinner) $55 per person. MC, V. **Amenities:** Restaurant; bar; babysitting; outdoor pool; tennis court; watersports equipment/rentals; Wi-Fi (free during restaurant hours). *In room:* A/C, CD player, kitchenette.

GREGORY TOWN

Gregory Town stands in the center of Eleuthera against a backdrop of hills, which break the landscape's usual flat monotony. A village of clapboard cottages, it was once famous for growing pineapples. Though the industry isn't as strong as it was in the past, the locals make good pineapple rum out of the fruit, and you can still visit the **Gregory Town Plantation and Distillery,** where it's produced. You're allowed to sample it, and we can almost guarantee you'll want to take a bottle home with you.

Where to Stay

The Cove Eleuthera ★★   This resort is among Eleuthera's most upscale and luxurious resorts. Positioned on rocky terrain above a pink-sand cove 2.5km (1½ miles) northwest of Gregory Town and 5km (3 miles) southeast of the Glass Window,

Crash Pad for Surfers

A short walk from Surfers Beach, the **Surfers Beach Manor** ((© 242/335-5300; www.surfersmanor.com) is a restored, laid-back inn offering nine air-conditioned bedrooms, with either twin or queen-size beds. In winter, doubles range from $109 to $139, with summer rates lowered to $89 to $129. A rental car can also be arranged for between $70 and $80 per day. An on-site restaurant and lounge serves Bahamian cuisine. Peter and Rebecca, your congenial hosts, offer free Wi-Fi in the lobby. Swimming, surfing (of course), and doing nothing are the pastimes here. American Express, MasterCard, and Visa are accepted.

this year-round resort is set on 11 hectares (27 acres) partially planted with pineapples; it consists of a main clubhouse and several simple, cement-sided bungalows, each containing four units nestled on the ocean side. They all have a spacious living area, tile floors, a relatively plush bathroom, a porch, and no TV or phone to distract you—except in the Point House suite, which does have a 36-inch TV to go along with its two bedrooms, two and a half bathrooms, and private deck.

The restaurant (below) carries hints of island posh, with an amiable bar area and a commitment to serving three meals per day. The lounge and poolside patio are open daily for drinks and informal meals. Kayaks, bicycles, two tennis courts, and a small freshwater pool compete with hammocks for your time. There's fabulous snorkeling right off the sands here, with colorful fish darting in and out of the offshore reefs.

Queen's Hwy., Gregory Town, Eleuthera, The Bahamas. www.thecoveeleuthera.com. (© **800/552-5960** in the U.S. and Canada, or 242/335-5142. Fax 242/335-5338. 26 units. Year-round $245–$295 double; $410 1-bedroom suite; $465–$490 2-bedroom suite; $995 Point House suite. AE, MC, V. **Amenities:** Restaurant; bar; exercise room; outdoor pool; 2 tennis courts; watersports equipment/rentals; Wi-Fi (free). *In room:* A/C, hair dryer, kitchenette (in some), MP3 docking station, no phone.

Where to Eat

The Cove Eleuthera ★★ BAHAMIAN/CONTINENTAL   Located in the previously recommended eponymous hotel 2.5km (1½ miles) northwest of Gregory Town, this spacious dining room is your best bet in the area, featuring gourmet Continental cuisine with surprising amounts of local flair. The restaurant is decorated with pastel colors in a light, tropical style. Lunch begins with the inevitable conch chowder. Follow it with a conch burger, a generous patty of ground seafood blended with green pepper, onion, and spices. Conch also appears in the evening, and we think this is the best cracked conch in town—it's tenderized, dipped in a special batter, and fried to golden perfection. Other menu items include char-grilled tenderloin steak with skewered prawns and field mushrooms, seared ahi tuna with pounded ginger sauce, and grilled chicken breast with papaya salsa and spicy coconut sauce.

Queen's Hwy. (© **242/335-5142.** www.thecoveeleuthera.com. Breakfast items $8–$14; lunch main courses $10–$25; dinner main courses $26–$46. MC, V. Daily 8–10:30am, 11:30am–2:30pm, and 6–8:30pm.

Exploring the Area: the Glass Window & Beyond

Behind a colorful facade on Queen's Highway in the heart of Gregory Town, the **Island Made Gift Shop** (© 242/335-5369) carries an outstanding inventory that owes its quality to owner Pamela Thompson's artistic eye. Look for one-of-a-kind

Drop-Dead Delicious Pineapple Tarts

Follow the smell of fresh-baked goods to one of Gregory Town's most enduring small businesses, **Thompson's Bakery,** Johnson Street (𝄞 **242/335-5053**), open Monday through Saturday from 8:30am to 6pm. Run by two local sisters, Monica and Daisy Thompson, this simple bakery occupies a lime-green wooden building near the town's highest point. Although it churns out lots of bread—including raisin, whole-wheat, and coconut—the best reason to stop by are the fresh pineapple tarts, priced at $3.25 each. They're among the best we've ever tasted. You might also find freshly baked doughnuts and cinnamon rolls.

paintings on driftwood or crafted on the soles of discarded shoes, handmade quilts from Androsian fabrics, Abaco ceramics, and jewelry made from pieces of glass found on the beach. There are extraordinary woven baskets made by the descendants of Seminole Indians and escaped slaves living in remote districts of Andros Island. Especially charming are bowls crafted from half-sections of conch shells.

Dedicated surfers have come here from as far away as California and Australia to test their skills at **Surfers Beach,** 4km (2½ miles) south of Gregory Town on the Atlantic side. The waves are at their highest in winter and spring; even if you're not brave enough to get out there, it's fun to watch.

South of town on the way to Hatchet Bay are several caverns worth visiting, the largest of which is simply called **the Cave.** It has a big fig tree out front, which Gregory Town's people claim was planted long ago by pirates who wanted to conceal the cave because they had hidden treasure in it.

Local guides (to get one, ask around in Gregory Town or Hatchet Bay) will take you into the cave's interior, where the resident bats are harmless even though they must resent the intrusion of tourists with flashlights. At one point, the drop is so steep—about 3.5m (11 ft.)—that you have to use a ladder to climb down. Eventually, you reach a cavern ornamented with stalactites and stalagmites. A maze of passageways leads off through the rocky underground recesses. The cave comes to an abrupt end at the edge of a cliff, where the thundering sea crashes around some 27m (89 ft.) below.

If you drive north out of Gregory Town, you'll come to the famed **Glass Window,** Eleuthera's narrowest point. A natural rock arch once bridged the land, but it's gone now, replaced by a constructed bridge. As you drive across it, pay attention to the contrast between the deep-blue ocean of the sound's windward side and the emerald-green shoal waters of its leeward side. The rocks rise to a height of 21m (69 ft.).

Often, as ships in the Atlantic are being tossed about, their crews look across the narrow point to see a ship resting quietly on the other side, hence the name Glass Window. Artist Winslow Homer was so captivated by this spot that he captured it on canvas.

Fishing & Other Outdoor Pursuits

Your best bet for fishing trips is **Capt. Z Fishing and Dive Charters** (𝄞 **242/335-5185;** www.fisheleuthera.com), located at the Cove House on Bay Street in Gregory Town. (Cove House is not to be confused with the entirely separate Cove Eleuthera resort described above.) This charter outfit offers some of the Bahamas' best spearfishing. Both half- and full-day fishing excursions are offered aboard custom-built boats. Call ahead for details or bookings.

A particularly popular outfitter for anyone interested in exploring the Eleutherian great outdoors is Gregory Town–based **Bahamas Out Island Adventures** (✆ **242/ 335-0349;** www.bahamasadventures.com). Depending on demand, it can be all things to all outdoors enthusiasts. Come here for activities as diverse as surfing or kayaking lessons, bird-watching tours, and treks through the scrub and low trees of the island's windswept terrain. Full- and half-day tours can be custom-organized for your individual preferences, abilities, and needs.

THE CURRENT

The inhabitants of the Current, a settlement in North Eleuthera, are believed to have descended from a tribe of Native Americans. A narrow strait separates the village from Current Island, where most locals make their living from the sea or from plaiting straw goods.

This is a small community that often welcomes visitors. You won't find crowds or artificial attractions here. Everything is focused on the sea, a source of pleasure for the visiting tourists, but a way to sustain life for the residents.

From the Current, you can explore some sights in North Eleuthera, including **Preacher's Cave,** northeast of North Eleuthera Airport. In this barren and isolated backwater, the Eleutherian Adventurers found shelter during the mid–17th century, when they were shipwrecked with no provisions.

Note that your taxi driver may balk at being asked to drive here; the road is hard on his expensive tires. As such, his round-trip asking price from, say, the ferryboat wharves servicing Harbour Island might be as much as $100.

If you do opt for a detour here, you'll find yourself within one of the most historically important sites in The Bahamas—the point from which the origins of the country emerged. Set amid scrub and bush, the Preacher's Cave looks something like an amphitheater, with niches carved into its walls for seating for the community's elders, and a central boulder allegedly used as either a pulpit or an altar. The devout Eleutherian Adventurers held religious services inside the cave, which is pierced by natural holes in the roof, allowing light and rainfall to intrude.

For several years after they were stranded on reefs near this site, the settlers developed an elaborate series of religious and cultural codes and bylaws, which in some ways factored into the legal and social codes of The Bahamas. The landscapes around this cave are rich with buried workaday artifacts from that early impromptu community, and much excavation work remains to be done, a project of ongoing interest to the Bahamian government. DNA tests of skeletons unearthed from the cave have drawn distinct links between the Eleutherian Adventurers and the modern-day residents of Spanish Wells (p. 230).

Another sight of interest to ecologists and marine scientists is **Boiling Hole,** part of a shallow bank on the island's Atlantic side that seems to boil and churn during changing tides.

Where to Stay

Sandcastle Apartments ☺ For escapists seeking a location far removed from the usual tourist circuit, these utterly plain but airy accommodations are a good bet. Its on-site kitchen, easy access to a simple grocery store within a 5-minute walk, and self-contained nature often appeal to families. Each modest unit has a double bed, a queen-size sleeper sofa in the living room, a small bathroom with a shower stall, and a view over shallow offshore waters, where children can wade safely for a surprisingly long distance offshore. The accommodations lie just across the road from the sea.

The Current, Eleuthera, The Bahamas. ✆ **242/335-3244.** Fax 242/393-0440. 2 units. Year-round $85–$90 double. No credit cards. **Amenities:** Bikes. *In room:* A/C.

HARBOUR ISLAND ★★★

One of the oldest settlements in The Bahamas, founded before the United States was a nation, Harbour Island lies off Eleuthera's northern end, some 322km (200 miles) from Miami. It is 5km (3 miles) long and 1km (⅔ mile) wide. The media have hailed this pink-sand island as the new St. Barts, a reference to how chic it has become. These days, beware: If you're jogging along the beach, you might trip over a movie star.

Affectionately called by its original name, "Briland," Harbour Island is studded with good resorts. The spectacular **Pink Sands Beach ★★★** runs the whole length of the eastern side of the island and is protected from the ocean breakers by an outlying coral reef, which makes for some of the country's safest swimming. Except for unseasonably cold days, you can swim and enjoy watersports here year-round. The climate averages 72°F (22°C) in winter, 77°F (25°C) in spring and fall, and 82°F (28°C) in summer. Occasionally, evenings are cool, with a low of about 64°F (18°C) from November to February.

To the amazement of even the island's most reliable repeat visitors, its clientele has gotten almost exponentially richer and more famous since the turn of the millennium. There's a building boom of ultra-upscale villas and a migration into the island by some staggeringly wealthy billionaires who have included Ron Perlman (CEO of Revlon) and India Hicks (a relative of England's royal family and former fashion model). Colin Farrell, Sylvester Stallone, and Sarah Ferguson, the Duchess of York, along with various titled aristocrats from the old houses of Europe, make discreet but strategic appearances throughout the winter months. This new influx of the mega-wealthy has led to prices going far upward and caused something of a run on building sites along "zillionaire's row," a deliberately rutted and potholed byway north of the town center. No one is thrilled with these changes, especially the deeply entrenched owners of the island homes, and any attempt at expansion by any of the local hotels is rigorously opposed by increasingly politicized contingents of local residents and homeowners.

Harbour Island Essentials

GETTING THERE   To reach Harbour Island, take a flight to the **North Eleuthera Airport,** which is only a 1½-hour flight from Fort Lauderdale or Miami, or a 30-minute flight from Nassau. See "Getting There" under "Eleuthera Essentials," at the beginning of this chapter, for details on which airlines provide service. From the airport, it's a 1.5km (1-mile) taxi ride to the ferry dock. The taxi costs about $5 per person if you share the expense with four or five other passengers. From the dock, you'll take a 3km (1¾-mile) motorboat ride to Harbour Island. There's usually no waiting because a flotilla of high-powered motorboats makes the crossing whenever at least two customers show up, at a cost of around $5 per person. If you're traveling alone and are willing to pay the $20 one-way fare, the boat will depart immediately, without waiting for a second passenger.

Another way to get to Harbour Island is by boarding a speedy 177-passenger catamaran in Nassau. Contact **Bahamas Ferries** (☎ 242/333-3113; www.bahamas ferries.com) for details. You can begin this 2-hour trip at **Potter's Cay Dock,** which is under the bridge leading from Paradise Island to downtown Nassau. The fare for one of these daily excursions is $131 round-trip or $68 one-way for adults, and $80 round-trip or $60 one-way for children 2 to 11. This ferry pulls up to Harbour Island's Government Dock, where taxis wait to take you to your hotel.

GETTING AROUND   Upon reaching Harbour Island, most visitors don't need transportation. They can walk to where they're going, rent **bicycles** (check your equipment carefully before renting—some bikes rented to tourists are way past their prime), or putt-putt around the island on electric **golf carts.** Most hotels offer these for rent or at least will make arrangements for a cart or bicycle; usually, they'll be delivered directly to your lodging.

Michael's Cycles, on Colebrook Street (☎ 242/333-2384), is the best place to go if you want some mobility other than your own two feet. The shop is open daily from 8am to 6pm. Bikes rent for $13 per day, two-seater motorbikes are $32 per day, and four-seater golf carts go for $50 per day. You can also rent kayaks for $40 per day, paddleboats for $40 per day (or $10 per hour), and jet skis for $85 per hour.

VISITOR INFORMATION   The **Harbour Island Tourist Office,** on Dunmore Street (☎ 242/333-2621), is open Monday through Friday from 9am to 5pm.

[FastFACTS] HARBOUR ISLAND

The **Royal Bank of Canada,** on Dunmore Street (☎ **242/333-2250**), has an ATM. The bank is open Monday through Thursday from 9:30am to 3pm, Friday from 9:30am to 4:30pm.

The **Harbour Island Health Centre,** South Street, Dunmore Town (☎ **242/333-2227**), handles routine medical problems. Hours are Monday through Friday from 9am to 5pm. The on-call doctor can be reached at ☎ **242/333-2822.**

Resorts sometimes provide **Internet access.** If yours doesn't, try **Arthur's Bakery,** Dunmore Street (☎ **242/333-2285;** www.myharbourisland.com/bakery.htm), in the center of town. You can use the computer there or bring your own laptop. Hours are Monday through Saturday from 8am to 2pm; the cost is $10 for 15 minutes.

You can get prescriptions filled at the Bayside Pharmacy, in the Bayside Café Plaza, Bay Street (☎ **242/333-2174**). It's open Monday through Saturday from 9am to 5pm.

The **police** can be reached at either ☎ **919** or 242/333-2111.

The **post office,** on Gaol Alley (☎ **242/333-2215**), is open Monday through Friday from 9am to 5:30pm.

Where to Stay
VERY EXPENSIVE

The Dunmore ★   This formal and exclusive colony of cottages is the quintessentially elegant hideaway, with 3.2 hectares (8 acres) of well-manicured grounds along the island's legendary 5km (3-mile) pink-sand beach. Extensive renovations have brought it up to the standards of Pink Sands. The interiors have a nostalgic feeling with custom-upholstered sofas, vintage rattan chairs, and grass matting on the floors, plus a collection of shells, books, and antique maps. All of the accommodations were slightly renovated in 2010, and some were enlarged. The Bahamian-style bungalows combine traditional furnishings and tropical accessories.

Breakfast is offered on a garden terrace under pine trees with a view of the beach. Dinner is served at one seating between 7 and 8:30pm; men should wear jackets (ties are optional). Bahamian and international cuisine is featured in a formal dining room with a high ceiling, louvered doors, expensive china, and windows with views over the blue Atlantic. A clubhouse is the focal point for socializing, while a living room, library, and ocean-view bar provide additional cozy nooks.

Colebrook Lane, Harbour Island, The Bahamas. www.dunmorebeach.com. ✆ **877/891-3100** or 242/333-2200. Fax 242/333-2429. 16 units. Nov–Apr $450–$650 double, $600–$800 suite for 2; May–Aug $350–$500 double, $500–$600 suite for 2. MC, V. Closed Sept–Oct. **Amenities:** Restaurant; bar; babysitting; bikes; tennis court. *In room:* A/C, ceiling fan, TV, hair dryer, Internet (free).

Pink Sands ★★★ Posh and sophisticated, and refurbished in 2011, this hideaway is just the place to sneak away to with that special (wealthy) someone. The elegant, relaxed retreat occupies an 11-hectare (27-acre) beachfront estate, located adjacent to a 5km (3-mile) stretch of pink sand sheltered by a barrier reef. Although it feels a bit like a pricey private club, it's less snobbish and a lot more hip than the Dunmore Beach Club. The resort's outrageous clubhouse is the most beautifully and imaginatively decorated room in the Out Islands. Guests here get some of the best meals on the island, an "A-B-C" fusion of Asian, Bahamian, and Caribbean cuisine. Dinner is an elegant four-course nightly affair. Lunches are much less formal, served in the Blue Bar, a postmodern beachside pavilion.

The airy, spacious accommodations occupy cement-sided cottages scattered throughout the grounds and gardens. Depending on the configuration and size, each cottage contains one or two separate units, with either an ocean or a garden view, mahogany furniture, and elaborate tile work. Each has a pressurized water system, walk-in closets, and private patios with teak furnishings. The interior design features marble floors with area rugs, oversized Adirondack furniture, local art, and batik fabrics. Fax machines and cellular phones can be supplied if you need them.

Chapel St., Harbour Island, The Bahamas. www.pinksandsresort.com. ✆ **800/407-4776** or 242/333-2030. Fax 242/333-2060. 25 units. Winter $600–$900 1-bedroom cottage for 2, from $1,400 2-bedroom unit; off-season $495–$750 1-bedroom cottage for 2, from $1,200 2-bedroom unit. 1- to 3-night minimum stay, depending on season. AE, MC, V. **Amenities:** 2 restaurants; 2 bars; babysitting; small health club; outdoor pool; room service; 3 tennis courts (lit for night play); watersports equipment/rentals. *In room:* A/C, TV/DVD, hair dryer, minibar, MP3 docking station and free use of iPod, Wi-Fi (free).

EXPENSIVE

Coral Sands ★★ ☺ When it was built in the 1970s, everyone wondered how this concrete behemoth would fit into a community otherwise composed of clapboard-sided houses and historic Out Island charm. Its present owners have spent barrels of money skillfully softening the lines of its angular structure, painting the outside a soft shade of pink, improving the gardens, and spiffying the place up to a family-friendly hideaway of enormous charm. It stands on 3.6 hilly hectares (9 acres) overlooking the beach and within walking distance of British colonial–style Dunmore Town. This is one of the island's most consistently reliable hotels, avoiding the glitter of some of the more volatile properties. It's a favorite of families, whereas some of the more posh resorts don't really cater to children.

Built with an airy design that features big-windowed loggias and arcades, it opens directly onto the famous 5km (3-mile) pink-sand beach. Casual elegance, with ample doses of charm and friendliness, permeates every aspect of this place. Improvements have revitalized the property and freshened up the decor. Many rooms have private verandas or terraces; all are eminently comfortable, allowing you to fall asleep to the soothing sounds of waves breaking on the shore. The most recently restored rooms are on the Caribe building's second floor; these have been converted into deluxe one-bedroom ocean-view suites, some with two bathrooms, and have a bedroom facing the ocean, plus a separate living room with sofa.

The hotel's restaurant offers fine cuisine based on the craftsmanship of chefs who usually hail from Europe and are in The Bahamas on medium-term contracts. Less elaborate food is also offered at the Beach Bar & Lounge, which is dramatically cantilevered high above the pale-pink sands.

Chapel St., Harbour Island, The Bahamas. www.coralsands.com. © **888/568-5493** or 800/468-2799 in the U.S. and Canada, or 242/333-2350. Fax 242/333-2368. 36 units. Winter season $335–$390 double, $450–$900 1-bedroom cottage or suite, $1,950–$2,250 2-bedroom cottage, $8,000 private villa home; off-season $250–$295 double, $455–$700 1-bedroom cottage or suite, $1,200–$1,500 2-bedroom cottage, $7,000 private villa home. AE, MC, V. Closed early Sept to mid-October. **Amenities:** Restaurant; bar; babysitting; outdoor pool; tennis court (lit for night play); watersports equipment/rentals. *In room:* A/C, TV (in some), hair dryer, kitchen, Wi-Fi (free).

The Landing ★★ This intimate inn is understated, tasteful, and lovely. Harbour Island's first doctor built the house in the 1850s as his private residence. It's a few paces from the piers where ferryboats arrive from Eleuthera. Virtually destroyed by a hurricane in 1999, it was restored nicely by its former part-owner, India Hicks, daughter of the famed London decorator David Hicks, the granddaughter of Lord Mountbatten of Burma (grandson of Queen Victoria), and a bridesmaid to Diana at her wedding to Prince Charles. Although a few of the decor statements made by India are still in place, new owners run the Landing primarily as a sophisticated restaurant (p. 226), with bedrooms coming as a rustically upscale afterthought. Accommodations, five of which lie within a pair of old, historic buildings nearby, are breezy, airy, high-ceilinged, and artistically old-fashioned, opening in most cases onto wraparound verandas that seem to expand the living space within. Expect bold, cheerful island colors mixed with tones of muted gray, accompanied by design touches that evoke the seafaring days of old Harbour Island.

Bay St., Harbour Island, The Bahamas. www.harbourislandlanding.com. © **242/333-2707.** Fax 242/333-2650. 12 units. Year round $225–$395 double. Extra person $50. AE, MC, V. **Amenities:** Restaurant; bar; babysitting; outdoor pool. *In room:* A/C, hair dryer, no phone, Wi-Fi (free).

Rock House Hotel ★★★ This hotel, originally an unpretentious B&B, is now one of Harbour Island's most glamorous properties. It benefits from hip and trendy associations with Miami's South Beach and by being a sophisticated adult venue where children under 17 aren't really welcome. It has a surprisingly posh repeat clientele, with an occasional scattering of celebrities. Painted a pale yellow, with a white roof that's visible from Harbour Island's ferryboat pier, the hotel sits on a low bluff above the harbor in the center of the island's only village. The property combines the original 1940s-era B&B with an adjoining site that had functioned for several decades as a Catholic schoolhouse. Each of its whimsical accommodations is outfitted with a unique name and airy, island-comfortable decorative style. Examples include the Reef Room, the Palm Room, the Asian Room, the Nautilus Room, the Pineapple Room, and the Parrot Room. Social life centers on the bar, the restaurant, and the lavishly landscaped swimming pool, whose edges are lined with the kind of tentlike cabanas that you might expect along the coast of Sardinia.

Bay and Hill sts., Harbour Island, The Bahamas. www.rockhousebahamas.com. © **242/333-2053.** Fax 242/333-3353. 10 units. Year-round $380–$495 double; from $575 junior suite; $725–$950 2-bedroom unit. Rates include continental breakfast. 3- to 5-night minimum stay. AE, MC, V. Closed Aug–Nov.

Children 17 and under not permitted. **Amenities:** Restaurant (p. 226); bar; exercise room; outdoor pool; room service. *In room:* A/C, TV/DVD, CD player, minibar, MP3 docking station, Wi-Fi (free).

Romora Bay Club & Resort ★★

In 2011, after the completion of a long-awaited 40-slip marina, and despite an ongoing series of management upheavals and continuing conflicts over its expansion plans, this cluster of cottages on the island's bay side is up and running, welcoming visitors to its oft-changing premises. The inn was originally developed as a private club for reclusive millionaires, but today is open to all. Built on a sloping hillside, a short golf-cart ride away from Pink Sands Beach, its clusters of pink, blue, and yellow cottages and gazebos are scattered about the landscaped grounds. Rooms have tiled floors and are cozily furnished with comfortable beds and private patios. The junior suites and water-view rooms are the most desirable, opening onto panoramic vistas of the bay. Within an open-sided ground-floor pavilion overlooking the harbor, an intimate, informal restaurant, Sunsets on the Bay, serves cheeseburgers, salads, and grilled lobster and grouper, along with stiff drinks and the promise of memorable sunsets. At presstime, plans had been postponed for the oft-announced construction of condominiums, which may or may not be reinaugurated when the economy improves.

Colbrooke St., Harbour Island, The Bahamas. www.romorabay.com. ⓒ **800/688-0425** or 242/333-2325. Fax 242/333-2500. 25 units. Year-round $250 double, $350 suite; AE, DC, MC, V. **Amenities:** 2 restaurants; 2 bars; outdoor pool; watersports equipment/rentals; Wi-Fi (free). *In room:* A/C, TV, hair dryer.

Runaway Hill Inn

Small and intimate, within a 1938 masonry building with rambling verandas and porches, this conservative, comfortable hotel overlooks acres of pink-sand beach. It has a huge lawn and is separated from Colebrook Street by a wall. The building retains its English colonial–style dormers and many other original features, including a black-and-white checkerboard-tile floor, which, we're told, was installed to emulate a sophisticated Cuban resort during the heyday of that island's pre-Castro tourism. In winter, a crackling fire sometimes burns in the hearth near the entrance. The social center is a cheerfully decorated, pastel-painted lounge/dining room/bar/reception with a sense of Bahamian whimsy. Dinners are served on the breezy rear porch overlooking the swimming pool, and nonguests are welcome to eat here (p. 227).

As for bedrooms, each one is different, giving the impression that you are in a private home—as indeed this used to be. Only two of the guest rooms are in the original house, and these are accessible via the building's original 18th-century staircase. The others are within comfortable annexes built during the 1970s and 1980s.

Colebrook St. (at Love Lane), Harbour Island, The Bahamas. www.runawayhill.com. ⓒ **843/278-1724** or 242/333-2150. Fax 242/333-2420. 11 units. Nov–May 15 $375–$425 double, $450 villa; May 16–Sept 1 $375 double, $400 villa. MC, V. Closed Sept–Oct. **Amenities:** Restaurant; bar; bikes; outdoor pool; watersports equipment/rentals; Wi-Fi (free in lobby). *In room:* A/C, hair dryer, no phone.

Valentines Resort & Marina ★ ☺

If Harbour Island has a mega-hotel, this is it. Since its inception as a small-scale haven for yachties in the 1980s, it has survived major shifts in both its ownership and its priorities. What you'll see today is a corporate-minded and somewhat anonymous enterprise that has survived many years of squabbling among its partners and with local homeowners. Some locals have objected—almost violently—to the construction of the resort's marina, which retains its status as Harbour Island's biggest and best accessorized. Much of the new construction associated with this place has been sold as condominiums to mostly absentee owners. They're rented out as hotel accommodations whenever possible.

Don't expect a candy-colored confection in tones of Valentine pink. The predominant colors here are tangerine and coral, all in a low-rise venue just across the sleepy harborfront road, a 10-minute golf-cart ride from Harbour Island's ferryboat piers. Whereas the resort's airy, sunny bar and restaurant lie on the piers directly above the harbor, its accommodations are within Neo-Georgian two-story structures on a sloping lawn uphill from the harbor. Each evokes a government ministry, each is painted a different pastel color, and each contains between 8 and 10 separate units.

Harbour Island, The Bahamas. www.valentinesresort.com. © **888/513-5974** or 242/333-2142. Fax 242/333-2135. 45 units. Winter $395–$875 one-bedroom suite for up to 4 occupants, $495–$1.025 two-bedroom suite for 6–8 occupants; off-season $195–$300 one-bedroom suite for up to 4, $350–$550 2-bedroom suite for up to 6. AE, MC, V. **Amenities:** Restaurant; bar; children's camp; marina; watersports equipment/rentals; Wi-Fi (free). *In room:* A/C, TV, kitchen or kitchenette.

MODERATE

Chef Neff's Getaway & Heron's Nest ★ 🏠   Harbour Island's most respected chef, a gastronomic genius originally from Ohio—with a resume that includes catering for Sarah Ferguson, Duchess of York—rents a duet of well-decorated rooms within her private home. Susan Neff, once the full-time chef at Coral Sands and now semi-retired, offers good value within her neat-as-a-pin private villa, a short walk from Romora Bay Resort near the island's southern end. Surrounded by lush landscaping and flowering shrubs, the house, rebuilt to her specifications in 1999, boasts a panoramic cupola, comfortable beds, private bathrooms, and the benefit of Susan's years of experience as a nurse, hospice counselor, and professional chef. Though it lacks the hands-on amenities of a deluxe hotel, many guests return year after year, drawn by rates significantly lower than what's charged for comparable accommodations at any of the island resorts. Each unit has a very small private patio. February sojourns are usually booked a full year in advance, so plan ahead.

Yellow Heron, off Queen's Hwy., Harbour Island, The Bahamas. www.vrbo.com/19186. © **242/333-3047** or 301/560-3166. 2 units. Year-round $155–$165 double per night or $925–$1,025 per week. No credit cards. **Amenities:** Wi-Fi (free). *In room:* A/C, TV, kitchenette or kitchen.

Sugar Apple Bed and Breakfast   One of the simpler inns on Harbour Island is this two-story motel, offering spacious suites, each with an up-to-date kitchen. You're a 5-minute walk from the pink sands of a beach and water that, in the words of the owner, varies in color "from the celluloid eyes of Paul Newman to that of Elizabeth Taylor." The suites come with a cozy sitting room, bedrooms with hand-crafted four-poster beds, and well-equipped kitchens. The suites are decorated with Kenyan art and fabrics. Do not expect the elegance and snobbery of many of the upmarket Harbour Island inns; it's way more downhome here. Accommodations are clean, comfortable, and inviting.

Colebrooke St., Harbour Island, Eleuthera, The Bahamas. www.sugarapplebb.com. © **242/333-2750.** 7 suites. Year-round $150–$435 suite. MC, V. **Amenities:** Golf cart rentals ($50 per day); Wi-Fi (free). *In room:* A/C, ceiling fan, TV, kitchen, no phone.

Where to Eat

If you don't want to dress up for lunch, head for **Seaview Takeaway,** at the foot of the ferry dock (© **242/333-2542**). Here you can feast on all that good stuff associated with old-time and ethnic Bahamian cuisine: pig's feet, sheep-tongue souse, and, most definitely, cracked conch. Everything tastes better with peas 'n' rice. Daily specials range from $3.50 to $11. It's open Monday through Wednesday from 8am to 5pm, and Thursday to Saturday from 8am to 10pm

Another casual drop-in spot for both visitors and locals is **Arthur's Bakery & Cafe,** Dunmore Street (© **242/333-2285;** www.myharbourisland.com/bakery.htm), owned by Robert Arthur, the screenwriter for *M*A*S*H*. Artists, writers, media people, and what Arthur calls "international lollygaggers" hang out here. There are only a few tables, and they fill up quickly with those catching up on local gossip. Arthur's Trinidadian wife, Anna, bakes the island's best Key lime tart and is also praised for her croissants and banana bread. At lunch, drop in for fresh salads and sandwiches. Many guests come here to use the Internet, too.

EXPENSIVE

Acquapazza Wine Bar & Ristorante ★★ ITALIAN/MEDITERRANEAN

Within marina-fronting premises, this is the best high-end restaurant on Harbour Island. It's the culinary statement of two expatriate Italians, Hagmo (from Bolzano) and Manfredi (from Módena), who wax eloquent about the menu items of the day. (Both are refugees from the now-defunct kitchen of the Windermere Island Club on nearby Eleuthera.) Italian wines by the glass are appropriate foils for lunch platters that include seared tuna with onions and capers, grilled grouper with homemade tartar sauce and fries, burgers, and Mediterranean-style lobster salad. Dinner main courses are far more elaborate, including linguine with lobster and fresh tomatoes, roasted lamb chops with a balsamic reduction, beef tenderloin with sautéed wild mushrooms, and a signature version of poached grouper with herbs and tomato broth. Lighter appetites appreciate the antipasti, served only from 5 until 10pm. Examples include fried calamari, sea scallops poached in lentils with truffle broth, and kebabs of spicy "pil-pil" shrimp. Some of the residents of the island's villas make it a point to find out when fresh spider crab arrives off the local fishing boats, claiming that some of the best of it is served at this restaurant.

Harbour Island Marina. © **242/333-3240.** www.acquapazzabahamas.com. Reservations not necessary. Lunch main courses $10–$24; antipasti $12–$22; dinner main courses $19–$48. AE, DC, MC, V. Restaurant daily 11am–10pm. Bar daily 11am–11pm.

The Landing ★ INTERNATIONAL

This restaurant occupies the ground floor and most of the garden of the previously recommended hotel (p. 223), a stately building on the dock's right as your ferryboat pulls into Harbour Island. Built around 1850 with a combination of thick stone walls and clapboards, incorporating an annex that's 20 years younger, it's a stylish place and noted by virtually every local restaurant professional as one of the island's best eateries.

The menu changes depending on the availability of fresh ingredients. You might begin with a salmon seviche with coconut, chili, lime, and cucumber-cilantro salad, or perhaps ravioli stuffed with goat cheese and shrimp and served with brown butter, pine nuts, and tea-soaked raisins. Among the more delectable main courses are chargrilled tuna steak with roasted tomatoes, spicy Thai-style green curry, or a New Zealand rack of lamb with saffron-flavored potatoes. Also worth trying are the pan-fried mahimahi and the tuna with a salad of soba noodles.

Bay St. © **242/333-2707.** www.harbourislandlanding.com. Reservations recommended. Main courses $39–$46. AE, MC, V. Thurs–Mon 6:30–10:30pm.

Rock House Restaurant ★★ INTERNATIONAL

Set on a covered terrace overlooking anchored boats bobbing in the harbor, this restaurant is the showpiece of what's probably Harbour Island's most stylish and trend-conscious hotel (p. 223). Inside, there's a hip bodega feel, with decor that features lots of varnished mahogany, vanilla-colored walls, and ceiling fans. In addition to the tables for two and four, the restaurant offers a large chef's table (with 16 seats), reputed to have been among the furnishings in the American Embassy in Paris and on which Winston Churchill signed lots of important documents during World War II's aftermath. Though lunches are charming, they're gastronomically simple affairs, with dishes that include burgers, rock-lobster salad, sandwiches, conch chowder, and savory pasta variations. Dinners are more elaborate; with a time-tested menu that, although flavorful and stylish, rarely changes. The best menu items include curried Junkanoo capellini with shrimp in a spicy arrabiata sauce with preserved lemons, cider-brined pork tenderloin, Colorado lamb chops with toasted couscous salad, seared yellowfin tuna, roasted lobster tail, and vegetarian arugula-pesto pasta. Especially flavorful is a crispy pan-fried "almost deboned" chicken breast with a citrus-flavored herb sauce.

Rock House Hotel, Bay and Hill sts. ✆ 242/333-2053. www.rockhousebahamas.com. Reservations recommended. Main courses $14–$24 lunch; $36–$58 dinner. AE, MC, V. Dec–mid-Mar daily 6–8:30pm; mid-Mar–July daily 6:30–8:30pm. Closed Aug–Nov.

Runaway Hill Inn ★ BAHAMIAN/AMERICAN/INTERNATIONAL   The dining room at this intimate inn (p. 224) presents a sweeping view over the beachfront. Inside, the decor features brightly painted, whimsical colors, with wicker and rattan furnishings and a fine collection of watercolors the owner has spent years collecting. The kitchen is known for succulent preparations of fresh-caught snapper, grouper, and tuna, any of which might be preceded with such well-prepared dishes as grilled prawns served with curried mangos, conch marinara, or tempura-crusted lobster with sweet Thai dipping sauce. A favorite dessert incorporates a freshly baked plum-and-pineapple tart with cranberries and vanilla ice cream.

Colebrook St. (at Love Lane). ✆ 242/333-2150. www.runawayhill.com. Reservations required. Lunch main courses $18–$35; dinner main courses $30–$45. AE, MC, V. Lunch daily noon–3pm, Dinner daily 6–8pm. Closed mid-Sept to November

Sip Sip ★ 🍴 BAHAMIAN/INTERNATIONAL   The only problem with this restaurant is that it's closed every evening (except for large parties), preferring instead to focus on lunch, when it gets extremely busy and crowded, sometimes serving as many as 200 clients during the lunchtime rush. (A few of these might be famous—a recent example includes Robert DeNiro.) Set at the top of a ridge overlooking Harbour Island's spectacular beach, it was built in 2003 in a traditional green-painted design with louvered shutters, a style that's evocative of much older Harbour Island buildings. Inside, the cuisine is the product of the Bahamian/American couple Jim Black and Julie Lightbourne, who met in Africa while Jim was working in the safari business. The brightly painted interior features mahogany doors, windows, and bar tops, the setting for a changing menu that, depending on the owners' whim, might highlight Bahamian, Italian, French, Thai, or Pacific Rim influences. The menu could include hummus with grilled pita bread, conch chili (a welcome variation on conch chowder), fresh salads, baba ganoush (a Lebanese eggplant specialty), seafood quesadillas, and a flavorful curried chicken salad with chunks of apple and mango chutney. Grouper filets, prepared at least two different ways, are usually available as well. The restaurant's name, incidentally, translates from local patois as "gossip."

Court St. ✆ 242/333-3316. Reservations not necessary. Main courses $15–$35. MC, V. Daily 11:30am–4pm. Closed Wed June–Nov.

INEXPENSIVE

Avery's Restaurant & Grill BAHAMIAN/AMERICAN   From the moment you enter, you get the sense that Avery's is a simple, friendly, family-run restaurant with absolutely no pretensions. It occupies a tiny wooden house, painted in tones of orange and yellow, near the public library. Inside, you'll find a clean, white-tiled room with no more than four tables and a deck with six more. Maria Campbell and her daughter, Murieta, are the owners. Their breakfasts nourish city employees all around town. The rest of the day, an unending stream of sandwiches and steaming platters of seafood and steaks emerge from the kitchen.

Colebrook St. (✆ **242/333-3126.** Reservations not accepted. Breakfast and lunch platters $7–$18; dinner main courses $10–$38. No credit cards. Thurs–Tues 6:30am–3pm and 6–10pm.

Sunsets Bar and Grille BAHAMIAN   At the previously recommended Romora Bay Club, this casual restaurant attracts both locals and visitors to its sunsets and Bahamian specialties. Arrive early for a sundowner drink in the bar where Goldie the parrot has been greeting guests for more than a half century. Hopefully, she'll be around to greet you too. At lunch, sample the Briland burger, made with Black Angus beef, or the grilled chicken Caesar salad or the Junkanoo chicken curry. At night you might opt for the Dockmaster's mixed grill with filet mignon and garlic-butter shrimp. If you were out fishing, the chef can cook your catch to your specifications. Pastas are a special feature, including one made with Italian sweet sausage and braised greens. There is live music three times a week, with no cover charge.

At the Romora Bay Club & Resort, Colbrooke St. (✆ **242/333-2325.** Reservations recommended for dinner. Main courses $11–$19. AE, DC, MC, V. Daily 11:30am–9pm.

Beaches & Outdoor Pursuits

Pink Sands Beach ★★★ is our favorite strand in all of The Bahamas; its sands stretch for 5 uninterrupted kilometers (3 miles). Although the beach is set against a backdrop of low-rise hotels and villas, it still feels tranquil and pristine. The sun is best in the morning (afternoons become shadowy), and the water is generally gentle, owing to an offshore reef that breaks waves coming in from the Atlantic. It has many good snorkeling spots and is also the island's best place for a long, leisurely morning stroll.

The diving in this part of The Bahamas is among the most diverse in the region. The most spectacular site, judged among the top 10 dives in the world, is **Current Cut Dive ★★★**, which is also one of the world's fastest (9 knots) drift dives. It involves descending into the water flow that races between the rock walls forming the underwater chasm between Eleuthera and Current Island. Swept up in the currents with schools of stingrays, mako sharks, and reef fish, divers are propelled 1km (⅔ mile) of underwater distance in less than 10 minutes. This dive may become one of the highlights of your entire life.

Valentines Dive Center, on the harborfront (✆ **242/333-2080;** www.valentinesdive.com), offers a full range of dive activities. It's centered in a blue-painted wooden building near the entrance to the marina at the Valentines Resort. Lessons in scuba diving for beginners are usually offered daily at 9:30am for $135 per person. Snorkeling trips cost $65 per half-day, including equipment. A two-tank 3-hour dive goes for $115. When four experienced divers can be assembled into one coherent group, Valentines offers a dive excursion to the maritime phenomenon described above, the "Current Cut." There, within the fast-moving waters between Current Island and Eleuthera, the excursion, priced at $195 per participant, includes equipment and three consecutive underwater transits through "the Cut."

Lil' Shan's Watersports, Bay Street (✆ **242/422-9343;** www.lswatersports. com), offers everything from scuba diving to boat rentals and fishing trips. A two-stop snorkeling jaunt goes for $65 per person, including gear. The staff here also offers special kids' programs.

If you're looking to rent a motorboat, try **Michael's Cycles,** Colebrook Street (© **242/333-2384** or 242/464-0994). Plan to spend about $80 for a full day on a 4m (13-ft.) boat, or $110 to $185 for a full day on a 7m (23-ft.) boat; rates do not include the gas charge. Kayaks go for around $45 per day.

To book fishing guides and charters, you can either go through your hotel or contact the previously mentioned **Valentines Dive Center** (© **242/333-2080;** www.valentinesdive.com), on the harbor side of the island in Dunmore Town.

Exploring Harbour Island

Dunmore Town, located on the island's harbor side, was named for the 18th-century royal governor of The Bahamas who had his summer home here. You can walk around the narrow, virtually car-free lanes in less than 20 minutes, or stroll slowly to savor the sight of the old gingerbread cottages lining the waterfront. Draped with orange, purple, and pink bougainvillea, white picket fences enclose wooden houses painted pastel blue, green, and lilac. Wind chimes tinkle in front of shuttered windows while coconut palms and wispy casuarina pines shade grassy yards.

Americans and Canadians own some of these houses, which have whimsical names, such as Up Yonder and Beside the Point, instead of house numbers. One of the oldest, **Loyalist Cottage,** was built in 1797. It survives from the days when the original settlers, loyal to the British Crown, left the American colonies after the Revolutionary War.

Just across the road from Loyalist Cottage, you can browse through straw goods, T-shirts, and fruits and vegetables at vendor stalls.

On Sundays, dressed-up residents socialize in clusters outside churches before and after services. Two of the first churches in The Bahamas are in Dunmore Town, still going strong: **St. John's,** the country's oldest Anglican church, established in 1768, and **Wesley Methodist Church,** built in 1846.

Spend some time wandering the streets—some hilly, some flat—away from the heart of town. You can see roosters doing their jerky marches through front yards and horses grazing in small fields. In this locals' area, you'll come across some unassuming but perfectly good Bahamian restaurants, bars, and nightclubs.

Shopping

Miss Mae's, on Dunmore Street (© **242/333-2002**), lives up to its billing as one of the island's finest clothing boutiques. **Briland's Androsia,** on Coconut Grove Avenue (© **242/333-2342**), sells Harbour Island's best selection of bathing suits; its bright batik fabrics are printed on the island of North Andros.

Blue Rooster, in the center of town (© **242/333-2240**), along with the Shop at the Landing (see below), offers what might be the island's most upscale and stylish collection of men's and women's clothing and casual eveningwear. Come here for something sporty and trim-looking to wear into a posh hotel's dining room, especially if the New England button-down look appeals to you. Finally, check out **Princess Street Gallery** (© **242/333-2788;** www.harbourislandgallery.com), where owner Charles Carey has restored an ancestral home and transformed it into a showcase to display works by local artists.

Harbour Island After Dark

Unpretentious **Gusty's,** on Coconut Grove Avenue (© **242/333-2165**), boasts sweeping sea and sunset views and a clientele that's drawn from every strata, top to bottom, of Harbour Island's complicated sociology. Inside is a sand-covered floor, while the outdoor veranda is sometimes the scene of fashion shows for local dress-makers. Live music is featured almost every night. Gusty's opens nightly at 9:30pm and then goes on rocking virtually until dawn.

Sea Grapes, on Colebrook Street (no phone), another favorite of locals, is where you can boogie down to the sounds of disco or catch a live band. Expect to be jostled and crowded on a Saturday night because everyone on the island comes here for a wild Bahamian hoedown.

Vic-Hum Club, on Barracks Street (© **242/333-2161**), established in 1955, is the quintessential Harbour Island dive. Its walls are layered with the covers of hundreds of record albums and sports posters that music-industry and basketball buffs find fascinating. The Vic-Hum is open 24 hours a day, catering to breakfasting construction workers in the morning, then locals meeting friends for a beer all afternoon. Some of them play basketball on an indoor court that is transformed later in the evening into a dance floor—the music begins at 10pm every Friday and Saturday.

SPANISH WELLS

Called a "quiet corner of The Bahamas," Spanish Wells is a colorful cluster of houses on St. George's Cay, 1km (⅔ mile) off the coast of northwest Eleuthera. You'll find sparkling bays, white beaches, sleepy lagoons, excellent diving, and a fine fishing colony here. Since it's not rich in facilities, many vacationers to Eleuthera view Spanish Wells as a day trip from "mainland" Eleuthera.

You can easily walk or bicycle through the village, looking at the houses, some of which are more than 200 years old. They have New England saltbox styling but bright tropical coloring. You'll also see handmade quilts in many colors, following patterns handed down from generations of English ancestors. Homeowners display these quilts on their front porches or out their windows, and they are for sale. No one locks their doors here, or removes ignition keys from their cars.

Getting There

To reach the island, you can fly to the **North Eleuthera Airport,** where taxis will be waiting to deliver you to the ferry dock.

A **ferryboat** (© **242/554-6268,** but be warned that the phone works only inter-mittently) runs between Gene's Bay in North Eleuthera to the main pier at Spanish Wells, departing whenever passengers show up. The cost is between $8 and $15 per person round-trip, depending on how many people are ferried across within your boatload. Regardless of the time of day you get there, a ferryboat will be either waiting for passengers or arriving shortly with a load of them.

Where to Eat

Anchorage BAHAMIAN   Though you won't find Spanish Wells written up in any gourmet guides, you can eat well enough here if you stick to locally caught fish and the like. Decent, clean, and unpretentious, this little eatery serves such home-cooked Bahamian-style items as cracked conch and grouper fingers. The island is known for its *langoustes* (Bahamian lobsters). For dessert, try a mud pie.

Along the waterfront at the Spanish Wells port. © **242/333-4023.** Reservations required Sat–Sun. Main courses $15–$23. No credit cards. Mon–Sat 9am–1:30pm; daily 5–10pm.

THE EXUMAS

The Exumas are some of the prettiest islands in The Bahamas. Shades of jade, aquamarine, and amethyst in deeper waters turn to translucent opal near sandy shores; the water and land appear almost inseparable. Sailors and their crews like to stake out their own private beaches and tropical hideaways, and several vacation retreats have been built by wealthy Europeans, Canadians, and Americans.

A spiny, sandy chain of islands, the Exumas begin just 56km (35 miles) southeast of Nassau and stretch more than 161km (100 miles) from Beacon Cay in the north to Hog Cay and Sandy Cay in the south. These islands have not been developed like the Abacos and Eleuthera have, so they are relatively inexpensive to visit. But they still have much to offer, with crystal-clear waters on the west around the Great Bahama Bank, the 1,500m-deep (4,921-ft.) Exuma Sound on the east, rolling hills, ruins of once-great plantations, coral formations of much beauty, and uninhabited cays ideal for picnics. Although they're crossed by the Tropic of Cancer, the islands have average temperatures ranging from the mid-70s to the mid-80s (mid- to upper 20s Celsius).

Most of our resort recommendations are in and around **George Town,** the pretty pink capital of the Exumas, on Great Exuma Island. A community of some 900 residents, it was once considered a possible site for the capital of The Bahamas because of its excellent **Elizabeth Harbour.**

Nearly all the other cays are uninhabited or sparsely populated. Over the years, remote accommodations have come and gone on these islands. Today, the only lodgings, which attract mostly the yachting set, are at Staniel Cay and Sampson Cay.

The cruising grounds around the Exumas, which are scattered over an ocean area of 233 sq. km (90 sq. miles), are among the finest in the Western Hemisphere—if not the world—for boating. The sailing rivals that of the Grenadines and the Abacos. If you don't come in your own craft, you can rent one here, from a simple little Daysailer to a fishing runabout, with or without a guide. Elizabeth Harbour's annual regatta in April has attracted such notables as Prince Philip and Constantine, Greece's former king. Yachters often say that the Exumas are "where you go when you die if you've been good."

Snorkeling and scuba-diving opportunities draw aficionados from around the world to the vast underwater preserve of **Exuma Cays Land and Sea Park** and to the island group's other exotic limestone and coral reefs, blue holes, drop-offs, and caves. Dive centers in George Town and Staniel Cay provide air fills and equipment.

The Perfect Beach

For years, boaters have known of a special beach, **Saddle Cay,** whose horseshoe-shaped curve lies near the small archipelago's northern tip. The only way to reach it is by private boat; there are no organized excursions or tours (the Exumas are much too laid-back for that).

However, if you own a boat, head for Saddle Cay and you won't be disappointed when you see this totally unspoiled beach of white sand and tranquil water. The cay is perfect for beachcombers, bird-watchers, and snorkelers—but don't expect any facilities.

The fishing, too, is superb here, and the "flats" on Great Exuma's west side are famous for bonefishing. You can find (if you're lucky) blue marlin on both sides of Exuma Sound, as well as sailfish, wahoo, and white marlin, plus others.

The Exumas are among the friendliest islands in The Bahamas; the people are warmhearted and not (yet) spoiled by tourism, seeming genuinely delighted to receive and welcome visitors. They grow a lot of their own food, including cassava, onions, cabbages, and pigeon peas, on the acres their ancestors worked as slaves. Many fruits grow on the cays, including guavas, mangoes, and avocados. At **Government Wharf** in George Town, you can watch these fruits being loaded for shipment to Nassau. The sponge industry is being revived locally, too; this product of the sea is found in shallow waters and creeks to the south side of the Exumas.

EXUMAS ESSENTIALS

GETTING THERE

BY PLANE   The region's major commercial airport, **Exuma International Airport** (GGT), in Moss Town, is 16km (10 miles) from George Town, the capital. The most popular way to get to the Exumas is to fly there aboard **Bahamasair** (📞 800/222-4262; www.bahamasair.com), which offers twice-daily service from Nassau to George Town. The first flight usually leaves Nassau in the morning sometime around 6:20am, depending on the day. The second flight is at 4pm. Be sure to call ahead—flight schedules are subject to change.

American Eagle (📞 800/433-7300 or 242/345-0124; www.aa.com) serves Exuma from Miami daily. **Continental Connection** (📞 800/231-0856 or 242/345-0280) flies three times daily to George Town from Fort Lauderdale. **Delta** (📞 800/221-1212; www.delta.com) offers twice-per-week service to George Town from Atlanta. Minor charter-based carriers serving the archipelago from other parts of The Bahamas and in some cases, the mainland of Florida, include **Flamingo Air** (📞 242/377-0354 or 954/839-8688) and **Western Air** (📞 242/345-0300).

For flights to the private airstrip at Staniel Cay, see "Staniel Cay," later in this chapter.

BY BOAT   One of two separate ferryboats, each designed for cars, building supplies, and freight, and each operated by **Bahamas Ferries** (📞 242/323-2166; www.bahamasferries.com), make an island-hopping transit twice a week from Nassau. Depending on the season, one or another of them arrives in George Town every Monday and Wednesday at 7:30pm, departing on Tuesday and Thursday. If you're transporting a car, the passengers accompanying the vehicle, up to a total of four, ride for only $5 each. Otherwise, the cost of a round-trip fare is $110 per person. There

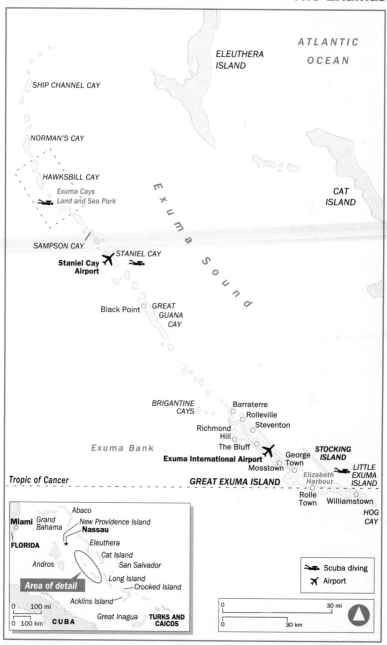

SHIP CHANNEL CAY

NORMAN'S CAY

HAWKSBILL CAY

*Exuma Cays
Land and Sea Park*

SAMPSON CAY

STANIEL CAY

**Staniel Cay
Airport**

Black Point

*GREAT
GUANA
CAY*

*BRIGANTINE
CAYS*

Barraterre
Rolleville
Steventon

Richmond
Hill
The Bluff

Exuma International Airport

Mosstown

George
Town

**STOCKING
ISLAND**

*Elizabeth
Harbour*

GREAT EXUMA ISLAND

*LITTLE
EXUMA
ISLAND*

Rolle
Town   Williamstown

*HOG
CAY*

*ELEUTHERA
ISLAND*

*ATLANTIC
OCEAN*

*CAT
ISLAND*

Exuma Sound

Exuma Bank

Tropic of Cancer

9

THE EXUMAS | Exumas Essentials

Area of detail

Miami Grand
Bahama

FLORIDA

Andros

0   100 mi

0   100 km   **CUBA**

Abaco

New Providence Island

Nassau

Eleuthera

Cat Island

San Salvador

Long Island

Crooked Island

Acklins Island

Great Inagua   **TURKS AND
CAICOS**

★

⚓ Scuba diving

✈ Airport

0   30 mi

0   30 km

are no overnight accommodations on board, so many of the passengers stretch out on the deck in sleeping bags.

In addition to the above-mentioned car and freight-laden ferryboats, two mail steamers, the **MV *Grand Master*** and the **MV *Captain C,*** sail from Nassau several days a week, stopping, depending on the schedule, at points that may or may not include Big Farmer's Cay, Staniel Cay, Black Point, George Town, and Barraterre (stopovers last no more than a few hours). Passengers, as well as small amounts of freight, are allowed onboard. It usually takes between 14 and 21 hours for either of the ships to make the full-circuit itinerary described above. Per person transit costs between $40 each way, with a supplement of $5 charged for use of an indoor bunk, crammed among dozens of others, for anyone who hopes to lie down and/or sleep during part of the journey. Since sailing schedules are subject to change due to weather conditions, quantities of mail on hand, and other factors, check departure times with the dock master at Nassau's **Potter's Cay Terminal** (*©* **242/393-1064**).

GETTING AROUND

BY TAXI If your hotel is in George Town, it will cost about $35 to get there in a taxi from the airport. Rides are often shared. Hotels can usually get you a taxi if you need to go somewhere and don't have a car. Otherwise, for taxi service, call **Leslie Dames** at *©* **242/357-0405.**

If you're going on to Stocking Island, an islet in Elizabeth Harbour, make prior arrangements with your hotel for boat transfers.

BY CAR It's also possible to rent a car during your stay, though the major North American agencies aren't represented here. Try **Exuma Airport Car Rental** (*©* **242/345-0090**), where cars start at $65 per day or $330 per week. A $200 deposit is required. Your hotel may also be able to arrange a rental car for you through any of several local residents.

The George Town area has only three gas stations: one near Exuma International Airport and the other two in or in the environs of George Town. They're generally open Monday through Saturday from 8am to 5pm, Sunday from 8am to noon, and on holidays from 8 to 10am.

BY BOAT For ferry service between George Town and the beaches on Stocking Island, call **Club Peace & Plenty** (*©* **242/336-2551**), which has departures twice a day. The ferries, which depart from the hotel's dock, are complimentary to Club Peace & Plenty guests. If you're not staying at that hotel, the cost is $12 round-trip for adults, free for children 10 and under. A less expensive, less formal alternative is provided by **Elvis Ferguson Water Taxi Service** (*©* **242/464-1558**), which operates from George Town's government pier at more or less hourly intervals (depending on business) every day from around 11am till the final return at between 6 and 8pm, depending on the season, for a fee of $4 per person each way. Be very clear with the ferryboat operator on your way over to the island about your intentions to return to the George Town "mainland" after your visit, so as not to be stranded on Stocking Island overnight.

ON FOOT George Town is designed for strolling, but don't expect sights that scream "tourist attraction." This is a handsome little waterfront village where the big draws are simply browsing at the tree-shaded straw market, sampling fresh conch salad at the dock, and mingling with residents and fellow vacationers over drinks and home-style meals. The most idyllic walk is around **Lake Victoria.**

GEORGE TOWN

The Tropic of Cancer runs directly through George Town, the capital and principal settlement of the Exumas, located on the island of Great Exuma. This tranquil seaport village opens onto a 24km-long (15-mile) harbor. George Town, partly in the Tropics and partly in the temperate zone, is a favorite port of call for the yachting crowd.

If you need to stock up on supplies, George Town is the place to go, as it has more stores and services than any other spot in the Exumas. There are dive centers, marinas, markets, a doctor, and a health clinic here. The town often doesn't bother with street names, but everything's easy to find.

George Town Essentials

GETTING THERE   Flights from Nassau and Miami come into nearby Exuma International Airport, 16km (10 miles) from George Town. See "Getting There" under "Exumas Essentials," above, for details on airlines and taxis.

VISITOR INFORMATION   The **Ministry of Tourism** maintains an office on the second floor of the Royal Bank of Canada, in Turnquest Plaza, beside Queen's Highway, Exuma (✆ 242/336-2457; www.exumas.bahamas.com), across from Exuma Market. It's open Monday to Friday 9am to 5pm.

[FastFACTS] GEORGE TOWN

Scotiabank (also known as the Bank of Nova Scotia, Queen's Highway, ✆ 242/336-2651), which has an ATM, is open Monday through Thursday from 9:30am to 3pm and Friday from 9:30am to 4:30pm. The Royal Bank of Canada (Turnquest Plaza; ✆ 242/336-3525) also has an ATM.

If you come to the Exumas aboard your own boat, **Exuma Docking Services,** Main Street, George Town (✆ 242/336-2578), has slips for 52 boats with water and electricity hookups. On the premises are Sam's Restaurant, a Laundromat, a fuel dock, fuel pumps, and a store with supplies for boats and people.

The government-operated **medical clinic,** beside Queen's Highway in George Town, can be reached by phone at (✆ 242/336-2088. You can go here to have a prescription filled.

To call the George Town **police,** dial ✆ 242/336-2666.

The **post office** is in George Town's government building ((✆ 242/336-2636); it's open Monday through Friday from 9am to 4:30pm.

SPECIAL EVENTS   In April, the **National Family Island Regatta** (✆ 242/336-2430; www.nationalfamilyislandregatta.com) draws a yachting crowd from all over the world to Elizabeth Harbour. It's a rollicking week of fun, song, and serious racing when the island sloops go all-out to win. It's said that some determined skippers bring along extra crewmen to serve as live ballast on windward tacks, and then drop them over the side to lighten the ship for the downwind run to the finish. The event, a tradition since 1954, comes at the end of the crayfish season.

The **Junkanoo Summer Festival** (www.exumas.bahamas.com) is held in the hot months, unlike the regular Bahamian winter Junkanoo. The festival runs for 3 loosely scheduled weeks at the peak of summer (dates vary), with events scheduled for every Saturday night in George Town. Bands play rake 'n' scrape music for street dancing, while small stands hawk fresh conch, grilled seafood, and plenty of rum punches. An onion-peeling competition celebrates Exuma's historic link to the cultivation of the bulb.

Where to Stay

VERY EXPENSIVE

February Point Resort Estates ★★★ *Island* magazine has voted Great Exuma one of the world's top five islands to inhabit, and surely this private 32-hectare (79-acre) estate on the peninsula was one of the reasons for that honor. The site opens onto panoramic views of Elizabeth Harbour, and the upmarket, gated, and guarded residential community is the most luxurious way to live in the Exumas. There are some 50 magnificent villas here, each privately owned. Of these, nearly a dozen are rented to vacationers on a temporary basis during the owner's absence. The villas, painted in Easter egg colors, offer everything from two to six bedrooms. Each has a full dining room and kitchen, very spacious bedrooms, and lovely views. Maids come in every day to keep the accommodations well maintained. Guests of the villas are allowed to use the community center, with its array of facilities, including a waterfront restaurant.

Queen's Hwy., George Town, Great Exuma, The Bahamas. www.februarypoint.com. ✆ **877/839-4253** or 242/336-2693. 12 units. Winter $650 2-bedroom villa, $850 3-bedroom villa, from $930 4-bedroom villa; off-season $500 2-bedroom villa, $750 3-bedroom villa, from $850 4-bedroom villa. MC, V. **Amenities:** Restaurant; bar; babysitting; concierge; exercise room; outdoor pool; 2 tennis courts (lit for night play); watersports equipment/rentals; Wi-Fi (free). *In room:* A/C, TV/DVD, kitchen.

Grand Isle Resort & Spa ★★★ ☺ Living within these well-managed rental units is like enjoying life in a luxurious home. A 20-minute drive south from the center of George Town, it is a compound of luxurious villas with 1, 2, 3, or 4 bedrooms, the latter ideal for families. The complex boasts one of the best spas in the Exumas, and there is also an infinity pool that opens onto views of the Atlantic. Lying only a short walk from the pool are the sands of the secluded Emerald Bay Beach, where guests can snorkel in the gin-clear waters or else go on kayak trips.

Couples find the resort a romantic getaway, especially for a honeymoon, although families also like to book those well-equipped villas with panoramic views from all accommodations. The decor is done in an elegant Caribbean motif, with a fully appointed gourmet kitchen with granite countertops. Plush furnishings are used throughout, and each unit comes with first-class marble-clad bathrooms.

Queens Hwy., Emerald Bay, The Exumas, The Bahamas. www.grandisleresort.com. ✆ **866/380-5213** or 242/358-5000. 78 villas, 66 of which are available as rental units. Winter $450–$500 double, $700–$1,200 2-bedroom, $1,000–$1,300 3-bedroom, $2,500 4-bedroom; off-season $350–$400 double, $550–$900 2-bedroom, $750–$900 3-bedroom, $1,500 4-bedroom. AE, DC, MC, V. **Amenities:** Restaurant; bar; children's programs; concierge; exercise room; outdoor pool; room service; spa. *In room:* A/C, TV/DVD, hair dryer, kitchen, Wi-Fi (free).

Hotel Higgins Landing ★ The beach at this resort is a major attraction. Higgins Landing is one of the first eco-resorts in The Bahamas and the more substantial of the two hotels on undeveloped Stocking Island. It takes great care to preserve the natural beauty of its surroundings on this gorgeous island. The solar-powered hideaway bills itself as one of the great escapes of The Bahamas, bordered by Elizabeth Harbour and the Atlantic on one side and the crystal-blue waters of Turtle Lagoon and its colorful reefs on the other. Other than the staff and management, you'll probably never see more than a total of 12 guests here at any time.

Cottages are exquisitely decorated with antiques, mirrors, and Higgins family heirlooms. They're furnished with queen-size beds, well-maintained private bathrooms, and island accents including cool tile floors and ceiling fans. The landscaped grounds are as colorful as your imagination, attracting many types of wildlife, from herons and hummingbirds to green sea turtles. Hotel ferry service from George Town provides access to the island. Rates include a first-rate candlelit dinner (nonguests are welcome, too, with advance reservations). The open-air bar overlooks the cerulean sea. Be warned that there is very little nightlife, if any, at this resort, where smoking is strictly prohibited and where the emphasis is on quiet communion with the natural (and stunning) environment—and the satisfied repeat visitors at this place wouldn't have it any other way. Management warns that the place is not appropriate for very young children.

Stocking Island, George Town, Great Exuma, The Bahamas. www.higginslanding.com. © **242/357-0008.** 5 units. Year-round $495 1-bedroom cottage; $875 2-bedroom cottage. Rates include dinner and transportation from George Town. 4-night minimum stay; 50% deposit required to secure reservation. MC, V. Children 5 and under not permitted. **Amenities:** Restaurant; bar; Internet (free); watersports equipment/rentals. *In room:* Ceiling fan, hair dryer, kitchenette (in some).

Sandals Emerald Bay Great Exuma ★★★ ☺

The quiet Exumas emerged from a centuries-long sleep with the official opening of this resort as one of the newest and most luxurious members of its chain in 2010. (It had first been launched as a posh branch of the Four Seasons chain in 2004, and between 2008 and 2009 was totally revamped.) Its sweeping ocean vistas and tropical beauty frame an experience unique in this part of the world; the Out Islands have seen nothing like this in their history, and the resort changed the archipelago's entire character. All accommodations here open onto private terraces and balconies with scenic views of either the bay or the widely varied plantings of the resort's botanical garden. For the big spender, the resort also offers a series of executive suites and beachfront properties with one or two bedrooms.

So much goes on at this resort that you may never get around to exploring the surrounding islands. The most spectacular feature is a championship 18-hole golf course designed by Greg Norman. The full-service spa and health club is the finest in The Bahamas, and you can swim either at the hotel's crescent-shaped white-sand beach or in one of two pools. The best marina in the Southern Bahamas operates here. And the cuisine is among the finest in the Out Islands, with both indoor and outdoor dining options and a selection of Italian, Caribbean, Bahamian, and international dishes. The main dining room is perhaps the Southern Bahamas' best, and it's accentuated by floor-to-ceiling panels and screens, opening onto views of the landscaped gardens and the stars overlooking Emerald Bay. On offer is a wide selection of Italian dishes, including locally caught seafood, and an impressive wine cellar. A children's menu is also available.

Queen's Hwy., Emerald Bay, Great Exuma, The Bahamas. www.sandals.com. © **888/SANDALS** (726-3257) in the U.S. and Canada. 183 units. Year round $3,700–$30,000 double, depending on the season and promotions which have reduced the official rates by as much as 65%. Rates are all-inclusive for 7 days. 3-night minimum. AE, DC, DISC, MC, V. **Amenities:** 7 restaurants; 6 bars; babysitting; children's programs; golf course; health club and spa; 3 outdoor pools; 6 tennis courts (lit for night play); watersports equipment/rentals. *In room:* A/C, TV/DVD, CD player, hair dryer, Wi-Fi ($15 per day).

EXPENSIVE

Augusta Bay ★

This is an intimate boutique hotel with an excellent staff who can arrange any number of activities for you, including beach picnics, snorkeling, sea kayaking, Hobie Cat sailing, reef fishing, golf tee times, bike tours, eco-tours, windsurfing, boat rides, even spa treatments and fishing charters, plus scuba diving and on-site car-rental services. For music and good food, head for Frankie Bananas, a restaurant and bar built over the water directly in front of the hotel and open to non-guests as well. Tranquil, and with a world-class reputation as a bonefishing resort, it opens onto 90m (295 ft.) of sandy beach that's noted for its snorkeling. Bedrooms contain Italian tiles salvaged from the inn's earlier incarnation and marble vanities in 10 of the 16 units. Balconies overlook Bonefish Bay and Elizabeth Harbour.

Harbourfront, George Town, Great Exuma, The Bahamas. www.augustabaybahamas.com. ©**242/ 336-2251.** Fax 242/336-2253. 16 units. Winter $225–$325 double; off-season $175–$225 double. Rates include breakfast. AE, MC, V. **Amenities:** Restaurant; bar; outdoor pool; watersports equipment/rentals; Wi-Fi (free). *In room:* A/C, TV, hair dryer, no phone.

Palm Bay Beach Club ★ 🏢   One of the archipelago's most tranquil accommodations, Palm Bay overlooks the waters of Elizabeth Harbour. This attractive resort offers beachfront villas with studios, one-bedroom units, or more luxurious and spacious two- and three-bedroom accommodations. The cottages are well appointed and tasteful, each individually decorated and outfitted with queen- or king-size beds, ceramic tile flooring, and comfortable tropical-style furniture. A shuttle bus carries visitors to and from George Town. Kayaks and paddle boats are available.

Elizabeth Harbour, George Town, Great Exuma, The Bahamas. www.palmbaybeachclub.com. © **888/396-0606** or 242/336-2787. 70 units. Winter $130–$375 double; off-season $130–$310 double. Extra person $40. Children 14 and under stay free in parent's room. AE, MC, V. **Amenities:** Beach bar; outdoor pool. *In room:* A/C, TV, kitchen or kitchenette, Wi-Fi (free).

MODERATE

Club Peace & Plenty   This attractive, historic waterside inn is a classic island hotel in the heart of George Town. Once a sponge warehouse and later the home of a prominent family, it was converted into a hotel in the late 1940s, making it the oldest in the Exumas. The two-story pink-and-white building has dormers and balconies opening onto a water view. The grounds, planted with palms, crotons, and bougainvillea, front Elizabeth Harbour, making it a favorite of the yachting set. The midsize accommodations are tastefully furnished, though a 1950s vibe lingers. A refurbishment has freshened things up a bit, with bright print spreads and draperies, along with furnishings in white wicker or rattan. Many units sport balconies opening onto harbor views; oceanfront rooms are the most desirable.

You can dine indoors or outside (see "Where to Eat," below), and calypso music plays on the terrace. There are two cocktail lounges, one of which was converted from an old slave kitchen and is now filled with nautical gear including lanterns, rudders, and anchors. The hotel faces Stocking Island and maintains a private beach club there, offering food and bar service, as well as kilometers of sandy dunes. A boat, free for hotel guests ($12 round-trip for nonguests), makes the run.

Queen's Hwy., George Town, Great Exuma, The Bahamas. www.peaceandplenty.com. © **800/525-2210** in the U.S. and Canada, or 242/336-2551. Fax 242/336-2093. 32 units. Winter $180–$325 double; off-season $155–$270 double. AE, DC, MC, V. **Amenities:** Restaurant; 2 bars; outdoor pool; Wi-Fi (free in lobby). *In room:* A/C, TV, fridge, hair dryer, no phone.

Regatta Point ★ ☺   This cozy inn lies on a small cay just across the causeway from George Town and opens onto a small, sandy beach. The cay used to be known as Kidd Cay, named after the notorious pirate. Set at the tip of a peninsula jutting out into Elizabeth Harbour, the present complex consists of six apartments, each with a full kitchen, making this a good choice for families. The units are not air-conditioned, although the cross-ventilation is good and ceiling fans help. Each of the pleasantly furnished, summery units comes with maid service, plus a small bathroom. Nearby grocery stores are fairly well stocked if you feel like making your own meals. Those who don't wish to cook can have dinner at one of the previously mentioned hotels in town or at a local restaurant. This colony hums in April during the Family Island Regatta.

Kidd Cove, George Town, Great Exuma, The Bahamas. www.regattapointbahamas.com. ℂ **888/720-0011** or 242/336-2206. 6 units. Winter $198–$238 double, $278 2-bedroom suite; off-season $162–$206 double, $234 2-bedroom suite. Extra person $25. No credit cards. **Amenities:** Watersports equipment/rentals. *In room:* Ceiling fan, kitchen, no phone.

St. Francis Bay Resort Established by an expatriate couple, George and Jill Godfrey, from South Africa, this is a very appealing place where guests do their best to get away from most aspects of civilization, spending quiet days on the spectacular beach and tranquil evenings left to their own devices. Accommodations are within a half-dozen side-by-side beige-fronted townhouses, each fronting the beach on one side and a sandy garden on the other. Other than beach activities and R&R, there's very little to do here, but that's exactly what many of the residents seem to cherish.

Stocking Island, George Town, Great Exuma, The Bahamas. www.stfrancisresort.com. ℂ **242/557-9629.** 6 units. Year-round $235 double. Rates include breakfast. AE, MC, V. Closed Sept–Oct. **Amenities:** Restaurant; bar; watersports equipment. *In-room:* A/C, ceiling fans, small refrigerators.

INEXPENSIVE

Coral Gardens Bed & Breakfast   If you'd like to go to the B&B route on Exumas, the choice is very limited. The Coral Gardens, within a generously proportioned white-sided house run by British expats Peter and Betty Oxley, is an exception. It stands in an elevated position at Hoopers Bay, opening onto vistas of the sea. It's not on the beach, so you'll need a car to reach the bars, restaurants, and shops of George Town. Upstairs are some comfortable, unpretentious, and tastefully furnished guest rooms with private baths. On the lower level are two apartments, each fully equipped with kitchenettes. In its price range, this is about as good as it gets on island.

Queens Hwy. (3 miles N of George Town), The Exumas, The Bahamas. www.coralgardensbahamas.com. ℂ **800/688-0309** or 242/336-2206. 8 units. Year-round $199 double; $135 apt. Rates include continental breakfast. No credit cards. **Amenities:** Watersports equipment/rentals arranged; Wi-Fi (free). *In room:* Kitchen (in some).

Where to Eat

With a few exceptions (listed below), the best places to eat in George Town are in the hotels reviewed above.

If you just want to grab a quick meal, there are several casual joints in George Town. **Towne Cafe,** in the Marshall Complex (ℂ **242/336-2194**), serves one of the

---

🎁 Fresh, Sexy Conch

The Exuma archipelago's best conch salad is at **Big D's Conch Spot No. 1** (ℂ **242/358-0059**), in a beach-fronting cabana in the hamlet of Steventon, a 25-minute drive along Queen's Highway from George Town, and a 5-minute drive from the Sandals Resort. "Fresh, sexy conch," as it's called here, is served daily, along with platters of other Bahamian food that includes baked chicken, fish such as stewed grouper, sandwiches, and burgers. The joint is open Tuesday to Sunday noon to around 9:30pm, later if a crowd has formed. Reservations are required only for parties of five or more.

city's best breakfasts. It's really the town bakery. Drop in any day but Sunday for a sandwich or a lunch of Exumian specialties such as stewed grouper or chicken souse.

MODERATE

Club Peace & Plenty Restaurant CONTINENTAL/BAHAMIAN/AMERICAN   Come to this resort (p. 238) for the finest island dining, with plentiful home-style cooking that leaves everyone satisfied. You might begin with conch salad or perhaps one of the salads made with hearts of palm or artichoke hearts, and then follow with local lobster. Bahamian steamed grouper regularly appears on the menu, simmered with onions, tomatoes, sweet pepper, and thyme. But you can also order such special dishes as an herb-flavored Cornish game hen that is juicy and perfectly roasted and flavored. Lunch options include homemade soups, conch burgers, a chef's salad, or deep-fried grouper. Breakfast offerings range from traditional French toast or scrambled eggs and sausage to truly Bahamian boiled fish and grits. As you eat, you'll sit under ceiling fans, looking out over the harbor. In the evening, candle-light and windows on three sides make the place particularly nice. And who knows who will be at the next table? It may be a celeb or two, or a crowd of yachters providing conversation and amusement.

Club Peace & Plenty, Queen's Hwy. ✆ **242/336-2551.** www.peaceandplenty.com. Reservations recommended for dinner. Breakfast items $10–$12; lunch items $9–$14; dinner main courses $18–$35. AE, DISC, MC, V. Daily 7:30–10:30am, noon–2:30pm, and 6:30–9:30pm. Closed Sept–Oct.

Pallappa Pool Bar & Grill ★ BAHAMIAN/AMERICAN   At the posh Grand Isle Resort, this pavilion opens onto the resort's pool and the scenic Emerald Bay. It's dining with a view. The chef features freshly caught native food such as conch, grouper, red snapper, and crab, which he turns into carefully crafted platters. Blackened wahoo is one of the best choices on the menu, although on most occasions you can also order Bahamian lobster which is tasty without challenging the superior Maine lobster. The lobster is grilled and served with a creamy, garlic-studded sauce. You might also enjoy the curried steamed mussels or the Caribbean style coconut shrimp. An array of beef and chicken dishes is also prepared by these experienced chefs. If featured, the lobster-studded corn chowder makes an excellent starter.

In the Grand Isle Resort, Queens Hwy., Emerald Bay. ✆ **242/358-5000.** Reservations not needed. Lunch main courses $12–$22, dinner main courses $14–$30. AE, DC, MC, V. Daily 8am–9pm.

INEXPENSIVE

Chat 'n Chill ★ BAHAMIAN   Locals tell you that when you've tasted Kenneth Bowe's conchburger, you'll never go back to McDonalds again. Yachties, fishermen, and visitors show up at what has been called a "waterside conch-salad shack." If Jimmy Buffet ever came this way, he'd probably write a song about the place. The conch is cracked and broken out of its natural shell right before your eyes. Kenneth also makes the best fresh conch salad on island, chopping it with onions, tomatoes, sweet peppers, and Bahamian sea salt and flavoring it with lime. You can also order the grilled fish of the day, usually grouper. Cooking is done over an outdoor grill. In winter there's a popular pig roast every Sunday at noon. Chat 'n Chill is also home to beach parties, bonfires, and volleyball competitions. The dive lies on the Point on Stocking Island in Elizabeth Harbour, ½ mile across from George Town and reached by a local boat, which leaves from Government Dock about every hour during the day.

Stocking Island. ✆ **242/336-2700.** www.chatnchill.com. Reservations not needed. Main courses $8–$15. No credit cards. Daily 11am–7pm.

IN SEARCH OF THE RED-LEGGED thrush

Under the protection of The Bahamas National Trust, **Exuma Cays Land and Sea Park** (© 242/225-1791) begins at Conch Cut in the south and extends northward to Wax Cay Cut, encompassing Halls Pond Cay, Warderick Wells, Shroud Cay, Hawksbill Cay, Cistern Cay, and Bell Island, as well as numerous other small, uninhabited islands. It lies to the northwest of Staniel Cay. If you call the number noted above, you'll likely be connected to the park's supervisor and administrator, Andrew Kriz.

The park is some 35km (22 miles) long, and much of it is a sea garden with reefs, some only 1 to 3m (3–10 ft.) beneath the water's surface. The park is reached only by chartered boat and is very expensive to visit.

This is an area of natural beauty that can be enjoyed by skin divers and yachties, but it's unlawful to remove any plant, marine, or bird life. Before 1986, visitors were allowed to fish for spiny lobster, hog fish, conch, and such, but the park is now designated a marine replenishment nursery.

Many bird-watchers visit the park, looking for the red-legged thrush, the nighthawk, even the long-tailed "Tropic Bird," plus many, many more winged creatures.

This was once the home of the Bahamian iguana, which is now found only on Allan's Cays, a tiny island group just north of Highborne Cay. The government is taking belated steps to protect this creature, which is found nowhere else in the world.

Cheater's Bar and Restaurant BAHAMIAN   Operated with panache by local resident Julian Romer (who everyone knows as "Cheater"), this unpretentiously raffish Bahamian bar is an amiable dive that attracts sailors, the crew from the local mail boats, and escapist residents of some of the island's hotels. Set in a simple house across Queen's Highway from the seafront, about 2 miles south of George Town, it serves beer, rum-based drinks, cracked conch, and platters of sandwiches and burgers. Breakfast, served only on weekends, is viewed by locals as a way to socialize and bond with friends, neighbors, and family.

Queen's Highway, 2 miles south of George Town. © **242/336-2535.** Reservations not needed. Sat–Sun 8:30am–noon; daily noon–10pm. No credit cards.

Kermit's Airport Lounge BAHAMIAN   Originally established by one of Exuma's most visible and extroverted taxi drivers and guides, the late Kermit Rolle, it's run today by one of his granddaughters, Franquisha Cartwright. Simple but appealing, it lies across the road from the airport's entrance. It's the semiofficial waiting room for most of the island's flights, and it might make your wait more convenient and fun. The cook will fry you some fish, and there's always beans and rice around. Johnnycake and sandwiches are also available, along with burgers and an array of tropical drinks. Until an airplane flies you to a better restaurant, this place can come in handy.

Exuma International Airport. © **242/345-0002.** Reservations not needed. Beer $4; cheeseburgers $6–$12; platters from $9. No credit cards. Daily 6:30am–5pm.

Beaches & Outdoor Pursuits
HITTING THE BEACH
Stocking Island ★, in Elizabeth Harbour, faces George Town from across the bay, less than 1.6km (1 mile) away. This long, thin barrier island has some of the most

gorgeous beaches in The Bahamas. Snorkelers and scuba divers come here to explore the blue holes, and it is also ringed with undersea caves and coral gardens. If you'd like to go shelling, walk the beach along Stocking Island's Atlantic side. Boat trips leave daily from Elizabeth Harbour at 10am and 1pm. The cost is $10 per person round-trip. However, guests of Club Peace & Plenty ride free.

The island, which used to be a private enclave, has a marine-activity center run by **Dive Exuma** (✆ 242/336-2893; www.dive-exuma.com), based at February Point Resort Estates (p. 236). Visibility is great in these waters, and there are many rainbow-hued fish to see. A 3-hour snorkeling trip, including all equipment, costs $70. A two-tank dive goes for $150.

Yachting types and other island visitors like to drop in at Kenneth Bowe's **Chat 'n' Chill ★** (✆ 242/336-2700; www.chatnchill.com), a laid-back place that manages to be both upmarket and a local dive. Many of the fresh-fish dishes are grilled over an open fire, and the Sunday pig roasts are an island event. The conch burgers are the best in the Exumas. But the seasonings? They're secret.

BOATING

Landlocked **Lake Victoria** covers about .8 hectares (2 acres) in the heart of George Town. It has a narrow exit to the harbor and functions as a diving and boating headquarters.

If you come to the Exumas aboard your own boat, **Exuma Docking Services,** Main Street, George Town (✆ 242/336-2578), has slips for 52 vessels, along with water and electricity hookups. You can also stock up on supplies here, get fuel, and do laundry.

If motorboats are more your speed, **Minns Water Sports,** based in George Town (✆/fax 242/336-3483 or 336-2604; www.mwsboats.com), rents boats ranging from 4.5 to 6.6m (15–22 ft.) for $120 to $260 per day. With your own boat, you can set out to explore some of the most stunning waters in The Bahamas, rivaled only by the Abacos. The best territory for recreational boating is the government-protected **Exuma Cays Land and Sea Park** (www.bnt.bs/parks_exuma.php; see p. 249), stretching south from Wax Cay to Conch Cay, which has magnificent sea gardens and coral reefs.

Getting around the archipelago of the Exumas is very difficult unless you're a yachtie or a skilled skipper of your own rented craft. If you're not a sailor, your best bet is to call Captain Steven Cole of **Off Island Adventures,** George Town (✆ 242/524-0524; www.offislandadventures.com), to book a half-day tour for $350 or a full-day tour for $600. He'll take you to remote spots in the archipelago, including such exotic locations as White Cay, where parts of the *Pirates of the Caribbean* movies were filmed. Day cruises usually stop at a remote beach bar for cocktails. You can also opt for a sunset or moonlight cruise.

FISHING

Many visitors come to the Exumas just to go bonefishing. Arrangements for such outings can be made at **Club Peace & Plenty,** Queen's Highway (✆ 800/525-2210 or 242/336-2551).

GOLF

The **Sandals Emerald Bay Golf Club ★★★**, Emerald Bay (www.sandals.com; ✆ 888/SANDALS [726-3257]), is one of the top oceanfront courses in all of the Caribbean. The par-72 Greg Norman design features 6 oceanfront holes and stretches a challenging 6,402m (7,001 yd.), yet was laid out to accommodate golfers of various skill levels. The course finishes on a rocky peninsula with a panoramic view of the sea. There's also a pro shop. Greens fees for 18 holes are a steep $125 to $200 for resort guests, $145 to $245 for nonguests. Reservations are required.

KAYAKING

You can best appreciate some of the most dramatic scenery in the Exumas from the peaceful perch of a sea kayak. In fact, many areas—including mangrove lakes, rivers, manta-ray gathering spots, and bonefish flats—are too shallow for other boats. Don't worry if you haven't hit the gym lately: Anyone in at least average physical condition, from children to seniors, can kayak with a smile. **Rolle's Sea Kayaking Adventures,** Queen's Highway in George Town (© 242/358-5115) rents sit-on-top kayaks for singles and doubles. Singles are $50 per half-day, $100 per day, and $300 per week. Doubles run $75 per half-day, $125 per day, and $400 per week.

For more adventure, book one of this outfitter's guided kayak trips. You don't have to spend the whole time paddling. During half- and full-day excursions, lunch and beverages are served, and the price covers all gear, including snorkeling equipment. You may end up watching a blizzard of fish swarm a shipwreck, searching for sand dollars on a deserted beach, snorkeling into a sea cave, or finding out about bush medicine while you hike along a nature trail. Guided trips begin at $85 per hour for adults and $45 to $65 per hour for children.

KITESURFING

Kitesurfing is all the rage, whisking riders across the pristine waters using a power kite and a device similar to a snowboard (but in very different climes). Both novices and experts can join in the glide, soaring over the shallow waters of the Exumas. For more information about how to link up with this new sport, contact **Exuma Kitesurfing** (© 242/524-0523; www.exumakitesurfing.com).

SNORKELING & SCUBA DIVING

Your best bet for snorkeling is the beautiful waters off the coast of **Stocking Island** (see "Hitting the Beach," above). Boat trips from George Town depart for the island twice daily. You can also rent snorkeling equipment for $10 per day at **Minns Water Sports,** George Town (© 242/336-3483); a $50 deposit is required.

Scuba divers will find plenty of attractions surrounding the Exumas, including fields of massive coral heads, eerie blue holes, and exciting walls covered with marine life. Many excellent reefs are just 20 to 25 minutes away from the George Town area, so long boat rides won't cut into your underwater time.

The main attraction here is the **Exuma Cays Land and Sea Park** (p. 249), which draws scuba divers to its 453 sq. km (175 sq. miles) of sea gardens with magnificent coral reefs, flora, and fauna. Call your hotel to ask whether it offers a room/dive package, or try **Dive Exuma,** based at February Point Resort Estates (© 242/336-2893; www.dive-exuma.com), for information on scuba-diving excursions. A two-tank dive costs $150.

Exploring George Town

George Town has a colorful history, despite the fact that it appears so sleepy today. (With so little street action, it doesn't even need a traffic light.) Pirates used its deepwater harbor in the 17th century, and those called the "plantation aristocracy," mainly from Virginia and the Carolinas, settled here in the 18th century. Over the next 100

WHY IS EVERYONE NAMED rolle?

The history of the Exumas is not much documented before the latter part of the 18th century. It is assumed that the island chain was inhabited by Lucayans at least until the Spaniards wiped them out. Columbus didn't set foot on this chain of islands. However, from the northern tip of Long Island, he is believed to have seen Little Exuma, naming whatever was in the area "Yumey." At least, that's how the island chain appears on a map of the New World from 1500.

By the late 17th century, Great Exuma had become a major producer of salt, and permanent settlers began to arrive. The sailing vessels of the salt merchants were constantly harassed by pirates, but some families from Nassau must have looked on this as the lesser of two evils. On New Providence they were subjected to the terrorism inflicted by both the pirates and the Spanish, and in the latter part of the 17th century and the first of the 18th, they fled to the relative peace of the Exumas (they still do!).

Some Loyalist families, fleeing the newly established United States of America after British defeat, came to the Exuma Cays in 1783, but nothing like the number that settled in Harbour Island, New Plymouth, and Spanish Wells. In the 18th century, cotton and salt were "king" on the Exumas. English plantation owners brought in many slaves to work the fields, and many of today's Exumians are direct descendants of those early slaves, who were mostly of African origin. The "king" did not stay long on the throne. Insects went for the cotton, and salt lands such as those of the Turks and Caicos Islands proved much too competitive for those of the Exumas, so these pursuits were eventually abandoned.

Most of the white owners went back to where they came from, but the slaves, having no such option, stayed on, surviving by working the land abandoned by their former owners and taking the names of those owners as their own. A look through the George Town directory turns up such names as Bethel, Ferguson, and especially Rolle, the same as those of the long-gone whites.

It becomes immediately apparent, however, that every other person is named Rolle. One elderly woman, sitting in front of her little shanty painted in florid tricolors, and wearing a Bahama Mama T-shirt, confided, "You're born a Rolle, all your cousins are called Rolle, you marry a Rolle and have children called Rolle, and you are a Rolle and all the mourners at your funeral, related or not, are called Rolle." She claimed that since everyone in the Exumas keeps track of their blood relatives, the locals know which Rolle is "real family" and which is not related by blood. "That's got to be kept in mind," she said, "when it comes time to get married."

At one time Lord John Rolle held much of the Exumas under a grant from the British Crown, giving him hundreds of acres. He is reported to have owned 325 slaves who worked this acreage, but Lord Rolle never set foot on his potentially rich plantation. Stories vary as to what happened to the slaves—whether they were, as some claim, freed by Lord Rolle and given the land by him, or whether, upon being released from bondage by the United Kingdom Emancipation Act in 1834, they took over the land, with or without Rolle's approval. Whichever, descendants of those same slaves are important Exumians today.

years, **Elizabeth Harbour,** the town's focal point, became a refitting base for British man-of-war vessels, and the U.S. Navy used the port again during World War II.

There isn't much to see here in the way of architecture except the confectionery-pink-and-white **Government Building,** which was inspired by the architecture of Nassau's Government House.

Shopping in George Town is a very casual event, especially at the **Exuma Straw Market,** open Monday through Saturday from 7am to 5pm. Here in the shade of an old ficus tree in the center of town, you can talk to the friendly Exumian women and perhaps purchase some of their handicrafts. They make straw baskets, colorful hand-bags, dolls, and other keepsakes. Bargaining is permissible, and prices go from $25 for a hat to $150 for an intricate basket.

Otherwise there's not too much shopping here, but there are a few places where you can purchase souvenirs and gifts. **Exuma Liquor and Gifts,** Queen's Highway (© **242/336-2101**), is the place to stock up on liquor, wine, and beer.

The **Sandpiper,** Queen's Highway, across from Club Peace & Plenty (© **242/336-2084**), features original serigraphs by Diane Minns, as well as a good selection of Bahamian arts and crafts, sponges, ceramics, watches, baskets, jewelry, books, post-cards, and Bahamian straw baskets and other hand-crafted works. Diane designs and silk-screens T-shirts here in the shop, and she welcomes anyone to watch her work.

Seeing More of Great Exuma

If you've walked around George Town and now want to see more of Great Exuma Island, you'll need either a taxi or a rental car to drive **Queen's Highway,** which runs the length of the island and is still referred to as the "slave route."

Forty-five kilometers (28 miles) north of George Town, **Rolleville** is named after Lord Rolle, a British plantation owner and, in his time, the chief employer on the island. This village is still inhabited by descendants of his freed slaves, whose land is never sold but instead passed from one generation to the next.

As you travel north along the highway, you'll see ruins of plantations. This land is called **"generation estates,"** and the major ones are **Steventon, Mount Thompson,** and **Ramsey.** You'll pass other settlements such as Mosstown (which has work-ing farms), the Forest, Farmer's Hill, and Roker's Point. Steventon is the last settlement before you reach Rolleville, which is the largest of the plantation estates. There are several beautiful beaches along the way, especially the ones at **Tarr Bay** and **Jimmie Hill.**

If you head south from George Town, you'll pass Flamingo Bay and Pirate's Point. In the 18th century, Captain Kidd is said to have anchored at **Kidd Cay.** You, how-ever, can stay at the Regatta Point (p. 238). **Flamingo Bay,** the site of a hotel and villa development, begins just 1km (⅔ mile) from George Town. It's a favorite rendez-vous of bonefishers and the yachting set.

George Town After Dark

The best place to head for some after-dark diversion is **Club Peace & Plenty,** George Town (© **800/525-2210** or 242/336-2093). Though summer nights are slow, something is usually happening here in winter, from weekly poolside bashes to live bands that keep both locals and visitors jumping up on the dance floor.

More ethnic, and more local in its focus, is **Eddie's Edgewater Bar and Restaurant,** Queen's Highway, George Town (𝄐 **242/336-3050**). Set within a simple house across the highway from Lake Victoria, it's a hangout and nerve center for local gossip. It's open Monday to Saturday from noon till around 10:30pm, or whenever everyone opts to go home.

LITTLE EXUMA ★

This is a faraway retreat, the southernmost of the Exuma Cays. Despite the fact that it's in the Tropics, it has a subtropical climate and lovely white-sand beaches. The waters are so crystal-clear in some places that you can spot the colorful tropical fish more than 18m (59 ft.) down. The island, about 31 sq. km (12 sq. miles), is connected to Great Exuma by a 182m-long (597-ft.) bridge. It's about a 16km (10-mile) trip from the Exuma International Airport outside George Town.

Less than a kilometer (⅔ mile) offshore is **Pigeon Cay,** which is uninhabited. Visitors often come here for the day and are later picked up by a boat that takes them back to Little Exuma. You can go snorkeling and visit the remains of a 200-year-old wreck, right offshore in about 2m (6½ ft.) of water.

On one of Little Exuma's highest hills are the remains of an old **pirate fort.** Several cannons are located nearby, but documentation is lacking as to when it was built or by whom. (Pirates didn't leave too much data lying around.)

Coming from Great Exuma, the first community you reach on Little Exuma is called **Ferry,** so named because the two islands were linked by a ferry service before the bridge was built. Ask around about visiting the private chapel of an Irish family, the Fitzgeralds, erected generations ago.

Along the way, you can take in **Pretty Molly Bay,** site of the now-shuttered Sand Dollar Beach Club. Pretty Molly was a slave who committed suicide by walking into

A ROMANTIC LEGEND & A movie star

On the road to Little Exuma, you'll come to the hamlet of **Rolle Town,** at the southern tip of Great Exuma. It was once, like Rolleville in the north, owned by Lord Rolle. Today, it is populated with descendants of his former slaves. This sleepy town has some 100-year-old houses.

In an abandoned field where goats frolic, you can visit the **Rolle Town Tombs,** burial ground of the McKay family. Capt. Alexander McKay, a Scot, came to Great Exuma in 1789 after he was granted 161 hectares (398 acres) for a plantation. His wife joined him in 1791, and soon after, they had a child. However, tragedy struck in 1792 when Anne

McKay, who was only 26, died along with her child. Perhaps grief-stricken, her husband died the following year. Their story is one of the romantic legends of the island.

The village also claims a more contemporary famous daughter, actress Esther Rolle. Her parents were born here (though they went to the U.S. before she was born). Rolle is best remembered for her role as the strong-willed mother on the '70s sitcom *Good Times.* She won an Emmy playing a maid in *Summer of My German Soldier;* Rolle's other film credits included *Driving Miss Daisy, Rosewood,* and *How to Make an American Quilt.* She died at the age of 78 in 1998.

There is an idyllic chain of five privately owned little islands in the Exumas, in the indigo waters of Exuma Sound to the east of Great Bahama Bank. They are called Big Darby (our favorite), Little Darby, Goat Cay, Bette Cay, and Guana Cay. These islands lie 458km (285 miles) southeast of Miami and 154km (96 miles) south of Nassau and are accessible only by boat or charter aircraft.

If you have time for only one, make it **Big Darby,** where you can hike to a decaying castle that's been abandoned for more than half a century—talk about *Gone With the Wind.* **Darby Castle** was built as a working plantation in 1938 by an Englishman known as Sir Baxter. As a plantation, it became the largest employer in the southern Bahamas during World War II; its workers helped produce palm oil, fruit, cotton, and even goats. Today, the castle is the stuff of legend, with many tall tales told about the Englishman and his mistress. (Was he a Nazi sympathizer?) Though the so-called castle is in ruins, you can take a potentially dangerous walk to the second landing and its large stone-built balcony, where you can enjoy one of the grandest panoramas in the Exumas.

Come to the Darby Islands for some of the most beautiful beaches in The Bahamas; the sand is the color and texture of sifted flour. On Little Darby and Big Darby, there are more than 10 good beaches. The best snorkeling and dive spot is the little harbor nestled between the two islands.

the water. The natives claim that her ghost can still be seen stalking the beach every night.

Many visitors come to Little Exuma to visit the **Hermitage,** a plantation constructed by Loyalist settlers. The last surviving example of the many that once stood in the Exumas, it was originally built by the Kendall family, who came to Little Exuma in 1784. The family established their plantation at **Williamstown** and, with their slaves, set about growing cotton. But they encountered so many difficulties having the cotton shipped to Nassau that, in 1806, they advertised the plantation for sale. The ad promised "970 acres more or less," along with "160 hands" (referring to the slaves). Chances are, you'll be approached by a local guide who, for a fee, will show you around. Ask to be shown the several old tombs in the area.

At Williamstown (look for the seaside marker), you can also visit the remains of the **Great Salt Pond,** a body of water in the center of the island that used to be the site of a flourishing salt-raking industry.

If you really have to see everything, you may be able to get a local to take you over to **Hog Cay,** the end of the line for the Exumas. It's just a spit of land, and there are no glorious beaches here. It's visited mainly by those who like to add obscure islets at the very end of the road to their list of explorations. Hog Cay is privately owned and farmed. The owner, whose house lies in the center of the island, seems friendly to visitors.

STANIEL CAY ★

Staniel Cay lies 129km (80 miles) southeast of Nassau at the southern end of the little Pipe Creek archipelago. It's a 13km (8-mile) chain of mostly uninhabited islets,

If you want a beach to yourself, one of the uninhabited islands surrounding Staniel Cay could indeed become yours for the day. In the unlikely event that another yachting party arrives, just sail on to another nearby island—chances are, it'll be deserted.

The local map given out by the Staniel Cay Yacht Club pinpoints the location of **Thunderball Grotto** ★, where part of the James Bond film *Thunderball* was filmed. This is one of the best places for snorkeling in the Exumas. To the north of Thunderball Grotto lies the curiously named **Big Major Cay,** where hungry pigs will chase you down the beach for a handout. There are also stray cats on the island who appreciate a snack (they're especially fond of canned sardines), as well as some fresh water.

Believe it or not, **swimming pigs** will even surround your boat here. They are harmless, but do expect them to beg for food. At another point on your nautical map, about 6.4km (4 miles) beyond **Major Spot**, a tiny, uninhabited island directly northwest of Staniel Cay, you'll come across shallow waters where tame (at least, we hope so) nurse sharks like to have their pictures taken. Food makes them even less camera-shy.

sandy beaches, coral reefs, and bonefish flats. There are many places for snug anchorages, making this a favorite yachting stopover in the mid-Exumas. Staniel Cay, known for years as "Stanyard," has no golf course or tennis courts, but it's the perfect island for "the great escape." It's home to just 80 full-time residents.

An annual **Bonefishing Tournament** is sponsored here every July, during the celebration of Bahamian Independence Day. There's a **straw market** where you can buy crafts, hats, and handbags.

The **Staniel Cay Yacht Club** (see below) arranges charter flights from Fort Lauderdale on **Watermakers Air** (📞 **954/771-0330;** www.watermakersair.com). Tickets vary widely depending on the season and on how many other parties are on the flight, but generally cost from $240 to $325 per person each way; flight time is 2 hours, but you should expect to spend up to another hour or so clearing customs. Call for more information.

Where to Stay & Eat

Staniel Cay Yacht Club   Staniel Cay is a pleasant and remote getaway, and the Staniel Cay Yacht Club—only a 5-minute golf-cart ride from the airstrip—is the place to get away to. Although once famous in yachting circles, drawing celebrities like the late Malcolm Forbes, the property became run-down and lost its chic clientele for several years. Since then, it has bounced back. Restored and improved, it again welcomes the yachting world to its get-away-from-everything location near a white-sand beach. The accommodations were remodeled and refurbished in 2009 and 2010, with plans for the addition of nine additional accommodations during the lifetime of this edition. The cottages, each of which is painted a different color, have west-facing balconies, which make for unimpeded views of the sun setting over the water. Locals joke that a glorious sunset is one of the few guarantees each day on Staniel Cay.

A Boston Whaler, available as a rental, docks outside each cottage, and guests get a map of local waters and are invited to sail on their own—many deserted islands surround Staniel Cay. The club can rent you anything from a 4m (13-ft.) Boston

In the northern Exumas, the best waters for private boating are found in the government-protected Exuma Cays Land and Sea Park, which stretches south from Wax Cay to Conch Cay—a distance of 35km (22 miles)—with magnificent sea gardens and coral reefs. The park is 13km (8 miles) wide and was inaugurated in 1958. The exact location is 35km (22 miles) northeast of Staniel Cay.

The park is often called the "Garden of Eden," with its unspoiled beaches, safe anchorages, numerous islets, and endless cays. Wherever you go, expect to see tropical birds flying overhead. As you wander the islands, you may even catch a glimpse of the endangered **Bahamian iguana.** The environment below is also fascinating, a water world of coral reefs, mysterious caves, and scores of marine animals (take along your snorkeling gear). Fishing, incidentally, is prohibited, as is handling the coral—touching it will kill it.

The best place for hiking is **Hawksbill Cay** or **Warderick Wells,** which is the site of ruins of Loyalist settlements from the 18th century. Pioneers during that era tried to make a living out of farming these islands.

It's best to visit the archipelago between dawn and dusk. Note that there are no facilities associated with any of the cay's beaches, and that you must bring your own water during your explorations.

Whaler for $150 (including fuel) to a 5.1m (17-ft.) boat for $235 per day. Snorkeling gear is available for $20. Since the island is only a kilometer (⅔ mile) wide, you can easily walk to the local village, which has a grocery store, straw market, church, and post office. An on-site clubhouse offers American and Bahamian cuisine for breakfast, lunch, and dinner, with a menu that features steaks and seafood—nothing too foreign or experimental.

Staniel Cay, Exumas, The Bahamas. www.stanielcay.com. © **888/343-7374** or 954/467-8920 in the U.S., or 242/355-2024. Fax 242/355-2044. 12 units. Nov 20–Sept 9 $165–$195 double; from $210–$255 suite; off-season $145–$178 double, from $225 suite. MC, V. **Amenities:** Restaurant; bar; outdoor pool. *In room:* A/C, fridge, hair dryer, no phone, Wi-Fi ($10).

SAMPSON CAY

Tiny Sampson Cay, located within a 15-minute boat ride northwest of Staniel Cay and just to the southeast of the Exuma Cays Land and Sea Park, has a certain charm, as well as a full-service marina and a small dive operation.

Besides Staniel Cay, Sampson Cay has the only marina in the central Exumas, so most visitors arrive in their own boats, and local guides taking out sportfishermen for the day provide the chief entertainment.

Sampson Cay is 124km (77 miles) southeast of Nassau and one of the safest anchorages in the Exumas. It is a natural "hurricane hole"—in other words, a fully protected anchorage with land all around. The cay lies near the end of Pipe Creek, which has been called a "tropical Shangri-La."

Where to Stay & Eat

Sampson Cay Club ★   This is a rather remote outpost, but once you get here, you'll see that it's a gem. The resort has considerably improved in recent years and is

Norman's cay: A SHADY PAST

Throughout the Exumas, you'll see islands with NO TRESPASSING signs posted. In the early 1980s, on Norman's Cay, these signs were extremely serious: You could have been killed if you had gone ashore.

Fortunately, the drug smuggling that used to occur here has been cleaned up, and the area is once again safe for travelers. However, private NO TRESPASSING signs should still be obeyed. Even without drug activity, the privacy of individual property owners has to be respected, of course.

Once upon a time, you might have run into Ted Kennedy, Walter Cronkite, or William F. Buckley, Jr., enjoying the island's pleasures. The remote outpost enjoyed great popularity with the Harvard clique.

During the 1980s, however, all that changed when German-Colombian

Carlos Lehder Rivas purchased most of Norman's Cay. According to experts, the island soon became the major distribution point for drug exportation to the United States. Millions of dollars' worth of cocaine was flown from Colombia here before being smuggled onward to America.

Eventually, the U.S. applied strong pressure on the Bahamian government to clean up the island. Lehder fled for Colombia, where he was captured and extradited to the U.S. He is now in prison.

Norman's Cay may one day realize its ritzy tourist potential yet again, but for now, it remains relatively quiet, visited only by stray yachting parties and the occasional cruise vessel.

now better than ever. Accommodations, which are scattered across the floor spaces of at least four large and separate houses, are comfortable, well furnished, and generally spacious. Two of them have king-size beds; the others have queen-size beds. All accommodations have private bathrooms with showers, and two of the units are right on the beach. Each of the houses are equipped with outdoor showers, each has its own dock, and most of them can be rented as an independent building during reunions of families or friends.

Community life here revolves around the grocery store and commissary, the fuel and dockage facilities of the full-service marina, and a bar and simple, well-scrubbed restaurant favored by visiting yachters. The restaurant and bar serve drinks and sandwiches any time of day to anyone who shows up, but reservations are required before 4pm for the single-seating dinner, which is served nightly at 7:30pm. The staff will rent you a 5.1m (17-ft.) whaler for $350 a day, as well as Hobie Cats and snorkeling equipment. Upon request, they can also point to walking trails that will link you up to one of seven beaches.

Sampson Cay, Exumas, The Bahamas. www.sampsoncayclub.com. © **877/633-0305** or 242/355-2034. Fax 242/355-2034. 10 units. Year-round $275–$400 double; $750–$1,500 villa. MC, V. **Amenities:** Restaurant; bar. *In room:* A/C, fridge, kitchenette, no phone.

THE SOUTHERN BAHAMAS

This cluster of islands on the southern fringe of The Bahamas is one of the last frontier outposts that can be reached relatively quickly from the U.S. mainland. Their remoteness is one of the most compelling reasons to visit—that, and a chance to see life in The Bahamas the way it used to be. Some of the islands are proud to proclaim that "we are as we were when Columbus first landed here"—an exaggeration, of course, but one that contains a kernel of truth.

The Southern Bahamas have a colorful history. In the 18th century, Loyalists from the Carolinas and Virginia came here with slave labor and settled many of the islands. They had thriving cotton plantations for about 20 years until blight struck, killing crops and destroying the industry. In 1834, the United Kingdom Emancipation Act freed slaves throughout the British Empire. When the Loyalists moved on to more fertile ground, they often left behind emancipated slaves, who then had to eke out a living as best they could.

With some notable exceptions, such as Long Island, tourism developers have stayed clear of these isles. However, they offer enormous potential, as most of them have excellent beaches, good fishing, and fine dive sites.

If you're considering visiting any of these islands, be forewarned that transportation is inconvenient and that accommodations are rather limited. For these and other reasons involving the scarcity of tourist facilities, yachters and other boaters comprise the majority of visitors, since they can eat and sleep aboard their vessels.

Many changes are in the wind for the Southern Bahamas. Right now, however, there's almost no traffic, no banks, no lawyers. There are, however, mosquitoes, so bring a good insect repellent and a long-sleeved shirt for protection.

CAT ISLAND ★★

Untainted by tourism, lovely Cat Island is the sixth-largest island in The Bahamas. The fishhook-shaped island—some 77km (48 miles) long and 1 to 6.5km (⅔–4 miles) wide—lies about 209km (130 miles) southeast of Nassau and 523km (325 miles) southeast of Miami. (Don't confuse Cat Island with Cat Cay, a smallish private island near Bimini.)

Cat Island, named after the pirate Arthur Catt (and not wild packs of marauding cats), is located near the Tropic of Cancer, between Eleuthera and Long Island. It has one of the country's most pleasant climates, with temperatures in the high 60s (low 20s Celsius) during the short winters, rising to the mid-80s (low 30s Celsius) in summer, with trade winds making the place even more comfortable. It is also home to some 2,000 people, among the friendliest in all of The Bahamas.

Many local historians claim that Cat Island residents were the first to see Columbus. Some believe that the explorer was welcomed here by the peaceful Arawaks. Regardless of whether Columbus stopped here, the island has a rich history of adventurers, slaves, buccaneers, farmers, and visionaries of many nationalities. But even now, Cat Island remains mysterious to some. It's known as a stronghold of unfamiliar-to-most practices such as obeah (West Indian witchcraft) and of having miraculously healing bush medicines.

With its pristine virgin beaches, the island is beautiful to see, yet little-visited enough that it remains relatively inexpensive and untainted. The north shore is wild and untamed. A straight asphalt road (in terrible shape) leads from the north to the south of the island. Along the way, you can select your own beach—and chances are you'll have complete privacy. These beaches offer an array of watersports, and visitors can go swimming or snorkeling at several places. Boating and diving are among the main reasons to go to Cat Island, and diving lessons are available for novices. **Fernandez Bay** is a fit-for-a-postcard white-sand beach set against a turquoise-blue sea and lined with casuarina trees.

Arthur's Town, in the north, is the island's major hub. It's also the boyhood home of legendary actor Sidney Poitier. He has many relatives still living on the island, including a few amazing lookalikes. Poitier shares memories of his childhood home in his book *This Life.*

CAT ISLAND ESSENTIALS

GETTING THERE   Cat Island is served by two airports, **Arthur's Town Airport** (ATC; ✆ 242/354-2049) and **New Bight Airport** (TBI; ✆ 242/342-2107). Arthur's Town is the island's largest settlement, while New Bight is the island's most scenic village. Although **Bahamasair** (✆ 800/222-4262 in the U.S; www.bahamas air.com) suspended flights into Cat Island in 2010, they'll sometimes reserve a spot for you on the two small-scale airlines which do make scheduled runs into Cat Island. These include **Sun Air** (✆ 877/226-2040; www.gosunair.com), which flies from Fort Lauderdale into New Bight Airport four times a week, round-trip; and **Sky Bahamas** (✆ 242/377-8993; www.skybahamas.net), which operates twice-daily flights from Nassau to both of the above-mentioned airports on Cat Island.

The island is also served by mail boat. One of them, usually the **MV *Worth Cat Island Special,*** which transports passengers for $50 one-way and $100 round-trip, departs Potter's Cay Dock in Nassau every Tuesday or Wednesday at 5pm, heading for Bennett's Harbour and Arthur's Town for an arrival early the following morning. Since sailing schedules are subject to change due to weather conditions, check departure times with the dock master at Nassau's **Potter's Cay Dock** (✆ 242/393-1064).

GETTING AROUND   Limited but quite adequate **taxi** service is available on Cat Island. Hotel owners, if notified of your arrival time, will have someone drive to the airport to pick you up. You can, however, rent a car from **Bridge Inn Car Rentals,** Bridge Inn, New Bight (✆ 242/342-3014). Prices begin at $75 to $95 daily, with unlimited mileage. Hours are daily from 6:30am to 7:30pm.

The Southern Bahamas

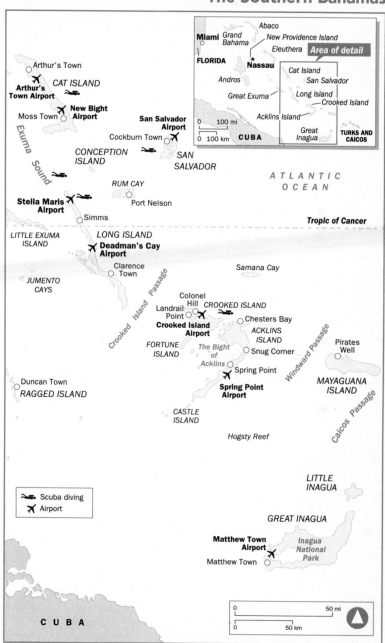

[FastFACTS] CAT ISLAND

There are three **medical clinics,** each among the simplest in The Bahamas. They are in Arthur's Town, Old Bight, and Smith's Bay, and they're not always open. In case of an emergency, notify your hotel staff immediately; someone will try to get in touch with a medical expert. Serious cases are flown to Nassau. If you're not in good health and might require medical assistance on vacation, Cat Island is not the island to choose, as there is no central number to call for help.

SPECIAL EVENTS   The annual **Cat Island Regatta** happens every summer, usually over 3 days at the end of July or beginning of August. It attracts the largest collection of visitors to Cat Island; the inns prove inadequate to receive them. Contact your local Bahamas Tourist Office (p. 298) for more information. Less formal but more musical is the **Cat Island Rake and Scrape Festival** (✆ **242/354-4085**), a 2-day event scheduled for the first weekend in June in a field near the Arthur's Town airport. As a celebration of the Southern Bahamas' indigenous musical traditions, it assembles into one convivial event many of the old-time aficionados of this waning musical form. Bands and old-time singers perform at loosely scheduled intervals within a venue otherwise devoted to food stalls and reunions of former island residents returning home for a brief visit with those relatives who remain.

Where to Stay & Eat

Bridge Inn   Set within a short stroll from a beach, the very relaxed and casual Bridge Inn occupies a cluster of simple and angular motel-like buildings which were substantially upgraded and renovated in 2010 and 2011. The inn offers babysitting services (at an extra charge) so that parents can play tennis or go diving, sailboarding, snorkeling, jogging, bicycling, fishing, or sightseeing with the knowledge that their youngsters are being carefully tended to. Bedrooms are modest and motel-style, but each unit can house three to four guests. Each of the high-ceilinged rooms comes with a private bathroom containing a shower stall. On the premises are a full bar and a restaurant that serves rather simple Bahamian and international cuisine. *Note:* It's always a good idea to confirm the prices listed below, as they may change over the life of this edition.

New Bight, Cat Island, The Bahamas. ✆ **242/342-3013.** Fax 242/342-3041. 12 units. Year-round $120 double; $250 villa. Extra person $10. MC, V. Rates include continental breakfast. **Amenities:** Restaurant; bar; babysitting; room service. *In room:* A/C, TV, kitchenette (in some).

Fernandez Bay Village ★ 🛏   Opening onto Fernandez Bay, this is Cat Island's best resort. Although rustic, it has a certain charm, mainly because of its position on a curvy beach set against casuarinas blowing in the trade winds. The beach is never crowded, so come here only if you *really* want to get away from it all; this place is far too laid-back for full hotel service. Things get done, but it takes time—and no one's in a hurry.

Fernandez Bay Village has been in the Armbrister family since it was originally established on a plantation in 1870. Its rusticity and seclusion are part of its charm. But if you wish, you can get acquainted with other guests whose interests match your own. Yachters, who moor in the water offshore—there are no marina facilities—often visit the resort to take advantage of the general store's fresh supplies. (Nearby Smith's Bay is one of the region's best storm shelters—even government mail boats take refuge there during hurricanes.)

The "village" consists of both villas and cottages, all with private gardens. Each villa contains two bedrooms, a full kitchen, and a washer/dryer—perfect for families or couples traveling together. There are also double-occupancy cottages, each built of stone, driftwood, and glass. Meals are served in a clubhouse decorated with antiques and Haitian art. This clubhouse, which opens onto a view of the beach and sea, also features a sitting area with library, stone fireplace, and overhead fans. You'll eat dinners here on a beach terrace adjacent to a thatched-roof tiki bar that runs on the honor system. On many nights, guests gather around a blazing bonfire near the water to hear island music.

1.6km (1 mile) north of New Bight, Cat Island, The Bahamas. www.fernandezbayvillage.com. © **800/940-1905** or 242/342-3043. 19 units. Nov–May $365–$425 villa, $270–$310 cottage; June–Aug $325–$395 villa, $235–$255 cottage. AE, MC, V. Closed Aug 15–Oct 31. **Amenities:** Restaurant; babysitting; bikes; watersports equipment/rentals. *In room:* A/C, ceiling fans, kitchen (in villas), no phone.

Greenwood Beach Resort ★   This resort's location, on a 13km (8-mile) stretch of the Atlantic bordered by pink sands, is idyllic, and there's good snorkeling right offshore. A German family has run this property since 1992, constantly making improvements. A group of modern buildings on the most isolated section of the island has a private beach and a freshwater pool. It's better run and more equipped than the Bridge Inn, and it attracts mostly divers. The small ocean-view double rooms are equipped with their own terraces.

The Cat Island Dive Center is the island's best, with 7.5m (25-ft.) and 11m (36-ft.) motorboats for diving excursions, plus complete equipment for 20 divers at a time. A two-tank dive costs $95 per person, including equipment. A half-day snorkeling trip costs $35, including equipment. The resort also has two boats available for bonefishing. The staff greets each arriving Bahamasair flight.

Port Howe, Cat Island, The Bahamas. www.greenwoodbeachresort.net. © **242/342-3053.** Fax 242/342-3053. 16 units. Year-round $110–$130 double. Breakfast and dinner $48 per person. AE, MC, V. **Amenities:** Restaurant; bar; babysitting; outdoor pool; watersports equipment/rentals; Wi-Fi (in clubhouse and on terrace). *In room:* A/C (in some), ceiling fan, no phone.

Hawk's Nest Resort & Marina   This remote getaway lies on Cat Island's southwestern side, fronting a long beach and containing its own runway for charter flights and private planes, plus a 28-slip full-service marina that attracts yachters. The intimate resort is set near the village of Devil's Point, lying some 16km (10 miles) west of Columbus Point close to the ruins of two once-flourishing but now-abandoned plantations, Richman Hill and Newfield. The clubhouse, the rooms, and the main house are all spacious and inviting. Bedrooms, with either two queen-size beds or one king-size bed, are well furnished and brightly decorated. They come complete with a patio for those late-afternoon toddies sipped while watching the sunset. If you bring the family, consider booking the two-bedroom house on the beach, which is separate from the other structures. The resort serves full cooked-to-order breakfasts, sandwiches for lunch, and a buffet-style dinner, with the unannounced fare changing nightly. A one-tank dive costs $70; a two-tank dive is $95.

Devil's Point, Cat Island, The Bahamas. www.hawks-nest.com. © **242/342-7050.** Fax 242/342-7051. 10 units. Year-round $165–$205 double. MC, V. **Amenities:** Restaurant; bar; bikes; marina; outdoor pool; watersports equipment/rentals; Wi-Fi (free in clubhouse). *In room:* A/C, TV/VCR, hair dryer.

Island HoppInn ★ 👜   This small all-suite resort is a real discovery. It overlooks the Atlantic with panoramic views over Fernandez Bay; from your front porch, you

10

THE SOUTHERN BAHAMAS │ Cat Island Essentials

can see one of the island's best sandy beaches. The suites are spacious yet cozy, much like those in an upmarket B&B. Half of the units are large enough for three or four occupants. They're all furnished in a tropical style, with four-poster beds along with rattan furniture, well-equipped kitchens, and outdoor showers in the garden. Lunches—featuring freshly baked bread, tasty main courses, and gourmet desserts—can be delivered to your front veranda while you enjoy the ocean view. Your hosts, Thom and Cathy Bencin, are both originally from Cleveland, and are the best on the island for arranging watersports, including fishing charters; they'll also arrange a car rental upon request.

Fernandez Bay, Cat Island, The Bahamas. www.islandhoppinn.com. ℰ **216/978-8800** in the U.S., or 242/342-2100. Fax 242/342-2101. 4 units. Year-round $225–$350 double. MC, V. **Amenities:** Restaurant; bar; room service; watersports equipment/rentals; Wi-Fi (free in lobby). *In room:* A/C, TV/DVD (in some), kitchenette.

Pigeon Cay Beach Club This pleasant and well-managed B&B fronts a tranquil bay at the island's northern end, about a 15-minute ride from the Arthur's Town Airport. The main building consists of a trio of units and a small store. Each unit comes with a fully equipped kitchen and one to three bedrooms. In addition, the property has some light-filled one- to three-bedroom cottages built of stucco and coral stone, with beamed ceilings and Mexican tile floors.

Pigeon Cay, Cat Island, The Bahamas. www.pigeoncaybahamas.com. ℰ/fax **242/354-5084.** 11 units. Year-round $140–$180 1-bedroom unit; $250–$275 2-bedroom unit; $375 3-bedroom unit. Rates include continental breakfast. AE, MC, V. **Amenities:** Dining area; bar; babysitting; bikes; room service; watersports equipment/rentals. *In room:* Ceiling fan, CD player, hair dryer, kitchen, no phone, Wi-Fi (free).

Sammy T's Beach Resort ★ 🛅 Sammy T's is the most tranquil resort on the island. Tucked away on a tiny cove opening onto an idyllic beach, the property offers one- and two-bedroom villas individually designed with rattan furnishings and tiled floors under beamed ceilings. Picture it as your tropical home, complete with ceiling fans, Bahamian art, full living room, and well-equipped kitchen. For such a small place, the resort offers plenty of recreational activities, including an excellent pool, a fitness center, and even kayaks. Island tours can be arranged, as can fishing and snorkeling. Conch is likely to be sizzling on the grill at lunch, and a lobster dinner awaits.

Bennett's Harbour, Cat Island, The Bahamas. ℰ **242/354-6009.** Fax 242/354-6010. 7 villas. Year-round $155 1-bedroom unit; $265 2-bedroom unit. MC, V. Closed Sept 1–Oct 15. **Amenities:** Restaurant; bar; exercise room; outdoor pool; watersports equipment/rentals. *In room:* A/C, TV/DVD, DVD library, kitchenette, no phone, Wi-Fi (free).

Shanna's Cove On lovely pink sands on the northernmost point of the island, this resort was established in 2009 by expatriates from Germany, Frank and Gabi Wolff, who conceived it as an outpost escape for urbanites looking to get away. Pleasant, well-managed, and well-maintained, it will appeal to adventure-seekers who appreciate the wild scenery and its isolated setting. Well-prepared food with a European flair is served as part of lunchtime platters priced at from $9 to $22 each, and evening meals cost around $40 per person. Rooms are clean and cozy, with colorfully tiled floors and wide verandas overlooking the scrublands and the sea.

Orange Creek, Cat Island, The Bahamas. www.shannas-cove.com. ℰ **242/354-4249** or 242/359-9668. Fax 242/354-4250. 6 bungalow-style cottages. Year-round $180–$200 double. No credit cards. **Amenities:** Restaurant; bar; watersports and scuba facilities. *In room:* A/C, fridge.

Exploring the Island

Points of interest on Cat Island include an **Arawak cave** at Columbus Point, on the island's southern tip. In addition, you can see the ruins of many once-flourishing plantations that saw their heyday during the island's short-lived cotton boom. Early planters, many of them British Loyalists, marked their property boundaries with stone mounds—some of which are now nearly 200 years old. The ruined plantations include **Deveaux Mansion,** built by Col. Andrew Deveaux, who led the fledgling U.S. Navy to recapture Nassau from the Spanish in 1783, and **Armbrister Plantation,** which lies in ruins near Port Howe.

You can also hike along nature paths through native villages and past exotic plants. You'll eventually reach the peak of **Mount Alvernia,** the highest point in The Bahamas, at a mere 62m (203 ft.) above sea level. For your efforts, you'll be rewarded with a spectacular view.

The mount is capped by the **Hermitage,** a religious retreat built entirely by hand by the late Father Jerome, the former "father confessor" of the islands, who was once a mule skinner in Canada. Interestingly, the building was scaled to fit his short stature (he was a very, very short man). Formerly an Anglican, this Roman Catholic hermit priest became a legend on Cat Island. He died in 1956 at the age of 80, and although the site has been more or less abandoned, his memory is kept very much alive here.

Cat Island Dive Center, at Greenwood Beach Resort (© **242/342-3053;** www.greenwoodbeachresort.net), takes visitors out on diving or snorkeling excursions and rents out snorkeling gear and other water toys. A single boat dive costs $75 per person, a double costs $110, and half-day snorkeling trips go for $35 per person. Our favorite diving spot is along the west coast, where **Dry Heads** is the finest reef. It gets its name because at low tide, a blanket of purple sea fans stands high and dry. The drop here is 7.6m (25 ft.), and as you plunge below, you'll meet butterfly fish and queen angels swimming over the coral heads.

SAN SALVADOR ★

This may be where the New World began. For some years, it has been believed that San Salvador is where Christopher Columbus left his first footprints in the Western Hemisphere, although some scholars strongly dispute this. The easternmost island in the Bahamian archipelago, San Salvador lies 322km (200 miles) southeast of Nassau. Much of its area—163 sq. km (63 sq. miles)—is occupied by water: There are 28 landlocked lakes on the island, the largest of which is 19km (12 miles) long and serves as the principal transportation route for most of the island's population of roughly 1,000. A badly maintained 64km (40-mile) road circles the island's perimeter. The island's highest point is **Mount Kerr,** at 41m (135 ft.).

The tiny island keeps a lonely vigil in the Atlantic. At South West Point, **Dixon Hill Lighthouse,** about 50m (164 ft.) tall, can be seen from 31km (19 miles) away. The light is a hand-operated beacon fueled by kerosene. Built in the 1850s, it is the last lighthouse of its type in The Bahamas.

Except for the odd historian or two, very few people used to visit San Salvador. Then, in 1992, **Club Med Columbus Isle** opened, and the joint's been jumping ever since—at least, at the Club Med property. Away from there, San Salvador is as sleepy as it ever was, though it's been known for years as one of the best dive sites in The Bahamas. The snorkeling, fishing, and lovely beaches are also excellent.

San Salvador Essentials

GETTING THERE **Club Med** (p. 259) solves transportation problems for its guests by flying them in on weekly charter planes from Florida. In winter, charter flights from New York and Miami come in once a week. You can also rely on commercial transportation by air (Bahamasair flights) or sea (government mail boats), but if you do, you'll have to wait a long time before getting off the island.

Bahamasair (☏ **800/222-4262;** www.bahamasair.com) provides flights to San Salvador either 6 or 7 days a week from Nassau, depending on the season. Departure times constantly change, so check with the airline for the latest schedule.

A mail boat, *MV Lady Francis,* departs from Nassau at weekly intervals (usually Tuesday evening), arriving at San Salvador very early on Thursday morning. For details about riding as a passenger on the mail boat, contact the dock master at Nassau's **Potter's Cay Dock** (☏ **242/393-1064**).

GETTING AROUND If you want to tour the island, ask your hotel staff to help with arrangements and **taxi** service. Through Club Med, an island tour costs around $35 per person for a half-day ramble. Club Med guests also have use of **bikes** for cycling around the property and for guided tours around the island. You don't need to rent a car on San Salvador unless you want to explore far-flung places on your own. If that's the case, **Riding Rock Inn Resort & Marina** (www.ridingrock.com; ☏ **242/331-2631**) can arrange a rental for about $85 per day.

[FastFACTS] SAN SALVADOR

The **San Salvador Medical Clinic** at Bonefish Bay (☏ **242/331-2105**), a 5-minute drive north of Club Med, serves island residents, but serious cases are flown to Nassau. The clinic, which also fills prescriptions, is open Monday through Friday from 8:30am to 4:30pm; only emergencies are handled on Saturday and Sunday.

To call the **police,** dial ☏ **242/331-2010.** Phones are scarce on the island, but the front desk staff at Riding Rock Inn will place calls for you.

Where to Stay

Club Med Columbus Isle ★★ This is one of the most ecologically conscious—and one of the most luxurious—Club Meds in the Western Hemisphere. Set at the edge of one of the archipelago's most pristine beaches, about 3km (1¾ miles) north of Cockburn Town, it's the splashiest resort in the Southern Bahamas. Its promoters estimate that more than 30% of the island's population works here.

The resort is built around a large free-form swimming pool. Most of the prefabricated buildings here were barged to the site in 1991. The public rooms are some of the country's most lavish and cosmopolitan, with art and objects imported from Asia, Africa, the Americas, and Europe, and assembled by a battalion of adept designers. Bedrooms each contain a private balcony or patio; furniture that was custom-made in Thailand, Indonesia (especially Bali), or the Philippines; sliding-glass doors; and feathered wall hangings crafted in the Brazilian rainforest by members of the Xingu tribe. Accommodations are large (among the most spacious in the entire chain) and durable, and contain mostly twin beds, though you might be able to snag one of the units with a double or a king-size bed if you're lucky. Dozens of multilingual GOs (guest-relations organizers, or *gentils organisateurs*) are on hand to help initiate newcomers into the resort's many diversions. Unlike many other Club Meds, this one

THE COLUMBUS mystery

In 1492, a small group of peaceful Lucayan natives (Arawaks) were going about their business on a little island they called Guanahani, where they and their forebears had lived for at least 500 years. Little did they know how profoundly their lives would change when they greeted three small, strange-looking ships carrying Christopher Columbus and his crew of pale, bearded, oddly costumed men. It is said that when he came ashore, Columbus knelt and prayed. Then he claimed the land for Spain and named it San Salvador.

Unfortunately, the event was not so propitious for the reportedly handsome natives. Columbus later wrote to Queen Isabella that they would make ideal captives—perfect servants, in other words. It wasn't long before the Spanish conquistadors cleared the island, as well as most of The Bahamas, of Lucayans, sending them into slavery and early death in the mines of Hispaniola (Haiti) in order to feed the Spanish lust for New World gold.

But is the island now known as San Salvador the actual site of Columbus's landing? Columbus placed no lasting marker of his landfall on the sandy, sun-drenched island. Hence, there has been much study and discussion as to just where he actually landed.

In the 17th century, an English pirate captain, George Watling, took over the island (there was no government in charge at the time) and built a mansion on it to serve as his safe haven. The island was listed on maps for about 250 years thereafter as Watling's (or Watling) Island.

In 1926, the Bahamian legislature formally changed the name of the island to San Salvador, feeling that enough evidence had been brought forth to support the belief that this was indeed the site of Columbus's landing. Then in 1983, artifacts of European origin (beads, buckles, and metal spikes) were found here together with Arawak pottery and beads and a shard of Spanish pottery. Though the actual date of these artifacts cannot be pinned down, they are probably from 1490 to 1560. The beads and buckles fit the description of goods recorded in Columbus's log.

National Geographic published two meticulously researched articles in 1986 that set forth the belief that Samana Cay, some 105km (65 miles) southeast of the present San Salvador, was actually Guanahani, the island Columbus named San Salvador when he first landed in the New World. The question may never be resolved, and there will doubtless be years and years of controversy about it. Nevertheless, history buffs still flock here hoping to follow in the explorer's footsteps.

does not encourage bringing children and deliberately offers no particular facilities for their entertainment.

The main dining room, where meals are an ongoing series of buffets, lies in the resort's center. Two specialty restaurants offer Italian and grilled food. Nonfat, low-calorie, and vegetarian dishes are also available. Nightly entertainment is presented in a covered open-air theater and on a dance floor behind one of the bars.

3km (1¾ miles) north of Cockburn Town, San Salvador, The Bahamas. www.clubmed.com. © **800/CLUB-MED** (258-2633) or 242/331-2000. Fax 242/331-2458. 236 units. Year-round, weekly double occupancy $3,200–$4,278. Rates include all meals, drinks during meals, and most sports activities. AE, DISC, MC, V. Closed Sept-Oct. No children 12 and under. **Amenities:** 3 restaurants; 3 bars; disco; large health club; outdoor pool; 10 tennis courts (lit for night play); watersports equipment/rentals. *In room:* A/C, TV, fridge, hair dryer, MP3 docking station, Wi-Fi ($15 per day).

Guanahani Beach Club　The island's newest resort, established in 2011, exudes almost as much European flair as the much larger Club Med, with which it cooperates in the administration of kite-surfing lessons for Club Med clients who pay extra. It features a restaurant, the Patio Restaurant and Bar, the resort's social center. Architecture here is postmodern, streamlined, mostly white, and angular in ways you might have expected on Miami's South Beach or at a beach resort in Italy. Simple, well-designed cottages are clustered into a compact compound adjacent to the sea—a total of three one-bedroom units and one two-bedroom unit. Expect France or Italy in the tropics, with water sports close at hand and lots of emphasis on recuperation from urban cares.

Snow Bay, San Salvador, The Bahamas. www.guanahanibeachclub.com. *C* **242/452-0438.** 4 units. Year-round, per week, with half board included $2,450–$2,860, 1-BR villa for two; $3,773–$4,284 2-BR villa for four. **Amenities:** Restaurant; bar; watersports equipment/rentals. *In room:* Ceiling fan, kitchenette, Wi-Fi (free).

Riding Rock Inn Resort & Marina　San Salvador's second resort is the motel-style Riding Rock Inn, which caters largely to divers. Its simple ambience is a far cry from the extravagant Club Med. Each guest room faces either a pool or the open sea. The most recent improvement is an 18-unit oceanfront building in which the rooms are decorated in a tropical decor with two double beds. An island tour is included in the rates, but after that, most folks rent a bike or a scooter from the hotel. An on-site restaurant serves routine Bahamian specialties (see "Where to Eat," below), and a bar features a seating area that juts above the water on a pier.

Many different dive packages are available—check with the hotel to find one that suits you. The resort specializes in weeklong trips that include three dives per day, all meals, and accommodations. Packages begin and end on a Saturday. Although most guests are already experienced and certified divers, beginners can take a $165 resort course on the first day of their visit and afterward participate in most of the daily dives. Full PADI certification can also be arranged for $425 to $499.

Cockburn Town, San Salvador, The Bahamas. www.ridingrock.com. *C* **800/272-1492** in the U.S., 954/453-5031 in Florida, or 242/331-2631. Fax 242/331-2020. 42 units. Year-round $150–$180 double; $165–$200 triple; $210 quad. Children 11 and under stay free in parent's room. MC, V. **Amenities:** Restaurant; bar; outdoor pool; tennis court; watersports equipment/rentals; Wi-Fi (free). *In room:* A/C, TV, fridge, hair dryer.

Where to Eat

Rock Inn Restaurant BAHAMIAN/AMERICAN　Sit on the deck overlooking the water or eat inside; either way, you'll dine on hearty portions of comfort food. Pancakes make a good breakfast choice, and sandwiches are on the menu for lunch. The fixed-price dinners include soup, salad, main course, dessert, wine, and soft, just-baked Bahamian bread. Launch your meal with the well-seasoned conch chowder or okra soup, and follow it up with steak, prime rib, chicken, or fresh fish. The Wednesday-night barbecues, featuring reggae music, are popular social events.

Riding Rock Inn Resort & Marina, Cockburn Town. *C* **242/331-2631.** Reservations recommended. Breakfast $15; lunch $18; dinner $35. MC, V. Daily 7:30–9am, 12:30–2pm, and 6:30–8:30pm.

Beaches & Outdoor Pursuits

If you prefer finding a stretch of sand where the only footprints are your own, rent a car or bike at **Riding Rock Inn Resort & Marina** (see above), or call a taxi. Empty beaches are everywhere. Just remember to take plenty of water and, of course, sunblock; you won't find much shade. Along the way, look for the island's various monuments to Christopher Columbus.

On the northeast coast, **East Beach** stretches for some 10km (6¼ miles). Crushed coral and shells have turned the shore a rosy pink. The deep-turquoise patches in the clear waters are coral heads, but the beach isn't good for snorkeling because of the presence of spotted sharks. Tall sea wheat or sea grass sprouts up from the sand. Off mile marker no. 24 on the main road, you can pick your way to the **Chicago Herald Columbus Monument** (p. 262).

Scuba divers flock to this remote island, as it's a major destination with some 40 dive sites that lie no more than 45 minutes by boat from either of the two resorts. A major attraction here is **wall diving**—diving where the sloping shoreline suddenly drops off and plummets to the ocean depths.

The Riding Rock Dive Center, associated with Riding Rock Inn and its twin dive boats, *Guanahani I* and *II* (© **242/331-2631**), offers dive packages as well as snorkeling, fishing, and boating trips. Divers can book an 8-day, 7-night getaway package year-round that costs from $1,462 per diver, including meals, transportation, dives, and rental gear. Prices are based on double occupancy. **Club Med Columbus Isle** should really be called an *almost*-all-inclusive resort because scuba diving is not covered by its rates. Diving courses at the resort run around $250, while certification courses are $475. A one-tank dive costs $80 and a two-tank $125.

With so many unspoiled and unpopulated kilometers of coastline, this area is ideal for swimming, shelling, and, of course, snorkeling. If you stay here a week, you've only begun to explore the possibilities. Places such as **Bamboo Point, Fernandez Bay,** and **Long Bay** all lie within a few miles of the main settlement of Cockburn Town on the island's more tranquil western side. At the southern tip of San Salvador are some of our favorite places for snorkeling: **Sandy Point** and nearby **Grotto Bay,** which has fine elkhorn coral reefs. Another wonderful spot for snorkeling is the wreck of the **SS *Frascate,*** which ran aground on January 1, 1902. Filled with such marine life as moray eels and grouper, it ranks as the area's best shallow wreck for snorkeling. Find it on the west coast, directly north of Riding Rock Inn.

Fishermen test their skill against blue marlin, yellowfin tuna, and wahoo on **fishing** trips, which you can arrange through Riding Rock Inn. The excursions run around $600 for a half-day and $900 for a full day. Bonefishermen enjoy **Pigeon Creek,** where some record catches have been chalked up. Rent a boat from a local or get your hotel to set you up.

Tennis players can head to Club Med, which offers 10 courts (3 lit for night play) that are open to nonguests who buy a day pass. Riding Rock Inn also has one (often empty) court.

Exploring the Island
COCKBURN TOWN

San Salvador's capital, Cockburn (pronounced "*Co*-burn") Town, is a harbor village that takes its name from George Cockburn, said to have been the first royal governor of The Bahamas to visit this remote island (he stopped by in 1823). Look for the town's landmark: a giant almond tree. Major San Salvador events, like the Columbus Day parade held every October 12, generally take place here.

Holy Saviour Roman Catholic Church   The New World's very first Christian worship service was Catholic. It thus seems fitting that the Roman Catholic Diocese of The Bahamas dedicated a new church on San Salvador in 1992, on the eve of the 500th anniversary of the Columbus landfall.

Cockburn Town. Free admission. Services Sun 10am.

New World Museum   This museum, 5.5km (3½ miles) north of Riding Rock Inn, has relics dating from pre-European times, but if you want to go inside you'll have to ask around until you find someone with a key. The museum lies just past Bonefish Bay in the little village of North Victoria Hill. Part of a large estate called Polaris-by-the-Sea, it's owned by a Columbus expert named Ruth Durlacher Wolper Malvin.

North Victoria Hill. No phone. Free admission. Open anytime during the day.

COMMEMORATING COLUMBUS & MORE

For such a small island, San Salvador offers a great deal of history as well as some sights that merit a look. Rent a bike, hire a taxi, or start walking, and see how many of the **Christopher Columbus monuments** you can hit. All of them are meant to mark the place where Columbus and his crew supposedly anchored the *Nina, Pinta,* and *Santa Maria* early that morning in 1492. Note that except for the party people at Club Med, San Salvador is mainly visited by the boating set, who live aboard their watercraft. If you're exploring for the day, you might come across one or two local cafes that serve seafood.

Just south of Cockburn Town, the **Tappan Monument,** a small four-sided stone pillar, stands on the beach at **Fernandez Bay** (mile marker no. 5 on the main road). The Tappan gas company embedded this monument here in 1951 in honor of Columbus.

The **Chicago Herald Monument** is located on the east coast at mile marker no. 24. To reach it, turn off the main road and drive 1.6 km (1 mile) to **East Beach.** Unless you meet a resident who can give you a ride in a four-wheel-drive car, you have to get out and walk. Turn right and hike 3km (1¾ miles) parallel to the beach until the sandy road ends. You'll see a cave to the left, at the water's edge. Follow the path to the right. Cupped by vegetation, a stone structure lies on the slice of land between the ocean and the bay. Although many historians dispute the claim, the marble plaque boasts, "On this spot Christopher Columbus first set foot upon the soil of the New World, erected by the *Chicago Herald,* June 1891." The only problem with the monument's claim is that the treacherous reefs here make this a dangerous—and thus highly unlikely—landing spot.

At Long Bay, the **Olympic Games Memorial** to Columbus, located 5km (3 miles) south of Cockburn Town, was erected in 1968 to commemorate the games in Mexico. Runners carrying an Olympic torch circled the island before coming to rest at the monument and lighting the torch there. The torch was then taken to Mexico on a warship. Another marker is underwater, supposedly where Columbus dropped the anchor of the *Santa Maria.*

Just north of the Olympic Games Memorial stands the **Columbus Monument.** On December 25, 1956, Ruth Durlacher Wolper Malvin—a leading U.S. expert on Columbus—established a simple monument commemorating the explorer's landfall in the New World. Unlike the spot marked by the *Chicago Herald* monument, this is actually likely to be the place where Columbus and his men landed.

Among the settlements on San Salvador are Sugar Loaf, Pigeon Creek, Old Place, Holiday Track, and Fortune Hill. **United Estates,** which has the largest population, is a village in the northwest corner near the Dixon Hill Lighthouse. The U.S. Coast Guard has a station at the island's northern tip.

In the northeastern portion of the island, **Dixon Hill Lighthouse,** built in 1856, sends out an intense beam two times every 25 seconds. This signal is visible for 31km (19 miles). The oil-using lighthouse rises about 50m (164 ft.) into the sky, and the keeper still operates it by hand. For permission to climb to the top, just knock on the keeper's door; he's almost always in the neighboring house.

After huffing and puffing your way up, you'll be surprised to see how tiny the source of light actually is. From the top of the lighthouse, take in the panoramic view of San Salvador's inland lakes, distant Crab Cay, and the surrounding islets. Ask the lighthouse keeper to show you the **inspector's log,** which has signatures dating back to Queen Victoria's reign. Be sure to leave at least a $1 donation when you sign the guestbook on your way out. The lighthouse is about a 30-minute taxi ride from Riding Rock Inn and Club Med.

At French Bay, **Watling's Castle,** also known as Sandy Point Estate, has substantial ruins that are about 26m (85 ft.) above sea level. The area is located some 4km (2½ miles) from the large lake on the southwestern tip of the island. Local "experts" will tell you all about the castle and its history. The only problem is that each one we've listened to (three in all, at different times) has told us a different story about the place. Ask around and perhaps you'll get yet another version; they're entertaining, at least. One of the most common legends involves a pirate who made a living either by salvaging wreckage from foundered ships or by attacking ships for their spoils.

Once upon a time, plantations—all doomed to failure—were scattered about the island. The most impressive and best-known ruins of one are at **Farquharson's Plantation,** west of Queen's Highway, near South Victoria Hill. In the early 19th century, some Loyalist families moved from the newly established United States to this island, hoping to get rich from farmland tended by slave labor. That plan collapsed when the United Kingdom Emancipation Act freed the slaves in 1834. The plantation owners moved on, but the former slaves stayed behind. A relic of those times, Farquharson's Plantation is where you can see the foundation of a great house, a kitchen, and what is believed to have been a jail. People locally call it "Blackbeard's Castle," but it's a remnant of slavery, not piracy.

San Salvador After Dark

Club Med (p. 258), just north of Cockburn Town, keeps its guests entertained every night, with musical revues and shows starring the vacationers themselves. At **Riding Rock Inn** (p. 260), also north of Cockburn Town, the Wednesday-night barbecue features reggae music, and many locals come to party. The hotel's **Driftwood Bar** is hot on Friday nights. If you're still game for some fun after the lodgings' festivities, head to **Harlem Square Bar,** in Cockburn Town (© **242/331-2777**). This friendly place is open daily from 7am "until food runs out."

Rum Cay & Conception Island

Where on earth is **Rum Cay?** Even many Bahamians have never heard of it. It's between San Salvador and Long Island, and is another cay, like Fortune Island (p. 273), that time forgot.

That wasn't always the case, though. The very name conjures up images of swashbucklers and rumrunners. Doubtless, it was at least a port of call for those dubious seafarers, as it was for ships that took on supplies of salt, fresh water, and food before crossing the Atlantic or going south to Latin America. The cay's name is supposedly derived from a rum-laden sailing ship that wrecked upon its shores.

Like many other Bahamian islands, Rum Cay once attracted British Loyalists fleeing the new United States. They hoped to establish themselves here as farmers and plantation overlords, but even those brave and homeless immigrants abandoned the island as unproductive. Salt mines were the mainstay of the island's economy before they were wiped out by a hurricane at the turn of the 19th century. After that, most of the inhabitants migrated to Nassau; by the 1970s, Rum Cay's population stood at "80 souls." Today, most of Rum Cay's 100 or so inhabitants live at **Port Nelson,** the island's capital.

The well-known underwater cinematographer Stan Waterman once described Rum Cay as the "unspoiled diving jewel of The Bahamas." For that reason, a diving club was opened here in 1983, but it closed, regrettably, in 1990.

Some maintain that Rum Cay was the next island where Columbus landed after he found and named San Salvador. He dubbed that second spot Santa María de la Concepción. However, many students of history and navigation believe that Columbus made his second landfall at what is today called **Conception Island,** which lies northwest of Rum Cay and northeast of Long Island. To get here, you'll have to travel via private boat.

Joseph Judge, a writer whose articles have appeared in *National Geographic,* believes that neither Rum Cay nor Conception was Columbus's second stop. He holds that, based on modern computer science and oceanography, the island the discoverer named Santa María de la Concepción has to be what's now called Crooked Island.

Still, the uninhabited Conception Island is under the protection of The Bahamas National Trust, which preserves it as a national park; it's a sanctuary for migratory birds. The most secretive scuba divers know of excellent dive sites here, and endangered green turtles use the beaches as egg-laying sites. Park rules are strict about prohibiting littering and removing any plant or animal life—so don't do it.

With the Rum Cay Club's demise, tourist traffic to the island came to a halt except for the odd yachting party or two. It's gaining renewed interest, however, and you can arrange for boaters on San Salvador to take you to see Rum Cay and Conception, which remain frozen in time.

LONG ISLAND

Most historians agree that Long Island was the third island Columbus sailed to during his first voyage of discovery. The Tropic of Cancer runs through this long, thin sliver of land, located 242km (150 miles) southeast of Nassau. It stretches north to south for some 97km (60 miles) and is 2.5km (1½ miles) wide on average, and only 5km (3 miles) wide at its broadest point. Long Island is characterized by high cliffs in the north, wide and shallow sand beaches, historic plantation ruins, native caves, and Spanish churches. The famed **diving sites ★** are offshore, including a blue hole of stunning magnitude that locals claim is bottomless.

Long Island's best beaches include **Deal's Beach, Cape Santa Maria Beach, Salt Pond Beach, Turtle Cove Beach,** and the **South End beaches,** the latter offering kilometers of waterfront scenery with powdery white or pink sands. Only recently has the island emerged as a minor tourist destination.

Long Island Essentials

GETTING THERE   There are two airstrips on Long Island. The **Stella Maris Airport** is in the north, and the other, called **Deadman's Cay Airport,** is in the south, north of Clarence Town. Be warned that it's important to know the location of your hotel on Long Island, since it's an expensive cab ride if you get off at the wrong airport. **Bahamasair** (© **800/222-4262** in the U.S.; www.bahamasair.com) flies once or twice a day from Nassau to Deadman's Cay. **Southern Air** (℗ 212/338-2095; www.southernaircharter.com) flies into both Stella Maris and Deadman's Cay from Nassau once or twice a day, depending on the day of the week and the season, and **Pineapple Air** (℗ 242/338-2070; www.pineappleair.com) flies to both of the island's airports from Nassau several times a week.

The mail boat **MV *Mia Dean*** sails every Tuesday, sometime in the late afternoon from Nassau to Clarence Town, a grueling journey of between 11 and 14 hours, depending on the weather and the season. Another mail boat, the MV *Island Link*, also departs from Nassau every Tuesday afternoon for Long Island's Salt Pond, arriving the next morning, very early, after a 12-hour trip. For information on mail-boat trips, contact the dock master at Nassau's **Potter's Cay Dock** (℗ 242/393-1064).

GETTING AROUND   The **Stella Maris Resort Club** (℗ 242/338-2051; www.stellamarisresort.com) can arrange to have you picked up at the airport upon arrival or get you a rental car. Otherwise, you can contact **Seagrape Jeep Rentals** (℗ 242/337-0249), **Allie's Car Rentals** (℗ 242/338-6036), or **Stan's Car Rental** (℗ 242/338-8987). Rental cars here are set up rather informally, with a car materializing unexpectedly, often culled from vehicles otherwise belonging to local residents willing to rent their family vehicles to someone from off-island. Rates usually run from around $65 to $85 a day.

[FastFACTS] LONG ISLAND

There's a local branch of the **Bahamas Tourist Office,** open intermittently, in the hamlet of Deals (℗ 242/338-8668). The **Bank of Nova Scotia** (℗ 242/338-2000) and the **Royal Bank of Canada** (℗ 242/337-0100) each maintain ATMs in Deadman's Cay. Hours of both facilities are Monday to Thursday from 9am to 1pm, Friday 9:30am to 3pm.

The **police** can be reached by calling ℗ 242/337-0999 or 337-0444.

SPECIAL EVENTS   In May or June, Long Island sailors participate in the big event of the year, the 4-day **Long Island Regatta,** held annually at Salt Pond since 1967. In addition to the highly competitive sailboat races, Long Island takes on a festive air with calypso music, reggae, and lots of drinking and partying. Many expatriate Long Islanders come home at this time, usually from Nassau, New York, or Miami, to enjoy not only the regatta, but also the rake 'n' scrape music. Call your local Bahamas Tourist Office (p. 298) for more information.

Where to Stay

Cape Santa Maria Beach Resort ★ ☺   This cozy nest has become the island's most luxurious resort, taking over the position long held by Stella Maris Resort Club (reviewed below). Two-room cottages are centered around a clubhouse, and the entire complex opens onto a stunning 6.5km (4-mile) strip of white sand. All units are only 18m (59 ft.) from the beach, where the snorkeling is great. Bedrooms have an airy, tropical feel, with marble floors and tasteful rattan furniture. As part of a multi-million-dollar development, the resort in 2006 added eight beachfront villas, each with luxury appointments such as jetted tubs and Internet service. There's also a screened-in porch with ceiling fans so you can enjoy the outdoors without the mosquitoes (the curse of the Southern Bahamas). The place is ideal for families, and several accommodations are configured so that children can have a separate bedroom. The hotel's 65-seat restaurant is also good, serving tasty Bahamian, North American, and seafood dishes.

Cape Santa Maria, off Queen's Hwy., Long Island, The Bahamas. www.capesantamaria.com. © **800/663-7090** or 242/338-5273. Fax 242/338-6013. 29 units. Winter $325 double, $795 2-bedroom villa; off-season $235 double, $595 2-bedroom villa. Breakfast and dinner $65 per person extra. Children 12 and under stay free in parent's room. AE, MC, V. Closed Sept–Oct. **Amenities:** Restaurant; bar; babysitting; bikes; exercise room; TV room; watersports equipment/rentals; Wi-Fi (free in TV room). *In room:* A/C, fridge, hair dryer, Internet (in villas), kitchen (in villas), no phone.

Chez Pierre ★ 🛅   Just south of the Tropic of Cancer, Montreal expats Pierre and Anne Laurence found their little bit of heaven on 3.2 hectares (8 acres) of land opening onto a wide crescent beach. Here they've built and attractively furnished a cluster of elevated bungalows overlooking the sea, each with a screened-in porch. A few steps from the beach cottages, an oceanfront restaurant serves the best food on the island. Dishes blend French, Italian, and Caribbean cuisines, incorporating island-grown produce along with fresh fish and seafood from local waters. This is the most eco-sensitive resort in the Southern Bahamas; it's powered by alternative energy, so the sun and wind keep it running. The location is halfway between Stella Maris and Deadman's Cay.

Simms, Long Island, The Bahamas. www.chezpierrebahamas.com. © **242/338-8809.** 6 units. Year-round $155 double. Rates include breakfast and dinner. AE, MC, V. **Amenities:** Restaurant; bar; babysitting; bikes; watersports equipment/rental; Wi-Fi (free). *In room:* Ceiling fan, no phone.

Gems at Paradise ★   This 6.5-hectare (16-acre) complex stands on a hill that opens onto a pink beach and the bay at Clarence Town's harbor. Lying just south of town, the hotel is owned by Shavonne Darville, who welcomes guests to her pristine little lodging. In such a faraway place, you'll discover quality furnishings, upmarket decorative accessories, art, Italian tiles, and stained woodwork. In addition to its array of attractively furnished suites and hotel rooms, one- and two-bedroom condos are available. Some of the suites open onto balconies, as do all the condos. There's no restaurant on-site, but the hotel will arrange the services of a local cook who will prepare meals for any resident who wants them.

Clarence Town, Long Island, The Bahamas. www.gemsatparadise.com. © **242/337-3016.** Fax 242/337-3021. 10 units. Year-round $130–$170 suite; $210 1-bedroom condo; $265 2-bedroom condo. AE, MC, V. **Amenities:** Bar; watersports equipment/rental; Wi-Fi (free in lobby). *In room:* A/C, TV, kitchen (in some), no phone.

Lochabar Beach Lodge   One of the most remote retreats listed in this guide, this lodge offers escapist studios for those fleeing the civilized world. You step from your studio to a pristine beach 23m (75 ft.) away, surrounding a blue hole in a natural cove. The only acceptable lodgings in the southern part of Long Island, these guest studios measure either 56 or 111 sq. m (603/1,195 sq. ft.) each. In lieu of ceiling fans, the studios were built to take advantage of the trade winds—just keep the Bahama shutters and double screen doors open to capture those breezes. If you like, a staff member will drive you to a nearby store to stock up on provisions.

Big Blue Hole, 1.6km (1 mile) south of Clarence Town, Long Island, The Bahamas. www.bahamas vacationguide.com/lochabarbeachlodge. © **242/337-3123.** Fax 242/337-6556. 3 units. Year-round $138–$180 double. Extra person $20. MC, V. **Amenities:** Watersports equipment/rentals. *In room:* A/C, TV, kitchenette, no phone.

Long Island Breeze Resort and Yacht Club ★   Built in 2008, with plans for the eventual construction of a marina, the full scale of this resort's business plan has

not yet fully manifested itself. Even so, it's now a prominent, well-respected establishment in the center of the hamlet of Salt Pond, midway up the length of Long Island, at its narrowest point. Accommodations, which evoke an unpretentious waterfront motel in Florida, are well-scrubbed and practical, set within a cluster of concrete-sided cottages and a three-story building that resembles an apartment complex, all compactly arranged around a sea-fronting deck with a freshwater pool and a gazebo overlooking two piers and the sea. There's a restaurant on-site, and, a simple bar as well.

Queen's Highway, Salt Pond, Long Island, The Bahamas. www.longislandbreezeresort.com. (C) **242/338-0170.** Fax 242/338-0172 Year-round $75–$200 double; price increases of between 30% and 50% during regattas. AE, MC, V. Closed Sept–Oct. **Amenities:** Restaurant; bar. *In-room:* A/C, TV/DVD, fridge, kitchen (in some), no phone.

Stella Maris Resort Club ★   Situated on a ridge overlooking the Atlantic, this durable and well-established resort, the most famous on Long Island, stands in a palm grove on the grounds of the old Adderley's Plantation. Though you can swim here, the beach isn't the best, so the hotel maintains a cabana at Cape Santa Maria, a gorgeous beach directly north, and offers shuttle service for its guests. Accommodations vary widely, ranging from rooms, studios, and apartments to cottages with one to four bedrooms. Each type of unit has its own walk-in closet and fully equipped bathroom; some are located directly on the water. All of the buildings, including the cottages and bungalows, are set around a central clubhouse and a trio of pools. The resort makes a great honeymoon destination; everything is relaxed and informal.

The on-site restaurant serves good Bahamian cuisine, as well as continental specialties. There are rum-punch parties, cave parties, barbecue dinners, Saturday dinners, dancing—and complete diving facilities. Divers and snorkelers can choose from coral-head, reef, and drop-off sites along the island's protected west coast, north side, and all along the east coast, as well as around Conception Island and Rum Cay. Water-skiing, as well as bottom- and reef fishing, are also offered; there are three good bonefishing bays nearby. Hotel guests can use the 3.5m (11-ft.) Scorpion and Sunfish sailboats at no cost.

Ocean View Dr., Long Island, The Bahamas. www.stellamarisresort.com. (C) **800/426-0466** or 242/338-2051; 954/359-8236 for the Fort Lauderdale booking office. Fax 242/338-2052. 47 units. Winter $195 double, $240 1-bedroom cottage, $360 2-bedroom bungalow, $590–$690 3-bedroom villa; off-season $180 double, $215 1-bedroom cottage, $330 2-bedroom bungalow, $555–$655 3-bedroom villa. Children 7 and under stay free in parent's room. AE, MC, V. **Amenities:** Restaurant; bar; bikes; 3 outdoor pools; watersports equipment/rentals. *In room:* A/C, fridge, hair dryer, kitchen (in some), no phone, Wi-Fi (free).

Where to Eat

Most of the inns listed above serve food, but you should call ahead for a reservation. One of our favorite stops is a little roadside dive called **Max's Conch Grill,** Deadman's Cay ((C) **242/337-0056**), which also serves some of the island's best conch. Daily specials are posted. Lunch platters range from $9 to $14, with dinners going for $12 to $22.

Another restaurant of note is the dining facilities within the previously recommended **Chez Pierre** (p. 266).

The Forest BAHAMIAN   Set beside the highway within a wood-built cottage with a wide outdoor deck and a thatched roof, this restaurant is one of the busiest all-Bahamian restaurants on Deadman's Cay. Its owner and founder, Dudley Dean, named it after its isolated position ("in the forest") near the airport, away from view of any of the Cay's other settlements. Come here for simple but flavorful versions of grouper fingers, burgers, cracked conch, barbecued chicken or pork ribs, and other foods that locals remember, usually with fondness, from their childhoods.

Queen's Highway, a 2-minute drive south of Deadman's Cay Airport. ℰ **242/337-1246.** Lunch main courses $6–$12; dinner main courses $10–$14. No credit cards. Mon–Sat 11am–9pm.

Fishing, Scuba Diving & Other Watersports

Many savvy anglers come to Long Island to fish, eschewing more famous places such as Andros and Bimini. The secret of good fishing here: the major North Equatorial Current, which originates in the Canary Islands and washes Long Island's shores. The current transports huge schools of blue marlin, white marlin, sailfish, rainbow runners, yellowfin tuna, blackfin tuna, wahoo, and dolphinfish. Wahoo is best hunted from September through November. Catches weigh from 4.5 to 41kg (10–90 lb.), and some yellowfin have weighed up to 68kg (150 lb.). The small blackfin tuna (July–Dec) weigh from 4.5 to 14kg (10–31 lb.). In addition, there are miles worth of reef fishing, with hundreds of species including snapper or grouper that have been known to weigh 45kg (99 lb.). A jewfish caught here weighed 226kg (498 lb.). In-shore fishing for bonefish is also possible.

Though there are no watersports outfitters on Long Island, the two major resorts, **Stella Maris Resort Club** (p. 267) and **Cape Santa Maria Beach Resort** (p. 265), fill the void and offer more watersports than you can do in a week. Bonefishing goes at a rate of $575 per day for four to five people, reef fishing costs from $680 per day for six to eight people, and deep-sea fishing is $950 per day for up to six people.

Snorkeling off the beach is complimentary at both resorts. However, snorkeling excursions from a boat usually cost around $25 per hour at either resort. Both also offer scuba diving at a cost of $110 per person per day, and equipment can be rented on-site. Both resorts also offer kayaks, windsurfers, Hobie Cats, and bicycles.

Exploring the Island

Most islanders live at the unattractively named **Deadman's Cay.** Other settlements have equally colorful names: Newfound Harbour, Burnt Ground, Indian Head Point, and, at the island's northern tip, Cape Santa Maria, generally believed to be where Columbus landed and from where he looked on the Exumas (islands that he did not visit). Our favorite name, however, is Hard Bargain, located 16km (10 miles) south of Clarence Town. No one seems to know how this place (now a shrimp-breeding farm) got its name.

Two underground sites that can be visited on Deadman's Cay are **Dunmore's Caves** and **Deadman's Cay Cave.** You'll need to hire a local guide to explore these. Dunmore's Caves are believed to have been inhabited by Lucayans and later to have served as a hideaway for buccaneers. The cave at Deadman's Cay, one of two that lead to the ocean, has never been fully explored. There are two designs that were chiseled into the cavern wall by long-ago islanders.

Try to visit **Clarence Town ★**, 16km (10 miles) south of Deadman's Cay along the eastern coastline. It was here that Father Jerome, the priest who became known as the islands' "father confessor," built two churches before his death in 1956: **St. Paul's,** an Anglican house of worship, and **St. Peter's,** a Roman Catholic church. The "hermit" of Cat Island (you can visit his Hermitage there; p. 257) was interested

RAGGED ISLAND & jumento cays

This, the most remote territory recommended in this guidebook, might come under the classification of "faraway places with strange-sounding names." The area is visited by very few tourists, except for stray people who come in on yachts.

The thing that's truly memorable here is the sunset, which, except in the rare times when clouds obscure the sky and the horizon, bursts forth in some of the most spectacular shades of gold, purple, red, and orange—and sometimes with a green flash reflecting in the crystal-clear waters.

This island group, a mini archipelago, begins with Jumento Cays off the west point of Long Island and runs in a half-moon shape for some 161km (100 miles) down to Ragged Island; Little Ragged Island is the southernmost bit of land at the bottom of the crescent. They comprise the southeastern limit of the Great Bahama Bank.

Ragged Island and its string of uninhabited cays are the backwaters of The Bahamas, since most of them are so tiny and so unimportant they don't often appear on maps. However, visitors who return from this area talk of the remarkable beauty of these little pieces of land and coral.

Sailing in this area in bad weather is dangerous because of the unrelenting winds. Otherwise, the cays would be better known among the boating crowd.

In summer it's usually a good place to cruise the waters.

Like nearly all the islands in this chapter, Ragged Island knew greater prosperity when hundreds of inhabitants worked its salt flats. Today Duncan Town, the little hamlet still standing on the island, is all that's left of the island's better days. Its people are hardworking and weather-beaten, and many have a difficult time making a living. Nassau seems to have forgotten this outpost of the nation.

Some of the little cays, from Jumento Cay around the semicircle toward Ragged Island, have names such as No Bush Cay, Dead Cay, Sisters Cay, Nurse Cay, Double-Breasted Cay, and Hog Cay. There's a Raccoon Cay, as well as a Raccoon Cut. A light tower stands on Flamingo Cay.

Visitors are so rare that anybody's arrival is treated as an event, and the townspeople are eager to help in any way they can. There's a 914m (3,000-ft.) paved airstrip here, but it's only accessible to private planes, so it's not used much.

A mail boat leaves Potter's Cay in Nassau on Tuesday at 5pm en route to Ragged Island, for $55 one-way. It returns on Thursday. For details about costs and sailing, contact the dockmaster at Potter's Cay Dock, Nassau (✆ 242/393-1064).

Regrettably, there are no hotel facilities.

in Gothic architecture. He must also have been somewhat ecumenical because he started his ministry as an Anglican but embraced Roman Catholicism along the way.

Many ruins recall the days when local plantation owners figured their wealth in slaves and cotton. The remains of **Dunmore's Plantation,** at Deadman's Cay, stand on a hill surrounded by the sea on three sides. There are six gateposts (four outer and two inner), as well as a house with two fireplaces and wall drawings of ships. At the base of the ruins is evidence that a mill wheel was once used here. The property was part of the estate of Lord Dunmore, for whom Dunmore Town on Harbour Island was named.

In the village of Gray's stand the ruins of **Gray's Plantation,** where you'll see the remnants of at least three houses, one with two chimneys. One was very large, while the other seems to have been a one-story structure with a cellar.

Adderley's Plantation, off Cape Santa Maria, originally occupied all the land now known as Stella Maris. The ruins at this cotton plantation comprise three structures that are partially intact but roofless.

ACKLINS ISLAND & CROOKED ISLAND

These little tropical islands, approximately 386km (240 miles) southeast of Nassau, make up an undiscovered Bahamian frontier outpost. Columbus came this way looking for gold. Much later, Acklins Island, Crooked Island, and their surrounding cays became hideouts for pirates who attacked vessels in the Crooked Island Passage (the narrow waterway Columbus sailed), which separates the two islands. Today a well-known landmark, the **Crooked Island Passage Light,** built in 1876, guides ships to a safe voyage through the slot. Also known as the **Bird Rock Lighthouse,** it is a popular nesting spot for ospreys, and the light still lures pilots and sailors to the **Pittstown Point Landing Resort.** A barrier reef begins near the lighthouse, stretching down off Acklins Island for about 40km (25 miles) to the southeast.

Although Acklins Island and Crooked Island are separate, they are usually mentioned as a unit because of their proximity to each other. Together, the two islands form the shape of a boomerang. Crooked Island, the northern one, is 181 sq. km (70 sq. miles) in area, whereas Acklins Island, to the south, occupies 311 sq. km (120 sq. miles). Both islands, which have good white-sand beaches and offer fishing and scuba diving, are inhabited mainly by fishermen and farmers.

In his controversial 1986 article in *National Geographic,* Joseph Judge identified Crooked Island as the site of Columbus's second island landing—the one the explorer called Santa María de la Concepción. Scholars are still arguing over the matter today.

Estimates say that by the end of the 18th century, more than three dozen working plantations were on these islands, begun by Loyalists fleeing mainland North America in the wake of the Revolutionary War. At the peak plantation period, there could have been as many as 1,200 slaves laboring in 3,000 acres of cotton fields, which were later wiped out by a blight. The people who remained on the island survived not only by fishing and farming, but also, beginning in the mid–18th century, by stripping the Croton cascarilla shrub of its bark to produce the flavoring for Campari liquor.

Acklins Island & Crooked Island Essentials

GETTING THERE   There's an airport at **Colonel Hill** on Crooked Island, and another airstrip at **Spring Point** on Acklins Island. **Bahamasair** (© **800/222-4262** in the U.S.; www.bahamasair.com) operates two flights a week from Nassau, on Wednesday and Saturday, to Crooked Island and Acklins Island, with returns to Nassau scheduled on the same day. Also from Nassau, **Pineapple Air** (© **242/338-2070;** www.pineappleair.com) operates twice-weekly flights (every Monday and Friday).

Mail-boat service on the **MV *United Star*** leaves Nassau, usually either late Monday night or early Tuesday morning, and heads for Acklins Island, Crooked Island, and Fortune Island (Long Cay) three times a month. Check the schedule and costs with the dock master at Nassau's **Potter's Cay Dock** (© **242/393-1064**).

GETTING AROUND   A government-owned **ferry** connects the two islands, linking Lovely Bay on Acklins Island with Brown's on Crooked Island. It operates six times a day, about every 90 minutes from 8:30am to 4pm; passage is free.

Once you arrive at Crooked Island, **taxi** service is available, but it's wise to advise your hotel in advance of your arrival—they'll probably send a van to meet you.

[FastFACTS] ACKLINS ISLAND & CROOKED ISLAND

There are several government-operated **medical clinics.** Phones are scarce on the islands, but your hotel desk can reach one of these clinics by going through the local operator. The clinic on Acklins Island is at Spring Point (✆ **242/344-3172**), while the clinic on Crooked Island is at Landrail Point (✆ **242/344-2166**).

The **police** on both Acklins Island and Crooked Island can be reached by dialing ✆ **242/344-2599.**

For more information, check www.crookedisland.biz.

Where to Stay & Eat

Casuarina Pine Villas   A cottage by the beach or oceanfront sounds idyllic, doesn't it? Okay, these are basic motel caliber at best, but well maintained and reasonably comfortable in this remote part of the Americas. The property opens onto half a mile of pristine sands lying between Pittstown Point Landing and Landrail Point. All of the cottages come with fully equipped kitchens and little verandas or decks facing westward. If you give the office sufficient notice, a Bahamian cook can prepare a dinner to be delivered to your door (wait until you try those pies). Snorkeling and scuba diving can be arranged, as can a rental car or fishing guide. At Landrail Point, you'll have such conveniences as a restaurant, gas station, and local market, which comes in handy if you want to cook in your cottage.

Landrail Point, Crooked Island, The Bahamas. ✆ **242/344-2036.** Fax 242/344-2525. 6 units. Year-round $135 1-bedroom cottage for 2 occupants; $220 2-bedroom cottage for 3–4 occupants. No credit cards. **Amenities:** Meals on request; watersports/equipment rentals. *In room:* A/C, TV, kitchen, no phone.

Crooked Island Lodge at Pittstown Point ★ 📖   Located on a beach at Crooked Island's extreme northwestern tip, this hotel is so isolated that you'll forget all about the world outside. For most of its early years, it was a well-guarded secret shared mostly by the owners of private planes who flew in from mainland Florida for off-the-record weekends. Even today, about 50% of the clientele arrives by one- or two-engine aircraft that they fly themselves as part of island-hopping jaunts around The Bahamas. The resort maintains its own 610m (2,001-ft.) hard-surface landing strip, which is independent from the one used for the flights from Nassau on Bahamasair or Pineapple Air.

Surrounded by scrub-covered landscape at the edge of a turquoise sea, Crooked Island Lodge lies 4km (2½ miles) north of Landrail Point (pop. 50) on a sandy peninsula. Within easy access are some of the weirdest historic sites in The Bahamas, including the sunbaked ruins of a salt farm, Marine Farms Fortress, which was sacked by U.S.-based pirates in 1812.

Spartan accommodations occupy three low-slung, cement-sided buildings. They lie directly on the beach, usually with verandas facing the sea. Because of the constant trade winds, not all bedrooms have air-conditioning, but they do contain paddle-shaped ceiling fans. The entire resort shares only one telephone line, which is reserved for emergency calls. Guests usually opt for the full meal plan here. Repasts are served in a stone-sided building that was erected late in the 1600s as barracks for the British West Indies Naval Squadron and later served as the country's first post office. The restaurant serves seafood, as well as American and Bahamian specialties. You'll usually see a scattering of yacht owners or aviators who drop in spontaneously for drinks and dinner.

Landrail Point, Crooked Island, The Bahamas. www.pittstownpoint.com. ℭ **242/344-2507.** Fax 242/344-2573. 12 units. Year-round $245 double. Full meal plan $65 per person. MC, V. **Amenities:** Restaurant; bar; bikes; watersports equipment/rental; Wi-Fi (free in lobby). *In room:* A/C (in some), no phone.

Exploring a Pirate Hideout & More

Crooked Island opens onto the **Windward Passage,** the dividing point between the Caribbean Sea and The Bahamas. When Columbus landed at what is now **Pittstown Point,** he supposedly called it Fragrant Island because of the aroma of its many herbs. One scent was cascarilla bark, used to flavor Campari as well as the native Cascarilla liqueur, which is exported.

For the best view of the island, climb **Colonel Hill ★**—unless you arrived at Crooked Island Airport (also known as Colonel Hill Airport), which has the same vantage.

Guarding Crooked Island's north end is the **Marine Farms Fortress,** an abandoned British fort that saw action in the War of 1812. It looks out over Crooked Island Passage and can be visited (ask your hotel to make arrangements for you).

Hope Great House is also on the island, with orchards and gardens that date from the time of George V of England.

Other sights include **French Wells Bay,** a swampy delta leading to an extensive mangrove swamp rich in bird life, and the **Bird Rock Lighthouse** (also called the **Crooked Island Passage Light**), built a century ago.

At the southern end of Acklins Island lies **Castle Island,** a low bit of land where an 1867 lighthouse stands. Pirates used it as a hideout, sailing forth to attack ships in the nearby passage.

Acklins Island has many interestingly named villages—Binnacle Hill, Delectable Bay, Golden Grove, Goodwill, Hard Hill, Snug Corner, and Lovely Bay. Some Crooked Island sites have more ominous names, such as Gun Point and Cripple Hill.

MAYAGUANA ISLAND

The least visited Bahamian island, sleepy Mayaguana, across the Mayaguana Passage from Acklins Island and Crooked Island, seems to float adrift in the tropical sun at the remote extremities of the southeastern edge of The Bahamas, 564km (350 miles) southeast of Nassau. It occupies 285 sq. km (110 sq. miles) and has a population of about 300. It's a long, long way from the development of Nassau and Paradise Island.

Standing in the Windward Passage, Mayaguana is just northwest of the Turks and Caicos Islands. It's separated from the British Crown colony by the Caicos Passage. Around the time of the American Civil War, inhabitants of Turks Island began to settle in Mayaguana, which before then had dozed undisturbed for centuries.

Mayaguana is only 9.5km (6 miles) across at its widest point, and about 39km (24 miles) long. Its beaches are enticing, but you'll rarely see a tourist on them, other than

The Ghost Island of Fortune

Lying off the coast of Crooked Island, **Fortune Island** is truly a place that time forgot. Your hotel can put you in touch with a boater who will take you here. Experts believe, based on research done for *National Geographic,* that Fortune Island (sometimes confusingly called Long Cay) is the one Columbus chose to name Isabella, in honor of the queen who funded his expedition. Its only real settlement is **Albert Town,** which is classified as a ghost town but officially isn't—some hardy souls still live here. **Fortune Hill,** visible from 19km (12 miles) away at sea, is the local landmark. Hundreds of Bahamians came here in the 2 decades before World War I, waiting to be picked up by oceangoing freighters, which would take them to seek their fortunes as laborers in Central America—hence the name Fortune Hill.

the occasional German. A few developers have flown in to check out the island, but to date, no new development has occurred.

Summer brings rain to Mayaguana. Combined with the heat and mosquitoes, it can get a little rough here. However, summer is also the best time to go fishing.

Getting There

Bahamasair (✆ 800/222-4262 in the U.S.; www.bahamasair.com) flies in from Nassau three times a week (every Monday, Wednesday, and Friday at around 9:15am); the trip takes approximately 1½ hours.

Mail-boat service on the **MV *Lady Mathilda*** leaves Nassau and heads for Acklins Island, Crooked Island, Fortune Island (Long Cay), and Mayaguana Island each week as part of a slow and meandering journey that takes at least 2 days, with many delays and interruptions en route. Check the schedule and costs with the dock master at Nassau's **Potter's Cay Dock** (✆ 242/393-1064).

Where to Stay & Eat

Few other outposts in The Bahamas are as remote as Mayaguana, which is the main reason many visitors come—to get away from everything. Tourists arrive by boat and just ask around for availability at one of the ultra-simple lodgings here. Some locals are willing to house you in one of their spare bedrooms for a rate that can be negotiated up or down to almost anything.

Baycaner Beach Resort In operation since 1996, this is the island's only hotel that can even lay a claim to being that. Its owner, Ernal Brown, is called "Shorty" by all the locals, and he's the man to see if you're one of the rare visitors who ever makes it to this part of the world. You can literally jump from your simply furnished bedroom right into the water. Accommodations contain a comfortable bed, a scattering of wicker furnishings, an air-conditioner, and a small but well-maintained bathroom. The lobby adjoins the dining room and bar (the latter is popular with locals). You might have the dining room to yourself, however. Dig into that Bahamian staple of brown pigeon peas 'n' rice. Most meals feature conch—perhaps in a chowder or freshly made salad—and the inevitable grouper, the most popular fish caught here. The cook bakes fresh bread daily.

Pirate's Well, Mayaguana, The Bahamas. www.baycanerbeach.com. ✆ **242/339-3726.** Fax 242/339-3727. 16 units. Sept–Apr $143 double; May–Aug $122 double. MC, V. **Amenities:** Restaurant; bikes; room service; watersports equipment/rentals; Wi-Fi (free in lobby). *In room:* A/C, TV, no phone.

Exploring the Island

The south coast's main town is **Abraham's Bay,** which has an excellent harbor. The other little settlement on Mayaguana is **Betsy Bay,** secluded and lost in time. Wild corn and saucy hummingbirds share this spot along with some little sun-worn cottages. At **Pirate's Well,** goats are now the chief residents, although buccaneers used to roam past here. Locals still dream of finding buried treasure. The best views of the Mayaguana Passage can be had from both Betsy Bay and Pirate's Well.

Fishing is good on the island. Locals will often take you out on one of their boats, but you've got to ask around. In summer and early autumn, temperatures can soar beyond 100°F (38°C). Winters, however, are ideal, and it never gets cold here, as it can in the northern islands.

Mayaguana might be called the "great outback" or "wild west" of The Bahamas. It's a rugged, salty environment. Sailing, deep-sea fishing, scuba diving, snorkeling, swimming, and walking are the main pastimes. The island is still too laid-back to have many organized outfitters. If you want to rent gear or hire a guide for an organized outing, your best bet is to inquire at your hotel; the staff can usually hook you up with the right person.

GREAT INAGUA ★

The most southerly and the third-largest island of The Bahamas, flat **Great Inagua,** some 64km (40 miles) long and 32km (20 miles) wide, is home to 1,200 people. It lies 527km (327 miles) southeast of Nassau.

This is the site not only of the **Morton Salt Crystal Factory,** here since 1800, but also of one of the Western Hemisphere's largest nesting grounds for **flamingos.** The National Trust of The Bahamas protects the area around **Lake Windsor,** where the birds breed and the population is said to number 80,000. Flamingos used to inhabit all of The Bahamas, but the birds have disappeared from most other places. This reserve can be visited only with a guide. Besides the pink flamingo, you can see roseate spoonbills and other bird life.

Green turtles are also raised here, at **Union Creek Reserve,** and then released into the ocean to make their way as best they can; they, too, are an endangered species. (Tours of the reserve are not well organized, and the operation is very informal, but if you're here, inquire about getting a look.) This vast windward island, almost within sight of Cuba, is also inhabited by wild hogs, horses, and donkeys.

Matthew Town is the island's chief settlement, but it's not of any great sightseeing interest, though it does have an 1870 lighthouse. Other locales have interesting names, such as Doghead Point, Mutton Fish Point, and Devil's Point (which makes one wonder what happened there to inspire the name).

Little Inagua, 8km (5 miles) to the north, has no population and is just a speck of land off Great Inagua's northeast coast. About 78 sq. km (30 sq. miles) in area, it has much bird life, wild goats, and donkeys.

Great Inagua Essentials

GETTING THERE   The **Matthew Town Airport** is served by **Bahamasair** (© **800/222-4262** in the U.S.; www.bahamasair.com), which departs Nassau on Monday, Wednesday, and Friday mornings. Flight time is approximately 2 hours.

The mail boat **MV *United Star*** makes weekly trips from Nassau to Matthew Town. The schedule varies, so call the dock master at Nassau's **Potter's Cay Dock** (© **242/393-1064**) for details.

GETTING AROUND   **Taxis** meet incoming flights from Nassau. If you need a **rental car,** check with one of the guesthouses, but don't expect the vehicles to be well maintained.

[FastFACTS] GREAT INAGUA

The **Inagua Hospital** can be called at ☎ **242/339-1249.** The **police** can be reached at ☎ **242/339-1263.**

Where to Stay

The choices of accommodations aren't great on this island, but most visitors are willing to forgo comfort to see the spectacular flamingos.

The Main House   Life here is casual and completely informal. This hotel is owned by Morton Bahamas Ltd., the salt people, so its employees often fill up all the rooms. Only six bedrooms are rented, and the furnishings are extremely modest, though everything is perfectly clean. You can order breakfast or lunch here—but no dinner. Unfortunately, the property sits near a noisy power plant.

Kortwright St., Matthew Town, Inagua, The Bahamas. www.inaguamainhouse.com. ☎ **242/339-1267.** Fax 242/339-1265. 6 units. Year-round $60–$85 double. No credit cards. **Amenities:** Restaurant; Wi-Fi (free in lobby). *In room:* A/C, TV, fridge.

Where to Eat

Cozy Corner BAHAMIAN/AMERICAN   The most consistently reliable restaurant, besides those at the guesthouses and hotels, is this lime-green stone house 2 blocks from the sea. Menu items include a simple roster of mostly fried foods that are almost always accompanied by french fries. Dishes include fried conch, fried chicken, burgers, and "whopper burgers," plus whatever sort of fried seafood is available from local fishermen on the day of your visit. If you call ahead and make arrangements, the eatery might serve you a Bahamian dinner.

William St., Matthew Town. ☎ **242/339-1440.** Lunch and dinner items $8–$15. No credit cards. Mon–Sat 11am–10pm.

Exploring the Island: Pink Flamingos & More

The island's vast number of **pink flamingos** ★★★ outnumbers its human population by far. They're so plentiful on Inagua that some of them even roost on the runway of the island's airport, as well as at thousands of other locations throughout the flat, heat-blasted landscape.

Dedicated bird-watchers who are willing to forgo comfort usually trek inland to the edges of the many brackish lakes in the island's center. About half the island is national park land, and Inagua's most viable industry involves distilling salt from the local salt flats.

To see the birds at **Inagua National Park** ★★ is reason enough to come here. The best time to see the feathered beauties is from November until June. Everyone entering the park must be accompanied by a warden, and reservations and a day pass ($25 for adults, $10 for students) must be obtained in advance. Get the passes either through The Bahamas National Trust in Nassau (☎ **242/393-1317;** www.bnt.bs) or by contacting one of the local wardens, Henry Nixon (☎ **242/339-1616**). In addition to the park fee, you're expected to offer the wardens a large tip; the usual payment is about $50 per day.

One of the island's best panoramas can be taken in from **Southwest Point,** 2km (1¼ miles) south of Matthew Town. From here, you can see Cuba on a clear day—it lies just 81km (50 miles) west. The best view of Cuba comes from the top of the **Inagua Lighthouse,** which dates from 1870 and is one of a quartet of hand-operated kerosene lighthouses left in The Bahamas. The reefs off this point are treacherous, as many a captain has fatefully learned.

WITH salt, PLEASE

Salt means a great deal to Great Inagua—not only because of the Morton Salt Company's extensive operations (the company produces more than 1 million tons of salt each year), but also for the unique local wildlife.

First, seawater is pumped into the island's interior and held by dikes. Great Inagua's salt ponds, about 80 of them, cover some 4,856 hectares (12,000 acres). As the water evaporates, it turns into heavy brine. The salt solidifies at night and melts during the heat of the day, and a crystallized bed forms at the bottom of the pond. During the final stage, any remaining water is drained and the salt is bulldozed into bleached-white mountains and then shipped around the world for processing.

As the water evaporates from these salt ponds, brine shrimp concentrate, providing hearty meals for the island's colorful pink flamingos.

PLANNING YOUR TRIP TO THE BAHAMAS

Y ou can be in The Bahamas after a quick 35-minute jet hop from Miami. And it's never been easier to take advantage of great package deals that can make these islands a terrific value.

If your papers are in order, flying to The Bahamas is like flying to Florida if you live on the Eastern Seaboard. Unless you run into transportation delays because of bad weather, it should be no hassle at all before you land on a beach strip.

For additional help in planning your trip and for more on-the-ground resources in The Bahamas, please turn to "Fast Facts."

GETTING THERE

Getting to The Bahamas

Lying off the east coast of Florida, the archipelago of The Bahamas is the easiest and most convenient foreign destination Americans can fly to unless they live close to the Canadian or Mexican borders.

Nassau is the busiest and most popular point of entry (this is where you'll fly if you're staying on Paradise Island). From here, you can make connections to many of the more remote Out Islands. If you're headed for one of the Out Islands, refer to the "Getting There" section that appears at the beginning of each island's coverage earlier in this book for details. Freeport, on Grand Bahama, also has its own airport, which is served by flights from the U.S. mainland, too.

Flight time to Nassau from Miami is about 35 minutes; from New York, 2½ hours; from Atlanta, 2 hours and 5 minutes; from Philadelphia, 2 hours and 45 minutes; from Charlotte, 2 hours and 10 minutes; from central Florida, 1 hour and 10 minutes; and from Toronto, 3 hours.

BY PLANE

From the U.S. mainland, about a half-dozen carriers fly nonstop to the country's major point of entry and busiest airline hub, **Lynden Pindling International Airport** (© **242/702-1010;** www.nas.bs). Some also fly to the archipelago's second-most-populous city of Freeport. Only a handful (see below) fly directly to any of the Out Islands.

Don't forget security precautions when packing for your trip. All liquids and gels—including shampoo, toothpaste, perfume, hair gel, suntan lotion, and all other items with similar consistency—are limited to 3 ounces or less (all packed into a 1-quart bag) in carry-on baggage. Pack larger items in your checked baggage. Carrying liquids of any sort to the screening checkpoint will cause you delays and will most likely result in the item being confiscated.

With the ever-changing security measures, we recommend that you check the **Transportation Security Administration's** website, **www.tsa.gov**, as near to your departure date as possible to make sure that no other restrictions have been imposed.

American Airlines (© 800/433-7300; www.aa.com) has several flights per day from Miami to Nassau, as well as between four and five daily flights from Fort Lauderdale to Nassau. In addition, the carrier flies several times daily from Miami to Freeport. It also offers between two and three flights daily from Miami to George Town and as well as a daily flight from Miami to Marsh Harbour.

Delta (© 800/221-1212; www.delta.com) has several connections to The Bahamas, with service from Atlanta, Orlando, and New York's LaGuardia.

The national airline of The Bahamas, **Bahamasair** (© 800/222-4262 or 242/377-8451; www.bahamasair.com), flies to The Bahamas from Miami and Fort Lauderdale, landing at either Nassau (with seven nonstop flights daily) or Freeport (with at least two nonstop flights daily).

US Airways (© 800/428-4322; www.usairways.com) offers daily direct flights to Nassau from Philadelphia and Charlotte, North Carolina.

JetBlue (© 800/JET-BLUE [538-2583]; www.jetblue.com) has one direct flight daily to Nassau, from JFK in New York. In addition, JetBlue offers daily nonstop flights from Westchester County Airport in New York to Nassau, serving area residents in Westchester and Fairfield counties. This is the first international flight service ever offered out of Westchester County.

Other carriers include **United Airlines** (© 800/231-0856; www.united.com), which has greatly expanded its link to The Bahamas through South Florida through its regional affiliate, Silver Airways. United operates flights between Fort Lauderdale and Andros Town on Andros, with four round-trip flights each week. The airline also offers daily service from Fort Lauderdale to both George Town and Governor's Harbour. In addition, it maintains frequent links between Fort Lauderdale, Freeport, Marsh Harbour, North Eleuthera, and Treasure Cay. **Air Canada** (© 888/247-2262; www.aircanada.com) offers scheduled service to Nassau from Canada. Direct flights from Toronto and Montreal leave daily; other flights from Toronto and Montreal, as well as other Canadian cities, make connections in the U.S. **WestJet** (© 888/937-8538; www.westjet.com) provides daily nonstop flights from Toronto to Nassau and seasonally from Calgary. It also offers nonstop service to George Town, Exuma once a week on Sundays.

British travelers opt for transatlantic passage aboard **British Airways** (© 800/AIR-WAYS [247-9297] in the U.S. or 0844/493-0787 in the U.K.; www.britishairways.com), which offers four weekly direct flights from London to Nassau.

The airline also has at least one flight daily from London to Miami. From here, many connections are available to Nassau and many other points within the archipelago on several carriers.

FLYING TO THE OUT ISLANDS

Many frequent visitors to The Bahamas do everything they can to avoid the congestion, inconvenience, and uncertain connections of the Lynden Pindling International Airport in Nassau. A couple of U.S.-based airlines offer service directly to some of the Out Islands. **American Eagle** (© 800/433-7300; www.aa.com) offers frequent service from Miami International Airport to the Abacos, Eleuthera, and the Exumas. **US Airways** (© 800/428-4322; www.usairways.com) flies nonstop every day from Fort Lauderdale to Eleuthera, usually making stops at both Governor's Harbour and North Eleuthera. US Airways also flies every day from West Palm Beach to the Abacos, stopping in both Treasure Cay and Marsh Harbour.

Getting Around

If your final destination is Paradise Island, Freeport, or Nassau (Cable Beach) and you plan to fly, you'll have little trouble reaching your destination. However, if you're heading for one of the Out Islands, you face more exotic choices, not only of airplanes, but also of other means of transport, including a mail boat, the traditional connecting link in days of yore.

As mentioned, each section on one of the Out Island chains has specific transportation information, but here's a general overview.

BY PLANE

The national airline of The Bahamas, **Bahamasair** (© 800/222-4262; www.bahamasair.com), serves 17 airports on 10 Bahamian islands, including Abaco, Andros, Cat Island, and Eleuthera. Many of the Out Islands have either airports or airstrips, or are within a short ferry ride's distance of one. You can usually make connections to these smaller islands from Nassau.

BY RENTAL CAR

Many travelers don't really need to rent a car in The Bahamas, especially those who are coming for a few days of soaking in the sun at their resort's own beach. In Nassau and Freeport, you can easily rely on public transportation or taxis. In some of the Out Islands, there are a few car-rental companies, but most rental cars are unusually expensive and in poor condition (the roads are often in the same bad state as the rental cars).

Most visitors need transportation only from the airport to their hotel; perhaps you can arrange an island tour later, and an expensive private car won't be necessary. Your hotel can always arrange a taxi for you if you want to venture out.

You may decide that you want a car to explore beyond the tourist areas of New Providence Island, and you're very likely to want one on Grand Bahama Island.

Just remember: Road rules are much the same as those in the U.S. and Canada, but you *drive on the left.*

For the Out Islands, turn to the relevant "Getting Around" sections of those chapters to determine if you'll want a car (you may want one to explore on Eleuthera or Great Abaco Island); perhaps you'll stay put at your resort but rent a car for only 1 day of exploring.

The major car-rental companies operate in The Bahamas, but not on all the remote islands. We always prefer to do business with one of the major firms if they're present because you can call ahead and reserve from home via a toll-free number, they tend to offer better-maintained vehicles, and it's easier to resolve any disputes after the fact. Call **Budget** (© **800/472-3325;** www.budget.com), **Hertz** (© **800/654-3001;** www.hertz.com), **Dollar** (© **800/800-4000;** www.dollar.com), or **Avis** (© **800/331-1212;** www.avis.com). Budget rents in Nassau and Paradise Island. Liability insurance is compulsory.

"Petrol" is easily available in Nassau and Freeport, though quite expensive. In the Out Islands, where the cost of gasoline is likely to vary from island to island, you should plan your itinerary based on where you'll be able to get fuel. The major towns of the islands have service stations. You should have no problems on New Providence or Grand Bahama Island unless you start out with a nearly empty tank.

Visitors may drive with their home driver's license for up to 3 months. For longer stays, you'll need to secure a Bahamian driver's license.

BY TAXI

Once you've reached your destination, you'll find that taxis are plentiful in the Nassau/Cable Beach/Paradise Island area and in the Freeport/Lucaya area on Grand Bahama Island. These cabs, for the most part, are metered—but they take cash only, no credit cards. See "Getting Around" in the chapters on each island for further details.

In the Out Islands, however, it's not so easy. In general, taxi service is available at all air terminals, at least if those air terminals have "port of entry" status. They can also be hailed at most marinas.

Taxis are usually shared, often with the local residents. Out Island taxis aren't metered, so you must negotiate the fare before you get in. (Expect to pay a rate of around $30–$35 per hour.) Cars are often old and badly maintained, so be prepared for a bumpy ride over some rough roads if you've selected a particularly remote hotel.

BY MAIL BOAT

Before the advent of better airline connections, the traditional way of exploring the Out Islands—in fact, about the only way unless you had your own vessel—was by mail boat. This service is still available, but it's recommended only for those who have lots of time and a sense of adventure. You may ride with cases of rum, oil drums, live chickens, or even an occasional piano.

The boats—21 of them composing the "Post Office Navy" under the direction of the Bahamian Chief of Transportation—are often fancifully colored, high-sided, and somewhat clumsy in appearance, but the little motor vessels chug along, serving the 30 inhabited islands of The Bahamas. Schedules can be thrown off by weather and other causes, but most mornings mail boats depart from Potter's Cay (under the Paradise Island Bridge in Nassau) or from Prince George Wharf. The voyages last from 4½ hours to most of a day, sometimes even overnight. Check the schedule of the particular boat you wish to travel on with the skipper at the dock in Nassau.

This is a cheap way to go: The typical fare from Nassau to Marsh Harbour is $60 per person, one-way. Many of the boats offer two classes of passenger accommodations, first and second. In first class, you get a bunk bed; in second, you may be entitled only to deck space. (Actually, the bunk beds are usually reserved for the seasick, but first-class passengers on larger boats sit in a reasonably comfortable enclosed cabin.)

Delivering goats, chickens, hardware, and food staples along with the mail, Bahamian mail boats greatly improve the quality of life for the scattered communities of the Out Islands. You can book passage aboard these vessels to at least 17 different remote islands. All 21 of the boats leave from Nassau, and in many cases, the round-trip takes a full day. For more information, consult an office of **The Bahamas Tourist Office** (© **242/326-9781** or 326-9772; see "Visitor Information," later in this chapter) or ask the dock master at the Nassau piers (© **242/393-1064**).

For information about mail boats to the Out Islands, contact the **Dock Masters Office** in Nassau, under the Paradise Island Bridge on Potter's Cay (© 242/393-1064).

BY CHARTERED BOAT

For those who can afford it, this is the most luxurious way to see The Bahamas. On your private boat, you can island-hop at your convenience. Well-equipped marinas are on every major island and many cays. There are designated ports of entry at Great Abaco (Marsh Harbor), Andros, the Berry Islands, Bimini, Cat Cay, Eleuthera, Great Exuma, Grand Bahama Island (Freeport/Lucaya), Great Inagua, New Providence (Nassau), Ragged Island, and San Salvador.

Vessels must check with Customs at the first port of entry and receive a cruising clearance permit to The Bahamas. Carry it with you and return it at the official port of departure.

Yachtsman's Guide to The Bahamas (Tropical Island Publishers), updated yearly, covers the entire Bahamas. Copies are available at major marine outlets and bookstores, and by mail direct from the publisher for $45, plus postage: Tropical Island Publishers, P.O. Box 12, Adelphia, NJ 07710 (© **877/923-9653;** www.yachtsmansguide.com).

Experienced sailors with a sea-wise crew can charter **"bareboat"** (a fully equipped boat with no crew). You're on your own, and you'll have to prove you can handle it before you're allowed to take out such a craft. You may want to take along an experienced yachter familiar with local waters, which may be tricky in some places.

Most yachts are rented on a weekly basis. Contact the **Moorings** (© **888/952-8420;** www.moorings.com).

TIPS ON ACCOMMODATIONS

The Bahamas offers a wide selection of accommodations, ranging from small private guesthouses to large luxury resorts. Hotels vary in size and facilities, from deluxe (offering room service, sports, swimming pools, entertainment, and so on) to fairly simple inns.

There are package deals galore, and they are always cheaper than "rack rates." (A rack rate is what an individual pays if he or she literally walks in from the street. These are the rates we've listed in the chapters, though you can almost always do better—especially at the big resorts.) It's sometimes good to go to a reliable travel

What the Hotel Symbols Mean

As you're shopping around for your hotel, you may see the following terms used:

- o **AP (American Plan):** Includes three meals a day (sometimes called full board or full pension).
- o **EP (European Plan):** Includes only the room—no meals.
- o **CP (Continental Plan):** Includes continental breakfast of juice, coffee, bread, and jam.
- o **MAP (Modified American Plan):** Sometimes called half-board or half-pension, this room rate includes breakfast and dinner (or lunch instead of dinner, if you prefer).

agent to find out what, if anything, is available in the way of a land-and-air package before booking particular accommodations.

There is no rigid classification of hotel properties in the islands. The label "deluxe" is often used (or misused) when "first class" might have been a more appropriate term. "First class" itself often isn't. For that and other reasons, we've presented fairly detailed descriptions of the properties so that you'll get an idea of what to expect. However, even in the deluxe and first-class resorts and hotels, don't expect top-rate service and efficiency. When you go to turn on the shower, sometimes you get water and sometimes you don't. You may even experience power failures.

The winter season in The Bahamas runs roughly from the middle of December to the middle of April, and hotels charge their highest prices during this peak period. Winter is generally the dry season in the islands, but there can be heavy rainfall regardless of the time of year. During the winter months, make reservations 2 months in advance if you can. You can't book early enough if you want to travel over Christmas or in February.

The off season in The Bahamas—roughly from mid-April to mid-December (although this varies from island to island and from hotel to hotel)—amounts to a sale. In most cases, hotel rates are slashed a startling 20% to 60%. It's a bonanza for cost-conscious travelers, especially for families who can travel in the summer. Be prepared for very strong sun, though, plus a higher chance of rain. Also note that hurricane season runs through summer and fall.

MAP vs. AP, Or Do You Want to Go EP?

All Bahamian resorts offer a **European Plan (EP)** rate, which means that you pay for the price of a room. That leaves you free to dine around at night at various other resorts or restaurants without restriction. Another plan preferred by many is the **Continental Plan (CP),** which means you get a continental breakfast of juice, coffee, bread, and jam included in a set price. This plan is preferred by those who don't like to look around for a place to eat breakfast.

Another major option is the **Modified American Plan (MAP),** which includes breakfast and one main meal of the day, either lunch or dinner. The final choice is the **American Plan (AP),** which includes breakfast, lunch, and dinner. At certain resorts you will save money by booking on either the MAP or AP because discounts are granted. If you dine a la carte often for lunch and dinner, your dining costs will be much higher than if you stay on the MAP or AP.

Dining at your hotel at night cuts down on transportation costs. Taxis especially are expensive. Nonetheless, if dining out and having many different culinary experiences is your idea of a vacation and you're willing to pay the higher price, avoid AP plans or at least make sure the hotel where you're staying has more than one dining room.

One option is to ask if your hotel has a dine-around plan. You might still keep costs in check, but you can avoid a culinary rut by taking your meals in some other restaurants if your hotel has such a plan. Such plans are rare in The Bahamas, which does not specialize in all-inclusive resorts the way that Jamaica or some other islands do.

Before booking a room, check with a good travel agent or investigate on your own what you are likely to save by booking on a dining plan. Under certain circumstances in winter, you might not have a choice if MAP is dictated as a requirement for staying there. It pays to investigate, of course.

The Right Room at the Right Price

Ask detailed questions when booking a room. Specify your likes and dislikes. There are several logistics of getting the right room in a hotel. In general, back rooms cost less than oceanfront rooms, and lower rooms cost less than upper-floor units. If budget is a major consideration with you, opt for the cheaper rooms. You won't have a great view, but you'll save your money for something else. Just make sure that it isn't next to the all-night drummers.

Of course, all first-class or deluxe resorts feature air-conditioning, but many Bahamian inns do not, especially in the Out Islands. Cooling might be by ceiling fans or, in more modest places, the breeze from an open window, which also brings the mosquitoes. If sleeping in a climate-controlled environment is important to your vacation, check this out in advance.

If you're being your own travel agent, it pays to shop around by calling the local number given for a hotel and its toll-free number, if it has one. You can check online and call a travel agent to see where you can obtain the best price.

Another tip: Ask if you can get an upgrade or a free night's stay if you stay an extra few days. If you're traveling during the "shoulder" periods (between low and high season), you can sometimes get a substantial reduction by delaying your travel plans by a week or 10 days. For example, a $300 room booked on April 12 might be lowered to $180 by April 17, as mid-April marks the beginning of the low season in The Bahamas.

Transfers from the airports or the cruise dock are included in some hotel bookings, most often in a package plan but usually not in ordinary bookings. This is true of first-class and deluxe resorts, but rarely of medium-priced or budget accommodations. Always ascertain whether transfers (which can be expensive) are included.

When using the facilities at a resort, make sure that you know exactly what is free and what costs money. For example, swimming in the pool is nearly always free, but you might be charged for use of a tennis court. Nearly all watersports cost extra, unless you're booked on some special plan such as a scuba package. Some resorts seem to charge every time you breathe and might end up costing more than a deluxe hotel that includes most everything in the price.

Some hotels are right on the beach. Others involve transfers to the beach by taxi or bus, so factor in transportation costs, which can mount quickly if you stay 5 days to a week.

The All-Inclusives

A hugely popular option in some other Caribbean nations, the all-inclusive-resort hotel concept finally has a foothold in The Bahamas. At these resorts, everything is included—sometimes even drinks. You get your room and all meals, plus entertainment and many watersports (although some cost extra). Some people find the cost of this all-inclusive holiday cheaper than if they'd paid individually for each item, and some simply appreciate knowing in advance what their final bill will be.

The first all-inclusive resort hotel in The Bahamas was **Club Med** (www.clubmed. com; © **888/WEB-CLUB** [932-2582]) on Paradise Island. This is not a swinging-singles kind of place; it's popular with everybody, from honeymooners to families with kids along. There's another mammoth Club Med at Governor's Harbour on Eleuthera. Families with kids like it a lot here, and the resort also attracts scuba divers. There's a third branch in San Salvador, in the Southern Bahamas, which has more of a luxurious hideaway atmosphere.

The biggest all-inclusive of them all, **Sandals** (www.sandals.com; © **888/SAN-DALS** [726-3257]), came to The Bahamas in 1995 on Cable Beach. This Jamaican company is now walking its sandals across the Caribbean, in Ocho Rios, Montego Bay, and Negril. This most famous of the all-inclusives (but not necessarily the best) recently ended its ban against same-sex couples. See chapter 3 for details on these resorts.

Rental Villas & Vacation Homes

You might rent a big villa, a good-size apartment in someone's condo, or even a small beach cottage (more accurately called a cabana).

Private apartments come with or without maid service (ask upfront exactly what to expect). This is a more no-frills option than villas and condos. The apartments may not be in buildings with swimming pools, and they may not have a front desk to help you.

Many cottages or cabanas ideally open onto a beach, although others may be clustered around a communal swimming pool. Most of them are fairly simple, containing only a plain bedroom plus a small kitchen and bathroom. In the peak winter season, reservations should be made at least 5 or 6 months in advance.

Hideaways International (www.hideaways.com; © **877/843-4433** in the U.S., or 603/430-4433) publishes **Hideaways Life,** a color magazine that's updated six times a year with articles about home rentals and holiday destinations, and with tips about how to organize your life and holiday as a temporary resident. Rental possibilities range from cottages to staffed villas, to whole islands! For most rentals, you deal directly with owners. At condos and small resorts, Hideaways offers member discounts. Other services include specialty cruises, yacht charters, airline ticketing, car rentals, and hotel reservations. Annual membership costs $195.

Sometimes local tourist offices will also advise you on vacation-home rentals if you write or call them directly.

The Bahamian Guesthouse

Many Bahamians stay at a guesthouse when traveling in their own islands. In The Bahamas, however, the term *guesthouse* can mean anything. Sometimes so-called guesthouses are really like simple motels built around swimming pools. Others are small individual cottages with their own kitchenettes, constructed around a main building in which you'll often find a bar and restaurant serving local food.

[FastFACTS] THE BAHAMAS

African-American Travelers   Agencies and organizations that provide information and resources for black travelers include **Soul of America** (www.soulofamerica.com), a comprehensive website with travel tips, event and family-reunion postings, and sections on historically black beach resorts and active vacations.

Like-minded organizations also include the **African American Association of Innkeepers International** (© 877/422-5777; www.africanamericaninns.com), and the **National Association of Black Scuba Divers** (© 800/521-NABS; www.nabsdivers.org). Established in 1991 for the promotion of underwater diving within the African-American community, it's open to anyone regardless of race, color, religion, gender, sexual orientation, or creed. For additional insights into travel patterns of African-American consumers, check out the following collections and guides: *Go Girl: The Black Woman's Book of Travel & Adventure* (Eighth Mountain Press), a compilation of travel essays by writers including Jill Nelson and Audre Lorde; *The African-American Travel Guide,* by Wayne Robinson (Hunter Publishing; www.hunterpublishing.com); and *Steppin' Out,* by Carla Labat (Avalon).

Area Code   The country code for The Bahamas is **242.**

ATMs   See "Money & Costs," p. 293.

Babysitters   Check with your hotel staff to make arrangements. Most first-class hotels can provide babysitters from lists that the concierge keeps. Remember to request a babysitter no later than the morning if you're going out that evening. In the small little ins in the Out Islands, arrangements for babysitting are made with the staff, usually owner-managers.

Business Hours   In Nassau, Cable Beach, and Freeport/Lucaya, commercial banking hours are Monday through Thursday from 9:30am to 3pm, Friday from 9:30am to 5pm. Hours are likely to vary widely in the Out Islands. Ask at your hotel for specific information. Most government offices are open Monday through Friday from 9am to 5pm, and most shops are open Monday through Saturday from 9am to 5pm.

Car Rental   See "Getting Around," earlier.

Cellphones (Mobile Phones)   See "Mobile Phones," p. 292.

Crime   See "Safety" later in this section.

Customs   Bahamian Customs allows you to bring in 200 cigarettes, or 50 cigars, or 1 pound (.45 kg) of tobacco, plus 1 quart (1L) of spirits (hard liquor). You can also bring in items classified as "personal effects" and all the money you wish.

Visitors leaving Nassau or Freeport/Lucaya for most U.S. destinations clear U.S. Customs & Border Protection before departing The Bahamas. Charter companies can make special arrangements with the Nassau or Freeport flight services and U.S. Customs & Border Protection for pre-clearance. No further formalities are required upon arrival in the United States once the pre-clearance has taken place in Nassau or Freeport.

Collect receipts for all purchases you make in The Bahamas. **Note:** If a merchant suggests giving you a false receipt, misstating the value of the goods, beware—the merchant might be an informer to U.S. Customs. You must also declare all gifts received while abroad.

If you purchased an item during an earlier trip abroad, carry proof that you have already paid Customs duty on the item at the time of your previous reentry. To be extra careful, compile a list of expensive carry-on items and ask a U.S. Customs agent to stamp your list at the airport before your departure.

For information on what you're allowed to bring home, contact one of the following agencies:

o **U.S. Citizens: U.S. Customs & Border Protection (CBP),** 1300 Pennsylvania Ave., NW, Washington, DC 20229 (📞 **877/227-5511;** www.cbp.gov).

o **Canadian Citizens: Canada Border Services Agency,** Ottawa, Ontario, K1A 0L8 (📞 **800/461-9999** in Canada, or 204/983-3500; www.cbsa-asfc.gc.ca).

o **U.K. Citizens: HM Customs & Excise,** Crownhill Court, Tailyour Road, Plymouth, PL6 5BZ (📞 **0845/010-9000;** www.hmce.gov.uk).

o **Australian Citizens: Australian Customs Service,** Customs House, 5 Constitution Ave., Canberra City, ACT 2601 (📞 **1300/363-263;** from outside Australia, 612/6275-6666; www.customs.gov.au).

o **New Zealand Citizens: New Zealand Customs,** The Customhouse, 17–21 Whitmore St., Box 2218, Wellington, 6140 (📞 **64/99278036** or 0800/428-786; www.customs. govt.nz).

Disabled Travelers   A disability should not stop anyone from traveling to The Bahamas. Because these islands are relatively flat, it is fairly easy to get around, even for persons with disabilities.

You can call the **Bahamas Association for the Physically Disabled** (BAPD; 📞 **242/322-2393;** www.bahamas.com) for information about accessible hotels in The Bahamas. This agency will also send a van to the airport to transfer you to your hotel for a fee and can provide ramps.

Many travel agencies offer customized tours and itineraries for travelers with disabilities. Among them are **Flying Wheels Travel** (📞 **877/451-5006** or 507/451-5005; www.flying wheelstravel.com), **Access-Able Travel Source;** www.access-able.com), and **Accessible Journeys** (📞 **800/846-4537** or 610/521-0339; www.accessiblejourneys.com).

Organizations that offer assistance to travelers with disabilities include **MossRehab** (📞 **800/225-5667;** www.mossrehab.com), the **American Foundation for the Blind** (AFB; 📞 **800/232-5463** or 212/502-7600; www.afb.org), and **SATH** (Society for Accessible Travel & Hospitality; 📞 **212/447-7284;** www.sath.org).

In the event that you're temporarily disabled after an illness or accident, one of the best (and most valuable) insurance services is provided by **AirAmbulanceCard.com** (📞 **877/424-7633**), a membership program which provides medical evaluation in the event that someone is hospitalized for an illness or trauma while more than 150 miles from home. Membership in the AirAmbulance program, which costs $195 per year for an individual and $295 a year for a family with up to two parents and five children, allows you to be air-evacuated, and reimbursed, to top hospitals anywhere you specify in the event of a medical emergency. The savings you'd realize through this card, in the event of a medical emergency far from home, is huge.

Also check out the quarterly magazine ***Emerging Horizons*** (www.emerginghorizons. com) and ***Open World*** magazine, published by SATH.

British travelers can contact the Royal Association for Disability and Rehabilitation (RADAR), Unit 12, City Forum, 250 City Rd., London, EC1V 8AF (📞 **020/7250-3222;** www. radar.org.uk).

For more on organizations that offer resources to travelers with disabilities, go to www. frommers.com.

Drinking Laws   Alcohol is sold in liquor stores and various convenience stores; it's readily available at all hours, though not for sale on Sundays. The legal drinking age in The Bahamas is 18.

Driving Rules   See "Getting Around," p. 279.

Drug Laws   Importing, possessing, or dealing unlawful drugs, including marijuana, is a serious offense in The Bahamas, with heavy penalties. Customs officers may at their discretion conduct body searches for drugs or other contraband goods.

Electricity   Like Canada and the U.S., The Bahamas normally uses 110–120 volts AC (60 cycles), compared to 220–240 volts AC (50 cycles) in most of Europe, Australia, and New Zealand. American appliances are fully compatible; British or European appliances will need both adapters and downward converters that change 220–240 volts to 110–120 volts.

Embassies & Consulates   The embassy of the **United States** is at 42 Queen St., P.O. Box N-8197, Nassau (© **242/322-1181;** http://nassau.usembassy.gov).

The consulate of **Canada** is at Shirley Street Plaza, P.O. Box SS-6371, Nassau (© **242/393-2123;** cdncon@batelnet.bs).

There is a **British High Commission** in Jamaica, at 28 Trafalgar Rd., Kingston (© **876/510-0700;** http://ukinjamaica.fco.gov.uk).

Emergencies   See "Police," later in this section.

Entry Requirements   To enter The Bahamas, **citizens of Britain** and **Canada** coming in as visitors *must* bring a passport to demonstrate proof of citizenship. Under new Homeland Security regulations that started December 31, 2005, **U.S. travelers** are required to have a valid passport to re-enter the United States.

Onward or return tickets must be shown to immigration officials in The Bahamas. Citizens of other countries, including Australia, Ireland, and New Zealand, should carry a valid passport.

For information about how to get a passport, see "Passports," later. The websites listed provide downloadable passport applications as well as the current fees for processing passport applications. For an up-to-date, country-by-country listing of passport requirements around the world, go to the "Foreign Entry Requirement" Web page of the U.S. State Department at **http://travel.state.gov**.

Family Travel   The Bahamas is one of the top family-vacation destinations in North America. The smallest toddlers can spend blissful hours on sandy beaches and in the shallow seawater, or in swimming pools constructed with them in mind. There's no end to the fascinating pursuits offered for older children, ranging from boat rides to shell collecting, to horseback riding, hiking, or even dancing. Some children are old enough to learn to snorkel and to explore an underwater wonderland. Some resorts will even teach kids to swim or windsurf.

Most families with kids head for New Providence (Nassau), Paradise Island, or Grand Bahama Island (Freeport). Look for our "Kids" icon, indicating attractions, restaurants, or hotels and resorts that are especially family-friendly.

See also "The Best Family Vacations," in chapter 1, for additional recommendations.

Every country's regulations differ, but in general, children traveling abroad should have plenty of documentation on hand, particularly if they're traveling with someone other than their own parents (in which case a notarized form letter from a parent is often required).

For details on entry requirements for children traveling abroad, go to the U.S. State Department website (http://travel.state.gov).

Recommended family travel websites include **TravelwithYourKids.com, Family Travel Forum** (www.familytravelforum.com), **Family Travel Network** (www.familytravelnetwork.com), and **Family Travel Files** (www.thefamilytravelfiles.com).

Gasoline (Petrol)   Gasoline is plentiful on New Providence Island (Nassau/Cable Beach) and Grand Bahama Island (Freeport/Lucaya), but be prepared to pay almost twice the price you would in the United States. In the Out Islands, service stations are not plenti-ful, so plan your itinerary accordingly. Some islands are small and compact, but others, such as Eleuthera and Andros, are very spread out, with gas stations few and far between. In addition, watch out for those Sunday closings.

Health   We list **hospital** and **emergency numbers** in each chapter under "Fast Facts." Even on the remotest island, you'll find, if not a hospital, a local medicine man (or woman, in many cases). Many Bahamians are fond of herbal remedies. But you don't need to rely on these treatments, as most resorts have either hospitals or clinics on-site.

The major health risk here is not tropical disease, as it is in some Caribbean islands, but rather the bad luck of ingesting a bad piece of shellfish, exotic fruit, or too many rum punches. If your body is not accustomed to some of these foods, or if they haven't been stored or cleaned properly, you may suffer diarrhea. If you tend to have digestive prob-lems, then drink bottled water and avoid ice, unpasteurized milk, and uncooked food such as fresh salads. However, fresh food served in hotels is usually safe to eat.

The Bahamas has above-average medical facilities. Physicians and surgeons in private practice are readily available in Nassau, Cable Beach, and Freeport/Lucaya. A dozen or so health centers are in the Out Islands. Medical personnel hold satellite clinics periodically in small settlements, and there are about 35 other clinics, adding up to a total of approxi-mately 50 health facilities throughout the outlying islands. (We've listed the names and telephone numbers of specific clinics in the individual island coverage throughout this book.) If intensive or urgent care is required, patients are brought by the Emergency Flight Service to **Princess Margaret Hospital** (✆ 242/322-2861; www.phabahamas.org) on Shir-ley Street, Nassau. Some of the big resort hotels have in-house physicians or can quickly secure one for you.

There is also a government-operated hospital, **Grand Bahamas Health Services** (✆ **242/352-6735**), on East Atlantic Drive, Freeport, and several government-operated clinics on Grand Bahama Island. Nassau and Freeport/Lucaya also have private hospitals.

Dentists are plentiful in Nassau, somewhat less so on Grand Bahama. You'll find dentists on Great Abaco Island, at Marsh Harbour, at Treasure Cay, and on Eleuthera. There aren't dentists on some of the remote islands, especially those in the Southern Bahamas, but hotel staff should know where to send you for emergencies.

Contact the **International Association for Medical Assistance to Travellers (IAMAT;** ✆ **716/754-4883,** or 416/652-0137 in Canada; **www.iamat.org**) for tips on travel and health concerns in the countries you're visiting, and for lists of local English-speaking doc-tors. The United States **Centers for Disease Control and Prevention** (✆ **800/232-4636;** www.cdc.gov) provides up-to-date information on health hazards by region or country and offers tips on food safety. The website **www.tripprep.com**, sponsored by a consortium of travel medicine practitioners, may also offer helpful advice on traveling abroad. You can find listings of reliable clinics overseas at the **International Society of Travel Medicine** (✆ **404/373-8282;** www.istm.org).

Getting too much sun can be a real issue in The Bahamas. You must, of course, take the usual precautions you would anywhere against sunburn and sunstroke. Your time in the sun should be wisely limited for the first few days until you become accustomed to the more intense rays of the Bahamian sun. Also bring and use strong UVA/UVB sunblock products.

In most cases, your existing health plan will provide the coverage you need. But dou-ble-check; you may want to buy **travel medical insurance** instead (see the section on insurance). Bring your insurance ID card with you wherever you travel.

We list **hospitals** and **emergency numbers** under "Fast Facts" in each chapter.

If you suffer from a chronic illness, consult your doctor before your departure. Pack **pre-scription medications** in your carry-on luggage, and carry them in their original containers, with pharmacy labels—otherwise, they won't make it through airport security. Carry the generic name of prescription medicines, in case a local pharmacist doesn't know the brand name.

For travel abroad, you may have to pay medical costs upfront and be reimbursed later. See "Insurance."

Hospitals On New Providence Island (Nassau/Cable Beach), patients are treated at the government-operated **Princess Margaret Hospital,** on Shirley Street, Nassau (© **242/ 322-2861;** www.phabahamas.org).

On Grand Bahama Island, patients are seen at the government-operated **Rand Memorial Hospital,** on East Atlantic Drive, Freeport (© **242/352-6735;** www.phabahamas.org), and at several government-operated clinics.

A dozen or so health centers are located in the Out Islands. Many resorts also have either in-house physicians or on-site medical clinics. We've listed the names and telephone numbers of specific hospitals and clinics in the individual island coverage throughout this book. If intensive or urgent care is required, patients on the Out Islands are brought to Nassau by the Emergency Flight Service.

Insurance For travel overseas, most U.S. health plans (including Medicare and Medicaid) do not provide coverage, and the ones that do often require you to pay for services upfront and reimburse you only after you return home.

As a safety net, you may want to buy travel medical insurance, particularly if you're heading to a remote or high-risk area where emergency evacuation might be necessary, in the event of an accident, and hugely expensive. If you require additional medical insurance, try **MEDEX Assistance** (© **800/537-2029** or 410/453-6300; www.medexassist.com) or **Travel Assistance International** (© **800/821-2828;** www.travelassistance.com),

Canadians should check with their provincial health plan offices or call **Health Canada** (© **866/225-0709;** www.hc-sc.gc.ca) to find out the extent of their coverage and what documentation and receipts they must take home in case they are treated overseas.

Travelers from the U.K. should carry their **European Health Insurance Card (EHIC),** which replaced the E111 form as proof of entitlement to free or reduced-cost medical treatment abroad. Call © **0845/605-0707,** or 44/191-212-7500 outside the U.K., or go to www.ehic.org.uk for information. Note that the EHIC only covers "necessary medical treatment."

Travel Insurance The cost of travel insurance varies widely depending on the destination, cost, and length of your trip, your age and health, and the type of trip you're taking, but expect to pay between 5% and 8% of the cost of the vacation. You can get estimates from various providers through **Insuremytrip.com** (© **800/487-4722**). Enter your trip's cost and dates, your age, and other information to get prices from more than a dozen companies.

U.K. citizens and their families who make more than one trip abroad per year may find that an annual travel insurance policy works out cheaper. Check **www.moneysupermarket.com** (© **0845/345-5708**), which compares prices across a wide range of providers for single- and multi-trip policies.

Most big travel agents offer their own insurance and will probably try to sell you their package when you book a holiday. Think before you sign. **Britain's Consumers' Association** recommends that you insist on seeing the policy and reading the fine print before buying. The **Association of British Insurers** (© **020/7600-3333;** www.abi.org.uk) gives advice by phone and publishes *Holiday Insurance,* a free guide to policy provisions and prices. You might also shop around for better deals: Try **Columbus Direct** (© **0870/033-9988;** www.columbusdirect.net).

Trip-Cancellation Insurance   Trip-cancellation insurance will help you retrieve your money if you have to back out of a trip or depart early, or if your travel supplier goes bankrupt. Trip cancellation traditionally covers such events as sickness, natural disasters, and State Department advisories. The latest news in trip-cancellation insurance is the availability of expanded hurricane coverage and the "any-reason" cancellation coverage—which costs more but covers cancellations made for any reason. You won't get back 100% of your pre-paid trip cost, but you'll be refunded a substantial portion. **TravelSafe** (© 800/523-8020; www.travelsafe.com) offers both types of coverage. **Expedia** also offers any-reason cancellation coverage for its air-hotel packages. For other options, contact one of the following recommended insurers: **Access America** (© 800/284-8300; www.accessamerica.com), **Chartis Travel Guard** (© 800/826-4919; www.travelguard.com), **Travelex Insurance Services** (© 800/228-9792; www.travelex-insurance.com), and **Travel Insured International** (© 800/243-3174; www.travelinsured.com).

For additional information on travelers insurance, trip cancellation insurance, and medical insurance while traveling, please visit http://frommers.com/planning.

Internet & Wi-Fi   Internet cafes are not common on the islands, but in Nassau you can try **Cyberjack the Incredible,** in the Mall at Marathon (© 242/394-6254), or **Fantasy Web Café,** East Street at Balfour (© 242/323-7363). In the Out Islands, your hotel may have a computer with Internet access for guest use.

If you're traveling with your own computer, Web access via **Wi-Fi** hot spots is increasingly common at hotels, even in the Out Islands. But if this issue is especially important to you, see our hotel reviews throughout this book and check with specific accommodations before booking.

More and more Bahamian hotels, cafes, and retailers are signing on as Wi-Fi (wireless fidelity) "hot spots." Mac owners have their own networking technology: Apple AirPort. **T-Mobile Hotspot** (© 877/822-SPOT [7768]; www.hotspot.t-mobile.com or www.t-mobile.co.uk) serves up wireless connections at coffee shops nationwide. **Boingo** (www.boingo.com) and **Wayport** (www.wayport.com) have set up networks in airports and high-class hotel lobbies. iPass providers (see below) also give you access to a few hundred wireless hotel lobby setups.

For wired access, most business-class hotels in The Bahamas offer dataports for laptop modems. In addition, major Internet service providers (ISPs) have **local access numbers** around the world, allowing you to go online by placing a local call. The **iPass** network also has dial-up numbers around the world. You'll have to sign up with an iPass provider, who will then tell you how to set up your computer for your destination(s). For a list of iPass providers, go to www.ipass.com and click on "Individuals Buy Now." One solid provider is **i2Roam** (© 866/811-6209 or 920/233-5863; www.i2roam.com).

Wherever you go, bring a **connection kit** of the right power and phone adapters, a spare phone cord, and a spare Ethernet network cable—or find out whether your hotel supplies them to guests.

To find cybercafes, check www.cybercaptive.com and www.cybercafe.com.

Aside from formal cybercafes, most **public libraries** in The Bahamas have Internet access. Avoid **hotel business centers** unless you're willing to pay exorbitant rates.

Most major airports now have **Internet kiosks** scattered throughout their gates. These give you basic Web access for a per-minute fee that's usually higher than cybercafe prices.

Language   In The Bahamas, locals speak English, but sometimes with a marked accent that provides the clue to their ancestry—African, Irish, or Scottish, for example.

Legal Aid   Americans, Canadians, and British visitors can contact their embassies in Nassau for a list of lawyers. In the Out Islands, you may use a local lawyer. Nearly all violations and transgressions against foreigners are drug-related in The Bahamas.

LGBT Travelers In addition to the destination-specific resources listed below, please visit Frommers.com for other specialized travel resources.

Generally speaking, The Bahamas isn't a gay-friendly destination. Think twice before choosing to vacation here. Although many gay people visit or live here, the country has very strict anti-homosexuality laws. Same-sex relations, even when between consenting adults, are subject to criminal sanctions carrying prison terms. If you would like to make visiting gay beaches, bars, or clubs part of your vacation, consider South Miami Beach, Key West, or Puerto Rico instead.

Of course, the big resorts welcome one and all, even if forced to do so. For many years, the all-inclusive Sandals Royal Bahamian on Cable Beach refused to accept same-sex couples and booked only heterosexual guests. However, rights groups in Canada and Great Britain lobbied successfully, and the Sandals people found they could no longer advertise their resorts, and their discriminatory policies, in those countries. As a result, Sandals capitulated and ended its previous ban. However, gay and lesbian couples looking for a carefree holiday should seriously consider whether they want to spend their hard-earned dollars in a resort like Sandals that did not voluntarily end its ban against gay and lesbian travelers until forced to do so by more liberal and far-sighted governments.

Single gays and gay couples should travel here with great discretion. If you're intent on visiting, the **International Gay & Lesbian Travel Association (IGLTA; ℂ 800/GAY-TRAVEL;** www.iglta.org) is the trade association for the gay and lesbian travel industry, and offers an online directory of gay- and lesbian-friendly travel businesses; go to their website and click on "Members."

Many agencies offer tours and travel itineraries specifically for gay and lesbian travelers. Among them are **Now, Voyager** (ℂ 800/255-6951; www.nowvoyager.com) and **Olivia Cruises & Resorts** (ℂ 800/631-6277; www.olivia.com).

Gay.com Travel (ℂ 415/834-6500; www.gay.com or www.planetout.com) is an excellent online successor to the popular *Out & About* print magazine. It provides regularly updated information about gay-owned, gay-oriented, and gay-friendly lodging, dining, sightseeing, nightlife, and shopping establishments in every important destination worldwide.

The following travel guides are available at many bookstores, or you can order them from any online bookseller: *Spartacus International Gay Guide* (Bruno Gmünder Verlag; www.spartacusworld.com) and *Odysseus: The International Gay Travel Planner* (Odysseus Enterprises Ltd.); and the *Damron* guides (www.damron.com), with separate annual books for gay men and lesbians. For more gay and lesbian travel resources, go to www.frommers.com.

Lost & Found Be sure to notify all of your credit card companies the minute you discover your wallet has been lost or stolen. Also file a report at the nearest police precinct: Your credit card company or insurer may require a police report or record of the loss. Most credit card companies have an emergency toll-free number to call; they may be able to wire you a cash advance immediately or deliver an emergency credit card in a day or two. **American Express** cardholders and traveler's check holders should call ℂ **800/221-7282.** **MasterCard** holders should call ℂ **800/307-7309.** The emergency contact for **Visa** is **800/847-2911.** For other credit cards, call the toll-free number directory at ℂ **800/555-1212.**

If you need emergency cash over the weekend, when all banks and American Express offices are closed, you can have money wired to you via **Western Union** (ℂ **800/325-6000;** www.westernunion.com).

Mail You'll need Bahamian (not U.S.) postage stamps to send postcards and letters from The Bahamas. Most of the kiosks selling postcards also sell the stamps you'll need to mail them, so you probably won't need to visit the post office.

Sending a postcard or an airmail letter (up to ½ oz. in weight) from The Bahamas to anywhere outside its borders (including the U.S., Canada, and the U.K.) costs 65¢, with another charge for each additional half-ounce of weight.

Mail to and from the Out Islands is sometimes slow. Airmail may go by air to Nassau and by boat to its final destination. If a resort has a U.S. or Nassau address, it is preferable to use it.

Medical Requirements Unless you're coming from an area suffering from an epidemic, inoculations or vaccinations are not required for entry into The Bahamas.

Mobile Phones A U.S.-based cellphone will work in The Bahamas, even though roaming charges and rates might be more than you had expected, and conventional cellphone coverage on some remote areas of The Bahamas might be either spotty or unavailable.

In advance of your departure from home, contact your cell phone provider to make sure that it offers phone coverage in The Bahamas. If your cellphone is on a GSM system (and these day, there's a high likelihood that it is) and you have a world-capable multiband phone, such as many Sony Ericsson, Motorola, ATT, or Samsung models, you can make and receive calls across civilized areas around much of the globe. Just call your wireless operator and ask for "international roaming" to be activated on your account. Unfortunately, per-minute charges can be high—in some instances, as much as $1 a minute, often charged for both outgoing and incoming calls. Be warned in advance that whereas phone service is usually clear and workable in Nassau, Paradise Island, and on most parts of Freeport/Grand Bahama Island, service gets spottier as you advance deeper into the Out Islands.

GSM phones function with a removable plastic SIM card, encoded with your phone number and account information. If you plan on using your phone a lot (although we are of the opinion that you might at least try to reduce your dependence on phones during your time away) you can purchase a "Cybercell" Bahamas Prepaid SIM Card from **BTC** (The Bahamas Telecommunications Company; ☎ **242/394-3391;** www2.btcbahamas.com). The SIM card, together with a prepaid GSM cell phone, will allow you to have a local cell phone number for the Bahamas while paying local rates (usually between 15¢ and 30¢ per minute, depending on the time of day) with no roaming charges and no service contract. Many local phone shops will unlock your home cell phone for a small fee and without much of a wait.

You can conveniently recharge the funds associated with your phone through the purchase of airtime vouchers, available at a wide variety of vendors displaying the Cybercell sign. Ask for airtime vouchers at one of these points of sale which include many gas stations, the post office and local shops.

If arranging for an on-site replacement of your SIM card is daunting or too much of a hassle, consider renting a prepaid cellphone, either on site from any of the vendors advertising their services in Nassau and Freeport, or before you leave home. North Americans can rent one before leaving home from **InTouch Global** (☎ **800/872-7626;** www.intouchglobal.com) or **RoadPost** (☎ **888/290-1616** or 905/272-4934; www.roadpost.com). Some of the solutions proposed by either of these outfitters might veer into the extremely hi-tech and as such, offer solutions for boatowners interested in expanding their phone links even when traditional GPS service is spotty.

Any of these outfitters proposing rental deals will, without charge, advise you on whether your existing phone will work in The Bahamas or within other points overseas.

Money & Costs Frommer's lists exact prices in U.S. dollars throughout this guide, as they are widely accepted throughout The Bahamas. The currency conversions quoted below were correct at press time. However, rates fluctuate, so before departing consult a currency exchange website such as **www.oanda.com/currency/converter** to check up-to-the-minute rates.

THE VALUE OF THE BAHAMIAN DOLLAR VS. OTHER POPULAR CURRENCIES

B$	US$	Can$	UK£	Euro€	Aus$	NZ$
1.00	1.00	1.00	.65	1.30	1.00	1.24

It's always advisable to bring money in a variety of forms on a vacation: a mix of cash, credit cards, and traveler's checks. You should also exchange enough petty cash to cover airport incidentals, tipping, and transportation to your hotel before you leave home, or withdraw money upon arrival at an airport ATM.

In many international destinations, ATMs offer the best exchange rates. Avoid exchanging money at commercial exchange bureaus and hotels, which often have the highest transaction fees.

Currency The currency is the **Bahamian dollar (B$1),** pegged to the U.S. dollar so that they're always equivalent. There is no restriction on bringing foreign currency into The Bahamas. Most large hotels and stores accept traveler's checks, but you may have trouble using a personal check. It's a good idea to exchange enough money to cover airport incidentals and transportation to your hotel before you leave home.

Be sure to carry some small bills or loose change when traveling. Petty cash will come in handy for tipping and public transportation. Consider keeping the change separate from your larger bills so that it's readily accessible and you'll be less of a target for theft. In general, prices are about the same as in urban America, but they are less expensive than costs in the U.K. Food is often more expensive, however, since so much of it has to be imported.

ATMs The easiest way to get cash away from home is from an ATM (automated teller machine). The **Cirrus** (© **800/424-7787;** www.mastercard.com) and **PLUS** (www.visa.com) networks span the globe; look at the back of your bank card to see which network you're on and then call or check online for ATM locations at your destination. Know your personal identification number (PIN) and your daily withdrawal limit. Ask your card carrier if your current PIN works in The Bahamas, particularly in the Out Islands. Every card is different, but some need a four-digit rather than a six-digit PIN to withdraw cash abroad.

Many banks impose a fee every time a card is used at a different bank's ATM, and that fee can be higher for international transactions (up to $5 or more) than for domestic ones. On top of this, the bank from which you withdraw cash may charge its own fee. To compare banks' ATM fees within the U.S., use **www.bankrate.com**. For international withdrawal fees, ask your bank. You can also get cash advances on your credit card at an ATM. Credit card companies do try to protect themselves from theft by limiting the funds someone can withdraw outside their home country, so notify your credit card company before you leave home. And keep in mind that you'll pay interest from the moment of your withdrawal, even if you pay your monthly bills on time.

On New Providence Island and Paradise Island, there are plenty of ATMs, including one at the Nassau International Airport. There are far fewer ATMs on Grand Bahama Island (Freeport/Lucaya), but those that are there are strategically located—including ones at the airport and the casino (of course).

WHAT THINGS COST IN THE BAHAMAS	US$
Taxi from airport to Nassau Center	28.00–32.00
Double room, moderate	150.00
Double room, inexpensive	under 100.00
Three-course dinner for one, no wine, moderate	30.00
Bottle of beer	3.50–12.00
Cup of coffee	2.75

Very few ATMs are in the Out Islands. If you must have cash on your Out Island trip, make arrangements before you leave Nassau or Freeport; outside of Freeport, we counted only about a dozen ATMs in the entire remaining Out Islands. This situation is fluid, however, and more ATMs may be added in the future.

Credit Cards   Credit cards are another safe way to carry money, but their use has become more difficult, especially in The Bahamas. They also provide a convenient record of all your expenses, and they generally offer relatively good exchange rates. You can usu-ally withdraw cash advances from your credit cards at banks or ATMs, provided you know your PIN. Keep in mind that you'll pay interest from the moment of your withdrawal, even if you pay your monthly bills on time. Also, note that many banks now assess a 1% to 3% "transaction fee" on **all** charges you incur abroad (whether you're using the local currency or your native currency).

There is almost no difference in the acceptance of a debit or a standard credit card.

Be aware: Some establishments in The Bahamas might not accept your credit card unless you have a computer chip imbedded in it. The reason? To cut down on credit card fraud.

Chip and PIN represents a change in the way that credit and debit cards are used. The program is designed to cut down on the fraudulent use of credit cards. More and more banks are issuing customers chip-and-PIN versions of their debit or credit cards. In the future, more and more vendors will be asking for a four-digit personal identification num-ber, or PIN, which will be entered into a keypad near the cash register. In some cases, a waiter will bring a hand-held model to your table to verify your credit card.

More and more places in The Bahamas are moving from the magnetic-strip credit card to the chip-and-PIN system. In the changeover in technology, some retailers have falsely concluded that they can no longer take swipe cards, or can't take signature cards that don't have PINs any more.

For the time being, both the new and old cards are used in shops, hotels, and restau-rants regardless of whether they have the old credit and debit card machines or the new chip-and-PIN machines installed.

Beware of hidden credit card fees while traveling. Check with your credit or debit card issuer to see what fees, if any, will be charged for overseas transactions. Recent reform leg-islation in the U.S., for example, has curbed some exploitative lending practices. But many banks have responded by increasing fees in other areas, including fees for customers who use credit and debit cards while out of the country—even if those charges were made in U.S. dollars. Fees can amount to 3% or more of the purchase price. Check with your bank before departing to avoid any surprise charges on your statement.

Traveler's Checks and Prepaid Debit Cards   You can buy traveler's checks at most banks. They are offered in denominations of $20, $50, $100, $500, and sometimes $1,000. Generally, you'll pay a service charge ranging from 1% to 4%.

The most popular traveler's checks are offered by **American Express** (𝄇 **800/528-4800** or 623/492-8427—this number accepts collect calls from overseas from cardholders—offers service in several foreign languages, and exempts Amex gold and platinum cardholders from the 1% fee), **Visa** (www.visa.com; AAA members can obtain Visa checks for a modest fee at most AAA offices or by calling 𝄇 **800/221-7282;** www.AAA.com), and **MasterCard** (𝄇 **800/223-9920**).

Be sure to keep a record of the traveler's checks' serial numbers separate from your checks in the event that they are stolen or lost. You'll get a refund faster if you know the numbers.

If for any reason travelers checks are inconvenient, some banks are offering pre-paid debit cards which a traveler can use progressively, for credit card transactions or for cash withdrawals from an ATM during the course of his or her trip. They're being offered these days with a wide array of pre-defined spending limits and transaction fees, each of which varies with the rules of the individual bank or financial agent that issues them. If you haven't spoken to your bank already about an application for one of these, MasterCard (𝄇 **800/223-9928**) will direct potential users to the networks of banks which offer them.

Newspapers & Magazines   Three newspapers are circulated in Nassau and Freeport: the *Nassau Guardian,* the *Tribune,* and the *Freeport News.* Circulation in the Out Islands is limited and likely to be slow. In Nassau, you can find such papers as the *New York Times,* the *Wall Street Journal, USA Today,* the *Miami Herald,* London's *Times,* and the *Daily Telegraph* at newsstands in your hotel and elsewhere around town.

Packing   For helpful information on packing for your trip, download our convenient Travel Tools. Go to www.frommers.com/tips/packing_tips and click on "Smart Traveler" for either domestic or international flights.

Passports   See www.frommers.com/planning for information on how to obtain a passport.

For Residents of Australia   Contact the **Australian Passport Information Service** at 𝄇 **131-232,** or visit www.passports.gov.au.

For Residents of Canada   Contact the central **Passport Office,** Department of Foreign Affairs and International Trade, Ottawa, ON K1A 0G3 (𝄇 **800/567-6868;** www.ppt.gc.ca).

For Residents of Ireland   Contact the **Passport Office,** Setanta Centre, Molesworth Street, Dublin 2 (𝄇 **01/671-1633;** www.foreignaffairs.gov.ie).

For Residents of New Zealand   Contact the **Passports Office,** Department of Internal Affairs, 47 Boulcott St., Wellington, 6011 (𝄇 **0800/225-050** in New Zealand or 04/474-8100; www.passports.govt.nz).

For Residents of the United Kingdom   Visit your nearest passport office, major post office, or travel agency, or contact the **Identity and Passport Service (IPS),** 89 Eccleston Sq., London, SW1V 1PN (𝄇 **0300/222-0000;** www.ips.gov.uk).

For Residents of the United States   To find your regional passport office, check the U.S. State Department website (http://travel.state.gov/passport) or call the **National Passport Information Center** (𝄇 **877/487-2778**) for automated information.

Pharmacies   Refer to individual listings under Fast Facts in each chapter.

Police   Dial 𝄇 **919.**

Safety   When going to Nassau (New Providence), Cable Beach, Paradise Island, or Freeport/Lucaya, exercise the same caution you would if visiting Miami. Whatever you do, if people peddling drugs approach you, steer clear of them.

Crime is increasing, and visitors should use caution and good judgment when visiting The Bahamas. While most criminal incidents take place in a part of Nassau not usually frequented by tourists (the "Over-the-Hill" area south of downtown), crime and violence have moved into more upscale tourist and residential areas.

Women, especially, should take caution if walking alone on the streets of Nassau after dark, particularly if those streets appear to be deserted.

In the past few years, the U.S. Embassy has received several reports of sexual assaults, including some against teenage girls. Most assaults have been perpetrated against intoxicated young women, some of whom were reportedly drugged. To minimize the potential for sexual assault, the embassy recommends that young women stay in groups, consume alcohol in moderation, and not accept rides or drinks from strangers.

Pickpockets (often foreigners) work the crowded casino floors of both Paradise Beach and Cable Beach. See that your wallet, money, and valuables are well secured.

Travelers should avoid walking alone after dark or in isolated areas, and avoid placing themselves in situations in which they are alone with strangers. Be cautious on deserted areas of beaches at all hours. Don't leave valuables such as cameras and purses lying unattended on the beach while you go for a swim.

If you're driving a rental car, always make sure your car door is locked, and never leave possessions in view.

Hotel guests should always lock their doors and should never leave valuables unattended, especially on beaches. Visitors should store passport/identity documents, airline tickets, credit cards, and extra cash in hotel safes. Avoid wearing expensive jewelry, particularly Rolex watches, which criminals have specifically targeted. Use only clearly marked taxis and make a note of the license plate number for your records.

You're less likely to be mugged or robbed in the Out Islands, where life is generally more peaceful. There are some hotels there that, even today, don't have locks on the doors.

The loss or theft of a passport overseas should be reported to the local police and the nearest embassy or consulate. A lost or stolen birth certificate and/or driver's license generally cannot be replaced outside the United States. U.S. citizens may refer to the Department of State's pamphlets, A Safe Trip Abroad and Tips for Travelers to the Caribbean, for ways to promote a trouble-free journey. The pamphlets are available by mail from the Superintendent of Documents, U.S. Government Printing Office, Washington, DC 20402; via the Internet at www.gpoaccess.gov; or via the Bureau of Consular Affairs' home page at www.travel.state.gov.

Senior Travel In The Bahamas, the standard adult rate usually applies to everyone 21 years of age and over. The careful, frugal travel shopper, however, might find some deals if arrangements are made before you go.

Members of **AARP,** 601 E St. NW, Washington, DC 20049 (© **888/687-2277;** www.aarp.org), get discounts on hotels, airfares, and car rentals. AARP offers members a range of benefits, including *AARP The Magazine* and a monthly newsletter. Anyone over 50 can join.

Many reliable agencies and organizations target the 50-plus market. **Road Scholar** (© **800/454-5768;** www.roadscholar.org), formerly Exploritas/Elderhostel, arranges study programs for those aged 55 and over.

Recommended publications offering travel resources and discounts for seniors include the quarterly magazine **Travel 50 & Beyond** (© **717/974-6903;** www.travel50andbeyond.com); *Travel Unlimited: Uncommon Adventures for the Mature Traveler* (Avalon); *101 Tips for Mature Travelers,* available from Grand Circle Travel (© **800/959-0405** or 617/350-7500; www.gct.com); and *Unbelievably Good Deals and Great Adventures That You Absolutely Can't Get Unless You're Over 50* (McGraw-Hill), by Joan Rattner Heilman. For more information and resources about travel for seniors, go to www.frommers.com.

Single Travelers Single tourists often find the dating scene better in The Bahamas during the winter when there are more visitors, especially unattached ones.

On package vacations, single travelers are often hit with a "single supplement" to the base price. To avoid it, you can agree to room with other single travelers or find a compatible roommate before you go, from one of the many roommate-locator agencies.

TravelChums (www.travelchums.com) is an Internet-only travel-companion matching service with elements of an online-personals site. Many reputable tour companies offer singles-only trips.

For more information, check out Eleanor Berman's guide *Traveling Solo: Advice and Ideas for More Than 250 Great Vacations* (Globe Pequot), with advice on traveling alone, either solo or as part of a group tour. For more information on traveling single, go to www.frommers.com.

Smoking The government is on a drive to crack down on smoking in public places. Health officials are now in the process of drafting legislation that will ensure that nonsmokers are not subjected to secondhand smoke.

Taxes A tax of between 10% and 18% is imposed on hotel bills; otherwise, there is no sales tax on any purchase made within The Bahamas. Visitors leaving The Bahamas pay a $20 departure tax ($23 for travelers exiting The Bahamas directly from Grand Bahama Island), a tariff that's automatically included in the price of any airline or cruise-ship ticket.

Telephones Though some of the Out Islands are still difficult to reach by telephone, direct long-distance dialing is available between North America and Nassau (New Providence Island), Grand Bahama Island, the Abacos, Andros, the Berry Islands, Bimini, Eleuthera, Harbour Island, Spanish Wells, the Exumas, and Stella Maris on Long Island.

To call The Bahamas:

1.   From the U.S. and Canada, dial 1. From other countries, dial the international access code: 00 from the U.K., Ireland, or New Zealand; or 0011 from Australia.
2.   Dial the country code: 242.
3.   Dial the seven-digit local number.

To make international calls from The Bahamas: First dial 00 and then the country code (U.S. or Canada 1, U.K. 44, Ireland 353, Australia 61, New Zealand 64). Next, dial the area code and local number. For example, if you wanted to call the British Embassy in Washington, D.C., you would dial 00-1-202-588-7800.

For local calls within The Bahamas: Simply dial the seven-digit number. To call from one island to another within The Bahamas, dial 1-242 and then the seven-digit number.

For directory assistance: Dial ℗ **916** if you're looking for a number inside The Bahamas, **0** for numbers to all other countries.

For operator assistance: To reach an international or domestic operator within The Bahamas, dial ℗ **0.**

Toll-free numbers: Numbers beginning with 881 within The Bahamas are toll-free. However, calling a normally toll-free number within the U.S. (that is, one beginning with 800, 866, 887, or 888) usually involves a charge if made from The Bahamas. In fact, it usually costs the same as an overseas call unless the merchant has made arrangements with local telephone authorities. *Note:* Major airlines generally maintain toll-free 800, 866, 887, or 888 provisions for calls made to them within The Bahamas. If you dial what you think is a toll-free phone number and it ends up costing the long-distance rate, an automated recording will inform you of this fact. In some cases, the recording will suggest a local toll-free alternative—usually one beginning with 881.

To reach the major international services of **AT&T**, dial ℗ **800/CALL-ATT** (225-5288), or head for any phone with AT&T or USA Direct marked on the side of the booth. Picking up the handset will connect you with an AT&T operator. These phones are often positioned beside cruise-ship docks for disembarking passengers. **MCI** can be reached at 🕻 **800/888-8000.**

Note that the old coin-operated phones are still prevalent in The Bahamas and do still swallow coins. Those old phones, however, are gradually being replaced by phones that use calling cards (debit cards) that come in denominations of $5, $10, $20, and $50. They can be bought from any office of **BATELCO** (Bahamas Telephone Co.). BATELCO's main branch is on Kennedy Drive, Nassau (🕻 **242/302-7102;** www2.btcbahamas.com), although a popular local branch lies in the heart of Nassau, on East Street off Bay Street.

Time　Eastern Standard Time (EST) is used throughout The Bahamas, and daylight saving time is observed in the summer.

Tipping　Many establishments in The Bahamas add a service charge, but it's customary to leave something extra if service has been especially fine. If you're not sure whether service has been included in your bill, don't be shy—ask.

Bellhops and **porters,** at least in the expensive hotels, expect a tip of $1 to $2 per bag. It's also customary to tip the **chamber staff** at least $2 per day—more if she or he has performed special services such as getting a shirt or blouse laundered. Most service personnel, including **taxi drivers, waiters,** and the like, expect 15%, or 20% for waiters in deluxe restaurants.

Toilets　Public toilets are few and far between, except in hotel lobbies, bars, restaurants, museums, department stores, bus stations, and service stations. Large hotels and fast-food restaurants are often the best bet for clean facilities. Restaurants in resorts or heavily visited areas may reserve their toilets for patrons.

Visas　The Commonwealth of The Bahamas does not require visas. On entry to The Bahamas, you'll be given an immigration card to complete and sign. The card has a carbon copy that you must keep until departure, at which time it must be turned in. You'll also have to pay a departure tax before you can exit the country.

Visitor Information　One of the best information sources to contact before you leave home is your nearest **Bahamas Tourist Office.** Start off by visiting the country's official tourism website at www.bahamas.com or calling 🕻 **800/BAHAMAS** (224-2627) or 242/302-2000. You can also contact or stop by any of the following branch offices:

In the U.S.: 1200 South Pine Island Drive, Suite 750, Plantation, FL 33324 (🕻 **800/224-3681)**

In Canada: 6725 Airport Rd., Mississauga, Ontario L4V 1V2 (🕻 **800/667-3777)**

In the U.K.: 10 Chesterfield St., London W1J 5JL (🕻 **020/7355-0800)**

You may want to contact the **U.S. State Department** for background bulletins, which supply up-to-date information on crime, health concerns, import restrictions, and other travel matters. Call 🕻 **888/407-4747** or visit www.travel.state.gov.

A travel agent can also be a great source of information. Make sure yours is a member of the **American Society of Travel Agents (ASTA).** If you get poor service from an ASTA agent, you can write to the ASTA Consumer Affairs Department, 1101 King St., Alexandria, VA 22314 (🕻 **800/440-ASTA** [2782] or 703/739-2782; www.asta.org).

Useful Bahamas websites include:

The Bahamas Ministry of Tourism (www.bahamas.com), the country's official tourism site.

Bahamas Out Islands Promotion Board (www.myoutislands.com), with a focus on the more remote isles.

Bahamas Tourist Guide (www.geographia.com/bahamas), for general information and listings.

Bahamas Vacation Guide (www.bahamasvacationguide.com), for general information and various service listings.

Nassau/Paradise Island Promotion Board (www.nassauparadiseisland.com), the official tourism site for these areas.

Water   Technically, tap water is drinkable throughout The Bahamas. Still, we almost always opt for bottled. Resorts tend to filter and chlorinate tap water more aggressively than other establishments; elsewhere, bottled water is available at stores and supermarkets, and tastes better than that from a tap. On many of the Out Islands, rainfall is the main source of water—so be sure to drink bottled water there.

Wi-Fi   See "Internet & Wi-Fi," earlier in this section.

Women Travelers   Should a woman travel alone to The Bahamas? Opinions and reports vary. A woman traveling alone in such countries as Jamaica faces certain dangers, and safety is often an issue. Women traveling alone in The Bahamas rarely encounter aggressive, potentially dangerous behavior from males and are usually treated with respect. However, some Bahamian men may assume that a woman traveling alone is doing so in order to find a male partner. To avoid such unwanted attention, dress a bit conservatively and don't go wandering the streets of Nassau unescorted at night. It's always advisable to wear a cover-up to your swimsuit when leaving the beach and heading into town.

Women Welcome Women World Wide (5W; ℂ 01494/465441; www.womenwelcome women.org.uk) works to foster international friendships by enabling women of different countries to visit one another (men can come along on the trips; they just can't join the club). It's a big, active organization, with more than 3,500 members from all walks of life in some 70 countries.

Also check out the award-winning website **Journeywoman** (www.journeywoman.com), a "real life" women's travel-information network where you can sign up for a free e-mail newsletter and get advice on everything from etiquette to safety; or the travel guide *Safety and Security for Women Who Travel,* by Sheila Swan and Peter Laufer (Travelers' Tales, Inc.), offering common-sense tips on safe travel. For general travel resources for women, go to www.frommers.com.

online TRAVELER'S TOOLBOX

Veteran travelers usually carry some essential items to make their trips easier. Following is a selection of handy online tools to bookmark and use.

○ **Airplane Food** (www.airlinemeals. net)

○ **Airplane Seating** (www.seatguru. com and www.airlinequality.com)

○ **Foreign Languages for Travelers** (www.travlang.com and www. rosettastone.com)

○ **Maps** (www.mapquest.com)

○ **Time and Date** (www.timeand date.com)

○ **Travel Warnings** (http://travel. state.gov, www.fco.gov.uk/travel, or www.voyage.gc.ca)

○ **Universal Currency Converter** (www.xe.com/ucc)

○ **Visa ATM Locator** (www.usa.visa. com), MasterCard ATM Locator (www.mastercard.com)

○ **Weather** (www.intellicast.com and www.weather.com)

AIRLINE WEBSITES

Major Airlines

Air Canada
www.aircanada.com

Air Jamaica
www.airjamaica.com

AirTran Airways
www.airtran.com

American Airlines
www.aa.com

Bahamasair
www.bahamasair.com

BMI Baby
www.bmibaby.com

British Airways
www.britishairways.com

Caribbean Airlines (formerly BWIA)
www.caribbean-airlines.com

Delta Air Lines
www.delta.com

JetBlue Airways
www.jetblue.com

Southwest Airlines
www.southwest.com

Spirit Airlines
www.spiritair.com

United Airlines
www.united.com

US Airways
www.usairways.com

Virgin America
www.virginamerica.com

Virgin Atlantic Airways
www.virgin-atlantic.com

WestJet
www.westjet.com

Index

See also Accommodations and Restaurant indexes, below.

General Index

A

Abaco Club on Winding Bay Ritz Carlton (Marsh Harbour), 181
Abaco Inn (Elbow Cay), for honeymooners, 10
Abaco National Park (Bahamas National Trust Sanctuary), 182
The Abacos, 173–203. See also specific islands
  accommodations
    Elbow Cay, 184–186
    Great Guana Cay, 191
    Green Turtle Cay, 197–198
    Man-O-War Cay, 189–190
    Marsh Harbour, 177–178
    Treasure Cay, 193
  beaches and outdoor activities
    Elbow Cay, 183, 187–188
    Green Turtle Cay, 200–201
    Marsh Harbour, 180–181
    Treasure Cay, 192, 194
  brief description of, 35–36
  getting around, 174
  getting there, 173–174
  restaurants
    Elbow Cay, 186–187
    Great Guana Cay, 191–192
    Man-O-War Cay, 190
    Marsh Harbour, 178–179
    Treasure Cay, 193–194
  weather, 173
Abacos Train Wreck (Marsh Harbour), 180
Abraham's Bay (Mayaguana), 274
Accommodations, 281–284. See also Accommodations Index
  the Abacos
    Elbow Cay, 184–186
    Great Guana Cay, 191
    Green Turtle Cay, 197–198
    Marsh Harbour, 177–178
    Treasure Cay, 193
  Andros, 164–168
  Bimini, 149–151
  Cat Island, 254–256
  Crooked Island, 271–272
  Eleuthera. See Eleuthera, accommodations
  George Town, 236–239
  Grand Bahama, 119–128
  Great Harbour, 156, 158
  Great Inagua, 275
  Long Island, 265–267
  Mayaguana Island, 273
  New Providence, 50–61
  Paradise Island, 95–103
  San Salvador, 258–260

Ace Tennis Center (Grand Bahama), 10, 138
Acklins Island, 270–272
Active vacations, 40–42
Adderley's Plantation (Long Island), 270
Adirondack (wreck), 180
African-American travelers, 285
Afternoon tea, at the governor-general's mansion, 66
Air travel, 277–279. See also specific destinations
Albert Lowe Museum (New Plymouth), 201
Albert Town (Fortune Island), 273
Albury's Ferry Service, 174, 184, 189, 190
Albury's Sail Shop (Man-O-War Cay), 190
Alice Town (Bimini), 146, 153
All Abaco Sailing Regatta, 31
All-inclusives, 284
American Airlines Vacations, 40
Andros Barrier Reef, 169–170
Andros Conservancy and Trust, 169
Androsia Batik (Andros Town), 171
Andros Island, 145–146, 159–172
  accommodations, 164–168
  beaches and outdoor activities, 169–171
  bonefishing, 41
  brief description of, 35
  emergencies, 164
  exploring, 171–172
  getting around, 163–164
  getting there, 160, 162
  layout of, 162–163
  nightlife, 172
  post office, 164
  restaurants, 168
  scuba diving, 3, 41–42
  visitor information, 164
Andros Island Bonefish Club, 41
Andros Town, 163
  accommodations, 165–166
Animale (Port Lucaya), 141
Annual Racing Time in Abaco (Marsh Harbour), 31
Aquaventure (Paradise Island), 98
Arawak cave (Cat Island), 257
Architecture, 20–21
Ardastra Gardens, Zoo & Conservation Center (Nassau), 76
Armbrister Plantation (Cat Island), 257
Art galleries
  George Town, 245
  Grand Bahama, 141, 142
  Harbour Island, 229
  Marsh Harbour, 182
  Nassau, 88
  New Plymouth, 201
Arthur's Bakery & Cafe (Harbour Island), 221, 226

Arthur's Town (Cat Island), 252
Atlantic Undersea Test and Evaluation Center (AUTEC), 170
Atlantis, continent of, 154
Atlantis (Paradise Island), tennis, 110
Atlantis Casino (Paradise Island), 98, 112
Atlantis Paradise Island, 111
  for families, 11
  nightlife, 13–14, 112–113
  tennis, 9
ATMs (automated-teller machines), 293–294
  Andros, 164
  Bimini, 148
  New Providence, 49
Aura (Paradise Island), 113

B

Babysitters, 285
Babysitting, New Providence, 49
Bacardi Billfish Tournament (Freeport), 30
Bahama Divers, 110
Baha Mar Resorts, 55
Bahamas Adventure Glass Bottom Kayaks, 38
Bahamas Billfish Championship, 31
Bahamas Divers (Nassau), 75
Bahamas Family Island Regatta (George Town), 30–31
Bahamas National Trust, 33, 38
Bahamas National Trust Sanctuary (Abaco National Park), 182
Bahamas Outdoors, 86
Bahamas Outdoors Ltd., 72
Bahamas Out Island Adventures (Eleuthera), 219
Bahamas Summer Boating Fling/Flotilla, 31
Bahamas Wahoo Championships (Berry Islands), 30
Bahamas White Marlin Open (Abacos), 31
Bahamian iguana, 249
Balcony House (Nassau), 78–79
Bamboo Point (San Salvador), 261
Bandolera (Port Lucaya), 141
Barbary Beach (Grand Bahama), 134
Barefoot Sailing Cruises (New Providence), 8, 72–73, 87
Bars
  Nassau, 92
  Paradise Island, 113
Bay Street (Nassau), 47, 88
Beaches, 36. See also specific beaches
  the Abacos
    Elbow Cay, 183, 187–188
    Marsh Harbour, 180
    Treasure Cay, 192, 194
  Andros, 169
  best, 2–3

Restaurants

917.2960
4
Frommer'

Frommer's Bahamas

DUE DATE   18.99
